Apocalyptic Ecologies

# *Apocalyptic Ecologies*

From Creation to Doom in Middle English Literature

SHANNON GAYK

The University of Chicago Press
Chicago and London

The University of Chicago Press, Chicago 60637
The University of Chicago Press, Ltd., London
© 2024 by The University of Chicago
All rights reserved. No part of this book may be used or reproduced in any manner whatsoever without written permission, except in the case of brief quotations in critical articles and reviews. For more information, contact the University of Chicago Press, 1427 East 60th Street, Chicago, IL 60637.
Published 2024
Printed in the United States of America

33 32 31 30 29 28 27 26 25 24   1 2 3 4 5

ISBN-13: 978-0-226-83760-4 (cloth)
ISBN-13: 978-0-226-83761-1 (paper)
ISBN-13: 978-0-226-83762-8 (e-book)
DOI: https://doi.org/10.7208/chicago/9780226837628.001.0001

The University of Chicago Press gratefully acknowledges the generous support of the Luetzelschwab-Burkhart Professional Development Fund at Indiana University toward the publication of this book.

Library of Congress Cataloging-in-Publication Data

Names: Gayk, Shannon Noelle, author.
Title: Apocalyptic ecologies : from creation to doom in Middle English literature / Shannon Gayk.
Description: Chicago ; London : The University of Chicago Press, 2024. | Includes bibliographical references and index.
Identifiers: LCCN 2024020856 | ISBN 9780226837604 (cloth) | ISBN 9780226837611 (paperback) | ISBN 9780226837628 (ebook)
Subjects: LCSH: English literature—Middle English, 1100–1500—History and criticism. | Environmental degradation in literature. | Apocalypse in literature. | Ecology in literature.
Classification: LCC PR275.E59 G39 2024 | DDC 820.9/001—dc23/eng/20240510
LC record available at https://lccn.loc.gov/2024020856

♾ This paper meets the requirements of ANSI/NISO Z39.48-1992 (Permanence of Paper).

*For my father and late mother,
who modeled the work
of attention and care*

If we still love such a world, we now love wounds, not delights.
GREGORY THE GREAT, Homily on Ezekiel 2:6

One of the penalties of an ecological education is that one lives alone in a world of wounds. Much of the damage inflicted on land is quite invisible to laymen. An ecologist must either harden his shell and make believe that the consequences of science are none of his business, or he must be the doctor who sees the marks of death in a community that believes itself well and does not want to be told otherwise.
ALDO LEOPOLD, *Sand County Almanac*

Contents

INTRODUCTION: Learning to Die 1
EXCURSUS: A Brief History of Medieval Climate Change 19

PART I Edenic Ecologies

1 Being Earth: Performing the "Fayre Processe" of Creation 29
2 "This Deadly Life": Elegy and Ecological Care after Eden 61

PART II Everyday Apocalypse

EXCURSUS: On Plague, Precedent, and the Punishment Paradigm 97
3 Becoming Beholden: Floods, Fires, and Acts of Attention 103
4 Ordinary Apocalypses: Wondrous Weather in Early England 151

PART III Apocalyptic Ecologies

5 Fifteen Ways of Looking: Signs at the End of the World 183
EPILOGUE: Learning to Love: Ecological Attention and the Work of Care 214

Acknowledgments 221
Notes 223
Abbreviations 263
Bibliography 265
Index 289

INTRODUCTION

Learning to Die

Omnis mundi creatura,
quasi liber et pictura
nobis est in speculum;
nostrae vitae, nostrae sortis,
nostri status, nostrae mortis
fidele signaculum.

(Everything in the created universe,
like a book or a picture,
serves as a mirror for us,
a faithful sign
of our life, our destiny,
our condition, our death.)

ALAN OF LILLE, "Book of Creation"

Nearly every spring since I was a child, I have sought out ephemerals, those short-lived blossoms on the forest floor that emerge and disappear in a quiet parade just as the days begin to lengthen. One could easily not notice them at all. In any other setting, or to an uninterested eye, they would be called weeds. But during the year's first warming weeks, they are the glory of the landscape. Unlike most of the spring cultivars that fill gardens, these flowers grow where they like. Unlike summer's showy annuals, most ephemerals are minuscule, pale, and unassuming. Though they appear delicate, they can weather spring's inevitable cold snaps. To the observer they seem to live subtle, short lives, inviting a game of hide-and-seek. A hint of white among last fall's papery leaves, a bud on a slender pink stalk, petals nestled under a green hood.

Becoming aware of ephemerals requires perceiving the world at a different pace and scale than many of us are accustomed to. When they begin to emerge in early spring, one must pass slowly through the woods, crouch close to the ground, sometimes even crawl, to search for small signs of new growth. In the hill country of southern Indiana, where I've lived for about twenty years, first come the barely perceptible, clustered buds of the harbingers of spring, then toothwort, bloodroot, and spring beauties. Next appear all those midspring blooms with their old-fashioned, folksy names: Dutchman's-breeches, bishop's-cap, jack-in-the-pulpit, nodding wake-robin. By the end of April, bluebells carpet the woodland, lifting their blossoms toward the sun.

Their very nature is in their name: ephemeral. Now you see them, now you don't. As I write, in early May, the fade has already begun. The undergrowth, only days ago teeming with umbrellaed mayapples and red trillium, is suddenly thinning and browning. New green in the treetops darkens the forest floor.

These tiny topographies are a landscape that I am only now learning to read. The appearance of spring ephemerals signals the shifting of seasons and offers hope for warming days and spreading greenness. Growing in the seeming dead of winter, they are signs of ecological resilience, of how new life can emerge from decay. Blooming only for a few days or weeks and waning as the overstory leafs in, they are also reminders of the senescence of all things. They perform the cosmic life cycle in miniature, from emergence to flourishing to decay in a matter of weeks. The blooms are wondrous because of, not in spite of, their transience. They provide an early habitat for pollinators and food for winter-starved wildlife. They improve soil health. They are also a fitting example of the story I aim to tell in this book about attention, ecological fragility, and collective flourishing.

I linger here on this most mundane of truisms—the ephemerality of flowers—because literature has long treated this ecological commonplace as a *memento mori*, an aid to remembering our own mortality. A reminder that we too are ephemerals.

The idea that humans are "like flowers of the field" is ancient. It functions nearly as a refrain in the Hebrew scriptures and the Christian New Testament. We find in the book of Isaiah (40:6–7) that "all flesh is grass, and all the glory thereof as the flower of the field. The grass is withered, and the flower is fallen, because the spirit of the Lord hath blown upon it. Indeed the people is grass."[1] The psalmist concurs: "Man's days are as grass, as the flower of the field so shall he flourish" (Psalms 102:15). The book of Job is full of proclamations of what one theologian calls our "vegetal evanescence."[2] Jesus advises, "Consider the lilies, how they grow" (Luke 12:27).

The transitory lives of flowers also inspired medieval poets and preachers. Many medieval texts adopt this biblical imagery as a metaphor for the fleeting nature of human existence. Take, for instance, a little lyric in a 1372 handbook for preachers by John of Grimestone:

> Man is but a frele þing
> Fro þe time of is genning
> Nou he is an nou e nis
> Als þe flour þat springet in gres.[3]

> (A human is only a frail thing
> From the time of his beginning
> Now he is, and now he is not,
> like the flower that springs in the grass.)

This tight quatrain develops a single image but waits to unveil the comparison until its final line: a human life is as brief as that of the flowers that spring up in the grass. Now we are. Now we are not.

Or consider the Latin lyric attributed to the twelfth-century poet Alan of Lille, that opens this introduction. Drawing on the common medieval trope of "the Book of Nature," Alan writes, "Everything in the created universe" is like "a mirror for us."[4] For Alan, ecological process is a series of signs in which we might read our lives and deaths, our destiny and condition. Alan focuses this analogy for the human condition on this central image: like a flower, a human being "withers even as it blooms" (*defloratus flos effloret*). Yet, the final five of the poem's nine stanzas examine this dying from a variety of perspectives, layering on other images of ecological transience. Attend closely to the world, Alan suggests, and you will be reminded that your life is as fleeting as a wilting bloom, a tide swelling in a harbor, or a day giving way to evening (*portum fluctus / mane claudit vespere*).[5] All nature's processes proclaim transience. Thus, what we discover when we contemplate the ephemerality of the world, according to Alan, are reminders of our own condition. The passing of time. Biological process. Vulnerability. Precarity. Contingency. Senescence.[6]

Alan's use of the trope also conveys a deep sense of likeness and reciprocity. In his cascade of metaphors equating the human with wilting blooms, fading daylight, and tidal flows, Alan emphasizes kinship. We don't just mirror nature; we *are* nature. Yet, he goes further: we don't just read nature; it reads us. A single flower, Alan writes, can be "an apt gloss on our state / a reading of our life" (*nostri status decens glosa / nostrae vitae lectio*).[7] This relation is reciprocal; we are *like* this world, part and parcel of it, and bound up with it. We are also in relationship with it: we respond to it; it responds to us.

Although the poem insists on the logic of likeness, Alan concludes by implying a crucial difference:

> Ergo clausum sub hac lege
> statum tuum, homo, lege,
> tuum esse respice,
> quid fuisti nasciturus,
> quid sis praesens, quid futurus
> diligenter inspice. (43–48)

(Therefore, bound by this law,
oh man, consider your condition;
contemplate your existence:
examine closely
what you were born to be,
what you are now, what you will become.)

Alan's commands—"lege ... respice ... inspice" (consider ... contemplate ... examine)—are urgent. Now is the time, he insists, to reflect on one's fragility. By instructing his audience to *read* this book, to contemplate it, Alan might appear only to be situating human beings as outside of and other than the rest of the world, as observers, interpreters, or consumers of it. Indeed, Alan asserts, we are different in one critical way from the more-than-human world, for we can "consider [our] condition ... contemplate [our] existence."[8] If understanding nature as like a book is predicated on likeness, our ability to contemplate it suggests one way we are different. We are both participants in and interpreters of the world.

Early poetry points out time and again that humans share in the fleeting nature of all created things and are distinguished primarily by awareness of this fact. We may wish to ignore or deny this kinship, but the world's growing and decaying vegetation, its waxing and waning moon, its shifting weather, the short chirring lives of cicadas, the destructive and generative heat of composting earth all remind us that the beauty and value of biological life are predicated on its mutability and mortality.

Now we are, now we are not.

The idea that contemplating the ephemerality of the more-than-human world can spur productive reflection on human transience, kinship, and responsibility is at the heart of this book, which explores how late medieval retellings of biblical narratives invite deep attention to what I call *apocalyptic ecologies*. *Ecology* needs little definition, though I like John Muir's description: "When we try to pick out anything by itself, we find it hitched to everything else in the universe," an idea with which, we will see, medieval writers were familiar even if they didn't name it "ecology."[9] My use of *apocalypse* may require a bit more explanation. We now often use *apocalypse* as a synonym for *catastrophe*, to emphasize a violent disruption, rupture, cataclysm, or overturning of natural or social order.[10] Many of the ecologies that fill the following pages are apocalyptic in precisely this sense. Focused on dying worlds, these texts imagine landscapes and their inhabitants devastated by floods, fires, storms, decay, and death.[11] But here I also hope to recover the earlier sense of *apocalypse* as an uncovering or unveiling, a making known of something that has been obscured, an event with revelatory and perhaps even revolutionary potential.[12] In this sense, *any* ecological change—that of unfurling ephemerals in the waning days of winter, of woodlands shattered by tornadoes, or of towns drowned by the Army Corps of Engineers—can be apocalyptic, even if we rarely treat such things as potential sites of revelation. Thus, to read apocalyptically is to look for openings, eruptions of potentiality, and invitations to imagine our relationship with the world differently. For apocalyptic ecologies make visible how fine the line can be between the quotidian and the catastrophic; they reveal how within emergency lies the possibility of emergence; and they call attention to how grappling with loss can invite new ways of being, forms of living, communities, or practices of care.[13]

And so, in the pages that follow I trace the apocalyptic edges of the premodern ecological imagination. To do so, I turn to what may seem an unlikely source: vernacular biblical literature.[14] I focus on literature written in Middle English during the century or so before the Reformation, a period of global cooling during which England suffered from a series of ecological catastrophes resulting in massive human casualties (droughts and deforestation, strong storms and flooding, earthquakes, and, most famously, the Black Death, a devastating epidemic of bubonic plague). Importantly, this was also a time of theological and literary experimentation in English.[15] It was a time in which writers riffed on biblical sources, turning them over, upside down, and inside out, reimagining the stories for their late medieval audiences. The texts I discuss in this book take biblical narratives as occasions to ruminate on the human relation to and responsibility for the more-than-human world. In so doing, they explore the tensions implicit in their scriptural sources: between revering creation and repudiating it, between valuing immanence and transcendence; between the goodness of the cosmos and its corruption, and between earth's apparent stability and its unpredictability.[16]

Ultimately, I hope to show how close attention to apocalyptic ecologies—in medieval literature and in our own moment—can draw us into these tensions, inviting us to relinquish any lingering modern fantasy of ecological stability—that the cosmos is a well-oiled machine, its processes stable, reliable, knowable, and largely distinct from human influence; that things will go on more or less as they always have done; and even that humans can always understand and manage ecological processes.[17] Apocalyptic ecologies can prompt us instead to imagine ecological flourishing in another way, finding value in the world's mutability, ephemerality, and interconnectedness. This approach chimes with recent environmental writing, which has increasingly looked for the humanistic roots of ecological thinking in other nonmodern traditions, especially Indigenous or non-Western cosmologies and ethics.

Yet this book suggests that even in the West before the advent of modernity, some popular religious literature encouraged audiences not only to imagine themselves as part of an interconnected, transient cosmos but also to see themselves as responsible to and for it. And in so doing, they offered a vision of ecological thriving that is *apocalyptic* in the richest sense of that term, in which every moment, every interaction holds the possibility of both ending and beginning anew.[18]

Dark Ecologies and the *Ars Moriendi*

> If we still love such a world, we now love wounds, not delights.
> GREGORY THE GREAT

If, as Alan suggests, the small daily dyings of the world—from fading flowers to vanishing light—invite attention to and awareness of our mortal condition, we might read the "Book of Nature" as an *ars moriendi*, a book that teaches us how to die.[19] In contemporary parlance, the created world is a "dark ecology," which, as Timothy Morton defines it, "thinks the truth of death."[20] By taking seriously the idea that the biological world can function as an *ars moriendi*, an aid to ethical reflection on perishability, I here attempt to suggest that medieval religious texts might help us reframe how we imagine living in our own age of unprecedented ecological precarity. As *artes moriendi*, apocalyptic ecologies can call us to deeper attention to questions of value and meaning.

These days, it almost a cliché to read our environmental situation through the lens of apocalypse. The biosphere announces cataclysm everywhere—from daily extinctions to prolonged droughts, catastrophic fires, warming air, and rising waters. Representing ecological catastrophes as signs of an imminent end, modern ecoprophets and polemicists periodically herald "the death of nature," but they do so in a culture that is both fatigued by such constant apocalypticism and also often uncomfortable with talking about mortality.[21] Meditating on disaster, decline, and death may feel like a macabre undertaking, but as medieval writers knew, it could also be ethically and affectively productive. For this reason, nonmodern texts can offer an important corrective, reframing how we think about ecological death today, as well as the options we have in responding to it. After all, we are not the first to feel that our world is ending.

The late Middle Ages fostered a large discourse about human suffering and dying. A central insight of the *ars moriendi* tradition is that to contemplate death is to reorient oneself toward life, to reflect on how to flourish in whatever time may remain.[22] By attending to moments when medieval biblical texts confront the transience of the cosmos, this book proposes that apocalyptic ecologies, as *artes moriendi*, may inspire reflection and action in the face of collective finitude. As the first chapter of this book shows, premodern writers often invited such scalar thinking, linking microcosm and macrocosm, human body and world.[23] Though the medieval *ars moriendi* focuses on dying human beings, here I want to suggest the trope's usefulness in helping us think about ecological transience on a larger scale. In rescaling the trope (shifting from microcosm to macrocosm, from individual mortality to planetary mortality), I take my cue from Roy Scranton's 2015 provocation, *Learning to Die in the Anthropocene*. Considering the existential problems that life in our ecologically unsettled age poses, Scranton writes:

> The question of individual mortality—"what does my life mean in the face of death?"—is universalized and framed in scales that boggle the imagination.... What does one life mean in the face of species death or the collapse of global civilization? How do we make meaningful choices in the shadow of our inevitable end?[24]

To begin to answer such questions, he argues, we must learn to die. By this he means, "letting go of the ego, the idea of self, the future, certainty, attachment, the pursuit of pleasure, permanence, stability," seeing such relinquishment as a first step toward a recovery of a sense of a larger collective and a means of interrupting and reorienting the processes that drive us toward catastrophe.[25] "The practice itself is the wisdom," he writes, drawing on Zen Buddhism. But, as Scranton clearly knows, this is also a rather medieval way of viewing things.[26]

Scranton's emphasis on the importance of contemplating mortality as a mode of resistance is not unlike Alan's insistence on deep examination of the world's transience. For both authors, rather than invite passivity, such attention to death encourages reflection, reformation, and response while there is still time. They both center practice and process. They both imply that although the medieval art of learning to die may encourage nonattachment to a dying world, it can also direct us toward an *ars vivendi*, a renewed practice of living with an eye toward the inevitability of one's end.

Indeed, one of the truisms about the medieval *ars moriendi* is that its real function is to force attention to life itself. A confrontation with our own mortality or that of a loved one often leads us to reflect on life's brevity and, by extension, what makes for a meaningful or good life. And it invites us into deeper practices of care, tenderness, and connection. In the final year of writing this book, I found myself often sitting with the dying, with a colleague who "rag[ed] against the dying of the light" until the very end, with my nineteen-year-old tabby in kidney failure, with a near stranger at the hospital whom I had once taught in a community poetry course, with my grandmother in the late stages of dementia. In late May, I sat with my dying mother, first in the hospital and then during her final week at home when she had been released to hospice care. Despite immunotherapy and clinical trials, her rare retinal cancer had metastasized. Outside her bedroom, my father's Appalachian garden was in full bloom. We opened all the windows so she could hear the birdsong and breathe in the greenness and growth. Casseroles began to appear on the kitchen countertops. My parents' friends flitted in and out. We sat. We sang old hymns and folk and protest songs to her. We reminisced, telling her stories she already knew, while wondering what she understood. We attended to her, offering spoonfuls of water and painkillers. But mainly we just sat, holding her gaunt hand, or stroking her head, speaking our love for her again and again. We sat and kept watch. It turned out that, in the end, little mattered to us other than presence, attention, and care.[27]

Though "death, dying, and the dead," as Jane Gilbert writes, "are good to think with," feeling comes first, and then also, perhaps, new modes of awareness and being in the world, however fleeting those might ultimately be.[28] Practical manuals on death and dying, from *The Visitation of the Sick* (1380) to the *Book of the Craft of Dying* (mid-fifteenth century), offered instructions for how to prepare well and emphasized cultivating an ongoing commitment to care, compassion, and generosity toward others.[29] Yet one of the tropes of *ars moriendi* narratives is that the protagonists realize the necessity of contemplating death far too late. Death appears as an unexpected disruption, as untimely, as unthought. As the protagonist of the fifteenth-century play *Everyman* complains to a personified Death, "thou comest when I had thee least in mind."[30] The point the play is making, of course, is that most of us avoid preparing for death until a catastrophe—a cancer diagnosis, a car accident, the death of a loved one—brings us face-to-face with our own fragility.

Even though late medieval culture was saturated with the imagery and rituals of death—from how-to manuals to the prayers of the Office of the Dead and the circulation and veneration of pieces of holy corpses—finitude remained as unthinkable to medieval people as it does to us. In his book *Arts of Dying*, D. Vance Smith explores how death presents a philosophical and formal problem: it is virtually impossible to imagine or represent our nonexistence. What can be thought and written, he notes, is *dying*.[31] I find Smith's distinction between thinking death (an impossibility) and thinking dying (a necessity) helpful for conceptualizing what the medieval *ars moriendi* might offer to modern thinking about ecological catastrophe and climate change. Many recent environmental theorists have suggested that one of the central hinderances to taking action is the near unthinkability of climate change.[32]

We struggle to imagine the nonexistence or finitude of a species, civilization, or planet viscerally enough to move us to action. But what we *can* see, feel, and understand is process, which is manifested in ongoing, quotidian particulars. And thus, the chapters that follow focus on representations of dying more than depictions of death, on how medieval biblical literature turns again and again to dynamic scenes of vanishing worlds to make urgent the need for preparation, reformation, and transformation before it's too late.

As I have already begun to suggest, in medieval texts, there are two main responses to transience—both of our lives and that of the cosmos. On the one hand, the *ars moriendi* encourages renunciation, or *contemptus mundi* (the contempt of the world). Like much medieval religious writing, it insists on nonattachment, that we must turn away from the world, looking for permanence beyond the mutability of the physical realm in the stability of a spiritual one. To take this approach is to read mortality, earthly ruin, catastrophe, and decay (what Gregory the Great calls the "wounds of the world") as the earth's own reminder *not* to love it. Medieval *artes moriendi* often advocate turning away from an ephemeral cosmos to the stability of heaven, associating the art of dying with learning distrust of the world rather than care for it. Yet, on the other hand, the *ars moriendi* also turns us back toward the world, reminding us of our responsibility to the other, the necessity of care, the work of mercy, of acknowledging suffering and loving the neighbor and stranger alike. In navigating this apparent tension between relinquishment of the world and engagement with it, this book argues, medieval biblical texts explore the complex moral demands of ecological attention and care.

Biblical Cosmology and Modern Environmentalism

> Cosmologies are a source of identity and orientation to the world. They tell us who we are.
> ROBIN WALL KIMMERER, *Braiding Sweetgrass*

The weave of western Christianity is threaded with the *contemptus mundi*. "Behold not the earth, but lift your eye up," commands one medieval morality play.[33] "This world is not my home / I'm just a-passing through," intones the old gospel song, a sentiment that was in the water where I grew up in the foothills of East Tennessee. Every Sunday morning in church I heard about how we should hope for a better, more enduring world than this one. Sunday afternoons I wandered in the woods or helped my veterinarian father tend to the motley creatures temporarily sharing our home—cats and dogs with their IVs on the kitchen window seat, but also wounded and orphaned wildlife: baby opossums and squirrels, ducks in the bathtub, owls on the piano—each of which was deserving of care. The fabric of the small world I inhabited was tightly woven with wonders and wounds, its warp and woof. Every encounter seemed to confirm that this mortal world was very much my home, worthy of devotion and care, not contempt.

This book is born in part of my lifelong attempt to reckon with the dualistic worldviews that shaped my early life, the tension between the world-denying religious tradition in which I was immersed and my persistent sense that one of our fundamental privileges as human beings is to contemplate, love, and care for the more-than-human world, ephemeral though it and we may be. I couldn't help but love *both* the biblical stories and the world they sometimes seemed to condemn. Both were sites of wonder and incomprehension, beauty, sublimity, tragedy, and occasionally horror. It was not until much later, when I began to study the material and religious cultures of the Middle Ages that I came to better understand that although Christianity in particular, and Western thought more generally, has often embraced dualistic worldviews, emphasizing spirit over body, heaven over earth, immortality over mortality, there have always been other ways of telling the story of creation, catastrophe, and resurrection, even in the West. There have always been counternarratives.

Apocalyptic Ecologies charts some of the counternarratives that circulated in the centuries leading up to the Protestant Reformation in England and explores how biblical cosmologies (accounts of cosmic beginnings) and eschatologies (accounts of cosmic endings) framed how medieval people understood the work of living and dying in an ecologically vulnerable world. Part of its aim is thus to make freshly visible the particular contributions that parabiblical and apocryphal literature once made to ecological thinking. And part of its aim is to respond to the often religious roots of contemporary climate change skepticism or disinterest, which are frequently articulated by those who welcome global ecological collapse as a portent of a divinely ordained apocalypse. In so doing, this book suggests that attending to how premodern biblical literature engaged the problem of origins and ends might not only help us recover a productive awareness of the world's fragility and of our deep kinship with it but also encourage us to respond with compassion and care while we still can.

In a sense, this book is a sustained rumination on some of the questions that Lynn White Jr., a historian of medieval science and technology, posed in his hugely influential 1967 essay in *Science*, "The Historical Roots of our Ecologic Crisis": "What did [medieval] Christianity tell people about their relations with the environment?" And why do these medieval religious ideas matter for modern thinking about the relationships between humans and nature?[34] White's article was published in an early moment of social concern about the relationship of technology and the environment not long after Rachel Carson's 1962 *Silent Spring*. Yet unlike other contemporaneous work, such as *Silent Spring*, which opens with a description of an imagined *future* world that is silent of birdsong, White's essay turned to the past, arguing for the importance of thinking historically in understanding *how* we have arrived at this point. White's answers to the question of the source of the crises proved to be both enduring and controversial. Most simply put, he argued that our current ecological crisis is rooted in medieval cosmology. "What people do about their ecology," he writes, "depends on what they think about themselves in relation to things around them. Human ecology is deeply conditioned by belief about our nature and destiny—that is, by religion."[35] To develop this claim, White considers what sorts of beliefs medieval Christianity imparted and identifies several ecologically problematic strands of thought. Christianity is fundamentally anthropocentric and instrumentalizing, he writes. It insists on a dualist vision of the world that endows human beings alone with soul and thus renders them superior to all other beings. He sees this foundational anthropocentrism as forming the deep roots of modern justifications for the human exploitation of the more-than-human world.[36]

Although more than fifty years old, White's essay is still widely read and taught, thanks in part to its inclusion in one of the first anthologies of environmental writing in 1996 and several subsequent anthologies.[37] Since its publication, scholarship on the relationship of religion and the environment has proliferated.[38] During this time, many medievalists and scholars of religion have challenged White's claims of dualism and anthropocentrism by calling attention to the interconnectedness of the human and nonhuman in the premodern world.[39] Much of this work, however, aims to show that the original scriptures do not necessarily support White's claims about dominion, dualism, and anthropocentrism. While I have found these responses useful, they are often limited by their tendency to treat the scriptures as a single, static text. I approach the issue from a slightly different angle, exploring the popular reception of those scriptures in literature and performance.

Many premodern biblical texts do support a narrative of human dominion, but as this book argues, others imagine the moral and ecological implications of creation and apocalypse with surprising ambivalence, emphasizing human fragility, dependence, and responsibility for ecological catastrophe.

This argument needs to be made in part because many modern thinkers continue to echo White's basic claim. Linking Christian apocalypticism with "deep ecology," Timothy Morton complains that both share "a fundamental lack of concern for the way things are going. Since the end of the world is nigh, or since we will all be extinct in the long run, there isn't much point in caring."[40] Likewise, writing of the contrast between the Jewish and Christian origin stories and Indigenous ones, the botanist Robin Wall Kimmerer reminds us that cosmologies "tell us who we are. We are inevitably shaped by them no matter how distant they may be from our consciousness. One story leads to the generous embrace of the living world, the other to banishment."[41] Kimmerer is certainly right, but I would offer that we shape those stories as much as they shape us. Moreover, stories and the way we tell them change. After all, the vitality of myth is in its interpretation and reinterpretation. Mythic cosmologies are dynamic rather than static, carrying within themselves all their old significances as well as the possibilities of new ones. And thus, here I study the ways in which biblical stories of cosmic beginnings and endings have been represented in premodern English literature—the innovations, improvisations, and accretions—in the hope that they might inspire our own rereadings, adaptations, and improvisations as we reckon with our losses, consider our responsibility for them, and confront our own precarious climatic situation. The past, Karma Lochrie writes, both conditions and critiques the present, and thus "forms the necessary basis for imagining a future."[42] As it turns out, we do not know how to imagine a future without drawing from the past. And as this book attempts to show, we never have.

Yet the larger questions that White's thesis provokes about the power of biblical cosmology and eschatology to shape ethics remain central to this book. Throughout, I ask: To what extent is our way of inhabiting the world formed by historically deep ways of imagining its beginnings and endings? How should we understand the relationships among cosmology, eschatology, and ethics? Between the stories we tell about the world and how we dwell in it and with it? To what extent do our myths contribute to or discourage our sense of responsibility for the world? These are thorny questions, and ones bound to generate many answers, some of them incommensurable. I do not pretend to have complete answers to them, but I offer a few thoughts in the pages that follow with the caveat that they are necessarily limited and partial.

Whereas White speaks generally about the medieval reception of the Judeo-Christian creation story from Genesis, I look at particular literary examples in premodern popular culture of the reception of biblical stories. There have been few considerations of how the medieval religious imagination might speak to the modern environmental imagination that don't reach for an idealized version of a preindustrial world or protoenvironmentalist saints. White himself offers Francis of Assisi as a medieval model for responsible ecological relations. Similarly, Pope Francis, in his 2015 papal encyclical *Laudato si'*, invokes Saint Francis as an ecological model in his impassioned call for a recommitment to the idea of "integral ecologies," advocating an ethic of care based on the interconnectedness of all things.[43] Other recent thinkers have looked to Britain's pre-Christian or Celtic pasts for more "green" medieval environmental thinking. Still others appeal to Hildegard of Bingen's notion of *viriditas* (greenness) or to a premodern feminization of the physical world as "mother nature."[44] Most recently, scholars of premodern ecologies have drawn from critical animal studies and object-oriented approaches to decenter the human and emphasize the ecological mesh of all living and nonliving things.[45] Though their gaze remains focused largely on the human, medieval biblical adaptations display a wide-ranging, imaginative, dramatic, and sometimes irreverent approach to many of the cosmological and ethical questions that preoccupied medieval thinkers, throwing into relief that ecological questions have long been moral questions. Yet their very variety serves as a helpful reminder that, as today, there is no single nonmodern ecological or environmental model. Rather, a diversity of ideas, images, and beliefs circulated about the relation of humans to the environments they inhabit.[46]

Forms of Ecological Attention

> A quality of attention has been given to you,
> When you turn your head the whole world
> leans forward.
> WILLIAM STAFFORD, "For People with Problems about How to Believe"

Rather than a work of biblical interpretation, *Apocalyptic Ecologies*, then, seeks to be a contribution both to what Jacques Le Goff calls a "history of the imagination" and to a history of ecological attention.[47] I aim to tell a story about how premodern reimagination of sacred history still haunts our ecological imagination, the images and stories that we use to envision our relation to the world, from a decline from utopic beginnings to a fear of apocalyptic ends. Yet it doesn't always tell the story we have come to expect of it. The *how* of these representations of biblical narratives is as important as the *what*. This book argues that medieval writers cultivate attention to apocalyptic ecologies and seek to inspire the moral imagination through literary forms. They offer apocalyptic ecologies as important objects of contemplation and use poetic diction and devices to encourage ways of seeing, meditating on, reframing, and responding to catastrophe. Thus, in the chapters that follow, I explore how religious ideas and ecological thinking are refracted through the lenses of form and performance.[48] I attend closely to plays, poems, and stories intended to stir the religious and moral imagination, to cultivate particular types of attention, to investigate the dynamics of contempt and care for the more-than-human world.

Although I focus on the stories that this early literature tells, I'm equally interested in the effects that its ways of telling might have on a reader's experience. Medieval biblical texts make use of a small set of literary devices and modes that I see as distinctively ecological: thick description, dilation, shifts in scale, lists and polysyndeton, antitheses, negations, repetition and refrain, elegy, pastoral. These are forms that slow or interrupt plot, even as they emphasize dynamic becoming rather than static modes of being. These forms ask us to linger, to notice, to be present. They shape a particular quality of attention, inviting us to read for relation, for process, for how the new emerges from the old. They are forms that prize accumulation and proliferation. This book thus approaches literary language as not just referential or mimetic but also as performative and affective. I see texts as capable of shaping not only attention but also a form of life or ethics, both by what they say and also by the feelings they invite.[49]

In the pages that follow, I aim to respond in kind, attending deeply to these elements of biblical adaptations, lingering with them, considering how they construct unlikely alliances, and observing their language, imagery, and style. My approach reflects the ecological hermeneutic that I think these forms encourage. In reading them, I attend to and draw out connections between small and large, then and now, being and becoming, quotidian and catastrophic, and human and nonhuman creatures. Ecologists have long asserted that ecological thinking requires systems thinking. From Aldo Leopold's "land ethic" to Timothy Morton's reminder that ecology *is* relation, an insistence on seeing the bigger picture and mapping its entangled relationships undergirds any ecological hermeneutic.[50] This ecological hermeneutic emphasizes uncovering surprising gatherings, connections, and kinships. It requires, in Donna Haraway's terms, "making oddkin," textually and temporally.[51] Thus, my method here relies on crafting new textual communities, assembling sometimes eclectic groupings of texts, centering texts and figures that have been seen as marginal, observing unlikely literary and biological kinships, and acknowledging that I, as a writer and reader, am embedded in the stories, pasts, and places I consider. As I gather texts and attend to them, I look for relationships, for how parts, even minor ones, affect wholes, for what might emerge from sometimes motley pairings, from how the past might interrupt or reread present values or assumptions.

In short, I approach these writings as invitations to reflection, to see the world through their lenses, to attend to their workings and their contexts. But I am also interested in what they might say to our moment, to notice (to use

Alan's phrase) how they might read me or us. I thus engage with these works as living things, active participants in ecologies of reading that embody, accrue, and shed meanings.[52] Although I aim to be attentive to what these works might have meant to their earliest readers, I am always equally interested in how they might speak to us now, and how the environments in which we dwell shape what we can see in these texts.[53] Yet here we should exercise caution. A purely presentist interpretation risks reproducing our own biases. Geoffrey Hartman warns, "The purpose of literary commentary cannot be simply amplifying the clichés of our predicament."[54] This is surely a temptation for the ecocritic. Many of the categories and terms I use here would have been unthinkable to the medieval writers with whom I seek to be in dialogue. That does not mean that they don't pertain to these writers, nor that they cannot help us better understand what is happening within these works or in our own world.

I try to lay claim here to my own situation and biases partly by writing in a personal voice. We all speak and write from a particular vantage; mine happens to be the midwestern soil of a college town where I have lived for about twenty years, a liberal dot in a largely conservative state. My own daily comings and goings are still relatively sheltered from the worst effects of climate change, but many of my neighbors suffer acutely from environmental disaster and degradation—from toxic land and polluted waterways, food scarcity, and inadequate shelter from increasingly frequent floods, tornadoes, and extreme heat. And together we inhabit a wounded landscape. The ground and waters are laced with polychlorinated biphenyls from electronics manufacturers that have long since moved their operations abroad. Not far from here, the limestone substrate has been excavated, leaving flooded ruins. Just beyond the county line, the land flattens into a sprawl of CAFOs (concentrated animal feeding operations) and industrial, monoculture farmland: soybeans and feed corn as far as the eye can see.

Though my here and now are insistently particular, I sometimes write with a rhetorical "we." In this, I do not mean to conjure a universal collective subject. As many Black and feminist scholars have pointed out, such collectivizing categories can erase differences in experience, standpoint, or history, implying that all contribute to or experience ecological suffering equally. Yet I also believe in the ethical value—even necessity—of moving beyond the individual, of inviting you to think with me about ecological attention and care as a shared endeavor. I use "we" *not* as homogeneous, but as relational, as composed of an "I" and a "you."[55] To allow the possibility of a "we" is to resist the tendencies in much modern thinking to emphasize only the "I" or, worse, to evacuate voice with an impersonal "one" or passive construction (both tendencies, notably, have ecological ramifications). I'm inspired by Maggie Nelson's reminder that "our entire existence . . . is built upon a 'we' instead of an 'I,' that we are dependent upon each other, as well as upon nonhuman forces that exceed our understanding or control. . . . The question is not whether we are enmeshed, but how we negotiate, suffer, and dance with that enmeshment."[56] And so, in the pages that follow, we will meditate on what medieval biblical texts say about how those before us have navigated precarious ecosystems and consider what they might have to offer our own efforts to "negotiate, suffer, and dance" with a vanishing world.

Stories of Making and Unmaking

> To think in deep time can be a means not of escaping our troubled present,
> but rather of re-imagining it; countermanding its quick
> greeds and furies with older, slower stories of making and unmaking.
> ROBERT MACFARLANE, *Underland*

Apocalyptic Ecologies begins in the garden, that prototypical scene of ecological flourishing, and ends with the apocalyptic de-creation of the world. It lingers in the long middle of sacred time, exploring how ecological catastrophes and the human response to them make and unmake the world.[57] Because it is partly a book about how these biblical narratives might speak to the experience of time and place in a precarious cosmos, its structure is both linear and reiterative. In apocalyptic ecologies, temporality can be multiple, fragmented, and mobile. Thus, even as the arc of the biblical teleology drives us forward, toward an ultimate end, these stories emphasize process and constantly cycle back, shifting between beginning and ending, creating and ruining, telling and retelling, lamenting and hoping. We will end and begin again and again as we circle around the fact that the literary ecologies this book explores are as haunted by their futures as they are by their pasts.[58]

This proleptic haunting and incessant process of generation and decay frame the book's first part, "Edenic Ecologies," which explores how retellings of the biblical story of Creation, Fall, and Expulsion speak to ecological process and loss. In it, chapter 1, "Being Earth," considers how literary performances of Eden cultivate attention to the vitality of the prehuman world and represent ecology *as* drama, as a dance of creation, proliferation, decline, and death. It then considers the status of the human in the "fayre processe" of the world, thinking about how biblical texts imagine humans and earth as kin, intimately entangled with the ecologies that they both inhabit and are. In chapter 2, "This Deadly Life," we turn from the practice of attention to the experience of loss and the work of care. We follow Adam and Eve out of the Garden and into the wilderness in order to consider how early treatments of postlapsarian life navigate two contradictory views of the fallen world, exploring both its corruption and its generative potential. Although these texts are interested in imagining a first encounter with a precarious world, they also meditate on Adam and Eve's sense of alienation from and culpability for that world's suffering.

In part 2, "Everyday Apocalypse," we attend to that suffering more directly, observing literary responses to ecological catastrophes—plagues, floods, storms, droughts, and earthquakes—in the biblical and medieval present. Although we might expect premodern religious literature to represent ecological disaster as a sign of God's judgment, I query this explanation in a brief excursus, "On Plague, Precedent, and the Punishment Paradigm," by glancing at how medieval treatments of plague invoke biblical precedent to consider the causes and meanings of catastrophe. Chapter 3, "Becoming Beholden," explores the surprising perspectives medieval writers take on two of the great catastrophes of the Hebrew Scriptures—Noah's Flood and the destruction of Sodom and Gomorrah. Rather than emphasize flood and fire as divine punishments, they invite readers to witness, meditate on, and even mourn the suffering produced by these disasters. In chapter 4, "Ordinary Apocalypses," I turn to the intersections of poetry and history in works that represent three medieval catastrophes: Matthew Paris's description of the effects of the "volcanic winter" of 1257, representations of the St. Maurus Day wind of 1362, and accounts of an earthquake that shook southern England in 1382. Examining what might be called medieval disaster literature, I explore how authors draw on literary form and convention to attempt to mediate the trauma of disaster by situating it in larger patterns (both historical and formal), by linking the ecological and the social, and by emphasizing the difficulty of meaning making in such circumstances.

My focus on the interrelation of attention, unknowability, and care in the midst of catastrophe come together in part 3, "Apocalyptic Ecologies," which focuses on a single late medieval apocalyptic motif: the Fifteen Signs of Doomsday, a popular catalog of ecological and cosmological signs that were believed to portend the Last Judgment. In chapter 5, "Fifteen Ways of Looking," I survey some of the sermons, lyrics, plays, and art that include this motif, and in doing so I read the Fifteen Signs as an *ars moriendi* for a wounded and dying world. I suggest that imagining the coming apocalypse by reflecting on natural disasters and strange phenomena in the material world not only reminds human beings of their participation in a larger ecology, and of the intersectionality of social ecology with environmental ecology, but also can invite them to reflect on their responsibilities to and sympathies with the more-than-human world.

Apocalyptic Ecologies ends with a brief epilogue, "Learning to Love," which considers how medieval texts think about the ambiguity of world love and the work of care in an age of catastrophe. I here consider the medieval dream vision *Piers Plowman*, focusing on its representation of a crisis of care and Kynde's (Nature's) pithy command at the poem's apocalyptic end. When the dreamer asks about what one should learn when confronted with both widespread moral indifference and a burning world, Kynde replies, "Lerne to love . . . and leef alle other" (learn to love and leave all other—that is, forsake all other pursuits). Reading this scene as a parable for our moment, this book, like *Piers Plowman*, thus ends with reflection on the relationship of attention and care, suggesting that attending to apocalyptic ecologies—in the past and today—might render visible the pressing need for relinquishment, new forms of community, and the difficult labor of love.

EXCURSUS

A Brief History of Medieval Climate Change

> Astronomyens also aren at her wittes ende;
> Of that was calculed of the clemat, the contrarie thei fynde.
>
> (Astronomers also are at their wits' ends;
> For what was calculated of the climate, they find to be the contrary.)
> WILLIAM LANGLAND, *Piers Plowman*

The biblical literature this book studies is the product of a period of climate change, of plummeting temperatures, strong storms, floods, famine, pollution, and plague. It is the product of a period of widespread suffering and mortality. Though life in the Middle Ages was always precarious, the fourteenth century was particularly catastrophic. John Aberth writes, "At no other time in history did so much variegated misery ... descend all at once."[1] There were many reasons for these catastrophes, but climate change contributed to them.

But on what grounds might we speak of "medieval climate change"? The phrase will surely seem anachronistic and oxymoronic to some readers, and perhaps even troublingly so. We might dismiss the notion, saying that for medieval people, there was only weather, not climate. Or perhaps suggest that such an attribution is anachronistic since the premodern notion of "climate" was very different from our own. And it is certainly true that until the sixteenth century, the term *climate* primarily indicated a region of the earth, as in the way we still speak of tropic climate zones or subarctic ones.[2] Climate in this sense is an aspect of geography. For this reason, it once made more sense to say that we could change our climate (for example, by traveling from one zone to another) than to say that the climate could change.

Or perhaps we might register discomfort about the social or political implications of describing environmental conditions as affected by climate change before the Anthropocene, since modern definitions of climate change understand it as fundamentally anthropogenic, the direct result of our post-industrial reliance on fossil fuels. The *Oxford English Dictionary*, for instance, locates the phrase *climate change* as emerging in the mid-nineteenth century and defines it as "an alteration in the regional or global climate; esp.

the change in global climate patterns increasingly apparent from the mid to late twentieth century onwards and attributed largely to the increased levels of atmospheric carbon dioxide produced by the use of fossil fuel."[3] To suggest the possibility of climate change before the Anthropocene may thus imply a troubling desire to decouple it from human agency. Or, worse, doing so may seem to suggest that, following the logic of some climate change deniers, if the climate has always been changing, there is no reason to be especially worried about the alterations we are seeing now.

Yet to acknowledge, as Brian Fagan puts it, that humanity "has been at the mercy of climate change for its entire existence" is not to diminish the imminent threat of anthropogenic climate change in our own moment, which is clearly altering the biosphere at a previously unfathomable rate and in urgent need of response.[4] Rather, to speak of "medieval climate change" is to suggest that what we experience as unprecedented is not absolutely singular, and indeed, as Fagan argues, the catastrophes and transformations wrought by premodern climate change may "offer precedent as we look into [our own] climatic future."[5] It is to remember that we are not the first to experience the ending of the world. Another climate historian suggests even that the catastrophic climate changes of the later Middle Ages "may be regarded as a trial run for global warning," since they allow us to consider how even minor shifts in climate can have significant social, economic, and political effects.[6]

After all, as this book explores, precedent can be a powerful tool for imagining new futures. When medieval thinkers looked for precedent for the unprecedented calamities of their times, they often turned to the stories of creation and fall, disaster, and salvation in the scriptures. If medieval climate change rarely rises to the surface of my argument, it both occasions and subtends the reflections on apocalyptic ecologies I consider here. Climate change is the dynamic bass that pulses underneath the treble of late medieval biblical adaptations. Thus, although the phrase "medieval climate change" may raise some eyebrows, it provides an essential historical context for the concerns of this book.

For the climate *was* changing in the fourteenth century, a period of transition between the "medieval warm period" and what some scholars call the "Little Ice Age." Paleoclimatologists and environmental historians tell us that from the ninth through the thirteenth centuries, Europe experienced a prolonged warming period marked by mild and relatively consistent seasons. Writers have variously called this period the "medieval climate anomaly," "medieval warm period," or "medieval climate optimum." Over the course of these four centuries, temperatures rose across northern Europe by 1 to 2 degrees Celsius (1.8 to 3.6 degrees Fahrenheit). This rise in temperatures in the Northern Hemisphere created a prolonged climate mildness suitable for agricultural development.[7] We might call it a climatic golden age. Under the gentler climes of this extended warm period, agriculture expanded massively. Lands that once would not been considered arable were transformed by the more temperate conditions. Marshes were drained. Coastal wetlands became croplands. Farmers began to cultivate cereal grains on what had previously been marginal land, from sandy-soiled lowlands to windswept moors and mountains. Vineyards thrived in England, which was warmer and dryer than it is now. It was also a period of exploration, particularly by sea. Iceland and Greenland, then green with scrubs and trees, were colonized by the Norse.

Across Europe, forests were cut down to increase agricultural area and growing capacity for the rapid population growth and development.[8] Nearly 80 percent of Europe was deforested between the tenth century and the end of the thirteenth century. New mines were dug, and millions of tons of stone were quarried. The wood and stone were used for massive building projects across Europe, including the new vaunting Gothic cathedrals: Notre Dame, Chartres, Lincoln, the choir at Canterbury (all begun in the late twelfth century).[9] Perhaps unsurprisingly, such growth came with a price. Widespread deforestation made cultivated land far more susceptible to flooding and erosion. Land was settled, developed, and farmed that would be marginal and uninhabitable with harsher weather. Although the warm period was a boon for rural farmers as well as for explorers and city builders, none of them could have anticipated how climate cooling would change everything.

A cooldown period, often called the "Little Ice Age," began in the early fourteenth century and continued until the nineteenth. During this time, temperatures in Europe dropped by as much as 2 degrees Celsius (about 3.6 degrees Fahrenheit). This relatively small decline was catastrophic for northern European ecosystems. The period of agricultural expansion and bountiful harvests came to an end. One can imagine that in its early decades most Europeans might have assumed the change in weather would be short-lived. After all, Europe had experienced several comparatively brief cooling periods before this climatic cooling began, the most catastrophic driven by volcanic activity. In 536 CE, the eruption of a volcano in Iceland led to eighteen months of ashen skies in Europe, causing temperatures to fall 1.5 to 2.5 degrees Celsius (about 2.7 to 4.5 degrees Fahrenheit). The coldest decade in the West in the past two millennia followed. Close on its heels was the Justinian plague (541), which decimated the Eastern Roman Empire. Seven hundred years later, as I briefly explore in chapter 4, the eruption of the Samalas volcano in Indonesia (1257) created another volcanic winter in Europe, resulting in years of devastating crop failure, famine, and disease. Yet compared to the Little Ice Age, these episodes were brief climatic hiccups.

Beginning at the end of the thirteenth century, changes in the North Atlantic Oscillation (NAO), pressure patterns in the atmosphere over the North Atlantic drove down temperatures and created wetter, more volatile weather across northern Europe. Unlike the Southern (El Niño) Oscillation, the NAO is notoriously unpredictable. Even with our advanced modeling technology today, predictions can rarely be "made more than a week or two in advance."[10] Although it's not entirely clear *why* the NAO fell at the end of the thirteenth century, most climatologists suggest in general that solar forcing (changes in solar radiation) affected a centuries-long lowering of the NAO, which led to sustained cold conditions in northern Europe and the northeast coast of what would become the United States. This resulted in not only lower temperatures overall but also climatological volatility. Such larger climatological shifts would have been unknowable to the medieval people who experienced them. Unlike us, they had no global framework for interpreting changing climate conditions. What people *did* notice were the local effects of these hemispheric changes: the rather more quotidian, environmental anomalies—unusual weather patterns, earthquakes, celestial wonders, strange animal behavior. As Eleanor Johnson has shown, medieval people did indeed have "a concept of ecosystemic peril," which they explored, in lieu of scientific language, through literature.[11]

There were plenty of signs that something was shifting, that there was a new normal. By the beginning of the fourteenth century, medieval chroniclers began to record that the weather was markedly wetter and cooler. English winters were so frigid from 1308 through 1312 that the Thames froze over in the winter of 1309–10. Astonished, an English chronicler observed that the freeze "lasted so long that people indulged in dancing in the midst of it near a certain fire made on the same and hunted a hare with dogs in the midst of the Thames."[12] Over the next few decades, the effects of cooling were widespread. Villages were deserted.[13] Greenland and Iceland became nearly uninhabitable. With fewer growing days each year, agricultural yields declined, even as the population initially continued to grow. Some crops, such as England's grapes, no longer grew at all. Arable land became marginal again, unable to sustain the cereal grains on which the late medieval diet largely depended.

England suffered a series of climate-related crises in the fourteenth century. The first was the Great Famine, which followed the failed harvest of 1315, though it was aggravated by the conditions of the previous decade: diminishing yields, longer winters, an extraordinarily wet and stormy summer that caused devastating flooding and prevented crops from being harvested or replanted, demographic pressures, and a social conservatism that made adaptation to the new conditions difficult.[14] After two years of frequent rain, the agricultural landscape was irreparably altered. Cereal grains and legumes spiked in price because of scarcity. Topsoil washed away. Mills and granaries had been destroyed by flooded rivers. Fruit crops were plagued by mildew and fungus. Disease ravaged livestock. Inflation ensued, leading to even broader ecosystemic precarity. The English chronicler Johannes de Trokelowe writes:

> Meat and eggs began to run out, capons and fowl could hardly be found, animals died of pest, swine could not be fed because of the excessive price of fodder. A quarter of wheat or beans or peas sold for twenty shillings, barley for a mark, oats for ten shillings. A quarter of salt was commonly sold for thirty-five shillings, which in former times was quite unheard of.[15]

In northern Europe, at least 10 percent of the population died of starvation, and surely many more suffered greatly from hunger and food insecurity.[16] Yet despite the complex ecosystemic and social causes of the famine, Trokelowe later explains it was the fulfillment of biblical prophecies made by Jeremiah (14:18).

Trokelowe was in good company in seeking precedent and explanation for the period's calamities in both the Bible and moral failure. Other writers also sought reasons for such sustained suffering and highlighted the particular precarity of the poor. The early fourteenth-century political poem, "Symonye and Covetise, or On the Evil Times of Edward II," opens with a catalog of a recent disasters and a promise to explain *why* they have inflicted the English people:

> Whii werre and wrake in londe and manslauht is i-come,
> Whii hungger and derthe on eorthe the pore hath undernome,
> Whii bestes ben thus storve, whii corn hath ben so dere,
> Ye that wolen abide, listneth and ye mowen here
>   The skile.[17]
>
> (Why war and destruction in the land, and death has come,
> Why hunger and famine on earth have seized the poor,
> Why beasts have starved, why grain has grown so expensive,
> You that will abide, listen and you may hear
> the reason.)

As he continues, the anonymous author explains that all these disasters are the direct effect of a failure of virtue at all levels of society, even as he notes that the suffering is unevenly distributed. In later chapters of this book, I will explore such interpretations in greater detail and from several perspectives, but, for now, a simple point will suffice: for many medieval people, what we might call "natural disasters" were not understood as natural but rather as anthropogenic, caused by human behavior. What medieval thinkers seem often to have believed about these ecological calamities was that, as Allan Mitchell writes, "human disorder" was the cause of "major upheavals in the totality of things."[18] Or, as Eleanor Johnson says, when medieval people saw "climate change and famine . . . they simply assumed it was in some way their fault, their doing, their own responsibility."[19]

Although the Great Famine has, at least in the modern imagination, been overshadowed by the bubonic plague, which ravaged England only three decades later, it haunted the cultural memory of those who survived it. The weather began to normalize after 1317, but the harvest of 1321 was again catastrophic. However, this time, agriculture was plagued by drought rather than flooding. The food supply didn't return to sustainable levels until 1325, when England's population had shrunk significantly because of starvation and disease. Little did survivors know that things would only get worse. Just around the corner was the Black Death (beginning in 1348), an epidemic that wiped out nearly half of Europe's population and that had widespread ecological and social effects. The final decades of the fourteenth century, as I'll discuss in chapter 4, were characterized by a series of unusual geological and meteorological events—storms, earthquakes, and other famines.

This is all to say that the fourteenth century in England was remarkably calamitous, unusual for the sheer volatility of its climate, the number of ecological disasters, and the huge mortalities they inflicted. These crises were exacerbated by the expansion, development, and ecological exploitation of the preceding period. But they were also intensified by the lack of cultural memory of a world that was or could be otherwise. Such forgetting had repercussions for social preparedness for a more precarious climate future. Late medieval culture, William Rosen writes, was "inclined to sacrifice the future in order to satisfy the present."[20] The lack of preparedness was caused not only by an appetite for growth but also by a failure of imagination, memory, and a reticence to adapt to a new climate reality.

The effects of these climate changes rumbled through literature, art, theology, and politics, where their traces remain. Most of the literature that this book studies was composed during the catastrophic first century of cooling, though it often has an indirect relation to this background. Many works engage catastrophe opaquely, as David Coley shows in his investigation of how the Black Death haunts the works of the *Pearl*-poet.[21] Yet other works confront the losses directly, exploring the social effects of ecological catastrophe. For example, the fourteenth-century alliterative dream vision *Piers Plowman* engages with trauma of the Great Famine decades later in its depiction of the ravenous appetite of Hunger, its anxiety about "wasters," and its description of the catastrophic wind of 1362. As *Piers* and other poems make clear, in the Middle

Ages, as now, ecological suffering was largely avoided by the propertied and experienced by the poor. For instance, a fifteenth-century nativity play, the Towneley "Second Shepherds' Play," opens with a scene of ecosystemic precarity, as a shepherd bemoans both the extreme cold and the exploitative social structures that compel him to work in such conditions.[22] The shepherd observes that his exposure to the extremities is compounded by the injustices poor laborers suffer at the hands of "gentry men" who oppress them by privatizing land (assarting), taxation, profligate consumption, and exploitative labor laws. Such complaints should remind us that in the Middle Ages, as today, ecosystemic suffering is exacerbated by unjust social, economic, or political factors, that it "is unequally distributed," as Jeffrey Jerome Cohen writes.[23] Then, as now, not all experience or contribute to ecological degradation equally.

Yet, perhaps even more evident than traces of climatological trauma and its social and economic causes and repercussions is the general sense of unpredictability and uncertainty that the tumultuous fourteenth century generated. We see such uncertainty in the lines from *Piers Plowman* that serve as the epigraph to this excursus, but this concern about the apparent disorder and unpredictability of weather lingers well into the fifteenth century, and perhaps even longer. In the final lines of the anonymous debate poem *Mum and the Sothsegger*, for instance, the narrator decries those who try to make predictions about meteorological events:

> For there nys wight in this world that wote bifore eve
> How the winde and the wedre wol wirche on the morowe,
> Ne noon so cunnyng a clerc that construe wel couthe
> Ere Sunneday a sevenyght what shal falle.[24]

> (For there is no person in this world that knows before evening
> how the wind and the weather will be in the morning
> nor so cunning a clerk that can construe
> before Sunday what shall befall that week.)

Although the narrator suggests that knowledge of weather on the immediate horizon is possible, he conveys a sense of uncertainty about predicting anything more. Yet, such uncertainty may be a lesson in itself. Even if we intellectually accede to the world's fundamental mutability and vulnerability, most of us tend to arrange our lives as if climate is predictable until catastrophe lands at our doorstep, as if sheer optimism about the orderliness of the world were potent enough to counteract any signs indicating otherwise or to withstand climatological or geological forces that still remain beyond our ken.

Yet, as climate historians remind us, we can only understand any given climate patterns as stable when our scales of time are as short as our cultural memory and modes of measurement, which, until recently, have spanned a lifetime or perhaps a few generations. When we take the long view, we see that climate has always been changing—what has shifted is the nature of our understanding of human responsibility for that change and of how (and even if) we can mitigate it. Though we may be optimistic about our ability to engineer a way out of most catastrophes, the late medieval view of nature was darker than ours has been for many centuries, and perhaps more realistic. Yet it is precisely because premodern writers are often deeply attuned to ecological instability and precarity that we, who also inhabit an age of climate catastrophe, may have something to learn from how they navigated an apocalyptic world.

PART I

Edenic Ecologies

Earth felt the wound.
JOHN MILTON, *Paradise Lost*

Even a wounded world is feeding us. Even a wounded world holds us, giving us moments of wonder and joy.
ROBIN WALL KIMMERER, *Braiding Sweetgrass*

1

Being Earth

Performing the "Fayre Processe" of Creation

> Death neither negates nor terminates life but gives birth to its intrinsic potentialities, especially its potentiality for appearance.... Death sets things in motion, including our desires. It is the generative source of nature's ceaseless movement into form.
> ROBERT POGUE HARRISON, *Gardens*

In late winter, I walk in the garden. I kneel close to the earth to brush aside decaying leaves and run my fingers through the composting soil underneath, loosening it. This time of year, there is little physical evidence that in a matter of months these empty beds will resemble Darwin's tangled bank, messy and overflowing with life: vegetable and animal, visible and microscopic. There's little to suggest that much could emerge at all from the cold earth. Except, perhaps, in the crumbling humus that I sift through my fingers and the reasonable expectation of sunshine, rain, and warming days. To garden is to trust in the reliability of precedent and process—that life will return because it has before, that the days will warm, that the rain will fall, that seeds will germinate and grow. It is to become intimate with the rhythms of the biological world. It is also to know that plants grow best in the decayed remnants of other living beings, to know that one must cut branches and nip off buds and stalks to encourage growth. To cultivate a garden is to welcome death, in Robert Pogue Harrison's terms, as "the generative source of nature's ceaseless movement into form."[1]

Subject to time, change, and decay, gardens are microcosms of a transient cosmos, not only different in the winter than in the spring but also different at dusk than they were at dawn. As I draft these words, in late May, I periodically pause my work and walk outside to stretch my legs and see what's new. I scrutinize the soil in the raised beds, looking for pea shoots, which are just beginning to unfurl. I puzzle over why so few carrots have sprouted. I marvel at the fuchsia peony that bloomed just two days ago that is already shedding its petals. And I pluck the tiny weeds that seem to emerge hourly (a Sisyphean task if there ever was one).

It is my growing intimacy with the rhythms of this particular place that makes it difficult for me to understand why writers, artists, and theologians have long fantasized about an archetypal garden, Eden, that is free from such patterns of growth, flourishing, and death. I am not alone in my incomprehension. In his lyric "Sunday Morning," the modernist poet Wallace Stevens depicts a young woman in her garden contemplating the paradox of longing for "some imperishable bliss."[2] She muses, "is there no change of death in paradise?" For Stevens, the supposed stasis of the Garden of Eden is problematic since "death," as the poem later insists, is "the mother of beauty." The present-day poet Eleanor Wilner also ponders the eerie silence of a primeval garden paradise where there is "no insect hum / of propagation, no busy messengers / of change."[3] So imagined, the Garden of Eden is a world outside of and not subject to time and its processes. Lacking agents of change, it is without death but also without birth, without decay but also without growth.

Yet the Edenic world was not always envisioned as such a static system. As this chapter will explore, there were at least two ways that medieval religious thinkers conceived of prelapsarian ecologies. Some imagined every living being—vegetable, animal, human—in the newly made world as peaceful and immortal. Others understood ecological change, competition, and mortality as intrinsic to what one late medieval Creation play calls the "fayre processe" (beautiful process) of the cosmos.[4] To put this another way, it was a medieval commonplace that the prelapsarian world was, in fact, shaped by "the change of death." The ecological rhythms of birth, growth, decay, and death were not only productive but also wondrous, a source of the world's beauty and value. In the pages that follow, I consider a few dramatic and lyrical treatments of these "fayre processe[s]," focusing first on how medieval biblical plays perform the flourishing, if ephemeral, world, staging it as a site of delight and wonder, and second on how these plays and transience poems imagine human bodies as part and parcel of these fleeting ecologies.

That ecology is bound up with transience and death will not surprise modern readers; that some premodern religious thinkers celebrated the processes of generation, proliferation, decay, and death as part of the goodness of the *original* creation might. After all, within modern Christianity, it's a doctrinal commonplace that the Fall ushered in death. Wikipedia baldly states this position: "According to Christianity, death is a consequence of the fall of man from a prior state of innocence, as described in the Book of Genesis."[5] There's some biblical support for this belief. Often quoted is Genesis 2:17, in which God warns the new humans that if they eat from the tree, they will die.[6] Moreover, after Adam and Eve consume the forbidden fruit, God curses them with suffering, earthbound labor, and the promise of mortality, which will return them to the earth: "for dust thou art, and into dust thou shalt return" (Genesis 3:19). If such passages are now frequently taken as positing an imperishable prelapsarian world, medieval theologians tended to read them as concerned only with *human* death. In fact, since the scriptures don't speak to the presence of death in the nonhuman world before the Fall, it was once reasonable to assume that the cycles of generation and decay were at work from the beginning, and perhaps even more strikingly, that even after the Fall, the more-than-human world remained unfallen, as inherently good in the present as it was on its first day.[7] Perishability was not equivalent to fallenness. It was far from a foregone conclusion that the Fall changed anything about the inherent goodness and beauty of the nonhuman world.

But this is to oversimplify the story. When it came to speculation about the Creation, medieval people inhabited a world of paradox, of "both/and" rather than "either/or." Paradox, Caroline Walker Bynum reminds us, "is not dialectical. Paradox is the simultaneous assertion (not the reconciliation) of opposites."[8] Questions about the nature of prelapsarian ecology—Was there death in Eden? Were its plants and animals immortal or temporal? Was the biosphere fallen? Or just the human relation to it?—drew thinkers into these paradoxes from the fourth century onward and had critical stakes for how later theologians and writers understood, used, and valued nonhuman beings.[9] From the earliest Christian literature on the six-day creation (*hexamera*) until the Reformation, many thinkers thus imagined the physical cosmos as a paradox: both wondrously orderly, full of life, even profligate in its beauty *and* intrinsically fragile, contingent, all its processes fueled by death. The hexameral corpus repeatedly affirms the human relation to the more-than-human world as multiple and contradictory: the created world is good yet perishable; humans are substantially the same as other creatures, their bodies microcosms of the larger cosmos, and yet somehow they are also like God; humans share bodily fragility and transience with all other creatures, yet they are granted sovereignty.

Such paradoxes shaped premodern ecological ethics and aesthetics, informing how people dwelled among and with the world's other beings. Modern studies of early attitudes toward the physical world often seek to resolve these paradoxes, arguing that medieval people favored one side or another. Many scholars settle these tensions by locating the origins of a hostile, perishable universe in a postlapsarian "fallen nature," a concept that was known to medieval theologians but seems to have only achieved theological ascendancy in the Reformation.[10] In this view, the prelapsarian cosmos is good, the postlapsarian is corrupt.[11] Others attempt to reconcile the paradoxes of human nature (the simultaneous likeness with and difference from the world's other creatures) by suggesting that the Creation was fundamentally a story of human exceptionalism. Versions of Lynn White's influential thesis follow, and biblical cosmology becomes the primary origin of Western belief in human dominion and entitlement.[12]

However, as this chapter aims to show, some late medieval treatments of this origin story communicated rather different lessons about the nature of the world and the human relationship to it. In emphasizing process, they raised questions about human vulnerability, why we suffer and die, why the world feels like such a precarious place, and whether it is possible to live more harmoniously with the rest of the world's inhabitants. The creation story served as a reminder of the humble origins of humanity and its kinship with the nonhuman world as well as asserting human power over it.[13] Human exceptionalism and dominion also find their roots in this narrative, though Genesis seems rarely to have been used to justify ecological exploitation until well after the Middle Ages. What I hope to show instead is that exceptionalism and dominion are only one strand of what was once a lively, multifaceted conversation. The paradoxes of human power and weakness, difference and likeness, were not always resolved, as White implies, by asserting dominion. Instead, representations of the origin story often highlighted human fragility, coexistence, and kinship with an inherently good, if perishable, ecology.

There may be no better site for contemplating the beauty and value of ecological perishability than the garden, the prototypical scene of diversity, beauty, and fecundity, where art and biology most amicably converse. As sites of human-plant-animal collaboration, gardens have long been associated with both care and art.[14] Traditionally, a gardener is a contemplative, a caretaker, and an artist, meditating on ecological processes, nourishing the garden, protecting it, and shaping the scene's ecologies in collaboration (and sometimes in competition) with all the garden's other inhabitants, the birds and bees, worms and aphids, kale, tomatoes, and roses. Gardens offer a model of mutual flourishing. Insofar as a garden is a microcosm of a larger world or philosophical laboratory, it can function as what Michel Foucault calls a "heterotopia," an other space, a place of alternatives and potential.[15] Indeed, when we dream of a thriving world, many of us have long pictured that world as a garden.[16]

The Garden of Eden looms large in the modern ecological imagination. It provides a site for both ecological nostalgia and hope. On the one hand, the myth of an original, garden paradise promises insight into who we are, where we come from, and why the world is as it is.[17] On the other hand, it has long offered a space for critiquing the status quo and imagining possible futures.[18] Eden, Alastair Minnis writes, gave "generations of writers the opportunity to imagine an alternative universe."[19]

If gardens help us dream about possible worlds, they first ask us to think about ecology formally—about its patterns and rhythms and relationships. After all, whether one is growing vegetables, cultivating roses, or encouraging native plants, as Susan Stewart writes, a garden requires "the wresting of form from nature."[20] It's no wonder that garden writing delights in catalogs and categorizing, in elaborate descriptions, dilation, and lists. Medieval rhetorical manuals find gardens to be particularly apt subjects for demonstrating such literary devices.[21] Yet, descriptive devices such as these can miss a central aspect of the garden—its dynamism and ephemerality—since they tend toward the static, representing a garden as a collection captured in a moment of time. As any gardener knows, unlike many other types of art, gardens are always in motion, always in flux. Not only do they undergo a seasonal cycle of generation, flourishing, and decay, plants migrate. They expand their footprint. They disappear and reemerge somewhere else. One year a bed is full of bee balm, and the next, rudbeckia has taken over. One year a hydrangea's blooms are a dusty rose, the next year, a lily white. Gardens share this mobility and changeability with performance. Like ecological processes (and indeed, like life itself), performance is ephemeral—it takes shape in bodies for a time, then disappears.[22] Like gardens, performance and drama create a space of potentiality, but there is also an unpredictability to the shape any performance might take.

Thus, although there is a large corpus of writing on medieval gardens and Eden, I here attend to those medieval biblical texts that depict garden ecology *as* drama, as a scripted process of coming into being and passing away.[23] While they make powerful use of descriptive modes, the medieval biblical plays and transience lyrics this chapter considers leverage the formal affordances of drama, presenting prelapsarian ecologies as embodied cycles of creation and cessation, of action and idleness, of presence and absence, of potential movement. The relationship I am positing between ecological process and dramatic process is thus more than an analogy. Ecology and performance intersect and interact in many of the works I will discuss in this chapter. For instance, the term *process* is not only frequently used to describe nature's work but, in the Middle Ages, it is also another word for a dramatic performance.[24] The term can indicate a narrative sequence or progression; it also emphasizes forms of becoming over static being.[25] By focusing on premodern performances of ecological processes, this chapter shifts away from what Margaret Ronda calls the "essentially observational and mimetic ethics" of much ecocriticism, which reads for "what *is*," to a hermeneutic of process and rhythm. I thus read for what is in motion, what is coming into or passing out of being.[26]

When medieval biblical plays stage prelapsarian ecologies, they perform the rhythms of creation, growth, and decay in word and embodied action.[27] Creation, these works insist, is unintelligible, perhaps even unthinkable, outside such cycles of change. Foregrounding the flux of matter, including the matter of human beings, some performances of medieval biblical texts treat change not as a flaw but as the source of creaturely potential and meaning. This focus is evident in both the content of the plays and lyrics and in their forms, which depict ecological cycles—from generation and proliferation to decay and death—as a "fayre processe." They both thematize the flux of the inhuman world and perform how word can contour movements, shaping chaos into cosmos. Through lists, medieval plays and lyrics present an ecological aesthetics of abundance that relies on cycles of change. Through rhythms and repetitions, they script ecological process and potentiality. Performing a generative, dynamic aesthetic that is appropriate to Edenic ecologies, these works celebrate the processes of proliferation and degeneration.

This chapter thus explores how premodern performances of the Creation and the Garden of Eden represent ecological transience as a fundamental aspect of collective flourishing. Opening with a consideration of theological and dramatic representations of prelapsarian ecology, I examine the representation of ecology as a dance of generation, proliferation, and decay, looking first at prelapsarian plant life and then at animal agency, suffering, and death in the York creation sequence and hexameral writings. The first half of the chapter focuses on the wondrous rhythms and diversity of the prehuman biosphere; the latter part turns to medieval reflections on creaturely likeness, considering how drama and lyrics represent the place of the human being within this mutable cosmos. Premodern plays and lyrics imagine people and earth as kin, representing humans as microcosms or "little worlds" intimately entangled with, inhabiting, and embodying larger ecological processes and rhythms.

"So Like Our Perishing Earth"

> Is there no change of death in paradise?
> Does ripe fruit never fall? Or do the boughs
> Hang always heavy in that perfect sky,
> Unchanging, yet so like our perishing earth.
> WALLACE STEVENS, "Sunday Morning"

Around midsummer's eve, beginning in the late fourteenth century and ending the mid-sixteenth, the northern English town of York staged an annual festival of plays. From before dawn until after dusk, a procession of pageant wagons wove a circuitous path through the city streets. On them, amateur actors from the local guilds performed the biblical story from the creation and fall of the angels to the apocalypse. Beginning in the early morning darkness near Mickelgate, the opening sequence of plays depicted the creation of the world.[28] As the sun broke onto the horizon, God once again separated the darkness from the light. The firmament again appeared. As the plays themselves describe it, the physical cosmos took shape in performance as a "fayre processe" of ecological flourishing, an iterative cycle in which creation depends on decay and death, and creaturely permanence requires perishability.[29]

Where most of the other extant English cycles of biblical plays offer a rather perfunctory treatment of the opening chapters of Genesis, surveying the Creation and Fall in a single play, York offers a sequence of six plays: the Barkers' "Creation of the Angels and the Fall of Lucifer," the Plasterers' "Creation," the Cardmakers' "Creation of Adam and Eve," the Fullers' "Adam and Eve in Eden," the Coopers' "Fall of Man," and the Amourers' "The Expulsion."[30] The only other subject given as extended a treatment is the Passion and Crucifixion of Christ. The York plays linger in the natal world as long as they can. They revel in amplification and dilation. As they do so, the plays meditate on the nature of creation and the place of humanity in it. They also draw the mythic scene of cosmic origins into the present. In performance, the plays stage the creation of the world as re-creation, imaginatively transforming York's urban streets from chaos into a flourishing garden.

Devoting an entire play to the second through the fifth days of creation (the making of the physical universe), York directs attention to a prehuman world. "The Creation" contains neither dialogue nor human characters. Instead, the actor playing God issues a lengthy monologue.[31] Day by day, element by element, he speaks being into being. His words give form and movement to matter, performing the creativity he celebrates. The beginning and the end of the play emphasize the creative power of God's speech.[32] God begins, "Noght by my strenkyth, but by my steuyn / A firmament I byd apere" (Not by my strength but by my voice, / I command a sky appear; 54/31–32). He concludes with the creation of the land animals on the fifth day, saying, "I with my worde hase wrothe" (I have created with my words, 58/160). That God is the master craftsman who creates via words is a commonplace of theological discussions of the Creation, but it here also aligns him with the creative potential of drama itself, in which scripts come to life in bodies, in which every performance is a new creation.[33]

Over the course of the play's 172 lines, the generation, formation, animation, and sustaining of matter unfurl as one long performative utterance. Through God's speech act, the York play performs creation as *poiēsis* and ecology as drama.[34] The play's subject is the origin, relations, and sustaining processes of the animal, vegetable, and mineral. Its actors—stars, water, plants, fish, birds, and animals—do not need to speak to perform ecological agency. Instead, the play invites its medieval audience to imagine a thriving ecology *without* humans, to meditate on the workings of the cosmos before human presence and influence. And what is this prehuman world like? Beautiful. Diverse. Flourishing. God characterizes it as "fayre" seven times in this short play.[35] In all this, the play implies a poetic rather than a mechanistic or instrumentalizing vision of the cosmos; it locates the world's value in beauty and intrinsic goodness more than usefulness.

God's words also initiate the cosmic dance of impermanence, spinning the world into its cycles of life, death, and regeneration. Perishability, the play shows, is a source of creaturely creativity. Unlike God, creatures don't create ex nihilo, but rather by reproduction.[36] God creates with his words; creatures perform the script with their bodies. Diverging creative modes also shape the play's depiction of permanence, both divine and creaturely. In the opening lines, God proclaims his eternal existence in heaven: "Withoutyn ende ay-lastandly" (Always lasting, without end; 54/4).[37] In the closing lines, he exhorts all creaturely life to continue "Ay furth in fayre processe" (Always in a beautiful process; 58/170). The play thus offers two models of permanence and creativity: one outside time and matter and one within it; one free from mutability, the other dependent on it.

Contrasting the rhythms of the "fayre processe" of the prehuman world with the stability of eternity, God's narration slows down the rapid narrative of Genesis, drawing together beginnings, middles, and ends. When he surveys his work in the penultimate stanza of the play, God pronounces:

> And so it sall be kende
> How all þat eme is ought,
> Begynnyng, mydes, and ende
> I with my worde hase wrothe. (58/157–60)

> (And so it shall be known,
> how all that is required,
> beginning, middle, and end,
> I have made with my word.)

On the one hand, the passage suggests the holistic nature of creation—the original contains everything required to sustain itself permanently. Yet, on the other hand, the reference to endings is curiously proleptic in this prelapsarian world. Indeed, for a play ostensibly about beginnings, "The Creation" has a surprising amount to say about the middles and ends of biological life. But this is, of course, the place where all living beings dwell; we are in the middle, in constant movement between beginnings and endings.

As the play opens, we find ourselves in the middle of things. Since the previous play, the "Fall of the Angels," had already performed the separation of light from darkness, the "Creation" focuses almost entirely on the elements of the earthly realm. After God recalls the action of the previous play, he speaks the firmament into being, naming it a middle space that "sal nough moue, / But be a mene" (shall not move, / but be an intermediary; 55/42–43). But it is here that the process begins, for middle earth beneath, like this play, will be defined by movement.

When God calls it into being, the physical cosmos is already caught up in the transient processes that will define it. In the eight stanzas devoted to the third through the fifth days of creation, God creates via descriptive litanies the emergence of lush, entangled, and ephemeral ecologies. On the third day, God separates the waters from the land and creates vegetable life. He says:

> Þe erthe sall fostyr and furthe bryng
> Buxsumly, as I wyle byde,
> Erbys and also othyr thyng,
> Well for to wax and worthe to wede;
> Treys also þaron sall spryng
> With braunchis and with bowis on brede,
> With flouris fayr on heght to hyng
> And fruth also to fylle and fede.
> And þane I will þat þay
> Of þemselfe haue þe sede
> And mater, þat þay may
> Be lastande furth in lede.
>
> And all þer materis es in mynde
> For to be made of mekyl might,
> And to be kest in dyueris kynde
> So for to bere sere burgvns bright.
> And when þer frutys is fully fynde
> And fayrest semande vnto syght,
> Þane þe wedris wete and wynde
> Oway I will it wende full wyght;
> And of þere sede full sone
> New rotys sall ryse vpright. (55–56/65–86)
>
> (The earth shall foster and bring forth
> Obediently, as I will bid
> plants and also other things,

to grow healthy and be worthily clad.
Trees also shall spring there,
with branches and with boughs extended,
with fair flowers to hang on high,
and fruit also to fill and feed.
And then, I command, that they,
from themselves generate the seed
and substance so that they may
be lasting in that place.

And all their substance in mind,
to be made of great power,
and to be cast in diverse types,
in order to produce diverse bright blossoms.
And when their fruit is fully developed,
and seems most beautiful to see,
then with windy and rainy weathers
I will make it go away very quickly.
And from these seeds, very soon,
new roots shall emerge upright.)[38]

Though we often read plant life as little more than background, this description works against any tendency toward "plant blindness" (a form of cognitive bias that makes it difficult to see or acknowledge the importance of the plants around us). The two stanzas direct us to attend to the biological cycles of plant life. They do so in part by rhetorical and biological accumulation. The passage gathers grasses and trees and branches and flowers and fruit through its series of "and" and "also." Yet this is no static portrait of a spring scene. God both describes and performs motion and change, inviting absorption in the horticultural process and wonder in its rhythm and beauty.

The complex, yet orderly, rhythms of creation are performed, in part, by the monologue's intricately constructed twelve-line stanza form, which weaves together alliteration, a semiregular iambic tetrameter, and end rhyme, performing both sonic sameness and variation. The stanzas themselves are structured by an "octet/quatrain" formula, a form in which, as Susanna Fein notes, the final quatrain sometimes functions as a miniature envoi, shifting from narration to direct speech.[39] The stanza structure works a bit differently in the York "Creation": the opening eight lines of each stanza often establish a scene of growth, and as the final quatrains bring in a new rhyme word, attesting to the continuance and fulfilment of divine purpose in the created thing.[40] The shift from the *abab* rhyme scheme to the final *cbcb* thus rhythmically echoes ecological repetition and difference—the new thing emerging from, but still part of, the old.[41] Note, for instance, how both of the foregoing stanzas describing the third day introduce the shift to the quatrain with a causal, "then" that moves the imagination to how these plants will regenerate: through the production of seeds that will fall to the ground and produce new roots. This process, these stanzas suggest, enables sustainable ecologies.

This formal structure also figures ecological process as a sacred performance. For the play's performance of beginnings and endings may also be indebted, as Pamela King suggests, to contemporary liturgical texts. King explains that the York creation sequence aligns with the liturgy for the first week of Lent, which frames the narrative retelling with an antiphony of voices through lesson, response, and versicle, rendering it "a constantly recursive process that moves between beginnings and endings."[42] The formal structures thus echo the script's description of how the permanence of these plants (that they may be "lastande") is dependent on change, not free from it.[43] In this, as I suggested before, a temporal permanence in which new beginnings require endings is juxtaposed against the characterization of God's eternal permanence as "Withoutyn end ay-lastandly" (55/4) in the play's opening lines.

Although the script's emphasis on the seed-bearing nature of plants is clearly aligned with its source (Genesis 1:11–12), it offers a significant expansion of the biblical account. It is also far more descriptive than most other vernacular English treatments of this scene. For comparison, consider the analogous passage in the Chester cycle, which offers a single stanza of description of the creation of plant life:

> I will one yearth yerbes springe,
> ichon in kinde seede-gevinge;
> trees diverse fruite forth bringe
> after ther kynde eachone;
> the seede of which aye shalbe
> within the fruite of each tree.[44]
>
> (I will that plants spring on earth,
> each one bearing seeds according to its nature;
> trees [to] bring forth diverse fruit
> each according to their nature;
> the seeds of which shall always exist
> within the fruit of each tree.)

The Chester play mentions seeds as part of a tree's fruit but lacks any engagement with the rhythms that enable biotic regeneration, other than noting how time passes on the third day.[45] If Chester's description of creation only implies the potentiality built into the Edenic ecology, York's play offers an expansive treatment, basking in the process of growth, death, and new life. In the York "Creation," God's pronouncement is dynamic rather than merely descriptive. He cascades out a series of images of natural growth and decline. His alliteration and rhyme themselves also formally reproduce the interconnectedness of this scene, weaving a sonic web, linking words and lines. The horticultural, the meteorological, and the formal collaborate in this venture of germination, as words give shape to matter and form. The York passage both describes the diversity, inherent vitality, potentiality, and growth of the plant world, and performs the process.

Such dynamic description is not unlike some of the more poetic passages in hexameral writing (theological treatises on the first six days of creation), which similarly relish the potential (*virtu*) inherent in these first plants and link the new world's fecundity with its beauty.[46] For instance, Ambrose's fourth-century *Hexameron*, which draws from ancient pastoral poetry, describes plant generation as a kind of adornment: "'Let the earth,' He said, 'bring forth the green herb after its kind.' And forthwith the earth in labor brought forth new plants; girding herself with the garments of verdure, she luxuriated in fecundity, and decked in diverse seedlings, she claimed them as her own fitting adornments."[47] This language of ornament appears throughout the Middle Ages in writing on the world's creation.[48] In such lavish, aestheticized descriptions, we also find ourselves not far from the perpetual spring of later medieval romance's *locus amoenus* (pleasant place).[49] To this point, Derek Pearsall and Elizabeth Salter write, "to exercise the imagination in such a way was not simply to exercise literary skills in the description convention of *locus amoenus*. It was, in addition, to confirm that benediction had not been quite withdrawn from created things."[50] However, as Gillian Rudd has pointed out, medieval literary imaginations of gardens, such as that of the *Romance of the Rose*, tend "to overlook the change and decay that is a necessary part of every growing thing," leaving such "undesirables" as labor, death, and age outside the walls.[51]

Unlike the idealized gardens of much contemporary writing, York's Creation play places death and decay within the newly created world. Its depiction of the prehuman world represents biological life in medias res. From the instant of its creation, the world's process of regeneration and reproduction seem already to be at work: trees are budding, flowering, and bearing fruit; wind and rain spread the seeds, which soon establish new roots. These things happen both simultaneously and in an orderly chronology. The complexity of this mixed temporality is evident in the passage's verb tenses.[52] Throughout, God employs the Middle English modal auxiliary verbs *shulen* (shall) and *willen* (will) to proclaim the world into being.[53] Although they may now seem to indicate a simple future, what *will* happen, and thus function proleptically, the ambiguity of these modal verbs is key. In Middle English, they carry a striking range of temporal possibilities. They can variously imply a past action with present meaning, a present command, or an ongoing or future condition (as in our modern "shall" or "will"). The terms can thus speak both to a present, a potentiality, and a future. For instance, when describing the creation of the heavens on the second day, God proclaims, "Þe firmament sal nough moue, / But be a mene, þus will I mene" (The heavens shall not move, / but be an intermediary, thus I will intend; 55/42–43). Here, God's eternal *now* intersects the world's temporality; the "sal" and the "will" indicate an efficacious intention that is both present and future; what God thinks and says is now and will be. Further emphasizing this layered temporality, the homographs, the nominal "mene" and the verbal "mene," briefly create a linguistic echo chamber, aligning intention with God's cosmic work. Divine intention creates the physical medium. The play's diction thus subtly yokes the present and future, the idea, word, and physical manifestation. In so doing, its very grammar performs the play of presence and potentiality that the stanzas describe.

This new world, as the York play imagines it, is thus *not* the scene of ecological stasis or subordination that we might expect from a description of prelapsarian botany. The first plants are bursting with potential. The initial creation of plant life is bound up with its own reproductive capacities, as the passage imagines the plants' regeneration through normal processes—they flower, fruit, bear seeds, distribute seeds, and establish new roots. This is a botanical world built around an innate, biological process. The passage insists that plants produce seeds so that "they may be lastande furth in lede" (so that they may last in that place; 56/75–76), not so they can nourish human beings. Productive but not yet instrumentalized, trees produce fruit that is meant to sustain their lives rather than those of human beings. Indeed, one of the most striking aspects of this play is that it avoids even alluding to the future presence of humans, let alone their use of or dominion over this world.

Such resistance to a purely utilitarian understanding of plant life is in keeping with many early hexameral works.[54] Noxious plants and animal predation before the Fall proved important test cases for theologians. Considering God's creation of poisonous plants, Basil (d. 379) asks, "shall we not reflect that not all has been created in view of the wants of our bellies?"[55] Influenced by Basil, Ambrose similarly reflects on how to think about poisonous plants:

> Some perhaps may say: how do you account for the fact that deadly poisonous plants grow along with those that are of use, for example, there is found along with wheat the poisonous hemlock, a plant discoverable among those that support life. Unless you are on your guard against it, this plant can injure

your health.... But would you find fault with the earth because not all men are good?... Some people act as if everything has to be created for our gourmandizing or as if there was just a trifling amount left by the kindness of God to minister to our appetites.... Each and every thing which is produced from the earth has its own reason for existence, which, as far as it can, fulfills the general plan of creation.... There is nothing without a purpose; there is nothing superfluous in what germinates from the earth.[56]

In Ambrose's account, even what we might consider nature's dangers are seen not as corrupt but rather as integral to the flourishing of the whole. Poisonous plants, like predatory animals and parasitic insects (as we will soon see), are to be valued not or not only for instrumental reasons but also because they have their "own reason[s] for existence," their own purpose. In one of his fifth-century homilies on Genesis, John Chrysostom notes that it was not merely for human use that creatures came into being, but rather a sign of God's prodigality and abundance and a source of awe.[57] In the thirteenth century, Robert Grosseteste reiterates this position, noting that vegetables exist for themselves and for their own propagation.[58]

Things will change, of course, with the arrival of Adam and Eve, who will be given the fruits of the new world for their food. But for the duration of the York Creation play, God invites the audience to imagine a world without humans, a world that is valued and delighted in for its own sake. The play celebrates the beauty of creation in part by marking its larger rhythms. It imagines a world in which organic matter is already perennial, already caught in the necessary cycles of generation, reproduction, and death. In emphasizing this process, it implies the productive necessity of change. Biological life in the natal world of the York play is not a frozen moment in time; it is not a perpetual spring. It is in motion, bound up with the same processes that continue to govern the postlapsarian world, even if the relation of human beings to those rhythms has changed.

Although death remains largely implicit in the play's representation of vegetal life, it is an essential part of the biological cycles of regeneration, the process that enables creation's *temporal permanence* (a process acknowledged by a gospel parable that would have been familiar to its medieval audience: unless a grain of wheat falls to the ground and dies, it remains alone, but if it dies, it bears much fruit [John 12:24]). The play's suggestion of the essential ephemerality of all organic matter is not limited to its depiction of coming into being. It also implies its passing away. As God completes the work of the third day, he notes how the earth now grows "with gres / and wedis þat sone away bese went" (with grass / and weeds that soon disappear; 56/89–90). As I considered in this book's introduction, in the Bible, grass and flowers are often associated with the fragility and fleeting nature of life. Jeffrey Jerome Cohen notes, "to live in the world is to dwell in uncertainty, plants know that precarity well."[59] Even in Eden, it seems, weeds and grasses are vulnerable, but also generative. For, in the York Creation play, the representation of weeds and grass and fruit and seeds speak both to the lush fecundity of Eden and to its productive transience.

Death in the Garden

> Every glistening egg is a *memento mori*.
> ANNIE DILLARD, *Pilgrim at Tinker Creek*

It is one thing to depict plant mortality in the Edenic world and another thing entirely to suggest that animals suffered and died before Adam and Eve were expelled from the Garden.[60] Although most hexameral writing acknowledged prelapsarian animal death, many late medieval vernacular representations of the Creation refused to imagine creaturely violence before the Fall. The fourteenth-century biblical paraphrase *Cursor Mundi*, for instance, insists that the first animals were meek and didn't harm each other, noting that wolves would have slept with sheep, and hounds lay down with hares.[61] Yet, the York "Creation" represents the world's first creatures as no tamer than those after the Fall and thus suggests that animal antagonism and suffering would have been part of the original goodness of the world.

After bringing earth's teeming landscapes into being, God turns to the animal realm, first populating the sea, then the air, and finally the land. In each of the three stanzas describing the fifth day of creation, the script issues a paean to biodiversity. Yet even as it emphasizes the dazzling variety and proliferation of animal life, it alludes to inherent creaturely antagonisms and pains. God first fills the seas with whales and other fish with various forms and dispositions:

> Of diueris materis more and myn –
> in sere maner to make and mell;
> sum sall be milde and meke,
> and sum both fers and fell (57/131–34)

> (Of diverse matters more and less –
> in different ways to mate and breed;
> some shall be mild and meek,
> and some both fierce and ferocious.)

Celebrating the diversity of life contained within earth's waters, the passage homes in on fishy diversity and behavior.[62] God describes species variation and difference through the pairings that conclude each line—more and less, mate and breed, mild and meek, fierce and ferocious—while also performing a sense of likeness, as the passage pulls through the alliterating *m*. This aquatic world evokes its own dramas of procreation and survival. It speaks to a vital but chancy ecosystem, where the meek and the fierce coexist, though not always peacefully.

For many medieval thinkers, the species diversity of the creation bore both aesthetic and spiritual significance; the "diverse natures" of animals lead humans to know the beauty of their Creator and move humans to greater love of God.[63] Yet any sense of awe in the face of an ecology such as that offered by the York play was surely double-edged, as likely to prompt disquiet as to prompt love. For the play offers neither the pacific paradise imagined by other biblical texts, where lions lay with lambs, nor the "peaceable kingdom" imagined by Golden Age narratives.[64] Rather, as becomes clear in the following stanzas, the York "Creation" paints a picture of a world of predators and prey, powerful creatures and more vulnerable ones.

York is far from unique in imagining prelapsarian animal predation. Many early theologians comment on the carnivorous nature of animals in the original creation. In his influential work *On the Literal Meaning of Genesis*, Augustine considers, "why brute beasts inflict injury on one another, for there is no sin in them for which this could be a punishment," and simply offers the following explanation:

> One animal is the nourishment of another. . . . Rightly considered, they are all praiseworthy, and all the changes that occur in them, even when one passes into another, are governed by a hidden plan that rules the beauty of the world and regulates each according to its kind.

As he continues, Augustine notes the "struggle for life" as animals do their utmost to "protect the material and temporal life that has been given them."[65] Eight hundred years later, Thomas Aquinas similarly comments on both the natural "antipathy" of some animals before the Fall and the fact that the Fall itself doesn't alter those propensities:

> Some say that animals which are now savage and kill other animals would have been tame in that state [before the Fall], and not only towards man but towards other animals too. But this is altogether unreasonable. For man's sin did not so change the nature of animals, that those whose nature it is now to eat other animals, like lions and hawks, would then have lived on a vegetarian diet. . . . So clashes and antipathy would have been natural between certain animals even then.[66]

As Aquinas's statement suggests, for many medieval theologians, "antipathy" was not sin; animal predation was not a sign of animal fallenness. The commonplace that there was animal death in Eden appears in art as well. Perhaps, most famously, Bosch's fifteenth-century painting *Garden of Earthly Delights* doesn't hesitate to depict animal ferocity in Eden, showing predators capturing and consuming their prey: in the foreground, a cat carries a mouse, two long-necked birds peck at a frog splayed out on the grass, and two frog legs protrude from another bird's mouth; in the distance, a lion gnaws on an antelope.

Yet even if some medieval artists and thinkers imagined the prelapsarian world as already marked by predation, they saw this diversity of creaturely form and disposition as a fundamental part of the beauty of the universe. In the York play, God's creation of the birds attests both to the distinction of species and to their shared grandeur:

> Also vp in þe ayre on hyght
> I byd now þat þore be ordande
> For to be foulis fayre and bright,
> Dewly in þare degre dewlland,
> With fedrys fayre to frast þer flight
> For stede to stede where þai will stande,
> And also leythly for to lyght
> Whoreso þam lykis in ilke a londe.
> Þane fysch and foulis sere,
> Kyndely I ȝow commande
> To meng on ȝoure manere,
> Both be se and sande. (57/137–48)
>
> (Also, up in the air on high,
> I command now that there be ordained
> birds, beautiful and bright,
> duly dwelling in their degree,
> with beautiful feathers to help their flight,
> from place to place where they will stand
> and also lightly to alight,
> wherever they like in every land.
> Then diverse fish and birds,
> I command you naturally
> to mate according to your manner
> both by the sea and the sand.)

Although it highlights the beauty of these animals—they are "fair fowls" with "fair feathers"—the description also, like the earlier creation of the plants and fish, emphasizes procreation and regeneration. God commands birds: "kyndely . . . meng" (naturally procreate). Like the botanical processes performed on the third day of creation, prelapsarian animal life comes into being already bound up in biological rhythms and cycles. These processes are, the play will soon insist, the creature's means of permanence in a transient world. In his fourth-century *Homilies on Creation*, Basil writes, "So nature, being put in motion by the one command, passes equally through birth and death in a creature, while it keeps up the succession of kinds through resemblance, to the end."[67] The orderly succession, self-preservation, and beauty of the avian world is a source of wonder and fascination in many medieval texts.[68] In the fourteenth-century poem *Piers Plowman*, the dreamer observes, awestruck, how birds build complex nests in bushes and trees to hide their eggs from predators: feathered, mammal, and human.[69] The York "Creation" also emphasizes avian agency and freedom, observing that the birds may alight "wherever they like."

Hexameral texts often imagine the land animals as more constrained, noting how the milder beasts, such as cattle, are of benefit for helping human beings, providing labor and food.[70] But rather than foreshadowing the possible human uses of animals, the York "Creation" continues to focus on their original diversity and their reproductive capacities. To fulfill his "forethought" of creation, God speaks into being:

> diueris bestis in lande to lende
> To brede and be with bale furth brught.
> And with bestis I wille be blende
> Serpendtis to be sene vnsoght,
> And wormis vpon þaire wombis sall wende
> To won in erth and worth to noght.
>
> (diverse beasts in the land
> to breed and be brought forth with pain [or: from the womb].
> And with the beasts I will add in
> serpents to be seen but not desired,
> and worms shall move on their wombs
> to dwell on earth and not have any value.) (57–58/151–56)

Though this description is less detailed than that of the creation of the fish and the birds, it introduces an intriguing possibility: prelapsarian creatures may experience pain. The author has punned on "bale," which is usually glossed here as "belly" but can also mean pain or suffering.[71] Only forty lines earlier, when God describes how vegetation responds to weather conditions, he notes, "So sall my creaturis / euir byde withoutyn bale" (so shall my creatures /

always live without suffering; 56/112–13). But could this echo suggest that even suffering is part of the "fayre processe" of creation, part of the goodness of the world? Could it be that, to use Stevens's phrase, this playwright understands the uncomfortable truth that "death is the mother of beauty"? Perhaps this is going too far. But perhaps not. The play's two mentions of "bale" remind us, as Minnis has explored in a discussion of animal death in Eden, that "not all *dolor* (this term covers both physical and mental pain, sorrow, or distress) is *pena* (a punishment)."[72] This bears repeating: Not all suffering is punishment; perishability is not corruption.

Indeed, the York "Creation" depicts the new world and all its creatures as beautiful because of its transience. As the play comes to an end and God concludes his creation of the first five days, he summarizes it, emphasizing again the ecological growth and process at work in the new world. Noting that he has set all the beasts in diverse degrees to move about on the earth, God bids all his animal creations—beasts, birds, and fish

> wax furth fayre plente
> and grathly growes, als I ȝow gesse.
> So multiply ȝe sall
> Ay furth in fayre processe,
> my blyssyng haue ȝe all. (58/167–71)

> (grow forth beautifully and plentifully
> and eagerly grow, as I intend.
> Thus you shall multiply
> always in a beautiful process,
> you all have my blessing.)

Emphasizing the continuance of what God has set into motion, the cycle play concludes with a vision of plentitude and possibility. It imagines the beauty not only of the newly formed world but also of a beautiful and iterative *process* that will enable its preservation and flourishing, a process that, perhaps, is itself the blessing with which the play concludes.[73] Yet, as I noted earlier, "processe" is also a term for a dramatic performance. Though God here blesses the cycles of the cosmos, his words of blessing also affirm the beauty of the play that has just performed the story of that process. In other words, this may well be a metatheatrical moment. God is speaking to the plants and the animals but also to the players and the audience, who are participating in and observing the process of the Corpus Christi plays. In the York Creation play, prelapsarian ecology is a drama, a "fayre process" of coming into being and passing out of it, a divine *poema*.

The Simplest Part of Earth

> I came to see myself as growing out of the earth like other native animals and plants. I saw my body and my daily motions as brief coherences and articulations of the energy of the place, which would fall back into it like leaves in autumn.
>
> WENDELL BERRY, "A Native Hill"

But what of the human in this transient but complex, diverse, and beautiful ecosystem? If the York Creation play imagines the flora and fauna of the unfallen world as vital, potent, fecund, yet ephemeral, already participating in the natural processes of birth, decay, death, and regeneration, we might expect the introduction of humans into this Eden to emphasize their exceptionality. Many hexameral texts do just that, describing humans as immortal beings in a mortal cosmos.[74] Yet, the next York play, "The Creation of Adam and Eve," *grounds* the human (quite literally) within this "fayre" ecology. Never describing them as "fayre," the play instead depicts the first human beings as humble and fragile beings, earthbound creatures who also, remarkably, even paradoxically, bear the divine image. The poetic form shifts accordingly. Though it remains in a loose iambic tetrameter, the magisterial, alliterative twelve-line stanzas of "The Creation" give way in "The Creation of Adam and Eve" to humbler nonalliterative quatrains in a simple *abab* format.

As we have seen, these first humans are born into a flourishing world. "The Creation of Adam and Eve" opens with a long monologue in which God reflects on his work of the previous days, on how the trees, grass, beasts, fowl, fish, and "all othyr thyng / Thryffe" (all other things / thrive; 59/11–12). He made this world, he explains, out of love ("For loue mad I Þis warlde alane"; 59/19). Yet, if the York Creation play performed divine love for the world and its creatures through articulations of delight in its "fayre processe[s]," God is more restrained in his first description of humans, which figures them as both emerging from this thriving ecology and distinct from it. Adam and Eve are paradoxically both "simpyll" (lowly) and "skylfull" (rational). In a striking passage in "The Creation of Adam and Eve," God explains his rationale for creating one more type of creature:

> To kepe þis warlde, bothe mare and lesse,
> A skylfull best þane will I make
> Eftyr my schape and my lyknes,
> The wilke sall worschipe to me take
>
> Off þe symplest part of erthe þat is here
> I sall make man, and for þis skylle:

> For to abate hys hauttande chere,
> Bothe his grete pride and oþer ille;
>
> And also for to haue in mynde
> How simpyll he is at hys makyng,
> For als febyll I sall hym fynde
> Qwen he is dede at his endyng.
>
> For þis reson and skyll alane
> I sall make man lyke onto me.
> Ryse vp, þou erthe, in blode and bane,
> In schape of man, I commaunde þe. (59/21–36)
>
> (To care for this world, both its great and its small,
> I will make a rational beast
> after my own shape and likeness,
> which shall worship me.
>
> From the humblest part of the earth,
> I will make man, and for this reason:
> to abate his arrogant demeanor,
> both his great pride and other ills.
>
> And so he will also have in mind
> how lowly he is at his origins,
> for equally feeble I will him find
> when he is dead at his ending.
>
> For this reason alone,
> I will make man like me.
> Rise up, you earth, in blood and bone,
> in the shape of a human, I command you.)

As if anticipating humanity's Fall, God frames Adam's creation in terms of his death, both thematically and rhythmically aligning his "making" with his "ending." The entire passage is structured by such alignments and juxtapositions. In Middle English, "skyll" is the intellectual faculty, the godlike capacity to reason.[75] Here referenced three times, the play repeatedly juxtaposes human "skyll" against human lowliness and humility, emphasizing that humans share their spirit with God and their substance with the earth. The passage shifts between assertions of divine likeness and earthy substance while also knowingly observing that humans will be more likely to claim their association with the divine than with the earth. Before God brings humans into being, he imagines them as humble "caretakers," as those who will "kepe þis warlde" (*kepen* in Middle English can mean to care for, to conserve, but also to possess).[76]

This is a striking depiction, but it's not necessarily the standard one. Other contemporary treatments of this moment from Genesis downplay the humble origins of human beings and emphasize dominion over caretaking. The analogous Chester play puts the paradox of the human in the mouth of the devil, who asks, "Should such a caytiffe made of claye / have such blisse?" (should such a wretch made of clay / obtain such bliss?).[77] In the Towneley play, the creation of human beings is immediately followed by a statement of their dominion over the rest of creation:

> Now make we man to oure liknes,
> That shall be keper of more and les,
> Of fowles and fysh in flood.
> *Et tangent eum.*
>
> Spreyte of life I in the blaw,
> Good and ill both shall thou knaw;
> Rise vp and stand bi me.
> All that is in water or land,
> It shall bow vnto thi hand
> And sufferan shall thou be.
>
> (Now we make man in our likeness,
> who shall be keeper of the great and small,
> of the birds and the fish in the sea.
> *And he touches him.*
>
> I blow the spirit of life into you
> [so that] you will know both good and ill.
> Rise up and stand beside me.
> Everything that is in the water or on land
> shall bow to your hand
> and you shall be sovereign.)[78]

Handling the creation of Adam in this way, the Towneley play emphasizes superiority and hierarchy—humans are to be lords over the nonhuman world, which will "bow" into their hands. There is no mention at all of Adam's earthiness. The fourteenth-century biblical paraphrase *Cursor Mundi* also uses the language of kingly dominion:

> Þese beestes coom him alle aboute
> As to her lorde him to loute
> Foule in fliȝgte fisshe on sonde
> Alle bowed him to foot & honde

> At his wille þei 3eode & cam
> As he had bene makere of ham.
>
> (These beasts came all around him
> as if to their lord to praise.
> Birds in flight, fish in the sea,
> bowed their feet and hands.
> They came and went at his will
> as if he had been the maker of them.)[79]

As in the Towneley play, the beasts bow to Adam, but here they go further, treating him as if he were their lord. Although *Cursor Mundi* describes Adam as made of the same stuff of creation in an earlier passage, here the human is markedly distinct from it, more aligned with God than with the animals he dwells among. The *Middle English Metrical Paraphrase of the Old Testament* puts this dominion in even stronger terms:

> Then sayd He to Hymself: "Make We
> a man that may bestes mys amend,
> For have power and pausté
> on bestes and fowls withoutyn end."[80]
>
> (Then he said to himself: "Let us make
> A man that may amend the beast's errors,
> To have power and dominion
> Over animals and birds without end.")

Such accounts follow the biblical source, "Let us make man to our image and likeness: and let him have dominion over the fishes of the sea, and the fowls of the air, and the beasts, and the whole earth, and every creeping creature that moveth upon the earth" (Genesis 1:26), which does not yet mention the human kinship with earth, only the human power over other creatures (which the next verse indicates that humans should "subdue" and "rule over"). As I noted in this book's introduction, scholars have long understood this biblical rhetoric of power and dominion as a source of both ecological exploitation and ecological stewardship. We might see it as the source of human exceptionalism in the West.[81]

Yet, as the York play suggests, though human dominion will become the dominant paradigm in Western Christianity, not all reimaginations of this origin myth offer the same emphasis. Although the York "Creation of Adam and Eve" will also later develop the idea of human dominion, it first calls its audience to understand the human being as a fundamentally middling and derivative creature, born of the earth, kin to beasts, yet also somehow reflecting the likeness of its creator. On the one hand, as God says in the play, human beings are "lyke onto me," made in divine likeness or image. On the other, he emphasizes that they are both rational "beasts" and made from "the humblest part of earth." Like the rest of the prelapsarian world, human existence is already bounded by death; unlike the rest of creation, it is the human awareness ("mynde") of both their "making" and their "ending" that is intended to keep them humble, to tie them to the earth (59/29–30, 32). Medieval theologians sometimes linked the frailty of humans with the effects of the Fall, but this playwright depicts human fragility and their awareness of their mortality as a fundamental part of the human condition.[82]

The very structure of God's speech in York's "Creation of Adam and Eve" emphasizes the central paradoxes of the human animal, alternating between articulations of divine likeness and creaturely affinity. The final stanza of the creation of humanity juxtaposes these two sides of the human: the opening reminder of divine likeness ("I sall make man lyke onto me") is immediately followed by a command to the earth itself to give shape to the physical body of the human. Though humans may be *like* God, they *are* earth. God here commands, "Ryse up, þou erthe, in blode and bane, / In schape of man" (Rise up, you earth, in blood and bone / in the form of a man; 59/35–36). If other creatures are articulated from nothingness into existence by divine command, the human is a secondary creature, called out of, shaped, and one might even say recycled from the material stuff of the already created world.

"Rise up, thou earth!" What might it mean to understand human beings not only as inhabiting the earth, but as earthlings? There is ample biblical precedent for this idea, but the play imbues the creation scene with fresh dramatic force.[83] In so powerfully linking the human with other creatures and with the dust of earth, the play suggests that remembering whence they come, remembering their kinship with nonhuman creatures will "abate" human pride, reminding human beings of the fragility of both their lives and their "skyle." Later in the play and in the following one, "Adam and Eve in Eden," God will give humans dominion over the created order, though it will be framed largely in the language of care and sustainability. He will call them to "saue and sett / Erbes and treys" and "susteyn beast and man, / and fewl of ylke stature" (save and set / plants and trees [and] sustain animals and humans / and birds of every type; 62/25–26, 28–29). Later, then, humans will be held responsible for sustaining the vegetable and animal life around them, but the first thing we learn of what it means to be human in the York cycle is that it means being bound in some physical way to the earth.[84] Frailty and earthiness come first, power and responsibility later.

Little Worlds

> I am a little world made cunningly
> Of elements and an angelic sprite
> JOHN DONNE, *Divine Poems*

This substantial connection to earth is an insight that contemporary ecocriticism has often stressed.[85] York's take on human origins supplies a version of what Stacy Alaimo calls "a trans-corporality," which emphasizes "the extent to which the substance of the human is ultimately inseparable from the environment."[86] The York Creation plays likewise advocate a position of humility and the work of care, values that many ecocritics increasingly emphasize must become central to our own ecological ethics and practices. Timothy Morton, for instance, promotes assuming a posture of humility given our decentered, networked place in the world, suggesting that "perhaps the ecological art of the future will deal with passivity and weakness; with lowliness, not loftiness."[87] Like many other medieval texts, this reminder of weakness and lowliness is precisely where the York plays begin.

Transcorporeality, coextensiveness, likeness, and humility are now rarely concepts we associate with Western modes of thought. Today such ideas may seem more intrinsic to Eastern or Indigenous spiritualities and philosophies, which sometimes emphasize what the Buddhist philosopher Joanna Macy has called the dynamics of "interbeing."[88] European philosophy, theology, psychology, and ecology have been overwritten by the potent legacy of Cartesian dualisms: of mind and body, of self and other, of spirit and world.[89] Most of us are far more accustomed to thinking of nonhuman creatures as the "Not Me," as Ralph Waldo Emerson so powerfully put it, than as the "Also Me" or the "Like Me."[90] Yet, nonmodern religious texts often emphasize kinship with the nonhuman world even as they articulate ambivalence about our shared perishability.

Lest we be tempted to imagine that human kinship with the transient cosmos was only metaphorical to many medieval authors, we turn now to a range of biblical texts and mortality lyrics that reminds us just how substantial medieval thinkers understood that relationship to be. Medieval texts frequently represented human beings as physical microcosms of the cosmos— composed of the same material stuff and even composed in much the same way. In this model, humans are in some fundamental way patterned on and part of the larger creation: we share in its substance, form, and rhythms. In his *De planctu naturae*, Alan of Lille explains this relation even more clearly. "The form of the human body," he writes, "assumes the image of the world" (*humani corporis forma mundi furatur effigiem*).[91] Alan's trope of the human body as "little world" (*minor mundi*), Kellie Robertson writes, makes "not just an aesthetic claim but an ontological one.... The body is the world miniaturized; the world, the body dilated."[92] In this model, the world embodies and contains the human, but humans also embody and contain the world. To use Robertson's term, human beings and the physical world are "coextensive." Much like Alaimo's notion of "trans-corporeality" or Macy's "interbeing," the medieval model of microcosm and macrocosm implies material likeness as well as figurative likeness.

That humans are "little worlds" is a commonplace of late medieval biblical, devotional, and didactic writing. For instance, in its description of the creation of the world, *Cursor Mundi*, offers a lengthy characterization of the human body as both made of and a mirror of the cosmos. It explains that Adam was composed not only of earth but of all four elements: his blood of water, his flesh of earth, his heat of fire, and his being of air. Surveying the human body from head to toe, the anonymous author details the ways in which the body mirrors the universe. There are seven openings in the head, the text explains, like the seven (then known) planets in the sky. Likewise, the human body is composed of the same materials as the stone, grass, and trees:

> Þe erþe makeþ him fele & Fonde
> Þat hardenes þat men han in bones
> Hit comeþ of þe kynde of stones
> On erþe as groweþ trees & gres
> So nayl & heer of mannes flesshe
> Wiþ beestes doumbe man haþ fele
> Of þing him likeþ euel or wele
> Of þese þinges I haue herde seide
> Was adames body to gider leide.
> For þese resouns þat 3e haue herde
> Man is calde þe lasse werde.[93]

(The earth makes him feel and test
that hardness that men have in their bones.
It comes from the nature of stones.
Like trees and grass grow on the earth,
so do nails and hair [grow] from human flesh.
With unspeaking animals, humans share feelings
of things that please them well or ill.
From all these things I have heard it said,
Adam's body was put together.
For these reasons that you have heard
the human is called a little world.)

Although it is surely metaphorical to describe hair or nails growing like grass and trees, on the whole, the comparison between the human body and the physical world is no mere analogy or metaphor. As the final lines of the passage indicate, many medieval authors understood human beings to be literally, physically, substantially made of the same stuff as the cosmos. The hardness of human bones is not like stone, but of the same "kynde," or nature, as stone. Human beings share basic sensations and desires *with* animals. The human body is interconnected with and indebted to the world in which it finds itself, which, before the Fall, is its kindred, indeed, even its very substance.

The anonymous author of the *Cursor Mundi* is far from unique in this understanding. In his translation of Ranulf Higden's universal history, John Trevisa reaches back to a sermon by Gregory the Great to comment on the "interbeing" of all created things:

> For Gregorio in an omelye seiþ þat man haþ beynge wiþ stones, lyuynge wiþ trees and herbes, felynge wiþ bestes, knowleche and vnderstondynge wiþ aungels. Also in manis body semeþ erþe in flesche and bones, water in blood and in oþer humours, ayer in þe longen, fuyre in þe herte; and hatte *homo* in Latyn and *antropos* in Grewe, þat is as hit were a tree.[94]
>
> (For in a homily, Gregory says that a human has being with stones, living with trees and plants, feeling with animals, [and] knowledge and understanding with angels. Also, in the human body, the flesh and bones seem of earth, the blood of water, and in the other humors: air in the lungs, fire in the heart. And [humans] are called *homo* in Latin and *Anthropos* in Greek, that is, as if it were a tree.)

This popular schematic is rooted in the biblical notion that human beings emerged from the earth, but it is also shaped by late medieval Aristotelian thinking about the vegetative, sensitive, and intellective souls. In his *De anima* (*On the Soul*), Aristotle examines how plants, animals, and humans all share soul, a substance "which has life in potentiality," though each type of soul has different intrinsic powers.[95] At the most basic level, humans share physical existence with stones. They share the quality of life with plants, of feeling with animals, and of reason with angels. They are simultaneously elemental, creaturely, and divine. For Gregory and his chroniclers, the universe is a continuum of linked types of both soul and substantial likeness.[96] This is sometimes called the *scala naturae*, the scale of nature.[97]

The coextensive, multiscalar nature of this relationship offers an alternative model or supplement to recent ecocritical use of the more Darwinian idea of entanglement or the Latourian suggestion of assemblage. In her consideration of the microcosmic/macrocosmic structure of medieval treatments of humans' relation to nature in Alan of Lille's *De planctu naturae*, Robertson suggests that "for Alan's Nature, humans' inability to recognize their coextensiveness with the rest of the physical world is the origin of their spiritual failings."[98] As Robertson observes of this medieval relation, "It is anthropomorphism but, simultaneously, the opposite of anthropomorphism, the turning of the human back into the rest of the world. The figure spatializes the relations of the human and nonhuman worlds in a way that resists the notion of a center."[99] What I, following Robertson, find so useful about this medieval model is that it prizes both likeness and difference; it maintains a sense of varying valuation while also insisting on mutuality, connection, and dependence.

If human coextensiveness with the physical universe was a commonplace of medieval hexameral commentary and literature, perhaps its most famous instantiation today is the fourteenth-century mortality lyric "Erthe toc of Erthe," which emphasizes not only likeness but also process.[100] The poem circulated widely and in a range of forms from the early fourteenth through the fifteenth centuries. It appeared in manuscripts and was inscribed on church walls.[101] The earliest and most well-known version of this enigmatic lyric is found in London at the British Library in Harley MS 2253, where it is grouped with other mortality lyrics, and consists of four lines:

> Erþe toc of erþe erþe wyþ woh
> erþe oþer erþe to þe erþe droh
> erþe leyde erþe in erþene þroh
> þo heuede erþe of erþe erþe ynoh
>
> (Earth took from earth earth with woe.
> Earth dragged other earth to the earth.
> Earth laid earth in an earthen place.
> Then earth had of earth enough of earth.)

Meditating on a line from the Latin Office of the Dead, "Remember, O man, that you are ashes and to ashes you will return" (*Memento, homo, quod cinis es, et in cenerem reverteris*), this little lyric relies on the polyvalence of "erthe" (which can mean ground, a human being, and the world itself) to spin out possible meanings.[102] In its relentless repetition of "earth," the poem, as D. Vance Smith writes, "seems to use up language, stressing a single word until it becomes virtually nonsensical because it is coming to mean so much. . . . It moves toward greater equivocation."[103] In this, I would add, the poem invites its readers or hearers to inhabit, however briefly, what we typically avoid thinking: the precarity and uncertainty of our earthly existence.

Yet the repetition is also immersive and absorptive. Even as it unsettles our ability to understand what it means to be earth, the lyric's droning rhythms and repetitions sonically enclose us. Where it denies our full comprehension, the lyric appeals to our senses. In so doing, its very form draws us back into that existential paradox we encountered in the York "Creation of Adam and Eve," the precarity of being both earth and like God, both creaturely and aspiring to rise above our creatureliness.[104] Our difficulty grasping its equivocations is a humbling reminder of just how aligned with the sensory realm of earth we are. In the lyric's shortest, most enigmatic form, as Rosemary Woolf writes, it lays this paradox out as the "bare history of man" (as born of earth, accumulating earth, and returned to the earth) through its repetitions of "erþe, which is substituted for every noun except *woh*."[105] Earth here is not just the backdrop for human life but life and death's ground and substance, its beginning and end.

Most of the expanded versions of this lyric go far beyond this "bare history," making even clearer that the riddling and rhyming repetitions of the term "erthe" are the legacy of Adam, who was taken from the ground and will return to it (Genesis 3:19: "you are earth and to earth you will go"). The lyric has long been read as a precis of the biblical Creation and Fall.[106] A fifteenth-century version of the poem makes this association explicit:

> And of the same erthe mad God man,
> And sethe he made that erth & callyd it Adam,
> For loue of erthe, the wych was woman,
> That erth in this erthe fyrst be-gan.[107]

> (And from the same earth God made man
> And afterwards he made that earth and called it Adam,
> because of his love of earth, which was woman,
> thus earth in this earth first began.)

Here "erthe" is explicitly identified as "man" and then as Adam, whose love of earth (woman), marks the beginning of human/earthly history. The expanded versions often tell a more complex story about human origins and aspirations. If the York play suggests that human earthiness is a means of abating human pride, in some of the expanded versions of this lyric, human attachment to the earth is bound up with a forgetting of human earthiness.

This forgetting is ultimately figured as the root of both pride and suffering. As this passage might suggest, the longer versions of this poem that circulated widely in the fifteenth century often attempted to resolve the equivocations of the four-line version by providing a more explicit moral or historical frame to the enigmatic verses. More diffuse and didactic and less repetitive and riddling, these versions, Ingrid Nelson argues, depend on dilation, an expansion that throws into relief "a relationship between form and practice."[108] If this dilation and amplification diminishes the formal power of the equivocating repetitions, it goes a long way in elucidating how medieval readers understood the poem. In the more than two dozen manuscripts in which the longer version is found, the poem typically develops a point about the danger of earth (the human being) forgetting it is earth (dust), that it is ephemeral, and attempting to lay claim to possess that which does not last (other earthly things). One popular version of the poem, for instance, articulates it this way in the opening lines: "Erthe upon erthe wines castles and towers / Than says erthe unto erthe, 'This es alle ourres'" (Earth on the earth possesses castles and towers / then says the earth to the earth, "This is all ours'"; 11–12).[109] Any belief in the power and permanence of the earth, be it the earthly body, its creations or other earthly creatures and elements, the tradition claims, is shortsighted. The fate of earth, the poem insists again and again, is to return to itself. The longer versions of the poem make clear a moral that is only implicit in the four-line version: that human acquisitiveness for earthly things receives its just deserts when humans are reintegrated into the earth. Again and again, in all its forms, the poem suggests that we would do well to remember, as the Kentucky agrarian Wendell Berry puts it, that "while we live, our bodies are moving particles of earth, joined inextricably both to the soil and to the bodies of other living creatures."[110] Earth to earth. Dust to dust.

Such earthiness was on full, if unintentional, display the first time I saw a performance of the cycle plays in York in 2012. Revived in 1951 for the Festival of Britain after four hundred years of dormancy, today the city of York stages a selection from the original forty-eight plays every four of five years in the Museum Gardens, in the nave of York Minster, or on the streets.[111] In 2012, a selection of twenty plays were performed in the lavish gardens, which have been planted in the ruins of the eleventh-century St. Mary's Abbey, once one of the wealthiest Benedictine foundations in the North.[112] Skeletal Gothic arches rise from the grass, incorporated as landscape features.[113] A stage had been constructed in what was once the abbey nave with its airy tracery. The abbey's ruined windows and walls frame the views, as if they were built to purpose. Reclining in the flowerbeds at the Marygate entrance are empty stone caskets, a striking *memento mori*. "Remember death," they seem to murmur to the bright flowers crowded around them. Old English has a word for the contemplation invited by ruins such as this: *dustsceawung*.[114] Dust to dust. There may be nothing that more potently reminds us of our own mortality, of transience and mutability, than the garden and the ruin.

These are potent juxtapositions, and ones that provide a particularly apt setting for the medieval biblical plays sometimes performed on these grounds, which begin with an idyllic garden and end with apocalyptic ruination. These understandings of the cyclical processes of earth and the intimate affiliation of the human body with the ground appear throughout late medieval religious writing. Other medieval sermons and religious literature engage the human connection with the ground: The prologue to the fourteenth-century *Northern Homily Cycle* says that God made man "Of erthe and lam" (from earth and clay).[115] In her *Revelations*, Julian of Norwich comments that God "tooke the slyppe of erth, which is a matter medlid and gaderid of all bodily things, and therof He made mannys bodye" (took the slop of earth, which is matter mixed and gathered from all bodily things, and from it he made the human body).[116] Not only are humans the children of the earth, but also, as the dramas and these brief examples note, made of its lowliest part: the slime and slop, primordial mud. Medieval texts saw the human body as hybrid and multiple, mixed up with the stuff of creation. Thus, although much recent scholarship, following Ian Hodder and Timothy Morton, has emphasized ecological entanglement, many medieval texts offer a slightly different, but no less ethically or formally important, approach—emphasizing both the autonomy, generative power, and beauty of the more-than-human world *and* human fragility, dependence, and likeness.

What, then, do we see when we look at late medieval representations of this origin story through an ecological lens? I think White is right that we find the seeds of the logic of dominion and exploitation that continue to govern much of modern interaction with the environment. Yet, as I hope this chapter has begun to show, we also find an attentiveness to ecological process, to interconnectedness, to endings as well as beginnings, and some thinking about the precariousness of all life. We are confronted with questions about the scope of human ethical responsibility. We are offered a picture of ecological thriving and a reminder of biological fragility. Such biblical accounts might also remind us how tenuous the hold of life is, how closely we are bound to and mixed up with the earth, and how important it is to continue to attend to our participation in the "fayre processe" of the more-than-human world.

That Other Fall

> The question that he frames in all but words
> Is what to make of a diminished thing.
> ROBERT FROST, "The Oven Bird"

In the fall, I walk again in the garden. It's late October, one of those blue-skied blustery afternoons. The first frost has already struck. It has been a season of death. The loss of my mother is an open wound. COVID-19 deaths continue.

A war rages in Ukraine. Even my elderly cat hobbles lopsided around the house, severely disabled by a series of strokes. I nurse her and count her days. She will hang on until the spring. Then, as the days warm, she will let go, and I will bury her under an apple tree near the fence.

When the leaves have begun to dry and descend, I will "put the garden to bed," a phrase that suggests an extended sleep. Yet in its earliest forms, "bed" already had equally close links with both gardening and death. It was a place dug out of the earth, perhaps a grave, a site of cultivation, or a place for humans or animals to pass the night. I think of this autumn work as the garden's yearly funeral, returning earth to earth, dust to dust. I will pull up and burn the tangled tomato vines, which are still covered with tiny green tomatoes, and feed the rest of the wilted plants to the compost pile, only leaving the dried bee balm, milkweed, coneflowers, and black-eyed Susans for the finches.

After the heat of a southern Indiana summer, I am ready for the seasonal change, for how life stills, for how everything speaks the generative quietude of death. That the world is fueled by death is uncomfortable to acknowledge if you, like me, love the world for its vitality and beauty. But when it comes to collective flourishing, as medieval thinkers might have said: though God might be the father of beauty, death is its mother and the "generative source of nature's ceaseless movement into form."[117] Awareness of this "fayre process" has never stopped us from imagining or longing for worlds free from death. Neither has it stopped us from mourning the losses we all suffer as mortal beings. *Not* to lament the darker ecologies of our world (both intrinsic and anthropogenic) would be to add to their tragedy.[118] For, as we will see in the next chapter, in the repetition of mourning lies both commemoration and the possibility of transformation.

Even so, I rarely mourn the loss when I put the garden to bed in the fall. But, as I turn the plants back into the earth, I wonder at the brevity of their lives, how they flame out, filling my garden with blossoms and fruit, and then dry up. All in a matter of months. It is an astonishing thing. We may have a tendency, as Harrison suggests, "to see the earth as the matrix of pain, death, corruption, and tragedy rather than the matrix of life, growth, appearance, and form," but medieval creation accounts offer a rejoinder to such a unidirectional association.[119] Instead, they ask: What if we were to accept it as both? What if we were to inhabit this paradox, and perhaps even come to see it as good? We dwell, they remind us, in a movable, unstable world, a world of incessant change, of profound losses, but also of generative rhythms and "fayre processe[s]" that call for our attention, processes of which we, like it or not, are a part. And it is in this world and in these processes that we must find ways to live.

2

"This Deadly Life"

Elegy and Ecological Care after Eden

> Gentle now king eider, river darter, sauger, burning bush, common
> merganser, limpet, mayfly nymph, cedar, turkey vulture,
> spectacle case, flat floater, cherry, red tailed hawk,
> don't add to heartache.
> JULIANA SPAHR, "Gentle Now, Don't Add to Heartache"

One afternoon, not too long ago, I was startled from my work by a shadow and a sharp cry in the woods just outside my window. A young red-tailed hawk had snatched one of the neighborhood's abundant squirrels. I watched the hawk descend, clutching its prey, and land on a fallen tree. Extending its wings, it encircled the animal still in its talons. Had I been able to see the squirrel, I surely would have turned away, unable to bear what followed. But the hawk's posture obscured the squirrel's final moments, and I observed, astonished, horrified, and transfixed.

It was late winter, and the day was bright and still. The woods seemed quieter than usual. No birdsong. No wind rustling papery leaves. The hawk was patient, even tranquil. It perched as rigid as a statue. It waited. I watched. Five minutes passed. Then ten. Then, having released its prey, the hawk hopped to a nearby branch and stretched out its talons, now bloody. It scraped them against the bark, inscribing a rubricated memorial. It returned to the body and began to peck and tear, ripping through the fur. Its beak grew rosy too. Its small eyes, alert and protective, monitored me through the window. Where I live, at the edge of a ten-acre wood, creatures often watch me warily as they go about their bloody business. I once saw a raccoon pluck frogs one by one from my tiny ornamental pond, stuffing them headfirst into its mouth, while barely breaking my gaze. Red in tooth and claw indeed.

That the cosmos we inhabit is often violent, driven toward and fueled by death is an old story. Now usually told as a Darwinian drama of strength and survival, this tale long predates the idea of natural selection.[1] Medieval thinkers often meditated on the apparent antagonisms of the world—on the quotidian violence of hungry hawks and doomed squirrels, on the catastrophic suffering inflicted by disasters, on the human struggle for survival in this hostile environment. Imagining the postlapsarian world as fallen, as fundamentally altered, many biblical texts located the origins of such corruption in Adam and Eve's transgression.[2] For instance, one Middle English lyric juxtaposes animal conflict with a prior Edenic flourishing:

> Foulys in the eyer, bestys in lond,
> All þei had therof a onde,
> Fysschys, erbys, frute and tre,
> All the wers forto be;
> Euery thynge, both more and les,
> For that synne lest ther godnes.[3]
>
> (Birds in the air, beasts on the ground,
> They all henceforth had an enmity,
> Fish, plants, fruits, and trees,
> Everything was worse;
> Every thing, both great and small,
> Because sin stripped them of goodness.)

The passage makes a simple point: if the created world was intrinsically good, its processes untinged by evil and judgment, the postlapsarian world is newly marked by creaturely hostility ("onde"). The Fall, to put this in modern terms, is a significant ecological disturbance, transforming the landscape and its processes.

Yet, as we saw in chapter 1, some premodern representations of the prehuman world imagined biological transience and animal predation as an integral part of the prelapsarian beatitude of creation, the means of creaturely permanence in a mortal cosmos. In this view, the Fall corrupted human *perception* of the more-than-human world. Blinded by sin, human beings become unable to apprehend the world's continued order, goodness, and beauty. Such accounts suggest that if the earth seems fallen to fallen humans, it is not that nature has changed, but rather the human relationship to it. However, this becomes a minority view by the later Middle Ages. The writers of the vernacular texts this chapter considers generally held humans responsible for the harsh ecologies of the postlapsarian world and the suffering of nonhuman beings.

In this chapter, I explore how several retellings of the story of the expulsion from Eden mourn a lost world and engage the challenges of living in a cosmos that humans now perceive as hostile. If chapter 1 focused on how dynamic descriptions encourage forms of attention to ecological process (performing ecology as drama), this chapter turns to how the language of ecological suffering and loss can catalyze new ways of being in the world.[4] I look at expressions of grief and nostalgia, examining how, by employing a series of elegiac forms—negation, antithesis, repetition, refrain, ecphonesis (affective exclamation)—medieval texts both evoke and recast a larger narrative of decline. Yet these texts also imply that in repetition may also lie the grounds of hope, reclamation, and renewal. In these works, forms of repetition function first as means of coming to terms with and accepting responsibility for what has been lost and next as means of moving forward in a precarious world.

The idea of the Fall as the ground zero of a corrupted cosmos is barely implied by Genesis's brief account of Adam and Eve's expulsion and post-Edenic existence. After narrating how Adam and Eve eat from the tree of knowledge of good and evil and realize their nakedness, the Bible explains that God issues a series of curses:

> To the woman also he said: "I will multiply thy sorrows, and thy conceptions: in sorrow shalt thou bring forth children, and thou shalt be under thy husband's power, and he shall have dominion over thee." And to Adam he said: "Because thou hast hearkened to the voice of thy wife, and hast eaten of the tree, whereof I commanded thee that thou shouldst not eat, cursed is the earth in thy work; with labour and toil shalt thou eat thereof all the days of thy life. Thorns and thistles shall it bring forth to thee; and thou shalt eat the herbs of the earth. In the sweat of thy face shalt thou eat bread till thou return to the earth, out of which thou wast taken: for dust thou art, and into dust thou shalt return." . . . And the Lord God sent him out of the paradise of pleasure, to till the earth from which he was taken. (Genesis 3:16–23)

Sketching a shadowy picture of the beginning of human history, this passage projects an existence marked by subsistence farming, labor, subjugation, and bodily suffering. It marks the point of human entry into what fourteenth-century theologian Julian of Norwich will call "this deadly life."[5] By the later Middle Ages, the Fall and Expulsion also evoked a story of profound ecological alienation and reclamation, the negotiations that follow catastrophe, and the challenges of dwelling in a care-filled world.

When late medieval vernacular texts retell the story of the Fall and Expulsion, they do not just meditate on the profundity of the loss, they also enflesh Genesis's skeletal narrative with lively representations of the newly diminished world, full of creaturely struggle and sorrow, unlikely ecological antagonists and kin, and hopeful futures. The narratives that we will encounter in this chapter—a Chaucerian lyric on the Golden Age, expulsion scenes from medieval cycle plays and the capacious biblical history of the *Cursor Mundi*, and penitential laments in the apocryphal legends of Adam and Eve's travails—offer glimpses of some of the ways in which late medieval writers imagined the origin of humanity's sense of difference from the rest of the earth and its creatures. The story of the Fall is fundamentally a human drama, but as these texts tell it, fallenness seeps into everything. For instance, the lyric presented earlier notes that suffering and sin spread into all created things ("among all thing it sprong"),[6] so that what humans see then in the present world, even at its best, is never more than a shadow of a lost paradise, a world that was truer, more fully alive, even more substantial.[7]

Such nostalgic narratives of ecological loss and decline will surely feel familiar to modern readers. We may not see ourselves as living in a "fallen" world, but declensionism has long been environmentalism's grand narrative and elegy its operative mode.[8] Environmentalists lament habitat loss, industrial pollution of skies and waterways, species extinction, overextraction of natural resources, the paving of paradise ("you don't know what you've got till it's gone," sings Joni Mitchell in her well-known ecological elegy).[9] Although, as we have seen, Lynn White located the origin of anthropogenic ecological deterioration in the biblical assertion of human dominion over creation, many recent scholars have found the roots of declensionism in the industrialization of the nineteenth century, seeing it as a particular effect of modernity.[10] Ecological decline is thus a not-so-hidden cost of the Enlightenment pursuit of technological progress and economic development, an ideal which, Carolyn Merchant argues, is bound up with a desire to recover a prelapsarian world of leisure and abundance, to make the world Edenic again (for some humans, if not for others or for nonhuman creatures).[11]

As we have already begun to see, the narrative of intertwined ecological and social decline has a much deeper history, a history that complicates any linear narrative of decline or progress.[12] By the late Middle Ages, declensionism had come to assume several conventional forms, including the interlinked motifs of the *senectus mundi* (the aging world) and the seven ages of history.[13] These motifs, which draw from biblical and classical models, as James Dean writes, represent humanity's "moral failings" as both initiating and perpetuating the world's decline.[14] Both biblical and classical mythologies narrate a shift from virtue to corruption, from order to disorder, from a sense of interspecies kinship to human alienation from the cosmos, from simplicity to complexity, from leisure to labor. Both narratives imagine the earth as wounded by and hostile toward human beings, who have come to understand dominion as oppression, who mistake wants for needs, and who, once they have lost a sense of connection and stewardship, begin to see the earth primarily in terms of profit.

Yet as interwoven as they become, biblical and classical narratives of history, human responsibility, and ecology ultimately diverge. This chapter explores how medieval biblical narratives tell a story of ecological disturbance that emphasizes resilience and reformation. I briefly compare this to Golden Age narratives, which relay a story of ecological decline that is bound up with technological innovation and a sense of snowballing alienation from the natural world. Both stories narrate a rupture of humans and the more-than-human world, but they deviate in how they imagine what life might look like in the wake of catastrophe.

If they differ in their approaches to history and temporality, both classical and biblical treatments of a diminished world typically frame their historical narratives in the pathos of elegy.[15] The elegiac mourns the absence of an ever-receding past and a still-arriving future. It represents the *now* as diminished from the *then*; it pulses with ubi sunt. Its forms often mimic its content, embodying the recursiveness of lament, returning again and again to scenes of absence and loss through repetition, antithesis, and ecphonesis. Although they often represent the Fall as an ongoing process, medieval writers particularly mourn its catalyzing, catastrophic event. They circle around loss, finding its traces in absences and marking its repetitions. Nostalgia for Edenic ecologies reverberates throughout these works the way a refrain echoes through a song: similar but sometimes modulated to a new key or with a subtle change in the lyrics. The rhythmic repetition of loss attempts to make order in chaos, to locate moments of emergence in the midst of catastrophe.[16] In early elegies for a prelapsarian world, the utopic past echoes across time and space. Imagined as an unbroken whole, its repetitions are diminishments and fragments but also moments of possibility of the emergence of something new.

For with the Fall, history begins, and with it a pattern of loss. Yet, postlapsarian elegies do not simply narrate a linear unraveling of a perishing cosmos. Many medieval religious texts suggest that the human experience of time is of inhabiting a world of echoes and shadows. Fortune turns her wheel, now lifting, next casting down, and then perhaps, raising again. The phoenix burns and is reborn, its life cycle one of endless repetition. Sacred history unfurls in shadowy similitudes—the world is created, humans fall, it begins again, human virtue declines, the world is destroyed in a flood, the survivors begin anew until the last age when it will all again be destroyed and re-created. Such patterns, Dean writes, suggested "a Boethian point about human mortality and the world's transience: human life and world history move according to the same basic design, and there is a penitential lesson, or perhaps lessons, embodied in each revolution."[17] Because the Fall is ongoing, these texts suggest, humans must also continually repent and begin again. To attend to the first Fall, for medieval writers, is both to better understand the present condition of the world and to anticipate its end. And to evoke postlapsarian or primitive life is to query how we understand loss and return within the patterns of history.[18]

In the following pages, we will trace the cyclical paths of some of these patterns, echoes, and refrains through late medieval writing about humanity's First Age: the epoch immediately after the Fall and Expulsion from Eden. Rather like an elegy, my argument in this chapter moves forward by circling back, attending to scenes of world loss and their aftermaths, examining them from different angles, and listening to stories by different tellers. We begin with a glance at the classical model of the Golden Age, which advances a powerful teleology of interlinked ecological and social decline. We then return to the biblical narrative to consider how medieval plays mark the loss of Eden by emphasizing the contrast between then and now, presence and absence, and them and us. If *what* is lost is embodied in contrasts, the laments in the legendary *Lives of Adam and Eve* make clear how the *feeling* of loss manifests in repetition. In these apocryphal texts, form and history become mirrors, each imagining human existence as bound up with repetition. Yet, it is in such cycles of ecological disturbance, of death, decay, and suffering—of care—that some medieval texts locate opportunities for recovery.

And it is in their reflection on the catastrophic ending of one world and entry into another that narratives of the Fall and Expulsion explore apocalyptic ecologies as ongoing, as tragic but also signs of the possibility of change. Throughout, this chapter considers a small set of questions: How do medieval understandings of the postlapsarian world as inherently diminished shape the representation of the human relationship to and responsibility for that world? How does the sense of recurrent ecological loss and lack both stymie and catalyze human action in the world, against the world, or on the world's behalf? What is at stake in falling and beginning again, over and over again?

The Old Ways

> I wolde that our tymes sholde torne ayen to the oolde maneris!
> (I wish that our era would return to the old ways!)
> CHAUCER, *Boece*

Although this book focuses on the reception of biblical narratives, by the later Middle Ages, treatments of the Edenic world, as Alastair Minnis writes, were "permeated by notions of the classical 'Golden Age.'"[19] Advanced by Hesiod's *Works and Days*, Virgil's *Georgics*, and Ovid's *Metamorphoses*, the motif was translated into medieval writing, finding new audiences in popular works by Boethius, Isidore of Seville, Deschamps, and Chaucer.[20] By the fourteenth century, the concept of a primitive utopia untouched by human industry and commerce, private property, and even agriculture would have been well known to readers of Latin literature and increasingly to readers of vernacular texts.

Unlike biblical narratives, which idealize life in the Eden but represent early postlapsarian existence as neither more nor less difficult than contemporary existence, Golden Age myths typically offer a rose-tinted vision of early life, finding in the first ages a pastoral ideal of which the contemporary age is only the faintest of shadows.[21] To put this another way, although biblical texts often represent the lives of the first humans as primitive, simple but full of hard labor and suffering, Golden Age texts tend toward the primitivist, romanticizing the leisure, innocence, and ecological harmony of the earliest human beings.[22] If the biblical narrative of the Fall and Expulsion from Eden explains why human labor on the land is difficult yet necessary, Golden Age narratives approach this issue from the opposite perspective, emphasizing how human action and making in the world—labor, industry, technology—contribute to the deterioration of both ecological and social harmony.[23] Indeed, the power of this classical narrative of decline derives in part from a long-assumed antagonism of *natura* and *techne*.[24] In Ovid's *Metamorphoses*, for instance, each subsequent age is characterized by technological developments that are paralleled by increasing alienation from the more-than-human world.

An interest in the shaping historical force of the mechanical crafts and knowledge inflects Geoffrey Chaucer's late fourteenth-century treatment of this mythology, which as Sarah Stanbury notes, "offers a critique of modernity that is particularly targeted at technology, or craft."[25] Yet, Chaucer's versions of the mythology also complicate any simple linear narrative of decline, partly because he only describes the First Age. He offers two versions of the Golden Age myth: first a relatively straightforward version in his *Boece*, a prose translation of Boethius's *Consolation of Philosophy*; and second, a versified and expanded ballade, now known as "The Former Age," that draws on the *Romance of the Rose* and Ovid's *Metamorphoses* as well as Boethius, and that invokes the pastoral mode to mount a critique of his time's covetousness.[26] In his *Boece*, Chaucer writes: "I wolde that our tymes sholde torne ayen to the oolde maneris!" And indeed, scholars have long argued that Chaucer's treatment of the "Golden Age" theme is inspired by the bleak instability and uncertainty of his own moment with its recurrent plagues, famines, wars, social upheavals and revolts, heresies, and growth in global commerce.[27]

At first glance, Chaucer's lyric may seem to be a paradigmatic example of the nostalgic idealizing of a lost past. Yet it ultimately offers an ambivalent exploration of the entangled nature of ecological and social decline and progress that subtly unfolds through description, negation, and antithesis. Much like its sources, the lyric's eight stanzas ostensibly describe a lost world. Developing a contrast between the then and now, the before and after, and the them and us, it opens with a pastoral description:

> A blissful lyf, a paisible and a swete,
> Ledden the peples in the former age.
> They helde hem payed of the fruites that they ete,
> Which that the feldes yave hem by usage. (650/1–4)
>
> (A blissful life, peaceable, and sweet,
> led the people in the First Age.
> They were contented with the fruit they ate,
> which the fields gave them without cultivation.)

Before we know anything about the setting, Chaucer tells us how it feels: life in this time and place is one of *otium*—blissful, peaceful, and sweet. Syntactically, feeling comes first, then the reason. The fields voluntarily produce and give their fruits for the food of humans, who don't need to labor to cultivate the land but who also are content with the simple diet it yields. This world presents itself as gift; humans only need to receive from it. Yet in this, the opening lines also imply that this ecology is uneven: the earth gives and humans take.

"The Former Age" cannot sustain a straightforward celebration of this pastoral state through a single stanza. By its fifth line, this first stanza begins to contrast the First Age with the present, first with a subtle negation: "They ne were nat forpampred with outrage" (they were not pampered with excess; 650/5). The implication here is that later peoples *will* be characterized by excesses. Here as throughout the lyric, Nicola Masciandaro writes, "the past effectively ceases to be understood as what was and becomes simply an image of what is not."[28] Negation and contrast soon become the dominant modes of the lyric, evoking historical difference more than a narrative of decline. And indeed, though the poem's implicit contrasts may first suggest that difference *is* decline, the poem's forms ultimately do not allow the reader to adopt a purely declensionist reading of history. To the contrary, they actively undermine such a reading, constantly circling back and forth from the then and the now. It is a poem built around a proleptic temporality; nearly every detail is anticipatory, demonstrating a knowingness about the dynamics of historical change, suggesting throughout that what some people perceive as progress may be for others loss, and vice versa.[29]

The entanglement of progress and decline becomes increasingly visible as later lines subtly question how blissful this primitive life would have been for early humans. The poet opens the next stanza with the ominous "Yit nas the ground nat wounded with the plough" (The earth was not yet wounded by the plow; 650/9). The remainder of the stanza develops the image of the plow-wounded land with a series of anticipatory negations, emphasizing the violence that will be done to the land: "No man yit knew the forwes of his lond . . . Unkorven and ungrobbed lay the vyne" (No man yet knew the furrows of his land . . . the vine was unpruned [lit. uncarved] and uncultivated; 650/12, 14). Later the poem will describe ships on the ocean similarly as carving the blue-green waves (651/21). In his reading of this poem, Karl Steel observes that "all these people act as though anything could suffer a wound."[30] But strikingly much of the agency here is obscured by the passive voice and displaced onto tools rather than the human beings who will wield them: the plow wounds the land; the ship carves the sea; ostensibly the shears prune the vines. Human responsibility for this wounding may be implied, but it is rarely directly claimed in these opening stanzas.

In the poem's repeated "yet," the present hangs over the past like a shadow, attesting to the inevitability of change. Used this way, "not . . . yet" is recursive but also anticipatory. On the one hand, the lyric constructs an idealized image of the First Age by means of an implicit contrast with the excesses of the present moment. Unlike the present, the people of the past are not ruled by greed, materialism, and a desire for dominion. On the other hand, as the poem will articulate even more clearly in the next stanza, the lives of those of the former age were characterized by scarcity. They "eete nat half ynough" (don't eat half as much as they need; 650/11). These gatherers eat the food of animals—nuts, berries, and pig slop—and drink water. As Steel suggests, moments like this attest to how the poem temporarily suspends hierarchy to explore "shared vulnerability" of all creation in the First Age, but in so doing, also makes clear that life under these conditions is wretched.[31] If we find nostalgia in these lines, we must also acknowledge how bleak this picture of early life is. As we will see, one of the Adam Books, the *Canticum de Creatione*, similarly emphasizes the wretchedness of the first humans by hypothesizing about primitive food. It notes that after Adam and Eve are expelled from Eden, they wander hungry for over a week, only finding the kind of food animals eat.[32] Though they are starving, they consider it unfit for their consumption. Chaucer's poem implies that these first humans not only eat the same food as animals but also consume the uncultivated crops *like* animals, noting that "corn up-sprong, unsowe of mannes hond / the which they gnodded" (corn sprang up, not sown by human hand / which they husked out of its ear; 650/9–10) since they have not yet invented even the basic agricultural technologies of the mill, hand mill, or plow.[33]

In details such as these, Chaucer's poem initially seems to suggest a correlation between ecological alienation and technological innovation, but it also raises the question of human agency and responsibility for the more-than-human world more generally. Several scholars have observed that Chaucer focuses on technology more than his sources. For example, Masciandaro writes, "the poem's ideal past is less an identifiable historical age intelligible in its own terms than a negation of contemporary technology and corruption."[34] This negation of *ars* and *techne* unfolds in a remarkable list of human innovations framed by anaphoric *nos*:

> No mader, welde, or wood no litestere
> Ne knew; the flees was of his former hewe;
> No flesh ne wiste offence of egge or spere.
> No coyn ne knew man which was fals or trewe,
> No ship yit karf the wawes grene and blewe,
> No marchaunt yit ne fette outlandish ware.
> No trompes for the werres folk ne knewe,
> Ne toures heye and walles rounde or square (651/17–24)

> (No red, yellow, or blue dyes were known to any dyer,
> for wool remained its natural color;
> no animal knew danger from a sharp point or a blade.
> Humans knew not of coins, which were false or true;
> No ships yet carved the green and blue waves.
> No merchants yet searched for foreign goods.
> People did not know the sound of battle trumpets,
> Nor of high towers nor square or round walls.)

Like the implicit critique of "excess" in the opening stanza, this list uses anaphoric negation (itself a formal excess) to critique the present world by imagining the relations between humans and the more-than-human world differently. In this passage we see a shift in in focus from what objects and tools might do to what human agents might do with them.

Each negation, each "no," "ne," and "un-," implies a question: What would the world be like without such things as dye, weapons, money, ships, fortified buildings? What would the world be like if humans didn't *know* such things could exist? Imagining a world in which human *ars* and *techne* were as of yet unthought, Chaucer invites the reader to consider how history might have chosen a different path, while not entirely telling us what that path might have been or whether it would have been an improvement on the current world. On the whole, the lyric narrates a history of what is not but which once might have been. It largely keeps that past in the past, even as the imagination of that past is entirely shaped by the present world.

The lyric's veneer of affective distance is broken in two ecphonetic moments, both beginning with the lament, "Alas," and both turning from the "they" to the "us." In the first, the speaker bewails, "Allas, than sprong up al the cursednesse / Of coveytyse, that first our sorwe broghte" (Alas, then all the cursedness of covetousness, which brought our first sorrow, sprang up; 651/31–32). The second outpouring echoes the first: "Allas, allas, now may men wepe and crye! / For in oure days nis but covetyse" (Alas, alas, now may men weep and cry! / For in our time is nothing but covetousness; 651/60–61). It is in these moments of mourning, which focus on "*our* sorrow" and "*our* days" (my emphasis), that Chaucer's lyric turns from ironic description built on difference to query what is at stake in writing a declensionist history. Although declensionism can only effectively enforce its nostalgia by frequent reference to a diminished present, as Chaucer's lyric shows, any attempt to represent the present's relation to a more utopic past is bound to be fraught with caveats. If the felt experience of loss characterizes our desire for a different world, in articulating that loss, Chaucer begins to suggest, we may find ourselves confronting the ways our experience of history is primarily one of change.

"What Was Becoming Lost"

> What I did not know as I sang the lament of what was becoming lost
> and what was already lost was how this loss would happen
> JULIANA SPAHR, "Gentle Now, Don't Add to Heartache"

Where classicizing narratives like Chaucer's reflect on the disappearance of a distant past, the medieval biblical texts that the remainder of this chapter considers narrate the moment of loss and its immediate aftermath. For many early writers and thinkers, the biblical Fall marked a catastrophic shift from an orderly world full of generative potential to a cosmos ruled by contingency. When medieval texts imagine the immediate aftermath of this catastrophe, they turn elegiac, drawing bleak contrasts between then and now, mourning the loss, and circling around the absence. In the York play "The Expulsion," for instance, Adam laments that while they had enough before, now they have nothing ("We hadde inowe, nowe haue we noghte," 70/44), severing the past and the present with his syntax.

The felt experience of a ruptured world is part of the human condition, shaped in part by how we experience loss in time. If you have lived long enough, you likely carry a pocketful of moments when you knew, or suspected, that the world would never be the same, that you were witness to the crux of before and after. I remember walking into my morning Old English class in graduate school to see the classroom TVs projecting images of a plane striking one of the Twin Towers in New York City. That day—September 11, 2001—I, like everyone I knew, somehow felt the death of a world. In a morning, we experienced the world shift even if we could not yet imagine the fearmongering, the atrocities, and the lost sense of safety that the coming years would bring. And, it has been more than three years since I sat in a café in Durham, North Carolina, reading news reports about the "novel coronavirus," quarantines abroad, overburdened hospital wards, and hoarding of toilet paper. The plane I boarded to return to Indiana was almost empty but saturated with the scent of disinfectant. As I sheltered at home and watched the world shut down, I had a sense, as many of us did, of bearing witness to such a moment, a sense bound up with a kind of anticipatory nostalgia for a world in which this spreading catastrophe was still unimaginable. My students now sometimes speak of the "before times," and of teetering on a threshold, even as memories of those early days fade and even as we have all more or less adjusted to a new normal, a normal that feels increasingly distant from the strictures, fears, but also the awareness produced by pandemic. Our experience is not too different from that of medieval authors who measured time with the phrase "since pestilence time."[35] Yet, as the Expulsion story reminds us, the fissures of past from present that we, like Adam, sometimes experience are rarely absolute. In the works that this section considers, Adam's sense of the insurmountable distance of then and now, of before and after, of there and here is driven by nostalgia for a vanishing homeland but also by a sense of the necessity of moving forward in a changed world.[36]

The temporal and spatial dynamics of nostalgia are powerfully evident in the twelfth-century Anglo-Norman *Play of Adam* (*Ordo representacionis Ade*), which stages the Creation, Fall, and Expulsion, and Adam and Eve's longing for a lost Eden.[37] In the play, Adam and Eve are always already fallen, always already anticipating a changed world. Even when describing the Garden to its new inhabitants, God frames the prelapsarian world through the lens of its postlapsarian condition. As Steven Justice writes, God depicts it "in terms of a world that the audience recognizes as its own. What masquerades here as information to the unfallen is in fact the nostalgia of the fallen."[38] Suggesting the near impossibility of imagining Eden *not* in contradistinction to the present, the play assumes a deeply elegiac stance toward an imagined place of safety from the cares of contemporary life.

Adam and Eve's nostalgia for Eden manifests in lament. The Latin stage directions indicate that shortly after they are expelled from the Garden, the couple interrupts their attempts at working the earth with mournful glances toward paradise (*flebiliter repicient saepius paradisum*). Adam looks back, raising his hands toward Eden, and cries:

> Oi, paradis, tant bel maner!
> Vergier de glorie tant vus fet bel veer!
> Jotez en sui par mon pecchié par voir.
> Del recovrer tot ai perdu l'espoir.
> Jo fui dedenz n'en soi gaires joïr.
>
> (Ah, Paradise, how lovely to live there!
> Sweet glade of glory, now you look so fair!
> My sins have thrown me out of your fresh air –
> No hope that I'll return, and I despair.
> Within its walls, I knew not my delight.)[39]

In these few lines, Adam poignantly gives expression to the felt experience of an epistemic shift. He longs for the ability *not* to know what he now understands. However, his lament also reflects that cliché that we can only appreciate things fully in hindsight. His previous joy is newly apparent when viewed through the lens of its absence. Juxtaposing past and present, he longs for return to the "before times," even as the impossibility of return is beginning to dawn on him. Adam's sense of externality and alienation is deeply nostalgic. Like the speaker of Chaucer's "Former Age," in struggling to articulate the experience of loss, Adam reaches for elegiac structures—affective exclamations, negations, and juxtapositions of then and now, there and here. His expressions are forms of partial return, means of navigating the felt experience of a before and an after.

It is difficult to find a medieval treatment of the Expulsion from Eden that is *not* structured by contrasts of then and the now, that does not adopt nostalgic or elegiac forms. Mournful antitheses even find their way into prose histories. Consider, for instance, John Trevisa's fourteenth-century Middle English translation of Ranulf Higden's universal history, the *Polychronicon*. Trevisa explains that after the Expulsion, humans passed:

> Out of hiȝe in to lowh, out of liȝt in to derknesse and slym, out of his owne londe and contray in to outlawynge, out of hous into maskynge and wayles contray and lond, out of fruit into wepynge and woo, out of preisynge in to deel and sorwe, out of merþe in to stryf.[40]
>
> (Out of high into low, out of light into darkness and mud, out of his own land and country and into outlawry, out of his home into wandering and a pathless country and land, out of fruitfulness into weeping and woe, out of praising into sorrow, out of joy into strife.)

Relying on a series of contrasts between before and after, Trevisa catalogs how change ripples through the physical world into the domestic spaces and the emotional worlds of the first humans, who find themselves homeless outlaws, wanderers, entirely bewildered by the land outside Eden. This is a world marked by externality; the most repeated formula of the passage is "out of . . . into." The movements the passage marks are at once spiritual, social, emotional, and formal. In the place of the Edenic ideals of *otium*, safety, and happiness, are now labor, danger, and sadness. Such antitheses and inversions emphasize how the medieval authors understood the Fall as catastrophe, as a fissuring of then and now, joy and sorrow.

Similarly marking the shift from the prelapsarian then to the postlapsarian now with antitheses and inversions, the late medieval York play "The Expulsion" grieves the loss in a sustained litany of sorrows. York is the only extant English cycle of biblical plays to include a play devoted entirely to the Expulsion, an inclusion that, as Pamela King has noted, is itself redundant. It is as if the play cycle itself is hesitant to move forward and instead lingers on the moment of loss. In the previous play, "The Fall of Man," the angel has "already effectively expelled Adam and Eve from Eden."[41] That play ends with Adam's lament, "Allas, for sorowe and care / Oure handis may we wrynge" (Allas! Out of sorrow and suffering, / we may wring our hands; 69/175–76). "The Expulsion" unfolds as an extended gloss on these lines, taking the shape of a highly stylized and affect-driven dialogue between an angel and Adam and Eve. The lament, like the otiose play itself, becomes a means of postponement through repetition, an extended pause or dilation that emphasizes and explores the implications of Adam and Eve's failure. It resists moving forward. Adam and Eve linger as long as they can in the shadow of the Garden.

Punctured by the language of loss and care, the Expulsion play obsessively rehearses sorrow through repetition, spiraling from expressions of sadness to articulations of what was lost, to a sense of responsibility. Indeed, over the course of its 168 lines, the play creates a linguistic echo chamber, returning repeatedly to several terms: *allas* (fourteen times), *now* (twelve times), *wrought* (seven times), *syte* (suffering, six times), and *lost* (five times). Even the play's stanzaic form circles back on itself, chaining its six-line stanzas together with linkwords and phrases as it builds a repetitive lexicon of lament. Alliteration echoes across the lines, sonically tying them together. On the level of form, then, the play performs mourning as suspension and deferral—there is no movement forward here, only a sense of absence, loss, and grief bound up with a growing awareness of human responsibility for what they have "wrought."

Through all this repetition, "The Expulsion" both mourns the loss of Eden and emphasizes human culpability. The angel tells Adam and Eve that they have "wrought" and "made al þis syte" (made all this suffering; 70/30). Adam later rhetorically asks, "what haue we wrought?" (what have we done? 70/41). One of the play's echoing terms, *wrought* is the past tense of *werken*, a particularly multivalent verb that can indicate physical labor, action, performance, or creative production.[42] The term darkly echoes God's own work, throwing into relief how much has changed after the Fall. In the two York Creation plays, divine work is efficacious and generative. God describes how he has "wroght þire worldys wyde, / Heueyn and ayre and erthe also" (made the wide world, / heaven and atmosphere and also the earth; 54/5–6). And as we saw in chapter 1, in the earlier York plays, God proclaims his "werk" to be "fayre," joyful, and complete. In the Creation plays, *werken* overwhelmingly assumes its nominal form; God's "werke" is a creative act completed. At the conclusion of "The Creation of Adam and Eve," God proclaims, "My warke is endyde now at mane / All lykes me will, but þis is best" (My work is now ended with humanity / everything pleases me, but this is the best; 61/87–88). In "The Expulsion," "wrought" echoes its initial divine articulation in the cycle; human making is a shadowy likeness of the divine creation. Yet humanity's work is always a verb in the "Play of the Expulsion," suggesting that, if creation is complete, labor is ongoing.[43] The world Adam and Eve now inhabit will be shaped by human activity, for both good and ill. The "wrought" that echoes throughout the play is a past act with continued repercussions; what humans have "wrought" is characterized by its incompletion, its repetitive and ongoing nature.

Thus, in the fallen world, human relations with the earth are marked by perpetual travail. At the end of the play of "The Fall," God tells Adam, "In erthe þan shalle ye swete and swynke / And trauayle for youre foode" (in the ground you will sweat and labor / and travail for your food; 68/161–62). After the angel leaves Adam and Eve alone in the new world, they grieve their loss and the "trauel" (labor/travail) that lies ahead of them.[44] Unlike the more general term "werk," "travail" is postlapsarian labor; it is the subjective experience of work as difficult or painful.[45] Medieval texts use the term both to describe the pain of childbirth and physical labor. "Travail" is work synonymous with suffering and care.

Yet rather than focusing on the labor that lies ahead of them, Adam and Eve's response to this curse is to lament the loss of its opposite: *otium*. It is difficult for them to look forward rather than backward, to relinquish the idea that the world is only a setting for human recreation. In a lengthy elegiac monologue, Adam mourns the disappearance of the "gamys" (recreation) and "welthe" (plentitude and well-being) of their Edenic life with exclamations of grief:

Nowe is shente both I and shoo,
Allas, for syte.

Allas, for syte and sorowe sadde,
Mournynge makis me mased and madde,
To thynke in herte what helpe Y hadde
And nowe has none.
On grounde mon I neuyr goo gladde,
My gamys ere gane.

Gone ar my games withowten glee;
Allas, in blisse kouthe we noȝt bee,
For putte we were to grete plente
At prime of þe day;
Be tyme of none alle lost had wee,
Sa welawaye.

Sa welaway, for harde peyne,
Alle bestis were to my biddyng bayne,
Fisshe and fowle, they were fulle fayne
With me to founde.
And nowe is alle thynge me agayne
Þat gois on grounde.

On grounde ongaynely may Y gange
To suffre syte and peynes strange. (71/79–100)

(Now both she and I are guilty.
Alas, for sorrow!

Alas, for anguish and deep sorrow!
Mourning makes me confused and angry,
to think in my heart what help I had,
and now have none.
I will never walk gladly on the ground.
My games are gone.

Gone are my games without glee;
Alas, we are not in the blissful homeland,
for we were given great plenty
at the prime of day
before noon we had lost it.
Alas!

So, alas for the hard pains!
All the beasts were obedient to my bidding,
fish and birds were very joyful

"THIS DEADLY LIFE" 77

> when they encountered me.
> But now all things that walk on the ground
> are against me.
>
> On the ground I must walk with hostility,
> To suffer anguish and strange pains.)

Adam's lament is punctuated with exclamations, many of them serving as the concluding line to a stanza and repeated as the opening line of the next: "Allas, for care" (45), "Allas for doole" (75), "Allas for syte" (61, 80, and 81), "Sa welawaye" (92 and 93). A characteristic element of elegiac verse, ecphonetic terms such as *alas* and *welaway* are nonmimetic; they perform emotion more than they represent it.[46] Adam moves between contemplating what he has lost and feeling the loss. The passage's exclamations perform grief while the passage narrates its source. Mimesis and ecphonesis, thinking and feeling, go hand in hand.

The play's stanzaic structure heightens these repetitions. Each six-line stanza begins with a version of the final line of the previous stanza, as if Adam is turning over ideas in his mind, circling back, repeating himself as he tries to understand and articulate his new position in the world. But these repetitions are dynamic: the final lines of the stanzas are short, usually only four or five syllables; the opening lines of the following stanza offer an expansion, grounding the phrase in a larger context. "Allas for siyte" becomes "Allas, for syte and sorowe sadde." "þat gois on grounde" becomes "On grounde ongaynely may Y gange" (On the ground I must walk with hostility). We might see these expansions as small steps forward, and indeed, the passage emphasizes his movement into this new world, his "going on the ground." If Adam is caught in his elegiac ruminations, the expanded phrases suggest that he is not entirely immobilized by his grief. For in this passage, Adam pivots between past, present, and future, returning to the "And now" and other images of passing time. He represents himself as standing on the seam of the *now* that fissures past from future, looking both backward and forward.

The Angry Earth

> The politics of coexistence are always contingent, brittle, and flawed.
> TIMOTHY MORTON, *Dark Ecology*

As Adam works through his grief, his monologue emphasizes his growing alienation from the physical world. Even while his lament charts the movement between then and now, between what was and what is, he initially continues to think of himself in some of the same terms with which he describes the beasts—they all are earthbound, "going on the ground." Yet missing here is any sense that he is kin to the earth, the ground on which they all walk and from which he came. This growing distance constitutes a shift. In this play as in others, Adam and Eve cease to see the earth as part of their substance, treating it instead as a character with whom they must engage. Earthbound labor is a key aspect of the curse, but the play frames the ongoing relation with the earth as fraught. On the one hand, the play emphasizes that the earth will continue to sustain humankind, who will continue to be *in* it, relying on it even though their relation to it has changed. Yet on the other hand, Adam's lament functions as a process of differentiation from the earth. It renders the mourning "I" or "we" as distinct from the object of lament, which begins to recede into the background.

This alienation—even antagonism—comes to the fore in the final two stanzas of Adam's elegy. Echoing an earlier moment in "The Creation" where God proclaims that all his creatures shall dwell without danger or suffering ("sall my creaturis / Euir byde withoutyn bale"; 56/111–12), Adam articulates how his new experience of suffering ("bale") now extends to the entire creation:

> Allas, for bale, what may þis bee?
> In worlde vnwisely wrought haue wee,
> This erthe it trembelys for this tree
> And dyns ilke dele!
> Alle þis worlde is wrothe with mee,
> Þis wote I wele.

> Full wele Y wote my welthe is gone,
> Erthe, elementis, euerilkane
> For my synne has sorowe tane,
> Þis wele I see. (72/111–19)

> (Alas, for suffering, what may this be?
> We have acted unwisely in this world.
> The earth trembles because of this tree
> and makes noise in every way!
> The entire world is angry with me,
> this I know well.

> Very well do I know that my well-being is gone:
> earth, elements, everything.
> Because my sin has tainted it all with sorrow.
> I see this well.)

Adam, who entered being *as* earth, now personifies the earth, seeing it as something ontologically different from himself, though also sharing the pain of his fall.[47] Like Adam, the earth resounds with the inarticulate noise of grief; its din is everywhere heard. Yet even as Adam attests to mutual suffering, his rhetoric differentiates him from the rest of creation. He speaks of "this erthe" and "this tree." In so doing, he distances himself from them, acknowledging that while he and Eve "vnwisely wrought" (acted unwisely; 72/112), the earth quakes because of the tree. We could read these lines as indicating that the earth is trembling out of kinship with the tree, sharing in its violation. Or, we might find in this formulation a displacement of culpability, with Adam implying that the tree is the cause of the fall. Either way, the line marks a key moment in Adam's reframing of the cosmos. What he ultimately takes from the world's disorder, its trembling and echoing noise, is its antagonism. He reads the world as angry with him: "Alle þis worlde is wrothe with mee, / Þis wote I wele" (The entire world is angry with me, / I know this well; 72/115–16). His relationship with the earth is broken, and he becomes increasingly estranged from the source of his substance.

The remainder of the play stages how estrangement begins to taint human relationships. Adam and Eve descend into bickering about who is to blame for the fall, until Eve says, "Be stille Adam, and nemen it na mare, / It may not mende" (Be still Adam, and speak no more of this, / it cannot be mended; 73/155–56). The world, like their marital harmony, seems to them to be irreparably torn. Their bickering and lament soon succumb to silence as Adam and Eve head out into the new world "withouten glee" (73/162), fearing that the sorrow alone will kill them. They also literally descend. At the end of the play, Adam and Eve would, presumably, come down from the stage and step into the crowd, walking from Eden into the world of late medieval England. In so doing, they perform the continuity of then and now that many accounts of the Expulsion narrate. The human condition they now embody is shared by those watching or reading the story of their fall. Walking into the postlapsarian world, Adam and Eve find themselves alienated from Eden, an ecology built on likeness and collective thriving. They enter the creation beyond, which they interpret as resistant, antagonistic, a world in which mutability has become instability, in which catastrophe, small and large, has become the pattern of existence. They enter the disquieting world of the present.

The personification of the angry, suffering, and resistant earth is a commonplace of early treatments of the postlapsarian ecological condition. For instance, the fourteenth-century Cornish play known as the *Ordinalia* similarly personifies the earth as intractable.[48] The first in the cycle of three late fourteenth-century plays, the *Ordinale de origine munde* (typically called the *Origo Mundi*) dramatizes key biblical narratives from the Creation to the building of Solomon's temple in 2,846 lines.[49] Meditating on the aftereffects of the Fall, the scenes depicting the Expulsion dramatize the human desire for complete possession of and dominance over an earth that actively resists such treatment.

The *Ordinalia* imagines the human condition as caught within a dissatisfaction with "enough" and an insistence on "more." It does so by treating the earth as a character in the drama with whom both God and Adam must negotiate. Initially, the earth is recalcitrant and resistant to being used to service human needs. The play's stage directions, which are in Latin, indicate that it cries out upon being hit by Adam's spade. "And he digs, and the earth cries: and again / he digs, and the earth cries" ("*et fodiet et terra clamat et iterum fodiet et clamat terra*"). Adam is initially flummoxed by this unexpected difficulty but not discouraged. He asks God to persuade the earth to allow him to "seek food" from it, expressing his wonder that the earth will not let him "break it."[50]

In response, God demands that the earth comply and assist in meeting Adam's basic needs, commanding it: "Allow Adam to open thee."[51] But, for Adam, the satisfaction of basic needs is insufficient. Over the next fifty lines he barters with God for more and more, first complaining that it will not be enough to feed both him and Eve and then, after God grants him permission to extract more from the ground, saying that it will still not be enough for their child and next, if more children come, they will surely faint with hunger. At this point, and perhaps acknowledging the inevitable, God concedes and allows Adam and his heirs complete use of the earth:

> Go, take all thou wilt
> Adam, of the world all around;
> It shall be indeed for thee,
> And that which comes out of thee.[52]

Following as it does such a sustained negotiation, I find it hard not to read God's response here as one of exasperation. Taking all that they desire from the world, humans may now treat dominion as exploitation. A medieval audience may well have not seen it this way, reading it instead as divine license and approval, though, as Chaucer's Golden Age lyric makes clear, wounding the land out of covetousness was even then a questionable act. Either way, Adam is finally satisfied. He thanks God and then turns to Eve and reports that he has been given "mastery over the world."[53]

Yet even as this scene dramatizes human possession and dominion of the earth, it also imagines a precedent for the idea of the tithe: the obligation to return part of the harvest to God by allowing it to remain uncultivated, fallow, waste. Shortly after ceding use of the land to Adam, God reinstates a limit to its use, commanding, "Leave the tenth part to me, / Still to remain waste."[54] While today we might think of waste as that which is left over after human consumption, God here suggests it as a limit to human consumption, a means of restraint.[55] As the *Ordinalia* uses it, waste is to be a theological and ecological sign, intended to serve as a visible reminder that the world does not belong entirely to human beings, that consumption and growth need restraints and limits. Yet, in other biblical works (and environmental history more generally), we see the devastating effects of this mythology of divine allowance of dominion: human beings will continue to take far more than they need, from the earth and from each other. In the *Ordinalia*'s version of this story, Adam and Eve's sense of grief has been replaced with acquisitiveness, their sense of loss with a desire for new forms of consumption, power, and wealth.

Beginning Again

> The world was all before them . . .
> They, hand in hand, with wandering steps and slow,
> Through Eden took their solitary way.
> JOHN MILTON, *Paradise Lost*

As Adam's negotiations with God and the earth in the *Ordinalia* suggest, many medieval writers understood the Expulsion as the beginning of the human story.[56] But what happened next? The fourth chapter of Genesis moves quickly from the curse and expulsion to the story of Cain and Abel. Filling in the gaps left by the biblical account, medieval writers imagined Adam and Eve simultaneously yearning to return to Eden and learning to make a home in a complex and unpredictable world. These first humans wrestle with their loss, they grieve it, but then they navigate their new material conditions. Yet, this is not a straightforward story of progress. As these apocryphal texts make clear, in sacred history, the Fall originates a pattern of ongoing disturbance and loss, but also of recovery.[57] In representing these early human trials, apocryphal literature often depicts the Fall echoing through the cosmos, bound to be endlessly repeated, while also suggesting that it is *in* the repetitions, in the losses, echoing grief, and the repeated failures, that redemption and repair just might begin.

If medieval plays emphasize the felt experience of the epistemic shift and dramatize the earth's pain, suggesting its anger and resistance to human use, the legendary *Lives of Adam and Eve*, sometimes called the "Adam Books," imagine what it might look like to move forward in a newly precarious world. This little-studied corpus of fourteenth- and fifteenth-century texts finds its origin in the ancient *Life of Adam and Eve* (*Vita Adae et Euae*), which imagines what happened in the years following Adam and Eve's exile from Eden.[58] Since the Bible has little to say about life immediately after the Fall, early thinkers had many questions. Both Talmudic and patristic commentaries mused on how Adam and Eve survived outside of Eden: What did they eat? How did they get along? Did they get sick? Did they continue to communicate with God or angels? Did they try to return to Eden?[59] Explaining how humans learned how to satisfy their most basic needs after a world-changing catastrophe, legends about the post-Edenic existence of Adam and Eve were in wide circulation in Europe and the Middle East throughout late antiquity and the Middle Ages.[60]

The story of Adam and Eve's first days outside Eden was well known in medieval England. The Latin *Vita* survives in more than twenty medieval English manuscripts, and there are at least two distinct versions of the Middle English legend in verse (the early fourteenth-century Auchinleck *Life of Adam* and the late fourteenth-century *Canticum de Creatione*) and three more in prose, including versions in the Wheatley manuscript (London, British Library, MS Addit. 39574) and the Vernon manuscript (Oxford, Bodleian Library MS. Eng. poet. a. 1).[61]

Some of these versions begin with the Creation, others with the moment of the Fall. Regardless, these Middle English Adam Books frame the tragic story of expulsion and exile with a focus on penance, though they also draw some conventions from medieval episodic narratives, such as saints' lives and romances.[62] Because some versions are included in household miscellanies, recent attention to these legends has focused on how these texts are particularly suited for such domestic contexts, offering intimate looks into the homelife and gender dynamics of the world's first family. As Cathy Hume has discussed, the tradition, like hagiography, depicts the first couple as examples for later readers, imagining them in situations in which they proleptically model later Christian practices such as penance and proper burial.[63] I am interested here in how these texts also gesture toward the changed relationship of humans and the rest of creation, and the use they make of formalized laments. For, like the drama, the Adam Books bring the complex and shifting relations of humans and the more-than-human world to the fore in elegizing scenes.

Although the Adam Books vary in their details, they generally share a tragic narrative of postlapsarian life, exploring the complex dynamics of human flourishing in a world on which people depend but of which they are largely ignorant and from which they increasingly feel alienated. After Adam and Eve are cast out of the Garden, the couple sorrowfully head westward and construct a basic shelter. Within a week, they grow hungry and frustrated. Eve wants to die, thinking that if she is gone, God will permit Adam to return to Eden. Adam rejects this idea and suggests instead that if they do penance for their sin they might be forgiven and given some food, or perhaps even be able to return to paradise. Satan appears to Eve as an angel, tempting her to forgo her penance by persuading her that God has already forgiven them. When Adam sees what she had done, he chastises both Eve and the devil, who explains why he has a vendetta for humanity (jealousy, being expelled from heaven, etc.). Adam and Eve separate for a time until Cain is born. Many of the texts also narrate the lives of Adam and Eve's children, including episodes of Seth's heroic quest to Eden for oil to anoint his dying father. As this summary might suggest, if Adam and Eve cannot return to Eden, they can't quite leave it behind either. This movement between lament for Eden's loss and desire for its recovery structures the Adam Books' series of narrative episodes, which also both anticipate and echo later biblical events, figures, and ideas. In these movements and echoes, the books frame the larger arc of sacred history as a story of fall, repentance, and beginning again.

The Adam Books emphasize how Adam and Eve first encounter the world as a place of suffering and scarcity, at least in comparison to Eden. Everywhere they turn, they find a landscape riven with danger and *care*. Nearly every Middle English version of the narrative punctuates the episodes with scenes of lament. The *Canticum de Creatione* emphasizes that God has sent them "Into þis worlde, to leue wiþ care" (into this world to live with care), and then describes how they spend the first week mourning: "Þere dwelled þeȝ sore waymantende / Sixe dayes fulle to þe ende, / Boþe in sorwe and in care" (They dwelled there lamenting bitterly / six full days / both out of sorrow and in pain).[64] The Vernon manuscript's prose *lyff of Adam and Eue*, emphasizes bodily precarity even more than their emotional pain, explaining how Adam and Eve "lyueden heore lyf in þe wrecched weopes dale. Ofte heo weoren a-cold and sore of-hungred; eddren mihte hem styngen, foules and beestes hem mihte to-tere; þe watur þat before hem bare mihte adrenche" (lived their life in the wretched dale of weeping. They were often cold and painfully hungry; snakes might sting them, birds and beasts might tear them apart; the water that they bore might drown them).[65] As James Dean points out, Adam and Eve are not necessarily stung or torn apart or drowned, but they imagine that they *might* be in this new world.[66] The possibility of harm looms large as humans perceive threats to their safety at every turn. They discover themselves to be strangers in the world, newly aware of suffering, pain, and risk. Yet in this world full of sorrows, they continue to hope that God will take mercy on them and, in Eve's words in the *Canticum*, "ȝeuen us aȝen þat place / Þat we were ynne" (give us again that place / that we were in; 66/58–59). Adam and Eve thus enter the new world entrenched in a sense of loss, longing, and uncertainty.

Their mourning of their loss is compounded by the fact that they are also ignorant of what is required to sustain life in this new world. When they have stopped grieving the loss of Eden, they realize how hungry they are. Thinking that they will die of starvation, Eve laments their condition ("Allas, Adam, for hunger we dye"; Alas, Adam, we will die of hunger!) and suggests that Adam slay her, believing that, once she is gone, God will allow Adam to return to Eden.[67] (He refuses.) They spend over a week looking for food, seeming to expect the angelic sustenance that God provided for them in Eden but only able to find "more & gras" (roots and plants) that land animals eat.[68] None of the Middle English texts suggest that Adam and Eve succumb to eating the same food as animals, implying instead that the couple sees such food as outside their domain, as not ordained for them, and "þat schulde þe beestes of þe lond ete, for god hit haþ ȝeuen to hem" (and land animals should eat that because God has given it to them).[69] Embedded in this statement is a sense of the difference that Adam and Eve now feel from nonhuman creatures, but also perhaps a burgeoning awareness that while animals continue to receive food as a gift, for humans it now is a product of labor. But this is not yet entirely clear to Adam and Eve; they do not yet know how to work the land. Their only recourse seems to be praying to God for help.

Humbled by their hunger, Adam and Eve employ lament for a different purpose: repentance and penance. Rather than mourning the precarious conditions in which they find themselves, they lament the actions that brought them to that state. In one of the most striking narrative episodes in this tradition Adam and Eve each submerge themselves in a river. Adam does his penance in the Jordan (where Jesus would be baptized) and Eve in the Tigris (one of the four rivers that flowed from Eden). As he stands in the Jordan, Adam acknowledges his guilt and the blamelessness of the natural world. In the Wheatley manuscript, Adam's cry is marked as a new section by a title: "Se now þe sorowynge of Adam here" (Now see here the lamentation of Adam), which is followed by his request that the water and animals share in his lament:

> I seye to þee, Iordan, gadere to-gydere þi wawis and alle lyuynge beestis wiþ-inne þee, and comeþ aboute me and maakiþ sorowe wiþ me. Not for ȝou-silf make ȝe sorowe, but al for me; for ȝe han not synned, but I wickidly aȝeyns my Lord haue synned. Neiþer ȝe diden ony defaute, neiþir ȝe ben bigylid fro ȝoure

sustenaunce, neiþir fro ȝoure metis ordeyned to ȝou; but I am bigylid fro my sustenaunce which was ordeyned for me.[70]

(I say to you, Jordan River, gather together your waves and all the living beasts within you, and come all around me and mourn with me. Don't lament for yourself, but only for me. For you have not sinned, but I wickedly have sinned against my Lord. Nor did you make an error, nor were you beguiled from your sustenance, nor from the foods ordained to you; but I was tricked from the food which was ordained for me.)

Submerging himself in the water up to his chin, Adam buries himself in it, submits to its flow, becomes part of it and like the other river creatures. He places himself in an even more vulnerable position than he was on dry land, and then calls for collaboration with the more-than-human world. He implies that he is the one that has wounded the world. Even so, there's more than a little self-pity in this passage, as Adam laments that the rest of the world has not lost its source of sustenance as he and Eve have. If he seems to be channeling Ambrose's idea that creation's groans (Romans 8:22) are in sympathy with the human condition, Adam is admittedly tone-deaf here in asking innocent creatures to mourn for his sins.[71]

Yet the lament is also infused with a continued assumption of kinship between the human and animal world. The structure of the passage suggests Adam's yearning for a sense of restored connection not only with God but also with his fellow creatures. Adam still sees the more-than-human world as his community, as an interlocutor. Addressing the river as a person, Adam treats it and its creatures as capable not only of action but also of emotion. In so doing, he also, quite strikingly, acknowledges that the physical world itself bears no blame. That the world is innocent is evident in the passage's series of juxtapositions, the *nots* and *neithers* that distance the fundamental goodness of creation from the misuse of it by human beings.

Unlike the elegies for the loss of Edenic bliss in the biblical plays, and unlike Adam and Eve's elegiac mourning earlier in the Adam Books, this lament emphasizes culpability: Adam and Eve here understand their precarity as the direct result of their wrongdoing (even if Adam hedges a bit by emphasizing beguilement). If the scene's imagery of Adam surrounded by animals is nostalgically Edenic, its aim is to model a ritual of confession and baptism that allows Adam to move forward into the new world.

The river and its creatures join him in lamenting, in a scene of shared sorrow. "Se now how alle lyuynge þingis sorowiden togydere wiþ Adam" (Now see how all living creatures lamented together with Adam), the next title in the Wheatley manuscript suggests. Look, it instructs its readers, at human-elemental-animal solidarity:

> Whanne Adam hadde maad al þis lamentacioun wiþ sikynge and soruful teeris, þanne alle lyuynge þingis on erþe, fisch, foul, and beest, camen aboute hym makynge sorowe wiþ hym, and þe watir also soruyngly stood stille in þat tyme of preiynge.[72]

> (When Adam had made all of this lamentation with sighing and sorrowful tears, then all the living things on the earth—fish, birds, and beasts—gathered around him and mourned with him, and the water also sorrowfully stood still in that time of prayer.)

Adam desires company in his grief if not in his guilt. He seeks community, and the river and fish answer, mourning for humanity. Other Middle English versions of this episode, like the *Canticum*, emphasize the sorrow of the animals even more emphatically:

> And alle þe bestis þat weren þor
> For him sorweden alle.
> Þus seuentene dayes and more,
> Alle þe fisches sorweden þore,
> And waymentide wiþ Adam.[73]

> (And all the beasts that were there
> all of them mourned for him.
> Thus for more than seventeen days,
> All the fish mourned there
> and lamented with Adam.)

The language shifts tellingly over the course of these lines. At first, the beasts mourn *for* Adam; a few lines later they are described as mourning *with* him. The passage moves from creaturely sympathy to empathy. The passage also emphasizes their solidarity with its repeated *all*. The earth's creatures, and even its elements, here offer a model for continued kinship, if only as an interspecies community of lament. For a moment, the young world is united in sorrow and in penance.

Perhaps not the entire world. While Adam is joined in his penance by the river and the animals, Eve does her penance alone in the frigid waters of the Tigris. She stands on her rock until Satan appears, disguised as an angelic messenger and tells her that she can leave the waters. She takes him at his word, and when she emerges from the river, the *Canticum* narrates how:

> Out of þe water she wente þo,
> as gras hire body was grene.

> For cold of þe water broun
> anon to þe erthe she fel adoun,
> as ded she hadde bene.[74]
>
> (When she went out of the water
> her body was as green as grass.
> Because of the chill of the brown water,
> she immediately fell down to the earth,
> as if she had been dead.)

The contrast between Adam's call of the animal and elemental world into communion and Eve's suffering in isolation is jarring.[75] The following lines in the *Canticum* mention that Eve lies alone for almost an entire day. Other versions emphasize that she nearly dies.[76] Yet, the passage's central simile, that she is as "green as grass," draws us back to another type of communion with the more-than-human world: our shared transience. As Dean writes, "Eve's greenness, compared with grass, is reminiscent of those biblical passages that compare flesh with grass."[77] Green is also the color of inconstancy, a moral failing that Eve embodies when she emerges early from the water. Regardless, where the tradition emphasizes Adam's spiritual suffering through lament, it emphasizes Eve's physical suffering and weakness.

Eve doesn't fully understand what she has done until later. When she tells Adam that she has been beguiled again, she is inconsolable. In the Latin tradition and the *Canticum*, she faints. In the Auchinleck *Life of Adam* she cries out, "Adam, Adam, wel is te, / And Adam, Adam, wo is me!" (Adam, Adam, well are you, / and Adam, Adam, woe is me!). Because Adam has completed his penance, she says, he can be glad. But, since hers was interrupted and incomplete, she cries:

> And ich may sing "allas, allas,"
> Icham wers þan ich was,
> For now ichaue eft agilt,
> Seþþen we were out of paradis pilt.
> Þerfore ichil now biginne
> Oӡain penaunce for to winne.
>
> (And I may sing, Alas! Alas!
> I am worse than I was,
> for now I have again sinned,
> after we were thrown out of paradise.
> Therefore I will now begin
> again to complete penance.)[78]

This affective outpouring is unique to the Auchinleck *Life*. Both elegiac and penitential, Eve's lament acknowledges her failing while also mourning that it's not only Eden that has been lost, but also a better version of her self. Strikingly, she calls this lament a song. And indeed, it is filled with songlike qualities: repetitions and internal rhymes as Eve circles around her loss, performing her pain with the repeated exclamation, "allas, allas," and the enjambed slant rhyme, which insists that just as she has fallen again, so too, she must "begin / again." Yet, it is also confessional. If we don't hear Eve's confession of her sin while she stands in the river, as we hear Adam's, we hear it now. But we also hear her understanding that penance must be ongoing. And we hear in her antitheses and repetitions her sense that in acknowledging blame and beginning again lie the seeds of hope.

Within every Middle English version of the apocryphal lives of Adam and Eve is some repetition of the story of Edenic bliss and the Fall, some reminder that although the Fall originates a pattern of loss, it also opens up the possibility of redemption. That one of Eve's first acts in the wild echoes her fatal transgression in Eden signals the repetitive nature of human history as imagined by these legends. Her and Adam's failed penance in this watery wilderness also foreshadows Christ's forty days in the wilderness, and perhaps also, by extension, the forty-day fast of Lent. This scene of Adam's penance anticipates two later biblical episodes: the Jordan is the river where John the Baptist would baptize Jesus, the new Adam; and, Adam's forty-six-day fast is suggestive both of Jesus's forty days in the wilderness and the six days of creation, an association that some versions of the text make explicit: "For in sex dayes and seuen niȝtt / All þe warld was maked and diȝt" (because in six days and seven nights / all the world was made and created).[79]

These narratives embody the problems and possibilities of typological temporality, which reads events as both anticipation and repetition.[80] Typology imagines history as a hall of mirrors in which original and repetition are difficult to disentangle. In imagining Adam and Eve's postlapsarian life, these writers retrospectively map future biblical events and ecclesiastical practices onto earlier moments, creating precedents that could inaugurate a pattern. As I have already suggested, Adam and Eve's watery penance prefigures multiply, anticipating both Jesus's baptism in the Jordan and his temptation in the wilderness. Likewise, Eve foreshadows the second Eve, the Virgin Mary. As in the annunciation, the archangel Michael appears to Eve and calls her "blessed."[81] In these legendary narratives, the rhythm of history, like that of lament, is recurrence. Adam and Eve inhabit a world that is haunted by the future.[82] Yet, as they learn to live in and with a perilous world, that recurrence, those echoes and hauntings can also be sources of hope, reminders that though humans may fall and fall again, the future is never an exact reiteration of the past, that every failure opens up the possibility of learning to do things differently, but only if they can accept responsibility for the harm they have wrought.

Disturbance, Reclamation, and Recovery

> In the notion of return, of cycle, of the reclamation of landscape, lies the futility and productive possibility of human making.
> SUSAN STEWART, *On Longing*

In the end, Adam and Eve do not recover Eden, of course. They move forward, both learning to survive and learning how prone they are to fall. Yet these premodern narratives of the Fall and Expulsion do not represent human history as the beginning of a simple story of decline but rather celebrate the possibility of resilience and (partial) recovery. With the Fall and Expulsion comes the "possibility of human making."[83] The idea of the Fall opens up the possibility of futurity itself, of the unfolding of life in time and space. For although there may have been time in Eden, there is no human history without the Fall. But that making, that history, from the time of the Fall is fraught. The story of Fall and Expulsion invites the imagination of a different world, even as it fuels its own sense of absence and incompletion. This inherent ambivalence about the Fall is threaded through medieval biblical writing, where it registers as a profound ecological disturbance even though the biblical tradition insists that it may well lead to systemic good. Rather than offering a declensionist narrative, medieval Christianity is driven by an optimistic structure, a belief that in the end, as the fourteenth-century anchoress Julian of Norwich puts it, "all will be well," that in the big picture, the Fall and the human presumption that led to it are so insignificant as to be considered "nought," a blip in the overall pattern.[84]

History easily demonstrates that such pious optimism has its dangers: it has often led the devout to focus on individual salvation rather than social or ecological justice, on quietism rather than activism or mutual aid, or, at the other end of the spectrum, the desire for conservative, and often repressive, theocratic regimes, such as Christian nationalism.[85] It has led some people to embrace a *contemptus mundi*—contempt of a world that can be abused because it is ephemeral or because we experience its patterns as regenerative—rather than to embrace a commitment to participation in a *recreatio mundi*—the hard work of repair, which understands that "all flourishing," as Robin Wall Kimmerer puts it, "is mutual."[86] Ultimately, if the possibility of the new emerges in repetition, as Patricia Clare Ingham writes, "everything depends on *how* things are repeated" (my emphasis).[87] It depends, we might say, on the forms and modes of repetition.

If elegy typically moves toward consolation, Timothy Morton observes that *ecological* elegy "must provide forms that undermine a sense of closure"; it is bound up in a sense of repetition. We cannot ever fully mourn a lost ecology because we *are* ecology and because the loss is in process and incomplete. And so, Morton writes, "ecological elegy asks us to mourn for something that has not completely passed."[88] Medieval elegies for the loss of an Edenic world already seem to know the incomplete process of loss, but they go one step further. For, as these medieval narratives remind us, elegy is almost never the last word, nor should it be. Raymond Williams argued more than fifty years ago that the backward glance of elegy may well serve as a site of resistance, change, and movement forward.[89] But what these medieval biblical texts suggest is perhaps that movement forward requires an acknowledgment of human responsibility for the world's wounding and a commitment to repair. If medieval biblical texts render it impossible to imagine a Fall without redemption, they also insist that redemption depends on acknowledging culpability and then attempting to live differently.[90]

However uncomfortable it may be to modern sensibilities, ongoing lament and acknowledgment of responsibility may well be one step toward avoiding the sort of dilemma Ursula K. Heise describes when she asks "whether it might be possible to move environmentalism beyond the stereotypical narrative of the decline of nature without turning it into progress boosterism. What affirmative visions of the future can environmentalists offer, visions that are neither returns to an imagined pastoral past nor nightmares of future devastation?"[91] The expulsion narrative as it is imagined by late medieval biblical writers invites one approach to such a question: because processes of decline and progress are entangled, lamenting the loss of an imagined ecological past cannot effect change unless paired with reflection on culpability for devastation and resolve to make a change. For it may be, as Harrison writes, that "it was only by leaving the Garden of Eden behind them that [Adam and Eve] could realize their potential to become cultivators and givers, instead of mere consumers and receivers."[92] It is in the apocalypse of the Expulsion that the need for *care* is activated, a point that is made time and again by accounts of Adam and Eve in their new world.

I hope that it is clear that I am not suggesting that Middle English narratives of postlapsarian life suggest a translatable model of ecological care for the more-than-human world. They don't. As we saw in the Adam Books, premodern concern with the cares of nonhuman creatures often remains resolutely, and troublingly, anthropocentric. These stories of post-Expulsion life narrate human alienation from and dominion of the earth. Instead, I wish to invite consideration of how, or even if, these narratives might have something to teach about *processes* of navigating a world that suffers because of human action. Rather than only elegize or seek to recover an imagined pastoral world or dream of a utopic future, and rather than tell a simple tale of either progress or decline, medieval biblical texts suggest that to flourish in a mutable, precarious world, one must be willing to acknowledge both vulnerability and culpability and be willing to try to do better, again and again. To put this another way, these texts encourage their readers to imagine human action and ecological change within a framework of iterative process rather than simple progress or decline.

Like most settled landscapes, the part of southern Indiana where I live is a profoundly disturbed ecology, one continually remade by human presence and labor. On the outskirts of my small city, the earth bears the deep wounds of centuries of limestone extraction, some of which forms the neo-Gothic architecture of the campus where I teach. The highlands were once old-growth forest, and the lowlands marshes. Farmers cleared trees and drained the wetlands to access the loamy soil underneath. Many of the area's valleys were flooded to provide water for the region. Radically altered by human presence, it is the kind of landscape that the editors of *Arts of Living on a Damaged Planet* write is "our disaster as well as our weedy hope."[93] This doubleness is a commonplace of both disaster theory and disturbance ecology, which invites us to reframe our understanding of ecological disaster, acknowledging that, as devastating as it may be, it is often the catalyst for a change rather than simply an ending. Profound ecological disturbances certainly may mean the loss of a world. Yet, they may also provide grounds for imagining how a different (and dare we hope, *better*) world may still emerge through repair and recovery. It is a risky and perhaps foolhardy hope, especially given how destructive our quotidian ways of inhabiting the world can be and how invisible much of that damage remains to us.

On Thursday nights, once a month, I make my way downtown to sit in a windowless conference room with others serving on my city's environmental commission. We hear reports on air quality, easements, tree plantings, and the removal of invasive species. We discuss our position on the news from the Planning Commission that a developer wishes to transform a 140-acre parcel of land on the southwest side of town into a subdivision. We all are familiar with this area, with its karst topography, thick forests, and wetlands, and we are all surprised that development is on the table given these geological and ecological features. Even in our small, progressive town, the push and pull of expansion and conservation is fraught. More affordable housing is needed. Developers buy up the remaining bits of unsettled land within city limits faster than conservation groups rewild farmland at the periphery. Here, as in so many other places, the cycle of ecological loss and repair is uneven but ongoing.

As my fellow commissioners fuss over *Robert's Rules of Order*, I find myself wondering where the deer that inhabit that parcel would go were it to be developed. The last few decades of suburban expansion have already destroyed enough of their local habitat that deer have moved into city neighborhoods, grazing on flower beds and sleeping in wooded patches all around town. Seeing them as a nuisance and even a danger, the city hires sharpshooters each year to cull the population. Several months after I watched the hawk and the squirrel, I was standing in my kitchen making granola when I heard a shot ring through the woods behind my home. I rushed outside, but initially saw nothing. I glanced down. Just feet from my porch, a doe was splayed on the leaves, twitching and spattered with blood. A minute or so later, three men emerged in plain clothes, one holding a rifle. I was irate. Noticing me, they explained that they were from animal control. "Its back legs were broke. We did the humane thing," they said. The doe continued to writhe on the ground. I wondered if I had seen her before, racing through the forest with her fawns or nibbling on my rudbeckia earlier in the fall. One of the men approached the body, prodding it with the tip of his boot until it stopped twitching and became still. I monitored him warily as he went about his bloody business. He dragged the corpse up a small hill to my neighbor's driveway, threw it into the back of a pickup truck, and drove away. I stayed and lamented her loss. This world is no Eden.

When I turn back to the commission's conversation, I hear that a subcommittee will gather more information, and we table the proposal for the time being. I ask about plans for more wildlife corridors in town. As I leave, I find myself thinking about Bean Blossom Bottoms, hundreds of acres of reclaimed farmland on the outskirts of town, not far from several former Superfund sites. I think about the deer I've watched feed there in the gloaming, about the herons who glide over the wetlands, the snakes who sun themselves on the boardwalk, the red-winged blackbirds who sing from the high branches, and the beavers who have shorn the trees, leaving pencil-sharp points. The land trust acquired the acreage in the early twenty-first century. They have nursed it, tending its wounds with great care. They committed to the work of repair.

Now, the only traces of the settlement of the land are the drainage ditches and the clusters of daffodils lining the gravel road in the spring.

In my darker moments, I wonder what good it does to tend to one wound when the whole body is plagued, to celebrate one restoration when habitat loss is ongoing. Yet, in the face of all that is becoming lost, I cling to it as a sign of resistance and repair, of the possibility that things could be different, that if we can lament the losses we have wrought, we might also be able to begin again.

PART II

Everyday Apocalypse

Leaks and eddies are everywhere. These leaks and eddies might help open passages for a praxis of care and response—response-ability—in ongoing multispecies worlding on a wounded terra.
>DONNA HARAWAY, *Staying with the Trouble*

Some people see scars, and it is wounding they remember. To me they are proof of the fact that there is healing.
>LINDA HOGAN, *Solar Storms*

EXCURSUS

On Plague, Precedent, and the Punishment Paradigm

> I never knew   near the end
> how the world closed   and whether it *was* ever open,
> punishment rustling everywhere . . .
>   JORIE GRAHAM, "Eurydice on History"

So we begin again. We grieve, we move forward, even as we continue to glance back. Having long since left the Garden of Eden behind, we find ourselves in a wounded and wounding world, a world in which we labor in search of stability, but which remains unsettled and unpredictable, shot through with suffering and loss.

In chapters 3 and 4, we enter the long middle of medieval sacred time. This precarious middle is haunted by its imagination of its beginning and ending. On the one hand, as Jeffrey Jerome Cohen writes, representations of catastrophe look backward: "Every doomsday arrives pre-narrated, the latest iteration of a tale from the unsurpassed past."[1] They also point to the future, functioning as portents. In his entry on "floods," Isidore of Seville writes that "when rivers rise higher than normal, they not only bring destruction in the present moment, but they also signify something yet to happen."[2] Premodern treatments of ecological catastrophe are pattern-seeking and pattern-making; they rely on an understanding of history as more repetitive than progressive or declensionist. They emphasize that it is very difficult to understand present catastrophes apart from how they echo past disasters or portend future ones. This is even the case when a catastrophe feels unprecedented.

I drafted much of this book in a time of almost unprecedented plague and widespread suffering, when many of us shared a sense of general precarity and loss. We dwelled in uncertainty. In the early days of COVID-19, when neither the cause nor the conclusion was clear, we learned how to navigate a changed world. We bought masks and air filters and hand sanitizer. Those of us who could work from home downloaded Zoom. Those who couldn't suffered daily risk of exposure. Our worlds became smaller. Workplaces closed. Jobs disappeared. Food banks' shelves emptied. Hospitals filled. Refrigerated trucks were brought in for the bodies. Death tolls filled the daily headlines for months. I sat on my porch and watched the woods behind my home regreen day by day that first spring, marveling at how the trees could go about their seasonal business so casually when the world just might be ending. Many of our previous certainties about safety and stability crumbled. Even as we mourned and worried and feared, some people looked for whom or what we might blame, for precedent. We became curious about other pandemics—the Justinian plague, the Black Death, smallpox, the Spanish flu—realizing how impoverished our collective memory had become.[3] We compared our experience; we analyzed the data, seeking understanding and meaning.

In some corners of American religious culture, this analysis took a decidedly apocalyptic tone. Fundamentalist groups often blame catastrophic events on moral decline, identifying these disasters as divine judgments for sin, warnings, or lessons. Unsurprisingly some preachers and pundits framed the coronavirus pandemic in exactly these terms.[4] For instance, a 2020 article in *Christianity Today* asked:

> Is this pandemic part of a larger pattern? Consider other catastrophes that have struck North America over the past 20 years: 9/11; Superstorm Sandy; hurricanes Katrina, Maria, Irma, and Harvey; California wildfire; Midwest tornado spikes; swine flu, and now COVID-19. Have we hardened our hearts so as to write off a warning as mere acts of nature? Shouldn't we rather ask if we could be under divine judgment?[5]

A medieval preacher might offer an analogous list, ask similar questions, and look for similar patterns. Considering the representation of the pestilence in *Piers Plowman*, Siegfried Wenzel writes that medieval preachers frequently explained that, "together with other natural disasters, the plague is an instance of divine action, carried out through natural agents, to punish evildoers but also—and more prominently so—to call erring mankind back from their wicked ways."[6] Although many medieval medical and scientific texts located the causes of plague in physical sources, it was common for medieval sermons and religious texts to attribute all kinds of ecological and climatological catastrophes to sin.[7] To put this another way, although medieval thinkers had a number of interpretive tools available to them when it came to understanding the causes of plague, they often reached for biblical precedent.

What they frequently took from that precedent was that *plague* (a catchall term for disaster) was a form of divine punishment, but also that it was a wounding of the world.[8] In late medieval England, the word "plage" has a distinctively biblical cast. Indicating both punishment and injury, it is used synonymously with "vengeaunce" and "wound."[9] In his elegiac dream vision

The Book of the Duchess, Geoffrey Chaucer refers to "the dismal / That was the ten woundes of Egypte" (the unlucky days / of the ten plagues of Egypt).[10] But the Middle English metrical paraphrase of Exodus opens its multistanza description of the Egyptian plagues by explaining that "God sent unto them venjance ten / so forto make theym turne theire moode" (God set them ten plagues / in order to make them change their minds).[11] Ecological and epidemiological wounds, in this model, *are* divine punishment. Wounding is vengeance is plague.

Biblical plagues like those in the story of the Exodus provided the archetypal patterns within which medieval disasters were commonly interpreted.[12] In some cases, the precedent was invoked mainly for comparison, providing a frame of reference for the scale of a catastrophe. For instance, a fourteenth-century Italian writer explains, "The plagues in the days of Pharaoh, David, Ezekiel, and Pope Gregory now seemed nothing by comparison, for this plague encircles the whole globe. In the days of Noah God did not destroy all living souls and it was possible for the human race to recover."[13] A chronicle from the Cistercian abbey of Louth Park draws a similar comparison between the Black Death and the biblical flood, noting that "it is thought that so great a multitude of people were not killed in Noah's Flood."[14] Precedent here is used primarily to emphasize the unprecedented magnitude of a current catastrophe.

Yet, in other cases, biblical plagues served as the precedents for interpreting plagues as punishment or divine vengeance. For instance, Thomas Brinton, the bishop of Rochester, explains multiple catastrophes of his time, including the Black Death and ongoing wars, as the result of human wrongdoing. In a 1375 sermon on the importance of watchfulness, he writes:

> Even so have the pestilence and other misfortunes come to pass in these days. Let those who ascribe such things to planets and constellations rather than to sin say what sort of planet reigned at the time of Noah, when God drowned the whole world except for eight souls, unless the planet of malice and sin.[15]

Denying cosmological causation, Brinton instead emphasizes calamity's spiritual and moral source by invoking the biblical precedent of Noah's flood. The agency here is clear: God drowns the world because of human sin.

Other scriptural exemplars also supplied powerful precedent for this interpretation of plagues. A fifteenth-century treatise on pestilence found in British Library, Sloane MS 965, offers a list of biblical disasters to make this point:

> It should be known to all Christians that pestilence, and every other manifestation of God's vengeance, arises because of sin. It was for that reason that God first took vengeance in Heaven, when Lucifer fell; secondly in paradise,

when Adam was driven out; thirdly throughout the whole world when all living things, except for those saved in Noah's ark, were destroyed in a cataclysm; fourthly when Sodom and Gomorrah were submerged by a river of fire; fifthly when Lot's wife was turned into a pillar of salt; sixthly when God took vengeance on the Egyptian Pharaoh and his people on numerous occasions, as can be found in the book of Exodus, and finally drowned him and his people in the Red Sea.... And therefore it follows from these examples that pestilence arises from a multitude of sins.[16]

The scriptural exemplars provided are those most frequently invoked as precedents for medieval disasters: the Great Flood, Sodom and Gomorrah, and the Exodus. Yet other preachers reach for other precedents. As Rosemary Horrox notes, medieval writers aiming to make sense of the massive suffering caused by the Black Death tended to compare it to "the plague which killed the firstborn in Egypt (Exodus 12); the plague in the reign of David which was halted by the king's prayers (2 Kings 24); and the various manifestations of God's vengeance described by Ezekiel" as well as the historical precedent of the Justinian plague in the time of Pope Gregory.[17] They looked for significance, in other words, in past events. There they found a straightforward equation of plague with punishment.

The scholar Kate Rigby calls this common model "the punishment paradigm." As she writes, for much of history, cultures have understood ecological catastrophe:

> as a response to human wrongdoing on the part of God, or the gods, or an indwelling power inherent in the sacred order of things. In this hermeneutic horizon, morality and materiality, social relations and natural phenomena, were understood to be interrelated: how people comported themselves with one another, and with other others, had environmental consequences; and environmental disturbances, especially big ones, had moral, religious, and political reverberations.[18]

In the "punishment paradigm," climatological and geological catastrophes are caused by human behavior and divine prerogative rather than explicable physical processes. Because "morality and materiality" are interrelated, human action affects the more-than-human world. Disorder in the human microcosm disorders the macrocosm.[19] Human wrongdoing arouses God's wrath. Ecological and epidemiological disasters are thus "acts of God," a phrase that is now employed by insurance companies to describe unpredictable or unpreventable events beyond human control, and thus possibly not covered under a policy.[20]

If premodern texts often interpreted flooding, earthquakes, and strong storms as the terrifying consequence of human actions, many people today attribute ecological and epidemiological catastrophes to a disinterested nature "out there."[21] In this modern framework, heat waves and hurricanes are caused not by any divine intention but by explicable and predictable geological and climatological forces. And thus, the only one culpable for ecological catastrophe is nature itself. As Rigby explores, since the Enlightenment, we have tended to naturalize ecological catastrophes, understanding them as deriving from physical causes rather than moral ones. This secular model has obviously been beneficial: it has encouraged the scientific study of catastrophes, promoted practical preparation for disaster, and limited the scapegoating of victims that often accompanied the "punishment paradigm."[22]

Yet, as Rigby suggests, the Enlightenment naturalization of disaster has transmitted its own mythology: a "mythic fear of nature as Other." Even though we live in a moment in which humans are shaping ecology and geology more than ever before, she writes, "the entanglement of morality and materiality, social relations and natural phenomena has been veiled."[23] In other words, the modern model can occlude the anthropogenic aspects of ecological catastrophe. In this dualistic model, ecological change is no longer necessarily a moral issue because it is seen as external to and other than the interior or social life of a human being. We inhabit environments that we remain distinct from, rather than participating in ecologies, in which we are entangled and to which we are responsible. The ecological repercussions of this mythology of "nature as Other" have been devastating, since, as William Cronon observes in his classic essay on the myth of wilderness, when we see "nature" as something outside of us and unconnected to our quotidian lives, we are less likely to care for and protect the lands and the beings that are closest to us.[24]

Although few people would want to recuperate the "punishment paradigm," some elements of this model may help us appreciate the hybridity of extreme climatic events, reminding us that disorder in the more-than-human world is often and increasingly affected by human action, that morality (or ethics) may indeed have something to do with materiality.[25] In other words, because some pre-Enlightenment models see environmental change as anthropogenic, they may still have something to teach us about the dynamic entanglements of human and nonhuman agents and about the importance of acknowledging our responsibility for and shared vulnerability with the more-than-human world. As Rigby notes, in leaving the "punishment paradigm" behind, we have also sidelined its focus on human responsibility.[26] Yet insofar as some nonmodern texts imagine the world as a vast web of connection, they propose human moral action and connection as intrinsic to the collective thriving of the earth and all its inhabitants.[27]

In the following chapters, we will be considering the dynamics of climatological interpretation and "response-ability" in representations of "everyday apocalypses"—floods, pestilence, fires, storms, and other bad weather. Although the "punishment paradigm" rustles beneath the surface of these narratives, writers are often less interested in exploring it than we might expect. Even when they turn toward biblical precedents and patterns for explanation, they also often see the future in the present, reading catastrophe prophetically, as a temporal punctus that can throw into relief wounding sociocultural practices and open up the possibility of new ways of being in the world. They explore the moral complexity of being present to catastrophe; they emphasize attending to the suffering created by disaster and allowing it to move the conscience. They suggest that acknowledgment of mutuality, of enmeshment (both material and temporal), and compassion are key foundations for responsibility. And although past and future haunt medieval accounts of ecological catastrophes, such accounts more often locate the significance of extreme climatological events in presence and response.

3

Becoming Beholden

Floods, Fires, and Acts of Attention

> These times called the Anthropocene are times of multispecies, including human, urgency: of great mass death and extinction; of onrushing disaster . . . of refusing to know and cultivate the capacity of response-ability; of refusing to be present in and to onrushing catastrophe in time; of unprecedented looking away.
> DONNA HARAWAY, *Staying with the Trouble*

In the midwestern town where I have lived for about twenty years, there's an oddity that has never been adequately explained: our limestone county courthouse is topped with a weathervane in the shape of a fish. My colleague Scott Russell Sanders has proposed one of the more whimsical origin theories. He muses that the "fish swam up out of our ancestral memory, recalling the time when Indiana and the whole heart of the continent lay beneath a vast and shallow gulf, which geologists call the Sundance Sea."[1] Remnants of that watery past are everywhere. From the impressive crevices that attract hikers to area parks, to the smaller sinkhole opening in my driveway, from the caves to the limestone quarries, the ground on which I make my home is unstable and holey, a honeycomb of gaps and pockets left empty by the subterranean rivers that once flowed through these parts. The rolling hills and rocky ravines of southern Indiana trace the paths of glacial retreat, the flotsam of the rivulets extending from that vast inland sea.

The European people who would later colonize this land fought to reclaim it from the water.[2] They cut down trees and dug ditches that made forests and wetlands arable. When their growing demand for drinking water and the need for flood control increased, they dammed up valleys until new lakes lapped up the hillsides, washing away the schools, farms, churches, and cemeteries that had filled the lowlands. There is now almost no trace of the communities that existed little more than half a century ago. The magnitude of the ruin is submerged below placid lakes. I often walk trails named for drowned towns, trying to imagine what might still lie underneath, wondering if somewhere beneath it all Salt Creek continues to wind its narrow path or whether even that source of the flood has been erased.[3]

It is a landscape so changed that it is hard to read. Yet, when the skies pour rain, as they often do in the spring and fall, I find it easy to imagine this land as sea bottom. The flooded valleys and bottomland speak to deep time, recalling for an instant their past lives as whale paths. They become a mundane reminder of the ease with which the contours of the known world can be erased and rewritten. Attending to this topographical palimpsest reminds me of the difficulty of seeing what is historically distant and has been covered over. I watch the transformation of the low-lying woods behind my home as they are riven by new creeks that pool in shallow lakes. Over the following days, the woodland becomes marsh. When the waters recede, I gather the detritus deposited along their winding paths, picking up trash as robins peck at the muddy ground for worms.

Such engineered and seasonal floods are, to be sure, mundane threats, rarely approaching the gravity of the catastrophic deluges that increasingly populate our news cycles. Our screens offer daily displays of the watery paths of hurricanes, the smoky skies of wildfires, the ravaged landscapes of war. We consume catastrophe with our morning coffee, gripped by the media reports or perhaps only half listening as journalists narrate the struggle for escape and survival. We watch as streets become rivers, trees blaze, floods transform shorelines, fires strip mountain ridges bare, or as displaced people and animals flee landscapes transformed beyond recognition. In an age of climate change, the weather is now, perhaps more than ever, the stuff of spectacle, clamoring for our attention even if it sometimes fails to hold it.[4] We find ourselves in a world in which devastating floods and fires have become quotidian, threaded through the weave of our ordinary lives. We regularly confront the challenge of how to see, understand, and react to continuous catastrophe occurring to someone else, somewhere else. How do we respond to floods and fires from afar, from which we are safe? How does seeing from a distance shape our understanding of disaster's causes, costs, or our responsibility?

Such questions do not offer up easy answers. But, as in earlier chapters, here I look to how medieval biblical literature calls forth deep engagement with these seemingly modern problems. This chapter finds in premodern treatments of biblical catastrophes—particularly Noah's flood but also the destruction of Sodom and Gomorrah—reflections on the ethics of observing ecological disaster, models of how art and story might help bridge the affective gap between victims and observers, and surprising examples of what can emerge in the wake of massive ecological disturbance.

It would be easy to dismiss these biblical stories of flood and fire as simply offering archetypal instances of what the scholar Kate Rigby calls the "punishment paradigm," for they do represent environmental disasters and the suffering that follows as punishments for moral failings.[5] Yet medieval treatments of the catastrophic destruction of the Flood and the annihilation of Sodom and Gomorrah often demonstrate far more ambivalence about the ethics of understanding natural disaster as mass punishment than do their biblical sources. When we attend closely to how medieval poets adapt these stories, we can discern the outlines of alternative models of response to catastrophe, counternarratives that attend to the "so what" of attending to destruction or suffering that is beyond one's reach. Rather than simply represent these biblical catastrophes as signs of divine wrath that celebrate a few, righteous survivors, medieval texts often force the reader or listener to imagine the process of destruction and its victims. In so doing, they invite their audience to navigate the tensions inherent in becoming beholden to the suffering they imaginatively behold.

How we apprehend suffering at a distance and how seeing or imagining others' suffering is affected by the moral and affective frameworks we bring to it are the central issues of this chapter. Although interest in the emotional landscapes of premodern culture has grown since the middle of the first decade of the twentieth century, until recently most studies of the dynamics of compassionate attention in medieval texts have focused on "affective piety," often in terms of attention to the suffering body of Christ.[6] My interest is in medieval attention to the suffering of more ordinary bodies in the wake of ecological catastrophe—human, animal, vegetable, even elemental.[7] If studies of meditation on Christ's suffering emphasize how devotional texts develop intimacy and encourage compassion, reflections on ecological suffering and catastrophe assume varying perspectival and affective positions, toggling between intimacy and distance, pity and horror.

The biblical adaptations I consider here—the fourteenth-century homiletic poem *Cleanness*, the earlier biblical paraphrase *Cursor Mundi*, and several biblical cycle plays—experiment with perspective and scale. They swerve from the close-up to the panoptic, from the miniature to the gigantic, from the lyric to the epic, and from sympathy to disinterest or even disdain. In attending to how thick description characterized by shifts in perspective, mode, and affective stance shapes these texts' engagements with the fraught dynamics of attention, this chapter builds on the analyses of *Cleanness* by Sarah Stanbury, who has shown that the poems of the collection in which it is contained, known as the Pearl Manuscript (British Library MS Cotton Nero A.x), are especially preoccupied with vision and perception, and David Coley, who attends to the poem's sustained interest in witness.[8] My consideration of the ethical dimensions of medieval representations of biblical floods and fires is also indebted to the recent work of Jeffrey Jerome Cohen and Julian Yates, who find in the story of Noah's ark a powerful narrative for thinking about climate change in our own world.[9] I also think these archetypal scenes of ecological disaster, survival, and resilience can inform the stories we tell in a world wrecked by ever-more-dangerous and ever-more-quotidian fires and floods.

Similarly committed to investigating how premodern biblical literature thematizes perception and attention, this chapter explores how accounts of biblical flood and fire probe the ethics of seeing ecological catastrophe and responding to the suffering it generates. It does so by reflecting on what Rob Nixon has called "the entangled politics of spectacle and witnessing."[10] Representing disaster, Nixon points out, requires making decisions about audience and perspective, about "who gets to see and from where" and "who counts as a witness."[11] It also demands that a writer choose what is deemed worthy of representation or memorialization. When we represent catastrophe, we decide what exactly readers or viewers look *at* by determining the scale, focus, and framing of the representation. For instance, while panoptic scenes of drowned cities and a photograph of the lone polar bear gazing plaintively from a fast-melting sheet of ice both communicate the threat of rising oceans, they likely invite different emotional engagements from their viewers. Where the particularity of the bear's suffering might generate a sense of intimacy and even empathy, the panoptic view can depersonalize, rendering the imagined future a thing of absence, horror, and loss.

Observing catastrophe and the suffering of others has long been an ethically, emotionally, and philosophically fraught exercise.[12] In his *De rerum natura*, the ancient poet Lucretius explores a metaphor of a spectator who is safe on the shore watching the terror of a shipwreck at sea. For Lucretius, the spectator represents the philosopher, who remains unmoved—experiencing neither delight nor sorrow—as he observes suffering from a philosophical distance, knowing that catastrophe and pain are part of the course of the world.[13] In a reassessment of Lucretius's image, the seventeenth-century writer Voltaire claims that people flock to the coast to watch the shipwreck out of intellectual curiosity.[14] For medieval thinkers, though, such curiosity about disaster was potentially problematic. From Augustine onward, thinkers were wary of inordinate or misdirected attention to such spectacles, understanding curiosity to risk a dangerous focus on surface rather than substance, on flesh rather than spirit. And curiosity often begins with visual perception. The thirteenth-century cleric Peter of Limoges, for instance, explores "how pernicious an excessive curiosity of the eyes can be."[15]

With roots in the Latin *cura* (care), curiosity speaks to what we care about or value and why. As Richard Newhauser explains, in the Middle Ages, curiosity could be either *bona* (good) or *malo* (bad): the danger lies in "misplaced *cura*, excessive care for worldly matters."[16] On the one hand, *vitiam curiositas* (the vice of curiosity) can take the form of an immoderate absorption in the spectacular, those external things that seduce the gaze to surfaces, like today's digital clickbait, which allows a viewer-consumer to scratch the itch for meaning without actually providing a lasting remedy for that itch. Yet, on the other hand, as Patricia Clare Ingham writes, "the very mobility of this category [*curiositas*] suggests an abiding, even obsessive, preoccupation with a wide range of ethical questions related to human knowing."[17] At the heart of the distinction between good and bad curiosity is what motivates it. *Why* and *how* we set our gaze on spectacular destruction or suffering matters, as does what we do with any knowledge we gain from that attention.

While today we typically understand curiosity to be an entirely positive term, some anxiety about the objects of curiosity and the relation of the viewer to those objects endures. We still employ a dismissive lexicon for such overly curious spectatorship—*gawking, goggling, rubbernecking, voyeurism*—all terms that suggest that there is a fundamental difference between passive, consumptive viewing and active, compassionate attention. As Susan Sontag observes:

> There is shame as well as shock in looking at the close-up of a real horror. Perhaps the only people with the right to look at images of suffering of this extreme order are those who could do something to alleviate it . . . or those who could learn from it. The rest of us are voyeurs, whether or not we mean to be. In each instance, the gruesome invites us to be either spectators or cowards, unable to look.[18]

But can we not *all* learn from what we see? Might curiosity, wonder, or the absorption of the gaze not also pull us out of ourselves, make us less narcissistic, or even more empathetic? Can beholding or imagining the suffering of others help us feel a kinship with them, deepen our care, or activate the ethical imagination? What does it take for attention to lead to action or practice? How do we move from feeling *for* to feeling *with*, and from there to doing acting on behalf of? Again, there are no easy answers to such questions, but also again, I think that the practice of meditating on or imagining the suffering body of Christ in late medieval affective piety may serve as a useful, if imperfect, parallel. As many scholars have reminded us, the intensity of the devotional gaze on a broken, bleeding, destroyed body was not only an inducement to compassion for a particular body but also an invitation to extend that pity more broadly to a world full of other suffering bodies, each of which was to be seen as an *alter Christus* (other Christ).[19]

Unlike general awareness, attention can personalize. It can put us in relationship to what we see. It can render the distant present and proximate. It can open our eyes to what might otherwise remain invisible. And, insofar as it invites *care* for those things we might otherwise not notice or deem worthy of our gaze, imaginative writing, Nixon suggests, "can help make the unapparent appear, making it accessible and tangible by humanizing drawn out threats inaccessible to the immediate senses."[20] Imaginative apprehension, Nixon writes, may thus bring "together the domains of perception, emotion and action."[21] In so doing, imaginative texts invite us in and may even, however momentarily, transform us from curious spectators to compassionate witnesses.

By turning our attention to how medieval biblical texts explore the relation of "perception, emotion, and action" in their representations of the Great Flood and the destruction of Sodom and Gomorrah, the chapter meditates on the aesthetic and ethical stakes of beholding the vanishing landscapes, wreckage, and losses of ecological catastrophes. In their medieval treatments, both biblical stories feature a virtuous patriarch, a family saved from a corrupt society, a recalcitrant or reluctant woman, and the destruction of the known world. Both stories are types of the Final Judgment, as biblical precedent suggests when pairing these two catastrophes. The gospel of Luke identifies both the "days of Noah" and the "days of Lot" as foreshadowing of the eschaton.[22] And 2 Peter characterizes the two episodes as key examples of divine judgment.[23] Although this chapter focuses primarily on *Cleanness*, the only Middle English text that pairs these biblical episodes, I also draw on several other late medieval representations of these catastrophes, including those in *Cursor Mundi* (*The Course of the World*) and several plays of Noah and the Flood. The opening sections of this chapter focus on how these texts use description to invite readers to imagine the disasters. It thus investigates how they configure the perilous art of *beholding* the wreckage of ecological catastrophe. I conclude by reflecting on what these works suggest about *becoming beholden* to it. Cultivating a poetics that is variously omniscient and intimate, these works use thick, naturalistic description to represent the harrowing stories of the Flood and the destruction of Sodom and Gomorrah. These descriptions frame spectacular environmental devastation within a set of tensions—between victims and survivors, stranger and kin, the human and the nonhuman, the local and the cosmic, the quotidian and the catastrophic, and judgment and mercy.[24] Rather than settling these tensions, they careen between extremities, inviting readers to enter the precarity of being suspended in-between, as we observe these devastating floods and fires at a safe remove but also with intimate access to the suffering they depict. But, as these works also ultimately suggest by depicting two women who behold the catastrophe, we cannot remain suspended. To behold wreckage is always to risk becoming beholden to it; we must choose whether we will become responsible or whether we will look away.

Wrecked

> the thing I came for:
> the wreck and not the story of the wreck...
> the evidence of damage
> worn by salt and sway into this threadbare beauty
> the ribs of the disaster
>   ADRIENNE RICH, "Diving into the Wreck"

There may be no late medieval poem that better exemplifies the fraught dynamics of beholding the wreckage of environmental catastrophe than the Middle English poem *Cleanness*. This long sermon in verse recounts God's wrathful judgment of the "impure" in a series of unsettling biblical stories and depicts a series of desolate wastelands resulting from God's anger. Opening with the parable of guests who are cast out of a feast because of their unclean clothes (Matthew 22) and a brief glance at the Fall of the Angels, which establishes some of the key terms, modes, and movements of the poem, *Cleanness* focuses largely on three biblical catastrophes: the Flood (Genesis 6:9–9:7), the destruction of Sodom and Gomorrah (Genesis 19), and Belshazzar's feast (Daniel 5).[25] In its more than 1,800 lines of alliterative verse, the poem uses these stories to inveigh against moral and physical filth, developing a case for "cleanness" primarily by drawing a series of contrasts with "uncleanness."[26]

Cleanness is one of four alliterative poems uniquely found in Cotton Nero A.x, a late fourteenth-century northern manuscript now held by the British Library that also contains the well-known Arthurian romance *Sir Gawain and the Green Knight*, the visionary poem *Pearl*, and another homiletic poem, *Patience*, which focuses on the story of Jonah.[27] Although these may seem an eclectic set, the four poems have a number of shared interests, including, as Sarah Stanbury has noted, the use of extensive description and references to sight to dramatize "the limitations of human experience, an effect that is created in part by structuring descriptive passages according to the mechanics of perception."[28] As David Coley has recently argued, the four poems offer an "insistently quiet witness" to the Black Death, "the defining event of their historical moment."[29] In a sensitive reading of *Cleanness*'s representation of response to the bubonic plague Coley writes that "as it focuses at once on the bodies of the dead, the terror of the doomed, and the suffering of the living, *Cleanness* emerges as a poem that speaks both to the necessity and the danger of standing witness."[30] Like Coley and Stanbury, I am interested in how the poem and other related treatments of drowned worlds use thick description and perspectival play to represent the dynamics of witnessing crisis and catastrophe. But I am also interested in how the poem frames *who* gets to see the wreckage, *how* they see it, and *what* kind of responses are invited by the process of beholding.

That *Cleanness* is a poem littered with the detritus of divine wreckage is evident in its frequent use of the verb *wraken*, which in Middle English can mean both to exact vengeance and to annihilate. Its nominal form, *wrake*, also suggests either destruction or suffering, signifying an event that happens to a person or society, an action taken, or an object.[31] The term memorably appears in the opening stanza of the most famous poem in *Cleanness*'s manuscript, *Sir Gawain and the Green Knight*, where it describes the ruined state of Britain, besieged by "werre and wrake and wonder" [war and wreck and wonder].[32] Here, "wrake" is ruin, suffering, and catastrophe. It bespeaks a landscape of loss. Yoked here with "wonder," it evokes the affective and cognitive remainders of catastrophe: awe, astonishment, and terror.

Cleanness also uses "wrake" to describe devastated landscapes. "Wrake" frames the poem. It appears, refrain-like, throughout. In the term's fifteen or so appearances in the poem, *wrake* takes on its full range of possible meanings, shifting between judgment, suffering, annihilation, and disaster.[33] *Wrake* threads through each of *Cleanness*'s three main didactic stories. In the narrative of the Flood, people flock to the mountains "for ferde of þe wrake" (out of fear of the destruction; 127/386) and the author describes the sorrow of the scene as "suche a wrakful wo" (such a sorrowful woe; 134/541). In the Sodom and Gomorrah episode, the destruction is characterized as "þe wrake þat no wyȝe achaped" (the destruction/punishment that no person escaped; 152/970). After the destruction, the land itself bears witness to "þat wykked werk, and þe wrake after" (that wicked work, and the devastation after; 155/1050). The opening sections of the third exemplum attribute Nebuchadnezzar's wartime atrocities (ripping open women's wombs and bashing babies' heads) in part to the "wrake" of God (162/1225). In *Cleanness*'s concluding lines, the author summarizes its contents, attempting to offer a sense of closure by explaining that

> vpon þrynne wyses I haf yow þro schewed
> Þat vnclannes tocleues in corage dere
>   Of þat wynnelych Lorde þat wonyes in heuen
>   Entyses Hym to be tene, teldes vp His wrake. (184/1805–8)

> (in three ways I have thoroughly shown you
> that uncleanness cleaves the core of the heart
>   of that great Lord who dwells in heaven,
>   [it] entices him to be angry and increases his wrake.)

BECOMING BEHOLDEN   111

As this passage suggests, the God of this poem is not moved by suffering but by anger. Yet even as the poet ultimately frames the poem's disasters as caused by a pitiless God's "wrake," as I hope to show, the poem itself invites a far more nuanced, sometimes even compassionate, attention to those who suffer that destruction.

If *Cleanness* ultimately seeks to contain the term's multiplicities, many particular uses of it are rather more ambivalent, as the brief account of the fall of the angels shows. The description of the rebel angels is not one of the central exempla of the poem, but it inaugurates the poem's development of the language of wreckage and models the poem's characteristic shifts in perspective. The poem describes the rebel angels as

> Sweued at þe first swap as þe snaw þikke,
> Hurled into helle-hole as þe hyue swarmez.
> Fylter fenden folk forty dayez lencþe,
> Er þat styngande storme stynt ne my3t;
> Bot as smylt mele vnder smal siue smokezz forþikke,
> So fro heuen to helle þat hatel schor laste,
> On vche syde of þe worlde aywhere ilyche.
> 3is, hit watz a brem brest and a byge wrache. (121/222–29)

> (Swirled at the first blow like thick snow
> hurled into the depths of hell, like a swarming hive.
> The fiend's folk mixed for the length of forty days,
> before that stinging storm might not stop;
> But like burning grain under a fine sieve creates thick smoke,
> so from heaven to hell that vile shower lasted,
> on every side of the world everywhere the same.
> Indeed, it was a terrible outrage and a big wreck.)

Setting into motion the poem's exploration of stormy climes, the fall of the angels establishes a typology and iconography of destruction. On the one hand, the episode introduces the poem's treatment of fall and destruction as cyclical, each catastrophe (or "wrake") will be a variation on a theme, a repetition of this first devastation. The angels are the first "hatel schor" (vile shower) of several in the poem. To figure their fall as forty days of stormy chaos is to foreshadow the forty days of the deluge.[34] On the other hand, these lines introduce the governing imagery of spiritual catastrophe as a tempestuous storm that is ongoing, that "stynt ne my3t" as it grows, extending outward. This small narrative thus initiates the poem's sustained interest in how wreckage is both an end and a beginning.[35] God wipes the slate clean and restarts. He erases and rewrites creation, transforming the landscape into a kind of palimpsest that tells the same story again and again and again, only with slightly different players, though each iteration opens the possibility that things might go differently this time.

The poem characterizes the angelic fall using three rather quotidian comparisons: the fallen angels are like a snowstorm, like a swarm of bees, and like grain sifted in a fine sieve generating thick smoke. Medieval writers often used homely images like these to describe the fallen host. In *The Golden Legend*, Jacobus de Voragine compares them to swarms of flies that fill the air.[36] Other texts imagine the angels as like specks of dust in the sun or as snow.[37] As James Morey has observed, this series of images of angels as "falling particulate matter" serve two main functions: they explain both the innumerability of the fallen and their pervasiveness in the world.[38] Taken together, these similes emphasize the angelic fall as cloudy, smoky, and stormy. They force readers to assume a different perspective, to picture this first, epic catastrophe as something as common as burning grain.

For even when compared with the quotidian beauty of John Milton's description of the fallen angels as "thick as Autumnal Leaves that strow the Brooks / in Vallombrosa," *Cleanness*'s descriptions are strikingly mundane, representing the catastrophic by means of ordinary ecological occurrences that become darkly foreboding.[39] These angels are still airborne, unsettled, and in motion, a movement emphasized by the "tumbling of syntax across quatrain boundaries," which evokes the angels' downward fall.[40] Though mundane, the imagery also registers the fallen as a continued, even growing, threat. It links the rebel angels both to the dangerous world outside and to domestic spaces within. Like thick snow, the angels barrel toward the earth, obscuring vision in icy chaos. Like swarming bees, they are a "stinging storm that can't stop itself." Like burning grain, they are an obscuring smoke. Listed one after another, these images fold into each other, communicating chaotic, cloudy, and stormy multiplicities. Yet, as A. C. Spearing writes, "the scene is also seen as if from an immense distance, through a series of precisely chosen similes from everyday life ... [which move us] in a panoramic shot [to] where we can see the whole world at once."[41] Their juxtaposition of the intimate and the distant, the quotidian and the catastrophic sets the stage for the poem's later attention to the tempestuous dynamics of the Flood and the destruction of Sodom. Thus establishing the pattern of the "brem brest" (terrible trespass/outrage) and the "byge wrache" (big wreck), the scene introduces how spiritual, social, and ecological catastrophe will be bound together in this poem's representation of the precarious order of the cosmos.

To wrap up this brief treatment of the fall of the angels, the poet-preacher evokes the pattern of stormy wreckage that the remainder of the text will be so committed to exploring. As the poem draws a parallel between the fall of the angels and the fall of humanity, it signals this pattern: "þat oþer wrake þat wex, on wy3ez hit li3t" (That other/second destruction that grows, it alights on people; 121/235). Humans enter a cosmos already well acquainted with wreckage. This preexistent "wrack" increases, and its language of uncontrolled growth will be echoed in the poem's introduction to the Flood story, where God complains that "euelez on erþe ernestly grewen / and multyplyed monyfolde immongez mankynde" (evils on earth grew earnestly / and multiplied manyfold among humanity; 123/277–78), and again in the final lines of the poem, where God's anger at uncleanness causes his "wrake" to increase. But the "wrake" that alights on humanity first appears as a malicious outside force at work in the world. There is no suggestion yet that human beings cause this "wrake," no attribution of responsibility. It is something that happens *to* humans, who initially are the passive objects of wrake's fury. Yet, if it first appears to be imposed on them, as we have seen in earlier chapters, human beings quickly become complicit in this growth of evil and in the destruction it yields.

Flotsam and Jetsam

> We can only be ethical toward what we can see, understand, feel, love, or otherwise have faith in.
>
> ALDO LEOPOLD, *Sand County Almanac*

Although many medieval writers understood human complicity in the devastation of the world to originate in the Garden of Eden, the story of the Great Flood became another classic example of how human sin can lead to cosmic catastrophe.[42] *Cleanness*'s treatment of the Flood differs in some significant ways from other contemporary vernacular treatments of the scene, such as those offered by the biblical play cycles. The poem shows virtually no interest in describing the building of the ark or its specifications, which were as endless a source of fascination for medieval thinkers as they continue to be for modern biblical literalists.[43] Neither is *Cleanness* especially interested in the incredulity of Noah's neighbors, a scene often dramatized in contemporary sources, including *Cursor Mundi* and several cycle plays. Instead, the poem offers long, harrowing descriptions of the weather, the landscape, and the horrors experienced by those who are not saved. It attends to the suffering of living beings—both human and animal—and emphasizes their cries of desperation and pain. Focused on depicting the wreckage of the catastrophe in vivid detail, it invites its audience to behold that destruction from a range of perspectives.

In contrast, the biblical source text reveals little about the nature of the flooding or the experience of its victims:

> All the fountains of the great deep were broken up, and the flood gates of heaven were opened: And the rain fell upon the earth forty days and forty nights.... And the waters prevailed beyond measure upon the earth: and all the high mountains under the whole heaven were covered. The water was fifteen cubits higher than the mountains which it covered. And all flesh was destroyed that moved upon the earth, both of fowl, and of cattle, and of beasts, and of all creeping things that creep upon the earth: and all men. And all things wherein there is the breath of life on the earth, died. (Genesis 7:11–12, 19–23)

Most of the medieval English biblical paraphrases diverge little from this source. In fact, they usually offer even sparser accounts of how the waters covered the land and its creatures. Compare, for example, the brief treatment in the thirteenth-century biblical paraphrase *Genesis and Exodus*, which cleaves to the biblical description:

> Ilc wateres springe here strengð undede,
> And reyn gette dun on euerilk stede
> Fowerti dais and fowerti nigt,
> So wex water wið magti migt;
> So wunderlike it wex & get
> ðat fiftene elne it ouer-flet
> Ouer ilk dune and ouer ilc hil
> ðurge godes migt and godes wil.[44]
>
> (Those waters spring their strength in waves[45]
> and rain falls down on every side
> Forty days and forty nights
> So grows the water with great power
> So astonishingly it grows and covers
> so that it overflows fifteen cubits
> Over dunes and over hills
> through God's might and God's will.)

As in the biblical passage, the emphasis here is on the growth of the flood, its power, its depth, and its prevalence. Mentioning only the wondrousness of the water, the description entirely elides its annihilation of all living beings. Such straightforward narration of the Flood is the norm in Middle English biblical paraphrases. The lengthy *Metrical Paraphrase of the Old Testament* does not offer even a glance at the suffering of the victims. It notes only that as the water rises over the highest of the world's hills, "Yt drownyd the pepyll in all partyse, bot aght that in the arch wer styll" (it drowned people everywhere, but only those eight in the ark lived).[46]

Chronicles tend to be equally disinterested in the victims, as the description in John Capgrave's fifteenth-century *Abbreviation of Chronicles* makes clear: "And in þis same 3ere was þe flood þat ouyrflew al þe world, for it was xv cubites | aboue þe hiest hillis; þis flood in party cam fro þe grete se clepid þe occean, and in parti from þe grete waters þat ar aboue" (And in this same year was the flood that submerged the entire world, for it was fifteen cubits above the highest hills; this flood partly came from the sea, called the ocean, and in part from the great waters that are above).[47] Perhaps unsurprisingly, given their commitment to representing the human drama of salvation history, the biblical plays also tend to make short shrift of the ecological suffering brought by the flooding.

Conversely, *Cleanness* elaborates at great length on the storm and its environmental impact, focusing on the horrific process of flooding even more exhaustively than on the aftermath of the flood and its few virtuous survivors. It also describes in detail "þe ende of alle kynez flesch þat on vrþe meuez" (the end of every type of being than moves on the earth; 124/303). Along with the early fourteenth-century biblical poem *Cursor Mundi*, it offers the fullest description of the catastrophic scenes of the biblical flood in Middle English writing that I have found.[48] Both *Cursor Mundi* and *Cleanness* seem to draw their particulars in part from the representation of the storm in the fifth-century treatise *De diluvio mundi* by Avitus, a text that likely also influenced the Old English poem *Genesis B* and Milton's *Paradise Lost*.[49] It is probably from *De diluvio* that *Cleanness* derives its commitment to displaying both creaturely suffering and the "whirlwind ocean of things" (*Oceanus vertex rerum*) destroyed by the flood.[50]

In *Cleanness*, the flood passage occupies nearly three hundred lines (122-34/249-544), many of which focus on representing the universality of the wreckage.[51] For although it is humans who have sinned, as the poem notes, the land also requires cleansing. Telling Noah to construct the ark, God explains that he will

> fleme out of þe folde al þat flesch werez,
> Fro þe burne to þe best, fro bryddez to fyschez;
> Al schal doun and be ded and dryuen out of erþe
> Þat euer I sette saule inne. (123/287-90)

> (banish from the land all those that wear flesh,
> from humans to animals, from birds to fish,
> all will drown and be dead and driven from the earth
> that I ever set a soul in.)

Mirroring the larger perspectival swerves of the poem, this passage's from/ to movement casts a wide net to emphasize the breadth of the punishment (though unlike many medieval theologians, the poet seems unconcerned here with how or whether fish would have been drowned by the flood).[52] As these lines reiterate, "all" will drown. The subsequent description of the storm and flooding heightens this depiction of universal destruction, largely through a sequential narrowing of focus, from the heavens to the earth to human beings and to animals. And in what medieval rhetoricians call "amplificatio," *Cleanness* devotes more than fifty lines to describing what happens to the rest of the world after Noah and his family are safely ensconced in the ark.

Extensive descriptions of storms are common in late medieval alliterative verse, but the sufferings of humans and animals are not typical elements of such scenes.[53] Creaturely suffering takes center stage in *Cleanness*. However, the passage begins by paying particular attention to the falling and rising of the floodwaters, which assume their own dark agency:

> Þen bolned þe abyme, and bonkez con ryse,
> Waltes out vch walle-heued in ful wode stremez;
> Watz no brymme þat abod vnbrosten bylyue;
> Þe mukel lauande loghe to þe lyfte rered.
> Mony clustered clowde clef alle in clowtez;
> Torent vch a rayn-ryfte and rusched to þe vrþe,
> Fon neuer in forty dayez. And þen þe flod ryses
> Ouerwaltez vche a wod and þe wyde feldez.
> For when þe water of þe welkyn with þe worlde mette,
> Alle þat deth moȝt dryȝe drowned þerinne. (126/363–72)

> (Then the abyss surged and began to rise up the hills
> each fountain poured out in wild streams;
> there was no bank that was not quickly breached;
> the great flowing lake reared to the heavens.
> Many clustered clouds split all in pieces;
> tearing apart each break in the rain clouds, and rushed to the earth,
> it never ceased in forty days. And then the flood rises,
> flows over every forest and the open fields.
> For when the water from the sky met with the water from the ground,
> everything mortal drowned therein.)

Adopting an omniscient point of view, the poem initially invites us to behold the movement of the waters from a distance. From the first surfacing of the groundwater to the torrents issuing from the clouds, the description emphasizes the agency of massive ecological forces. Water envelops the dry land. Floods swell up out of the abyss, surging and rising up the hillsides. Throughout, the poet draws on a wide-ranging lexicon for bodies of water: *abyme* (abyss), *walle-heued* (fountain/spring), and *loghe* (lake/flood). The description's verbs give shape to the manifold ways that water gathers and moves in the depths of the earth and the skies: the floodwaters *bolned* (surged), *ryse* and *rered* (rose), *waltes* (pour), *stremez* (stream), and are *lauande* (flowing). Other terms emphasize the terrestrial and celestial boundaries that the water readily transgresses. It rises up *bonkes* (hills), is undeterred by any *brymme* (bank), rearing up even to the *lyfte* (skies). As the groundwaters reach up, the next lines turn to the waters that descend from the skies, describing how clusters of clouds crack open, releasing torrents that rush to the earth. With the meeting of the waters from heaven and those rising out of the ground comes a horrific sense of enclosure. Water closes in on and squeezes out space for creaturely life.

Yet for all its precision of description, the landscape itself is decidedly imprecise. This place could be any place. The storm could be any storm. Lacking topographical particularity, the passage focuses instead on the powerful movements of climatic forces. The landscape and its inhabitants register as little more than a barely visible background of a great atmospheric drama. Thus framing the human drama in this grand scale, emphasizing the power of the nonhuman cosmos, the poet foregrounds the smallness and fragility of human beings before he telescopes in to give us a series of intimate snapshots of creaturely suffering.

The biblical paraphrase *Cursor Mundi* offers a similarly detailed description but develops the scene in more explicitly apocalyptic terms, characterizing the rising waters and the destruction of cities in much the same language as do the Fifteen Signs of the Doom, a widespread eschatological motif that we will encounter in chapter 5 of this book. After a lengthy characterization of the building of the ark that explains where exactly the various animals are kenneled, *Cursor Mundi* focuses attention on the onset of the deluge:

> Stormes roos on euery syde
> Sonne & moone þe liȝt gan hide
> Hit merked ouer al þis world wide
> Þe reyn fel doun so wondir fast
> Þe welles wex, þe bankes brast
> Þe see to ryse, þe erþe to cleft
> Þe springes alle oute to dref
> Leityng fel wiþ þondur & reyn
> Þe erþe quook & dened aȝeyn
> Sonne & moone lost her liȝt
> Al þe world turned to nyȝt

> Þat sorwe to se was greet awe
> Þe bildyngis fel boþe heȝe & lawe
> Þe watir wex ouer Þe pleynes
> Þe beestis ran to mounteynes
> Men & wymmen ran hem wiþ.[54]

> (Storms rose on every side.
> The sun and the moon began to hide their light,
> and darkness spread over the entire world.
> The rain fell down so remarkably fast;
> the wells filled; the banks burst;
> the sea rises, the earth splits open;
> the springs spilled over.
> Lightening fell with thunder and rain.
> The earth quaked and resounded again.
> The sun and the moon lost their light.
> All the world turned to night.
> So that it was sorrowful to see that great wonder.
> The buildings fell, both tall and short.
> The waters grew over the plains.
> The beasts fled to the mountains.
> Men and women ran with them.)

Cursor Mundi depicts the storm primarily as a list of linked disasters and responses: images cascade like the waters, which crash like tidal waves against and over the hills. The short line and parallel syntax generate a quick-paced, nearly breathless rehearsal of the cataclysm. The use of anaphora links the watery components of the storm (rain, wells, sea, springs) and the objects of destruction (land, buildings, beasts). In so doing, its watery catalogs build a sense of the unthinkable scale of the catastrophe. The incomprehensibility of the disaster becomes further evident in the poem's insistence that much of this devastation occurs in at least partial darkness. Four lines comment on the shrouding of the light of the sun and the moon, and of a world that fallen into an untimely, unnatural night (111/1763–64, 1771–72). No longer mere objects of human apprehension, nature and weather do their dark work in growing obscurity, beyond the reach of human knowing.

Even so, unlike *Cleanness*, *Cursor Mundi* insists that there is still something that must be seen, remarking "Þat sorwe to *se* was greet awe" (my emphasis). On the one hand, the phrase "sorwe to se" is a commonplace of medieval devotional writing: it frequently appears in lyrical complaints from the cross, as Jesus calls attention to his broken and suffering body.[55] But here it attests to a more general cosmic sadness. It imagines the sublime horror of watching the world dissolve back into chaos. The line's syntax is evocatively imprecise. Drawing together sorrow and awe, it invites us to consider whether one should feel pity or horror upon beholding this sight. The phrase functions as a pause in the lengthy description and marks an affective rupture that draws readers or listeners out of the stormy, inhuman scene and back into the realm of the human. In so doing, it suggests that seeing or imagining such a scene should provoke a response, perhaps implying that curiosity about such wonders might lead to compassion. Understood here as intimates rather than opposites, sorrow and awe invite readers to pause and consider their own responses. Fittingly, the passage also suggests how imaginatively to behold the scenes unfolding within these lines. For after this orienting pause, this invitation to affective attention, *Cursor Mundi* turns from the environmental to the creaturely, narrating the crumbling of buildings and the flight of animals and people to the mountains.

There are no similarly explicit interjections of visual instruction or affective orientation in *Cleanness*'s description of the deluge. Yet when the poem describes the human response to the tempest, *Cleanness* also rescales its perspective, narrowing from a panoptic view of the scene to a more intimate one. First people and then animals try to escape, though they soon understand that there is no refuge to be found: "Þer watz moon for to make when meschef was cnowen, / Þat no3t dowed bot þe deth in þe depe stremez" (Pleas were made when the situation was understood / that there was no escape from dying in the deep streams; 127/373–74). As the floodwaters climb, the poem describes how homes and buildings disappear. But rather than emphasize the physical destruction of cities, *Cleanness* invites its readers to imagine the survival instinct in action as it surveys the ways that people attempt to escape the rising waters:

> Fyrst feng to þe fly3t alle þat fle my3t;
> Vuche burde with her barne þe byggyng þay leuez
> And bowed to þe hy3 bonk þer brentest hit wern,
> And heterly to þe hy3e hyllez þat haled on faste.
> Bot al watz nedlez her note, for neuer cowþe stynt
> Þe ro3e raynande ryg, þe raykande wawez,
> Er vch boþom watz brurdful to þe bonkez eggez,
> And vche a dale so depe þat demmed at þe brynkez.
> Þe moste mountaynez on mor þenne watz no more dry3e,
> And þeron flokked þe folke, for ferde of þe wrake. (127/377–86)
>
> (First, all that could flee, fled;
> each mother with her child leave their buildings

and fled to the high hills where it was steepest,
and quickly to the high hills that held secure.
But it was all pointless, because the rising rains never did stop
the raining tempest, the sweeping waves
Before every valley was brimful to the edges of the hills,
and every dale so deep that it was filled to the brinks/edges.
The greatest mountain on the earth then was no longer dry,
And still people flocked to it out of fear of the wreck.)

In a telling aside, the narrator notes that those who are able to flee are the first to seek higher ground, thus subtly reminding readers of the hopelessness of the physically and socially vulnerable or place bound.[56] Returning to its earlier from/to structure, *Cleanness* guides our attention from groups (*all that can flee*) to individuals (*each mother with her child*), back to the groups as the poem begins to build affective momentum. When it calls our attention to the child, the poem surely invites pathos. Yet our broad perspective also never permits us to forget that escape efforts are futile. We have seen how the rain fills first the deep valleys ("vche a dale so depe"), and how the waves lap against hills that are now the banks of an ever-expanding sea. We observe how the water climbs and then covers the hillsides, ultimately surmounting even the highest mountaintops. Even as we watch people flee, babes in arms, we already know that there is no place of refuge, no chance of survival, and ultimately no hope for those fleeing the rising floodwaters. We already know that they, too, will soon be submerged.[57]

For the human and animal victims of *Cleanness*'s flood, who cry out to God for salvation, there is no mercy to be found. After describing the panicked flights of people, the poem extends its gaze to the duress of the animals, who also seek shelter from the storm:

> Syþen þe wylde of þe wode on þe water flette;
> Summe swymmed þeron þat saue himself trawed,
> Summe sty3e to a stud and stared to þe heuen,
> Rwly with a loud rurd rored for drede.
> Harez, herttez also, to þe hy3e runnen;
> Bukkez, bausenez, and bulez to þe bonkkez hy3ed;
> And alle cryed for care to þe Kyng of heuen,
> Recouerer of þe Creator þay cryed vchone,
> Þat amounted þe mase His mercy watz passed
> And alle His pyte departed fro peple þat He hated. (127–28/387–96)

(Next the wild forest animals floated on the water;
some swam there that tried to save themselves,
some climbed to a high place and stared up toward heaven,

> (and) pitifully, with a loud cry roared out of fear.
> Hares and deer both ran to the heights;
> Bucks, badgers, and bulls scrambled up the hills;
> and all cried out to the King of heaven because of their suffering,
> each one cried to the Creator for safety,
> that created confusion. His mercy was gone
> and all his pity gone for people he hated.)

Alternating between general ("some" and "all") and the individual ("each one"), the scene imagines the destruction and suffering in both universalizing and particularizing forms. It does so with a repeated focus on the question of whether this suffering is "pitiable."[58] The poem evokes the possibility of pity, characterizing the beasts as roaring *pitifully* ("rwly") to the heavens. Yet even as the poem suggests that the animals' cries are pitiful, this is the only gesture in the passage indicating the possibility of sympathetic response to their suffering. When the passage shifts to narrate the human response, its "all" and "vchone" seems to encompass both human and animal and it continues the focus on the cries of the dying—indeed, words for *cry* appear three times in this short passage.[59] Two lines of verse emphasize these dying pleas: they *all* cry out because of "care" (suffering), they *each* cry out for relief and help ("recouerer"). It is to no avail; for, as the narrator so coldly pronounces, "God's mercy has passed." Is there no place for pity in this poem, then? Is the reader really expected to align her gaze and feelings with those of an apparently merciless God?

Although it may not be invited as explicitly as it is in *Cursor Mundi*, it is hard not to see some sort of affective engagement with the victims' suffering as central to the poet's aims, especially when he draws our attention to the last breaths of those who are submerged by the rising waters. In the following lines, the *Cleanness* poet offers one more description of the human response to the inevitability of death before he returns to the macrocosmic, distanced view of the drowned world:

> Bi þat þe flod to her fete floȝed and waxed,
> Þen vche a segge seȝ wel þat synk hym byhoued.
> Frendez fellen in fere and faþmed togeder,
> To dryȝ her delful destyne and dyȝen alle samen;
> Luf lokez to luf and his leue takez,
> For to ende alle at onez and for euer twynne. (128/397–402)

> (When the flood flowed and grew to their feet
> then each person saw well that they would sink.
> In fear, friends came together and embraced,

>   to suffer their sorrowful destiny and die together;
>   Lover looks to his beloved and says his goodbye
>   to end life all together and be parted forever.)

Animals and landscapes vanish, submerged under the watery depths. In a series of horrific tableaux, these final scenes of people seeking solace in their friends and lovers are particularly affecting. In such depictions, the poem seems interested not only in helping readers imagine the suffering of the victims but also to *feel* their desperation. Scholars do not tend to agree on the desired effects of those feelings. Charlotte Morse notes that in highlighting "frendez," the poem "adds a sentimental twist to the exhilaration that those not directly involved—like Noah, like the audience of the poem—feel when witnessing a disaster."[60] Spearing observes "an odd contradiction of feeling here," but suggests that ultimately the poet "imagines [the flood's] consequences to them, and to animals, with a compassion that seems almost a reproach to God."[61]

Yet not all readers of the poem have understood these lines as inviting sympathy or compassion. David Wallace writes that *Cleanness* "takes pains to complicate and intensify our experiences of terror" by aligning us not with the survivors but with the victims, who "share the fate of drowning creation."[62] Eleanor Johnson similarly sees the poem as building a sense of "participatory horror."[63] Ad Putter writes that the poem's tendency of "lingering on the death throes of human beings combines a recognition of human suffering with a cold-blooded precision of observation. Seeing the Flood both from the point of view of its victims and the unblinking eye of God, they give us neither the comforts of sentimentality nor of detachment."[64] While Putter is certainly right that these shifts in perspective unsettle readers, might it be possible that rather than giving us neither option, the poem gives us both? That it offers compassion and indifference as possibilities? That its perspectival swerves between distanced, omniscient views and intimate snapshots of suffering place its readers as *witnesses*, inviting a range of possible responses—curiosity, horror, delight, apathy, pity—rather than dictating a position? To put this another way, might the poem's tensions not be invitations?

Cleanness's insistence on the starkness of God's unrelenting anger and his refusal of pity for the suffering world is thrown into harsh relief when we compare its treatment of the pathos of the drowning world to that of *Cursor Mundi*. Unlike the more deterministic structure of *Cleanness*, *Cursor Mundi* both emphasizes that salvation remains a possibility even as the waters begin to rise and represents Noah as a figure of warning, witness, and compassion for those who are ultimately subsumed by the flood. When God first announces the flood to Noah, the patriarch is saddened and begins to preach to his doomed contemporaries, warning them of the imminent "wreche" (109/1731). Perhaps unsurprisingly, he is met with ridicule and scorn, as they ask him why he is so afraid of an impossibility ("Why he was so ferde for nou3t," 109/1738).

When the ark is complete, and the rain begins, *Cursor Mundi* turns this "nou3t" on its head, using the phrase to emphasize the impossibility of escape. "Al for nou3t" (111/1779) the people rush to the hills, and

> *For nou3t* fled beest & man
> Al to late þei hit bigan
> In þat watir soone þei swan
> Side bi syde wolf & man
> Þe lyoun swam bi-syde þe hert
> Dude no beest to oþere smert
> Þe sparhauke bi þe sterling
> Þei tented oþere no maner þing
> Þes ladyes tented not þo to pride
> Þei swam bi her knaues syde
> For lordshipe was þere no strif
> Was no man gelous of his wyf
> Oþere to help was noon so sly
> Alle þei drenched bi & by.
> Alle þei drenched euerychone (111/1783–97, my emphasis)

> (For naught, beasts and people fled
> but they began far too late
> in that water they soon swam
> side by side wolf and human
> the lion swam beside the deer.
> No beast sought to harm another.
> The sparrowhawk [swam] by the starling
> they thought about no other thing.
> The ladies did not think of pride
> when they swam by their servant's side
> For lordship was there no striving.
> No man was jealous of his wife.
> none were so cunning as to help.
> They all drowned eventually.
> Every one of them drowned.)

Surveying the process of "nought-ing" or unmaking of creation, the passage imagines the growing sea, strewn with human and animal bodies in the tropes of the *memento mori*. It is, as contemporary mortality lyrics insist, "Al to late" (entirely too late).[65] The realization that escape is futile and the acceptance of impending death generate fleeting utopian moments: wolves, humans, lions, deer all tread water together, too focused on their own preservation to harm each other. Hawks and starlings momentarily are kin rather than predator and prey. Pride and jealousy among classes and sexes disintegrate in the waters. In this watery dance of death, disparate creatures find themselves "bi syde" each other, but "alle" meet the same fate, a point emphasized by the reiteration, "Alle þei drenched," in the final lines. Mortality and the quest for survival are the great levelers.

But where do we readers stand here? On the one hand, we imagine this scene as if from the distance; we have a God's-eye view of the drowning world. But the poem also directs our attention to specific moments in the creaturely fight for survival and then further narrows the frame to focus on Noah, who witnesses the scene and offers an example of response. When he observes the victims left outside to drown, *Cursor Mundi*'s Noah mourns. He is "not al in ese of hert" (not at ease; 113/1804), but rather "wiþ sore wepynge" he prays night and day for the souls of the dead (with painful weeping; 113/1814–18). The poem devotes more than a dozen lines to Noah's prayer, which specifically asks that "Siþ þei were perisshed so rewely / On her soulis to haue mercy" (Since they perished so pitifully, / to have mercy on their souls; 113/1825–26). Because they suffered so much in this life, Noah suggests, they should be free of divine vengeance in the afterlife.

As I mentioned earlier, it is difficult to find similar models of pity or compassionate witness for the flood victims within *Cleanness*. Ensconced safely within the ark with his family, Noah offers no such prayers for the victims. Neither does he gaze on the wrecked world. He reminds blind to the suffering all around him. He is seemingly ignorant of and indifferent to the floating bodies of the dead that so many medieval artists depicted encircling the ark, as an image from the early fourteenth-century Holkham Picture Bible shows (figure 3.1). If our gaze is drawn first to Noah releasing the dove and the raven, it soon drifts below the waters where we see the corpses of the victims, which the narrative of salvation often renders absent. Because the poem's God has also refused to pity or offer mercy to the victims, it is only us readers capable of offering a compassionate response.[66] Yet even as the poem directs our gaze to the suffering bodies of victims and narrates their cries, it refuses to dictate such a response. We might say that it invites curiosity about those left behind but resists encouraging a move toward compassion for them.

However, in the moralization following the tale, the poet inserts a somewhat surprising reading of God's perspective on his destruction of the earth.

FIGURE 3.1. Noah releases the dove and raven. From the Holkham Bible Picture Book (before 1350). British Library Additional MS 47682, fol. 8r. Photograph © The British Library Board.

Although Genesis explains that God sent the flood because he was sorry that he made humanity, in *Cleanness*, God mourns both his initial creation and his rash destruction of it: "Hym rwed þat He hem vprerde and raȝt hem lyflode; /And efte þat He hem vndyd, hard hit Hym þoȝt" (He lamented that he created them and gave them life; / and also that he undid them. It seemed to him to be unfeeling/severe; 135/561–62).[67] And then, "quen þe swemande sorȝe soȝt to His hert" (when the grievous sorrow pierced to his heart; 135/563), he makes a covenant with humanity to never destroy the entire world again. In a moment indicative of what scholars have seen as the humanization of *Cleanness*'s God, the poem offers the unsettling possibility that God could make a mistake worthy of regretting. Although divine regret for mass extinction may offer little consolation to the modern reader, it functions as an affective opening, albeit a small one. For, if the divine perspective on things may be mutable, then readers, too, might hold contradictory feelings as we navigate how to witness and respond to that which remains distant.

Smoldering Soil

> everything, in a place we knew, every thing, we knew, little and large and mine and ours, except horror, all of it, everything could flame up that quickly, could flare and be gone.
> CAMILLE DUNGY, "this beginning may have always meant this end"

Given *Cleanness*'s development of this divine remorse and the promises of the covenant, it might come as a surprise that the next biblical exemplum is another tale of divine judgment resulting in mass ecological destruction. In its treatment of a biblical episode often read for its homophobia and sexual violence, the poem's description of the destruction of Sodom and Gomorrah amplifies its ecological violence, extensively elaborating on the two biblical verses that describe the scene: "And the Lord rained upon Sodom and Gomorrah brimstone and fire from the Lord out of heaven. And he destroyed these cities, and all the country about, all the inhabitants of the cities, and all things that spring from the earth" (Genesis 19:24–25). This story is far less common in Middle English biblical literature than that of the Flood, though it is a popular scene for visual depiction. Indeed, *Cleanness* offers the fullest treatment of it in Middle English that I have yet found.[68] In *Cleanness*, the description of the wreckage comes as the spectacular conclusion to the narrative of Abraham and the three visitors and Abraham's failed negotiation with God to spare the wicked cities of Sodom and Gomorrah (Genesis 18). In the *Cleanness* poet's hands, these linked episodes are lessons in hospitality, in what it means to welcome strangers as honored guests and what it means to fail to do so. However, following directly on the heels of the narrative of the Great Flood and God's promise not to destroy the entire world ("He schulde neuer for no syt smyte al at onez" [he would never again kill everything at once; 135/566]), the destruction of these towns is also a warning of the more localized wrack that divine vengeance maintains the right to inflict on the disobedient, inhospitable, or spiritually unclean.

In a strikingly literalizing move, *Cleanness* associates the "filth" of the citizens of Sodom with environmental conditions: "þe wynd and þe weder and þe worlde stynkes / Of þe brych þat vpbraydez þose broþelych wordez" (The wind and the weather and the world stinks / because of vomit that those vile words generate; 147/847–48). Language and weather both manifest their vileness as a stench. Foreshadowing the fetid fumes that will soon emit from the Dead Sea, which forms in the wasteland of the destroyed cities, this description implies that even after the catastrophe, some elements of the landscape might persist. But it is not only the putrid air that presages the fate of these cities; the destruction of Sodom in *Cleanness* begins with an ominous sky portending "þe vglokest vnhap euer on erd suffred. / Ruddon of þe day-rawe ros vpon vȝten / When merk of þe mydnyȝt moȝt no more last" (The most gruesome misfortune ever suffered on earth. / Dawn rose red in the early morning / when the dark of midnight could last no longer; 149/892–94). The poet writes of the destruction in superlatives, naming it one of the most gruesome misfortunes that had been suffered on earth, even though, as a regional event, clearly it is not as severe as the drowning of the entire world. Even so, the poet communicates the sense that every "wrake" is the worst destruction, as each surely must feel to those who experience it.

While Lot, his wife, and his two daughters flee the city to the surrounding hills before the dawn breaks, with the morning light come catastrophic winds and fiery showers for the inhabitants of Sodom and the four cities of the plains (Gorde, Gomorrah, Admah, and Zeboim). As with its description of the annihilation of the world by flood, *Cleanness* greatly expands the biblical description of the storm of fire on the five cities:

> Þe grete God in His greme bygynnez on lofte
> To waken wederez so wylde; þe wyndez He callez,
> And þay wroþely vpwafte and wrastled togeder,
> Fro fawre half of þe folde flytande loude.
> Clowdez clustered bytwene kesten vp torres,
> Þat þe þik þunder-þrast þirled hem ofte.
> Þe rayn rueled adoun, ridlande þikke
> Of felle flaunkes of fyr and flakes of soufre,
> Al in smolderande smoke smachande ful ille,

> Swe aboute Sodamas and hit sydez alle,
> Gorde to Gomorra, þat þe grounde laused,
> Abdama and Syboym, þise ceteis alle faure
> Al birolled with rayn, rostted and brenned,
> And ferly flayed þat folk þat in þose fees lenged. (151/947–60)

> (The great God in his anger begins on high
> to wake the wild weathers; he calls the winds
> and they angerly rise up and wrestle together,
> from the far side of the world they loudly strive.
> Clouds clustered between cast up as towers,
> that the thick thrusts of thunder often pierced.
> The rain poured down, thickly sprinkling
> many fiery sparks and flakes of sulfur,
> all in smoldering smoke smelling very awful,
> fell around Sodom and all its sides,
> from Gorde to Gomorrah, so that the ground galloped,
> Admah and Zeboim, all four of these cities,
> were all covered with rain, roasted and burnt,
> and the people that lived in those cities horribly terrified.)

This storm of fire echoes the smoky fall of the rebel angels and the descriptions of the massive storm that begins the Great Flood. Yet even as they transport us back to earlier scenes of ecological catastrophe, these images of cataclysm are equally visceral. The poet draws the readerly gaze first to the heavens to describe the disquieting atmospheric disturbances that presage the disaster. Clouds cluster. Thunder rumbles. Thick rain pours. Angry winds wrestle. As in the Flood, both heaven and earth tremble with divine wrath. The atmosphere thickens with clouds. The darkening sky shakes with thunder. Then the heavens break open and gush rain like liquid lava, sulfurous and smoking. Soon, the valley is drowning in flames and the people trapped within are subsumed by a fiery sea. The poet intensifies this terrifying description with heightened alliteration—many lines contain four alliterative stresses rather than the more common three. Some are particularly tongue-twisting ("Þat þe þik þunder-þrast þirled hem ofte"), their sonic intensity pulling us deeper into the smoky chaos.

Next, the poet homes in on the terrestrial response. The depths of the earth react to the climatological turmoil, as a personified Hell bursts open to receive the burning, sinking cities of the plains:

> For when þat þe Helle herde the houndez of heuen,
> He watz ferlyly fayn, vnfolded bylyue;
> Þe grete barrez of þe abyme he barst vp at onez,

> Þat alle þe regioun torof in riftes ful grete,
> And clouen alle in lyttel cloutes þe clyffez aywhere,
> As lauce leuez of þe boke þat lepez in twynne.
> Þe brethe of þe brynston bi þat hit blende were,
> Al þo citees and her sydes sunkken to helle. (151–52/961–68)

> (For when Hell heard the hounds of heaven,
> he was marvelously pleased, and opened immediately
> the great barriers of the depths he broke open at once
> so that all the region tore asunder in massive rifts
> and split into little pieces the cliffs
> like the loose leaves of a book that bursts apart.
> When the breath of the brimstone had stopped
> all the cities and their surrounds sank to hell.)

Where the inhabitants of the city were "ferly flayed" (greatly terrified), Hell is "ferlyly fain" (marvelously pleased).[69] An affective inversion, this verbal echo layers contradictory feelings onto the scene, inviting us to briefly inhabit the perspective of the broken landscape that consumes them. The poem turns us away from the pathos of the terrified victims to wonder at the astonishing geological spectacle. As the personified Hell yawns open the mouth of the abyss, it generates a series of earthquakes that rattle the earth, exploding its rocky cliffs, and opening a gaping crevasse that swallows the towns. The gulf between hell and earth is temporarily breached.

These unsettling details may have their source in medieval apocalyptic texts describing the Final Judgment. The *Apocalypse of Thomas* similarly describes the opening of the abyss and the heavens and "the stench of brimstone," before depicting the end of the world as the closing of a book.[70] The *Cleanness* poet transforms this bookish simile: Sodom's ground is violently ripped open like a manuscript cracked, bursting its binding, scattering its leaves. Closure here is construed as rupture and loss. The stories this landscape contained are now broken fragments and will soon succumb to the oblivion of forgetfulness as any remaining signs of the cities and their inhabitants succumb to the watery depths. It is difficult to remember what one can no longer see.

Thus, the landscape and diverse lives of the victims are submerged first by the fiery spectacle and then by the waters. As soon as they become aware of the futility of trying to escape this "wrake," the helpless people of the city cry out. Unlike the Flood narrative, there is here no differentiation between groups. There are no affecting interactions. There is only their shared vulnerability, emblematized in a single outcry. Even so, it is a pitiable scene. The narrator comments that "such a ȝomerly ȝarm of ȝellyng þer rysed" (such a miserable outcry of yelling was raised there; 152/971), that the clouds clattered, and Christ himself might have had pity ("þat Kryst my3t haf rawþe," 152/973).[71] The skies resonate with the suffering, mirroring it back. Yet if the poem briefly entertains the possibility of pitying the pain of the victims, imagining the possibility of Christ's compassionate response to it, the poem again forecloses on that possibility nearly as soon as it evokes it. For as we will see, as these cries echo outward to the hills and up to the clouds, the sound of them stirs Lot's wife to turn and behold the wreckage—an act of attention, perhaps of curiosity or even kinship or compassion, that will be fatal.

Staying with the Trouble

> Noah's wife, I am wringing
> my hands not knowing how to know.
> MAYA C. POPA, "Letter to Noah's Wife"

If *Cleanness* uses extensive description to force our attention to the fraught dynamics of attending to ecological wreckage, it and other medieval texts also sometimes write unlikely witnesses into these two biblical narratives. In the medieval tradition, stories of the Flood and the destruction of Sodom and Gomorrah frequently depict women who cannot help but look back, women who mourn the loss of the vanishing world. Figures of resistance, curiosity, and compassion, the wives of Lot and Noah model other ways of perceiving, feeling, and responding to the catastrophe, modes of being that are consistently evoked, if never endorsed, by the patriarchal narratives in which they are framed. They do so, I argue, first by embodying and then articulating an expansive notion of kinship, one that extends to other humans, to animals, and to the landscape itself. Insisting on unlikely kin making, they model what Donna Haraway has called the practice of "staying with the trouble," which requires "learning to be truly present, not as a vanishing pivot between awful or Edenic pasts and apocalyptic or salvific futures, but as mortal critter entwined in myriad unfinished configurations of places, times, matters, and meanings."[72] For in their characterization of the "disordered" affections of Noah and Lot's unnamed wives, medieval texts emphasize that the attachment and entanglement that lead to their backward glances reveal what might be at stake in beholding and becoming beholden to a wrecked world.

The stories of both wives originate in the Bible but are greatly expanded in later writings. A single verse in Genesis provides the account of Lot's wife's backward glance: "And his wife looking behind her, was turned into a statue of salt" (19:26). Scarcely mentioned before this moment, and barely at all afterward, she vanishes as quickly as she appears. She briefly resurfaces in the gospels when Jesus commands his followers, "Remember Lot's Wife," as a reminder to prepare for the Last Days (Luke 17:32). The story of Noah's wife is an invention, but a popular one in England by the fourteenth century, where it seems to be at least partly shaped by the comic fabliau figure of the shrewish wife.[73] The Bible only mentions that Noah has a wife, who is saved with him. Although the details vary, medieval texts generally depict her as cantankerous, skeptical of the ark-building venture, and reluctant to leave behind her friends and her work for what she sees as an endeavor born of madness. Like second Eves, both she and Lot's wife question the divine command by attending to the catastrophe and mourning its losses. Both wives remain nameless, defined only by their relationships to their more righteous husbands. They are both middle figures, caught between a vanishing world and the promise of a salvation contingent on limiting their loves. And here is where the wives' paths diverge. Despite their shared backward glances, they meet different ends. Noah's wife is pulled onto the ark and saved from the flood, even though she wishes to remain with her companions.[74] Lot's wife attempts to escape the wreckage with her family but is doomed by a single glance at the world she is leaving behind. Although medieval texts typically portray both women negatively, treating them as emblems of disobedience, the two wives embody the human impulse to look back. Their act of witness thus brings into focus a set of questions I suggested on the opening pages of this chapter: What is the difference between a witness, spectator, audience, and voyeur? What is so dangerous about attending to the wreckage, of turning to behold it?

As we will see, *Cleanness* and *Cursor Mundi* both expand the narrative of Lot's wife, but neither mentions Noah's wife's resistance to boarding the ark.[75] However, Noah's wife takes center stage in medieval dramatizations of the Flood. When she appears in the five extant Middle English plays of the Flood, it is typically as a figure of recalcitrance. In the York and Chester play cycles, she resists joining her family on the ark out of concern for her friends and relatives. In the Towneley cycle, she refuses to board partly because she has work to do. In a fragment from the Newcastle Flood Play, she is tempted by the devil to distract Noah from building the ark.[76] Only in the N-Town play is she piously compliant.[77] Scholars have long read these plays through the lens of typology, seeing the Flood as a type of redemption or baptism, Noah as a type of Christ, the ark as the church, and Noah's wife as representing the fallen, rebellious, but still redeemable sinner.[78] More recently, critics have observed that the characterization of Noah's wife complicates this typology, making visible its felt injustices.[79] For example, Jane Tolmie writes, "The story of the ark has its obvious cruelties; the inclusion of Mrs. Noah's resisting voice is one way of making the cruelties present and real for the audience ... her resistance makes a space in the play within which the abstract fictions of the situation are punctured by the reality of the loss of life."[80] The wife's very presence in these narratives offers an alternative mode of response to the Flood that the plays neither endorse nor entirely deny. Yet I am interested primarily in the significance of her embodiment of cosmic disorder. I read her kinship with the unruly heavens and its creatures as engendering her metaphorical backward glances toward them. Attending to the ecologies in which she is embedded and to which she responds allows reflection on the possibilities and risks of being beholden to those whom we are not tied by ancestry or even species.

The wife's status as a sign of the larger ecology comes into greatest focus in the Towneley Noah play, in which she resists coming onto the ark because she has work to do. In the play she also functions as the figure through which we see the coextensiveness of celestial and terrestrial disorder. On the one hand, the Wife is a particularly earthbound creature. Early in the play, she places herself in the landscape, both identifying with it and laying claim to it. When Noah asks her to join him on the ark, she says she will sit "on this hill" and spin "on my rok" (39/488–89), a lithic affiliation that returns in a dark echo later in the play when Noah threatens to make her "still as stone" (42/586) if she does not board the ark.[81] The simple act of placing herself, of grounding herself, is a radical gesture in a tale so dependent on the willingness to move, to be displaced. Sitting on her hill, she temporarily becomes an image of terrestrial stability in a world characterized by the movement of pouring rain and rushing waters.

She explicitly binds herself to the land, but the play soon implies her kinship with the heavens as well. As V. A. Kolve first observed, the play depicts the domestic disputes between Noah and his Wife as a microcosmic reflection of the larger disorder of the cosmos.[82] After Noah has boarded the ark and is trying to convince his Wife to board as well (she continues stubbornly spinning at her distaff on her rock even as the thunder crackles and the rain pours), he asks her to look to the heavens:

> Behold to the heuen!
> The cateractes all,
> That ar open full euen,
> Grete and small,
> And the planettys seuen
> Left has thare stall,
> Thise thoners and levyn
> Downe gar fall

>Full stout,
>Both halles and bowers,
>Castels and towres;
>Full sharp ar thise showers,
>That renys aboute (39/495-507)

>(Look up to the heavens,
>to all the cascades,
>that have opened entirely,
>great and small,
>and the seven planets
>have left their places
>These lightning and thunder
>crash down
>very fiercely,
>both halls and bowers
>castles and towers
>very sharp are these showers
>that rain all around.)

Of this scene, Kolve writes that "to this macrocosmic anarchy the drama relates the microcosm. God's great world is turned upside down just as is man's little world."[83] Noah's Wife mirrors the physical cosmos. Like the planets, she is out of place, manifesting chaos. Originally, a sign of disorder—recalcitrant, clinging to her hilly perch, resisting patriarchal authority—once she is on the ark, even if she comes kicking and screaming, her place in the domestic hierarchy is reasserted. It is only after the Wife boards the ark that the universe's order returns. She observes the fact, stating that "I se on the firmament / Me thynk, the seven starnes" (I think I see the seven stars in the sky; 42/610-11). Although the cosmos has returned to its regular order, she retains a sense of uncertainty. "I think," she demurs about her celestial observation, as if not yet willing to commit entirely to this new normal. But this new world is also a repetition of the old one: mirroring the second day of creation, this Second Age opens with God distilling order from the stormy chaos of an inchoate cosmos.[84]

If in the Towneley play, Noah's Wife is metaphorically entangled with her rock and with the hills and the stars, the Chester Noah play throws into relief the Wife's understanding of her kinship with a motley creaturely community, one that embraces what Haraway calls "oddkin."[85] The Chester play is unique among the Noah plays in offering an extended catalog of animals being led onto the ark. Lisa Kiser has shown that the lengthy lists of creatures adhere to a strict structure. Noah's sons begin the inventory, listing animals in easily discernible groups and types, all of which are associated with "political governance (with the lion and leopard), plowing, crop production, large animal husbandry, trade (of animal commodities, such as wool), and hunting."[86] The animals in their inventories reflect traditionally masculine practices and virtues. The two daughters-in-law each list the ark's avian guests, which are also carefully ordered by type ("here are fowles lesse and more" [here are smaller and greater birds; 50/181]) and reflect traditionally feminine or domestic concerns. Noah's Wife's selection of animals is rather more difficult to categorize:

> And here are beares, wolves sett,
> Apes, owles, maremussett,
> Wesills, squerrells, and fyrrett;
> Here the eaten there meate. (49/173–76)
>
> (And here are bears and wolves set,
> apes, owls, and monkeys,
> weasels, squirrels, and ferrets;
> they eat their food here.)

At first blush, this creaturely quatrain may seem much like those surrounding it. Yet, about this list, Kiser observes, "Noah's wife violates a number of principles that inform the catalogues of the other characters. First and foremost, not a single one of her animals contributes to the household economy. None performs worthwhile labour."[87] The Wife's inventory also lacks the orderly hierarchies evident in those of her children. Her list includes large animals and small ones, beasts and birds, wild and tamed. Rather than contribute to the ark's economy, these creatures will consume more than they give. Moreover, their association with the Wife clearly suggests something about her character. On the one hand, most of these animals, as Kiser details, have masculine, "comical and sinister associations."[88] But on the other hand, the Wife's set of animals is one of "oddkin;" it is a mismatched and motley assemblage that is as unruly as she is. It mirrors her disorder, her resistance, and her nonconformity. Like her very presence, it disrupts the orderly classification of the animals by her sons and their wives.

For it is precisely the mayhem of her creaturely inventory that gives us a sense of the radical inclusiveness of her kin making, an inclusiveness that will later create friction with her husband and his plans. Her inventory reminds us that not only the virtuous, orderly, or useful creatures are granted refuge. In so doing, it throws into relief the fundamental difference between animal and human salvation. This motley assemblage of creatures is as expansive as is the Wife's sense of whom should be permitted on the ark. This is made clear when, at the conclusion of the listing of the animals, the Wife proclaims, as if to add another set of creatures to the lengthy inventory: "But I have my gossips everyechone, / one foote further I will not gone" (unless I have every one of my friends, / I will not go one foot further; 50/201–202). Given the immediate context, it is a reasonable demand. If the ship can be filled with creatures fair and foul, wild and tame, useful and useless, why not a few more human companions, who would likely be a more practical choice than some of the animal species already aboard? In its larger context, this demand is framed in terms of reciprocity and kin love:

> I will not owt of this towne.
> But I have my gossips everyechone,
> One foot further I will not gone.
> They shall not drowne, by saynte John,
> And I may save there life.
> The loved me full well, by Christe. (50/200–205)

> (I will not leave this town
> unless I have every one of my friends,
> I won't go a foot further.
> By St. John, they will not drown,
> and I may save their lives.
> By Christ, they loved me very well.)

Despite the pleas of her husband and sons, she refuses to board, insisting instead on her mutual responsibility to those who loved her. Her rhetoric is adamant: I will not leave; I will not go; they shall not drown. She asserts her resistance and refusal on their behalf. And in so doing, she not only articulates her obligation to them, she also holds out the hope that sheer force of will and recalcitrance may be their salvation. But we know how this story ends. As in the other plays, she is pulled into the ark at the last possible moment, leaving her friends to drown.

As the floodwaters rise, the Chester play gives bodily presence and voice to these gossips, inviting the audience to behold their suffering. In the First Age's final hours, it is these women's voices that we hear. Speaking as a chorus, the gossips unite by drinking away their sorrows:

> The fludd comes fleetinge in full faste,
> One everye syde that spredeth full farre.
> For fere of drowninge I am agaste;
> Good gossippe, lett us drawe nere.
> And lett us drinke or wee departe,
> For oftetymes wee have done soe. (52/225–30)

> (The flood comes rushing in quickly,
> on every side it spreads very far.
> For fear of drowning, I am aghast.
> Good gossips, let us draw near.
> And let us drink before we depart
> as we have so often done.)

We only glimpse the surging floodwaters through the gossips' eyes. Both resistant and melancholic, their call to drink is a stay against catastrophe, a stubborn return to the quotidian practices of community and friendship in the face of their inevitable ending. But the gossips are also an assemblage in which the individual and the communal blend. They function like a chorus, their shared song beginning with an individuated "I" that soon opens into a welcoming "us." In a play dominated by imperatives and enclosures, the gossips extend an inclusive set of invitations—"let us draw near . . . let us drink"—and in so doing model kinship bonds based on invitation rather than obligation, on proximity rather than biology. Their kinship is characterized by friendship rather than bloodlines, and their communal song functions like the image of lovers embracing in *Cleanness*, humanizing them by performing their care for one another as death looms.

The voluntary nature of this community becomes even clearer when Japhett, one of Noah's sons, appeals to his mother's sense of familial bonds. Come aboard, he pleads, "for we are here, your owne childer" (for we are here, your own children; 52/237). What counts as kin, he seems to say, is family alone. But the Wife rejects his narrow association of kinship with biological family, reiterating that she will not come aboard until her gossips can enter with her (52/241–42). Ultimately, her resistance avails little. Only a few lines later, she is forcibly brought onto the boat, apparently against her will, and is not heard from again.

Like Chester, the York version of the Flood play gives particular focus to who counts as kin, with the Wife employing an even wider lexicon of kinship. As in the other Flood plays, the York Noah's attempts to coax his Wife onto the ark are initially thwarted. When he reminds her that God has commanded the destruction, she simply responds that she would like to gather friends and relatives to join them:

> Nowe, certis, and we shulde skape fro skathe
> And so be saffyd as ye saye here,
> My commodrys and my cosynes bathe,
> Tham wolde I wente with us in feere. (86/142–45)
>
> (Now certainly, if we could manage to escape harm
> and so be saved, as you have said here

I should like both my relatives and my friends
to accompany us.)

As in Chester, Noah's Wife seeks to broaden access to the refuge that Noah is promising here. Noah's logic (following the divine command) is an either/or proposition. It is either us or them, family or friends, here or there, life or death. Conversely, Noah's Wife is driven by the connective and expansive logic of the "and." She wishes to include relatives *and* friends. These conflicting senses of kin lead to a bitter exchange of words between Noah and the Wife. She laments that she has lived to see the day when she receives news that she will be saved while others perish (82/147–48).[89] Even after she has been pulled on to the ark, she continues to grieve the loss of her friends, though her daughters-in-law urge her to be grateful for her immediate family's salvation:

> I FILIA: Dere modir, mende youre moode,
>   For we sall wende you with.
> UXOR: My frendis that I fra yoode
>   Are overeflowen with floode.
> II FILIA: Nowe thanke we God al goode
>   That us has grauntid grith.
> III FILIA: Modir, of this werke nowe wolde ye noght wene
>   That alle shuld worthe to watres wan. (82/149–56)

> (DAUGHTER 1: Dear mother, amend your mood,
>   for we will go with you.
> WIFE: My friends that I left
>   are drowned by the flood.
> DAUGHTER 2: Let us now thank God, all good
>   who has granted us protection.
> DAUGHTER 3: Mother, even now do you not still believe about this work
>   that all should be covered in the dark waters?)

Previously calling them "commodrys and my cosynes," the Wife here calls them "frendis," and in so doing continues to expand the lexicon of kindship to encompass both voluntary and biological relationships. She speaks in the plural, opening up the possibilities of the multitudes that have been submerged by the rising waters. The daughters, in contrast, insist on an insular "we" that only includes the immediate family. They present the Wife's grief as a problem of comprehension or belief rather than one of feeling. And in so doing they lay bare the great distance between her mourning for the lost world and their detachment from it.

After her children usher the Wife aboard, we hear little more from her until the end of the play. When the family exits the ark into a brave new world, she looks around and asks:

> For wrekis nowe that we may wynne,
> Oute of this woo that we in wore,
> But Noye, wher are nowe all oure kynne
> And companye we knwe before? (89/267–70)
>
> (For wreckage now that we may escape
> from the sorrow that we were in.
> But, Noah, where are all of our kin now,
> and the company that we knew before?)

Although she has already mourned their loss, she continues to ask after her friends, to evoke them as "kin" and "company" (two new additions to her lexicon of kinship). She looks for them. She asks for them. Unlike her shipmates, Noah's Wife continues to remember and mourn the drowned world.[90] In answering her questions, Noah avoids the language of kinship, bluntly responding, "Dame, all ar drowned, late be thy dyne" (Woman, everyone has drowned, stop making noise about it; 89/271). Could there be a more detached and unfeeling response to his wife's pain and to the mass destruction experienced by the larger world? In it, Noah, always obedient, implies that such fellow feeling is misplaced or inordinate.

When Noah later links the Flood to the Last Judgment, pedantically explaining that the world will be destroyed by fire, his Wife again names her sorrow for the future disaster. "Owre hertis are seer," she laments, "For thes sawes that ye say here" (our hearts are broken / for these things that you are saying here; 90/303–4). She speaks for others, even when she alone seems to feel the loss. Because she is entangled with the world, because she had cultivated kinship with it, the play implies, she is also the one who is fated to grieve it. So although she is usually taken as a second Eve, in her pity, she also evokes Mary, as the suffering mother of the pietà, the embodiment of sorrow and compassion.

I am not alone in reading Noah's Wife as a site of resistance, as the origin of a counternarrative that privileges connection and kinship. Sarah Novacich writes, she is "a sign of possibility, a woman . . . whose eventual correction does not erase her ghostly presence and transgressive potential."[91] Daniel Birkholz similarly argues that "dissatisfaction seems too mild a term for the robust heroism *Uxor Noe* exhibits in her henpecking of tepid Noah. Beneath her comic bluster are principled objections to the notion of reserving 'lyfe' for the family, with dispassionate 'drowning' for the neighborhood."[92] For even when we acknowledge the comic potential of the domestic brawl between Noah and his wife, and even if we see her as a fabliau-type character, it is difficult not to read the wife's resistance as born of care and connection. She models compassion whereas Noah models obedience. But, in these plays, as in *Cleanness*, compassion remains a lesser virtue, perhaps even a failure of virtue.[93] Framed as an unstable emotion, it is bound to the unreliable, embodied female gaze.

The Backward Glance

> Dark thighs of smoke opened
> to the sky. She meant to look
> away, but the sting in her eyes,
> the taste devouring her tongue,
> and the neighbors begging her name.
> NATALIE DIAZ, "Of Course She Looked Back"

This dangerous gaze is imagined even more explicitly in the story of the destruction of Sodom and Gomorrah, which does not appear in any of the cycle plays.[94] Lot's wife's backward glance is, however, frequently memorialized both in medieval art and in biblical paraphrases. Consider, for example, the depiction offered in William de Brailes's *Picture Bible* from the early thirteenth century (figure 3.2). The burning city of Sodom occupies the lower portion of the miniature, and the upper register glistens with gold and streaming fire. Lot and his two daughters exit the frame to the right. Guided by the hands of an angel, they walk off the page itself and into another story. Lot's Wife, though, is caught inside the frame as she glances down at the tumbling towers. She returns the gaze of the eyes beseeching her from beneath the rubble. The image captures the moment of her transformation: her body is already becoming mineral, already reflecting the waves of the great, salty sea that will subsume this burning town and lap at her stony feet. But not yet. For now, the tongues of fire flow like flaming rivers, connecting heaven and earth.

As fascinated as the iconographic tradition is with representing the transformation of Lot's Wife, what the images can't or don't do is explore *why* she turns and looks. Vernacular biblical literature, however, is interested in precisely this question. Like some other Middle English translations of this

FIGURE 3.2. Lot and his daughters flee Sodom and Gomorrah while Lot's Wife looks back. From William de Brailes's *Picture Bible* (ca. 1230). Manuscript W.106, fol. 4r. Photograph courtesy of Walters Art Museum, Baltimore, MD (Creative Commons CC0 1.0).

episode, *Cleanness* and *Cursor Mundi* supply a reason for the turn beyond what Genesis provides, emphasizing her friendship with the townspeople. Consider, for instance, the opening lines of the stanza devoted to the destruction of Sodom and Gomorrah in the *Middle English Metrical Paraphrase of the Old Testament*:

> Thos cytes sanke ther certan,
> and the sownd was herd, a hydwyse bere.
> The wyf then wyst hyr frendes wer slayn
> and lokyd agayn with sympyll chere.
> For scho dyd that owtrage
> that God bad dame do never.[95]
>
> (Those cities sank there truly,
> and the sound was heard, a hideous outcry.
> The wife then knew her friends were slain
> and looked back with a sad expression.
> Because she did that offense
> that God commanded the woman never do.)

In the biblical account, there is no outcry. No reason for the wife to turn her head other than curiosity. But here, as in *Cleanness* and *Cursor Mundi*, the Wife's backward glance is a response to the sound of suffering rising up out of the valley below. And that suffering maps onto her own face in her "sympyll chere" (sad/humble expression), a description that emphasizes her sorrow and sense of loss.[96] Because she hears the outcry, she turns toward the suffering, and because she risks turning toward it, she is doomed to share in it. To be sure, her turn is transgressive; she has been told to ignore that impulse. But should she be faulted for turning toward the sound of pain?

Medieval biblical texts often sidestep this question by describing rather than moralizing her gaze. *Cleanness*, for instance, emphasizes the responsiveness of Lot's Wife to the "bale" (suffering) as well as to the moment of connection offered by her backward glance. On the one hand, Lot's Wife's fleeting glance toward the smoking cities offers us an example of what Stanbury calls the poet's "eyewitness technique": it gives us a witness within the narrative itself, though in this case the eyewitness offers an example of how *not* to look.[97] But on the other hand, the glance aligns Lot's Wife with the object of her gaze, solidifying her kinship with the vanishing cities of the plains. For *Cleanness* insists on a kind of tragic poetic justice: Lot's Wife transforms into a pillar of salt after gazing on the destruction of her home because she leavened and salted the bread of their angelic visitors against their wishes (146/820–25). Further, her salty body stands as a monument above a salty sea—the wasteland resulting from the sinking of the cities.

This transformation begins with a blush. Despite being instructed "Bes never so bolde to *blusch* yow bihynde" (be never so bold to glance behind yourself; 149/904, my emphasis), Lot's wife cannot seem to help herself. She

> *blusched* byhynden her bak þat bale for to herkken.
> Hit watz lusty Lothes wyf þat ouer her lyfte schulder
> Ones ho *bluschet* to þe burȝe, bot bod ho no lenger
> Þat ho nas stadde a stiffe ston, a stalworth image,
> Al so salt as ani se—and so ho ȝet standez.
> Þay slypped bi and syȝe hir not þat wern hir samen-feres. (152/980–85, my emphasis)
>
> (glanced behind her back to attend to that suffering.
> It was Lot's lusty wife who glanced once to the city over her left shoulder,
> but she remained no longer
> before she stood there a hard stone, a stalwart statue,
> as salty as any sea—and there she still stands.
> Her companions slipped by her and did not see her.)

Only a few lines later, the poet repeats the moment of her rebellious gaze in strikingly similar terms: "ho *blusched* hir bihynde, þaȝ hir forboden were" (she glanced behind, although it was forbidden to her; 153/998, my emphasis). The poem repeats the Middle English verb *blush* (or *blishen*) four times in twenty lines. In Middle English, this word has several senses. It can indicate to gaze or to glimpse. In its nominal forms, it indicates radiance or brightness, or, as we now use it, the rosy face of shame or embarrassment.[98] *Cleanness's* insistence on the Wife's "blush" conflates these meanings. Though the poet may have chosen the word for its alliteration with "behind," it carries with it this range of possible meanings. It is a word frequently used to indicate the resplendence of sunbeams, or the glimmer of light and fire.[99] And so here, the Wife's "blusch" also evokes the warm red glow that the flaming cities would have cast on her turned face. Her transgression is a moment of kinship, in which she not only sees but takes on the attributes of what she sees. Briefly aflame, her forbidden glance is both the blush of radiance and the blush of shame. In her act of disobedience, she shines.

Although "blush" also carries a sense of ephemerality (still today we say, "at first blush," to indicate a fleeting glimpse), the Wife's "blusch" doesn't tell the entire story of her moment of transgressive beholding. For to reduce her gaze to a brief glance is to overlook, as David Coley observes, that Lot's Wife also "harkens," or attends to, the destruction. She may not then be "the biblical equivalent of a freeway rubbernecker," but rather a witness to the catastrophe.[100] Even so, the poem equivocates about the object of her attention: "bale" can mean both calamity and suffering.[101] Is her turn motivated by compassion? Curiosity? Both?

Because *Cursor Mundi's* treatment of the backward glance more explicitly frames the Wife's gaze as an act of curiosity, it offers a bit of context here:

> Loth wif þis cry herde
> And longed to se how þei ferde
> Wondres fayn wolde she fynde
> And as she loked hir bihynde
> A stoon she stondeþ bi þe way
> And so shal do til domes day (171/2849–54)
>
> (Lot's wife heard this cry
> and longed to see how they fared.
> She would gladly have found wonders
> and as she looked behind her,
> she became a stone standing by the road
> and will remain so until doomsday.)

In this account, Lot's Wife's motivations are rather more ambivalent. Spurred by the cry emerging from the city, Lot's Wife turns to see how its inhabitants "fared." Though this act initially seems to be born of compassion and connection, *Cursor Mundi* quickly clarifies that what really motivates her is a desire to see wonders. The key word here is "fayn," which means "gladly, eagerly, joyfully."[102] It shifts the tone of the entire scene. Is she desiring to see the spectacle of destruction or, perhaps, looking for a miracle that God has stayed his hand?[103] The former seems more likely. What could have been a gesture of compassion becomes a mark of vain curiosity. She is drawn to the spectacle of the disaster. It impossible not to see her as a gawker, a voyeur. Yet when we lack such prompts explaining her feelings toward the scene, we readers are left only with the act itself.

So how are we to read the tragic gaze of Lot's Wife in *Cleanness*? Coley is surely right when he argues that Lot's Wife "emerges as both witness to and victim of a traumatic event."[104] She is also a memorial of the catastrophe. For, representing her as an "image of sorrow," some Middle English biblical poems monumentalize Lot's Wife's "sympyll chere" as well as her transgression. Reified, her body becomes a sign not only of disobedience but also of suffering and loss, and a physical *part* of the salty landscape. She *becomes* what she beholds. In an Ovidian-like metamorphosis, Lot's Wife becomes mineral, a transformation that is simultaneously ontological, moral, and allegorical. In many medieval manuscript illuminations, she looks ghostly, like an alabaster statue.[105] Her continued presence and stony gaze blur the human and the mineral, and in so doing, they capture a scene of the perils of being beholden to a dying world.[106] The message here is not only, as we might expect, "don't be like Lot's wife," but rather, that there is a risk in bearing witness to catastrophe, there is a risk in "staying with the trouble": you just might be subsumed by it, become part of it. The suffering of others might become your own.

Yet in the example of Lot's wife, we are also reminded that refusals to look at suffering and loss are often as powerful a testament to its claims on us as is curiosity about it. Lot's wife's salvation requires looking away. It requires choosing not to see, not to understand oneself as beholden to or "responseable."[107] Like Noah's wife, she is surrounded by those who refuse to look until they are far from the scene of the catastrophe. For after Lot and his daughters have escaped, *Cleanness* tells us that Lot "sende toward Sodomas þe sy3t of his y3en" (directed his gaze toward Sodom; 153/1005), where he discovers that the once paradisal space is now a vast stinking lake, bubbling with deadly black water. His belated gaze is all the more troubling when we recall, as Stanbury writes, that "Lot not only refuses to look on the cities, he refuses to see his wife once she has turned"; the poem tell us that "þay slypped bi and sy3e hir not þat wern hir samen-feres" (those that were her companions slipped by and did not see her; 152/985).[108] Indeed, his salvation is contingent on his refusal to turn to see the cities of the plains or even his wife in the process of fleeing the suffering. Yet, Lot looks back after he escapes from the burning city.[109] He observes the smoking ruins long after they can assert any claim on him. Lot's Wife attends to the horror while it is happening. Readers of *Cleanness* might occupy both of these positions: the during or the aftermath. But are we like Lot or like Lot's Wife? Do we observe the ruination with disinterested distance? A sense of justice? Or, do we mourn what is being lost? Feel responsible for it? Regardless, as Penelope Anderson observes of a slightly later reimagining of this narrative, by attending so closely to the thick description of the destruction, the "reader must do the very thing for which Lot's wife is punished."[110] To read this story is to look, to turn toward the suffering that the poetic lines depict with such urgency and intensity.

Writing of Lot's wife, Daniel Birkholz observes that "she works as a negative exemplum, obviously, from the perspective of doctrine. But from a less rigidly historicist perspective . . . Lot's Wife commemorates something else: an impulse to resistance."[111] Birkholz argues that the image of Lot's Wife is a "monogram of a possible alternative history," of the possibility of seeing "the world another way."[112] Might not both of these recalcitrant women function this way? Unlikely figures of resistance, they offer alternative responses to catastrophe. Both see the world as kin. Both turn to engage it, even as they are told that their own well-being and lives depend on turning away. They continue to look and connect even when others turn away. They model attention *as* connection. Doing so doesn't end well for them. They pay a great price. Both are silenced and subsumed, though in different ways. This is all the more reason, I think, for us to attend to narratives and figures that model the fraught dynamics of attending to disaster. Medieval reimaginations of Noah and Lot's wives, as I hope I have begun to suggest, offer a stark reminder of what might be at stake in being beholden to a dying world. As exemplary figures, they invite us to turn our gazes back on ourselves and ask: To what are we beholden? To what are we "response-able"?

The story of Lot's wife has continued to provide an opportunity for reflection on the risks inherent in looking back and becoming beholden. Consider, for example, a poem by a modern Indigenous writer, Natalie Diaz, that re-reads and retells the scene of the backward glance. "Of course she looked back," Diaz writes, as she paints a picture of a woman turning toward the city she is leaving behind. "Her husband uttered *Keep going.* / Whispered *Stay the course*, or / *Forget about it.* She couldn't."[113] Much like the medieval poems, Diaz invites us to see the catastrophe through the eyes of Lot's wife. Lot's Wife here thinks of what she is leaving behind, the quotidian life in the valley below oblivious to the imminent catastrophe—pigeons, dogs, children, the worry that she's forgotten to turn off the oven. And in so doing, she invites us to attend to and *feel* the loss of a world; to question the justice of the catastrophe; and to respond, by "staying with the trouble" rather than "staying the course" even though doing so may require great personal risk.

Becoming Beholden

> Standing witness ... creates an openness to the world in which the boundaries between us can dissolve in a raindrop.
> ROBIN WALL KIMMERER, *Braiding Sweetgrass*

How, then, might we think about beholding or being beholden to ecological suffering that is beyond our influence or that we *cannot* see? To what extent do witnesses and survivors bear responsibility to that which has been obliterated, erased, or transformed by the catastrophe, covered by the waters of the flood, destroyed by the fire? Although we live in times in which our vision extends much farther and deeper than a medieval audience could have imagined, such range can hinder engagement rather than catalyze it. In our moment, so riven with quotidian catastrophes, disaster is quickly forgotten or diminished. We clear the wreckage. Time transforms it. Those of us lucky enough to see and survive it are the archivists, the ones who choose which stories to tell and which to leave wrecked at the bottom of the sea, becoming visible only when remnants rise to the surface, as witnesses to lives and losses long submerged.[114]

Ultimately, these accounts of flood and fire suggest that we must reckon not only with what is being lost but also with what remains—the artifacts and stories that endure.[115] For the remnants shape what comes after. In Noah's postdiluvian world, everything is erased and rewritten. The only trace of what existed before is in the bodies of the survivors. The Flood obliterates the past, offering a hard reset. But the destruction of Sodom and Gomorrah leaves wreckage: the dark memorials of a salty monument and a salty, unproductive sea. And in so doing, it reminds us of how wrecked landscapes embody their own histories of suffering and loss but also, I want to suggest on these final pages, the possibility of reclamation and transformation.

The idea that wrecked landscapes function as their own memorials is elaborated by the *Cleanness* poet in the lengthy description of the Dead Sea, which comes to cover the fire-scorched plains. The poem depicts the sea as a wasteland, an absence created by the divine vengeance "þat voyded þise places" (that voided these places; 153/1013). Following the destruction of Sodom and Gomorrah, *Cleanness* describes the postapocalyptic scene, explaining that "Alle þyse ar teches & tokenes to trow vpon ȝet, / & wittnesse of þat wykked werk, & þe wrake after" (All these are signs and tokens to think about / and witnesses of the wicked deeds and the resulting wrake; 155/1049–50). The wrecked landscape here stands as witness. At first glance, what remains after this total annihilation seems to be a wasteland, apocalyptic in its description, a dead place that reeks even more than the vomit-scented winds generated by the Sodomites' violent words.[116]

Drawing on commonplaces of contemporary travel literature, including that of *Mandeville's Travels*, the *Cleanness* poet brings a striking naturalism to his depiction of this languishing landscape, just as he did to his descriptions of catastrophic storms:

> hit is brod and boþemlez, and bitter as þe galle,
> And noȝt may lenge in þat lake þat any lyf berez,
> And alle þe costez of kynde hit combrez vchone.
> For lay þeron a lump of led, and hit on loft fletez,
> And folde þeron a lyȝt fyþer, and hit to founs synkkez;
> And þer water may walter to wete any erþe
> Schal neuer grene þeron growe, gresse ne wod nawþer. (154/1022–28)

> (it is broad and bottomless and bitter as gall,
> and nothing may linger in that lake that carries any life,
> and it destroys all of nature's qualities.
> For if you lay a lump of lead there, it floats to the top,
> and rest a light feather on it, and it sinks to the bottom;

> And where its waters may flow to wet any ground
> vegetation will never grow there, neither grass nor wood.)

The laws of nature no longer hold here. What remains, in A. C. Spearing's words, is "a landscape of perverse contradictions, where lead floats, feathers sink, and delicious fruit turns to ashes."[117] The description itself is paradoxical, though the sea is bottomless, a feather will sink to its "founs" (floor). Its ashen fruit is an inversion of the Edenic apple. At first blush, the site seems inherently unproductive. Like an atomic wasteland, nothing is growing, and nothing ever will. The landscape is stripped of life of vitality and possibility. And, the poet claims, it is actively destructive.

But, yet. There is always a "but, yet," always a story that begins in the emptiness left by another story's ending. In her work on disturbance ecologies, the anthropologist Anna Lowenhaupt Tsing suggests the helpfulness of reorienting our expectations about the aftermaths of significant ecological disturbances by acknowledging that ruins are also sites of emergence of new possibilities.[118] And even the *Cleanness* poet seems to hint that destruction is not the end of this story. Following this general description of the unnatural properties of the deadly water, he inserts a catalog of the site's geological oddities. The poet first lists the rocks and minerals that can be found along coastlines and in the waters:

> And as hit is corsed of kynde and hit coostez als,
> Þe clay þat clenges þerby arn corsyes strong,
> As alum and alkaran, þat angre arn boþe,
> Soufre sour and saundyuer, and oþer such mony;
> And þer waltez of þat water in waxlokes grete
> Þe spumande aspaltoun þat spyserez sellen;
> And suche is alle þe soyle by þat se halues,
> Þat fel fretes þe flesch and festres bones. (154/1033–40)
>
> (And as it is cursed by nature and also its coasts
> the clays that cling nearby are strong corrosives,
> like alum and bitumen, that are both bitter,
> sour sulfur and sandiver, and many other like them;
> And where the water surges in huge waxy curls
> the foaming asphalt that spice merchants sell;
> and such is all the soil that borders the sea,
> that violently devours the flesh and festers bones.)

Though it is surely intended to be off-putting, this description sketches the surprising afterlives of this scarred topography. For even though it is devoid of life, this ruined landscape is nonetheless still useful; from it can be salvaged the materials of human medicine, shelter, and production. Sources as varied as Josephus, Pliny, and Mandeville all attest to the practical and medicinal uses of the Dead Sea's byproducts. Sandiver (or sandever), for instance, is an alkalized mineral used often in late medieval medicinal recipes.[119] The exceptionally salinic water has long been harvested for table salt. *Cleanness* itself gestures toward how contemporary spice merchants sell the asphalt, which has been used for millennia as an adhesive, sealant, mortar, medicine, and embalmment.[120] Still today, blocks of asphalt periodically rise to the surface of the Dead Sea.[121] Thus, despite the poet's claims about the landscape's dead emptiness, the symbolism here is ambivalent. Although many of the qualities the poem describes are accurate and although the landscape is indeed a desolate one, the Dead Sea has never been an unproductive wasteland.[122] It is a scarred landscape, but of course, scarred landscapes (like bodily scars) are signs not only of past wounds but also perhaps of their regeneration and healing.

In this, scenes of disaster and catastrophe invite us to reflect on what can emerge from emergency. What remains is both *wreckage* and *salvage*. These two terms are intimately entwined. Wreckage from one perspective may be salvage from another. To salvage is to reclaim. In the language of the Bible, we might even call this redemption, resurrection, or re-creation.

Some days when I walk the rocky shores of the reservoir that covers the Salt Creek valley just a few miles south of my home, I crouch to examine the stony brachiopods, the tubular crinoids, and trilobite tracings that litter the coastline of the vast lake. Those strange sea creatures memorialized in stone, resurfacing only after the waters returned, speak to deep time. Their once lively bodies are now mineral. The geodes strewn across the shore, too, their crystal-filled orbs embodying the pressures that eons placed upon the earth. Most days, soft waves lap against these remnants, pulling them back into the deeps or casting them out again. Other days, when the lake is placid, I amble over its fossil-laden shores. The past crackles underfoot. The lake's rocky edges are strewn with these remnants and wreckage of the Paleozoic era, when it was covered by that vast shallow sea, long before the engineers flooded these valleys again in the latter half of the twentieth century.

Just down the road is a cemetery where the human remains of those who once inhabited this valley have been moved. In 1962, all eight cemeteries in the eleven thousand acres that would soon be submerged were dug up; their coffins reburied on higher ground. The communities of those who would remember them were scattered and displaced. These were not my people, I am not native to this place, but I am becoming beholden to it. When I walk the trails named for the drowned towns, when I happen upon ruined buildings at its edges, when I dig in the sand for fossils, when I scoop up the waters, letting them trickle through my fingers, I glance back. Attending deeply to this place, learning to look beyond its present form, is shaping my sense of responsibility for it.

Donna Haraway writes that the Anthropocene is a time "of great mass death and extinction; of onrushing disasters, whose unpredictable specificities are foolishly taken as unknowability itself; of refusing to know and to cultivate the capacity of response-ability; of refusing to be present in and to onrushing catastrophe in time; of unprecedented looking away."[123]

Yet if the history of disaster is often written by those who flee or look away, the medieval biblical poems this chapter has considered both advocate such turning and do not entirely allow it. They frequently suspend their readers between compassionate witness and voyeurism, between curiosity and care, between intimacy and distance. And in doing so, they situate readers as both wrecked and beholden, and they invite presence. They call us to "stay with the trouble."

To be beholden is, in our usual modern sense, to be obligated or indebted by some sort of connection, intimacy, or oath. The word derives from the Old English *bihaldan*, which introduces this sense of holding, or holding together. But, in Middle English, the verb *beholden*, like our *behold*, also means to hold the gaze, to see, to focus, to turn one's thoughts or attention to something, to contemplate.[124] Like "wrake," the multiplicity of "beholden" undergirds my understanding of these texts. For we often become beholden to that which we behold, whether or not we acknowledge the fact. In medieval optical theory, this association was literalized. In the theory of intromission, the objects of the gaze were understood to enter into the eye and imprint on the mind and heart of the observer. In a sense, then, the viewer quite literally embodies what she sees.[125] To behold is to become beholden, to hold an object or scene within ourselves. For good or ill, it becomes part of us.

Such lessons may not be particularly profound, but when it comes to disaster, as these texts seem to know, profundity is far less important than presence and attention. One way we can process catastrophes too large for us to fully comprehend—pandemic, disastrous floods and fires, climate change—is do exactly what these writers have done: retell the old stories, the archetypal ones, and see how they might resonate differently when read in our moment. Doing so, quite simply, reminds us we are not alone. It reminds us that we, too, are beholden—to people and ideas and stories long gone. It draws us into a temporally deep community of victims and survivors; it invites us to bear witness, and to look at stories and our own world from new perspectives. And in retelling, we may also be able to begin to articulate something about our shared dilemmas of inhabiting a world marked by catastrophe and loss. For, perhaps, in the end, *more* backward glances—toward devastated landscapes, toward suffering, toward the past—are exactly what we need.

4

Ordinary Apocalypses

Wondrous Weather in Early England

> With wederes and with wondres he warneth us with a whistlere.
> (With weather and with wonders, he warns us with a whistler.)
> WILLIAM LANGLAND, *Piers Plowman*

In June I walk under a flat sky. The air is steeped in ash. Even though I inhale through a mask, the taste of smoke is on my tongue. It reminds me of the lingering scent of a campfire, how it clings to your clothes and hair for days. Until now, I have only witnessed wildfire from afar. It is one thing to see images of it, another to breathe it in. Air quality warnings caution of the risks of going outside. Newspaper photographs from cities farther north and east show burnt orange skies, apocalyptic but luminous. Here the air tends toward the ashen, softening everything, turning the distant horizon into a J. M. W. Turner painting.

Perhaps, I think, this is what it is to be like Lot, far from the fire, in relative safety but not immune to its effects. The scale of the fires consuming the Canadian wilderness hundreds of miles north challenges comprehension and even imagination: 18.4 million hectares, larger than the state of North Dakota; nearly nine times the area incinerated in any normal Canadian fire season. In southern Indiana, I inhale relics of destroyed forest with every breath; the particles agitate my eyes. Ashes to ashes. Later in the fall, a friend will call me as she drives through Appalachia, where flames are lapping up foothills near Interstate 40. It all feels portentous. The burning world that prophets and scientists have long predicted, already here. Even those of us far from the epicenter live downstream from disaster. What happens when we find ourselves no longer witnesses of the catastrophe, but in the thick of it . . . as we, in fact, are? How do we make sense of and dwell in a world in which catastrophe has become ordinary? What is at stake in acknowledging what we once would have seen as extraordinary weather as the "new normal," a phrase, Zadie Smith writes, that may be "the most melancholy of all the euphemisms"?[1]

In our moment, it does not take a disaster of the scale of the Canadian wildfires to trigger such questions.[2] Modern climate catastrophe registers as both chronic and acute. The more quotidian signs of a warming world are everywhere: in snowless winters where there once was always snow, in the rise of dangerous storms, in parched fields, in flooded fields, in the growing tide of climate migrants who seek more livable lands. We inhabit a world that is deeply unsettled, a world in which apocalypse is quotidian. Even so, increasingly frequent ecological catastrophes can continue to register as exceptions to a larger rule of climatic predictability. In this chapter, I'm interested in how medieval texts navigated these tensions between exceptional and ordinary catastrophes, in how they tried to make sense of seeming disorder. How did they understand and depict natural disasters in an ecologically precarious age?

People have long interpreted unusual weather both proleptically and metonymically, judging and forecasting larger patterns from local events, even when they name an extreme weather event as unprecedented. To interpret the weather this way is roughly analogous to how we read a book or poem.[3] We scan for patterns, likenesses, and repetitions. We look for causes and precedents. We piece together part and whole. We search for significance, even if we suspect there may be no deeper meaning to be found. That we seek to locate apparently anomalous events within larger patterns suggests a shared horizon of expectation about what weather or climate *should* be like.[4]

Such expectations about climatological predictability are deeply rooted in our mythologies, literature, and histories as well as in our experience.[5] Even *Cleanness*, a poem so committed to making visible the horror of extraordinary catastrophes, insists that they are exceptions to a rule. After describing the devastation wrought by the biblical Flood, the poet inserts a lyrical passage emphasizing the climatological regularity of the world:

> Sesounez schal yow neuer sese of sede ne of heruest,
> Ne hete, ne no harde forst, vmbre ne droȝþe,
> Ne þe swetnesse of somer, ne þe sadde wynter,
> Ne þe nyȝt, ne þe day, ne þe newe ȝerez,
> But euer renne restlez. (133/523–27)

> (Seasons shall never cease for you, neither the planting nor the harvest,
> neither the heat, nor the hard frost, clouds nor drought,
> neither the sweetness of summer, nor the somber winter,
> neither night, nor day, nor new years,
> but will always run restlessly.)

In the wake of the near-universal catastrophe of the Flood, a promise of a return to order should provide comfort. Yet, this passage unsettles. Its concatenation of climate conditions articulates one thing—that the world will henceforth be predictable—and embeds another in its form and syntax: that the world still pulses with precarity. Extending the structure of its source text, Genesis 8:22 ("All the days of the earth, seedtime and harvest, cold and heat, summer and winter, night and day, shall not cease"), *Cleanness* frames its catalog of seasonal cycles within doubled, then tripled, then quadrupled negations: "never cease ... ne ... ne ... ne." This piling up of negation opens—even insists on—the possibility of the world being otherwise, insofar as it implies that seasons *could* cease. We can only receive this vision as an image of hope when we understand compound negation as affirmation.[6] Even in doing so, that repeated "ne" jars as it echoes in the memory, undermining what the passage affirms, straining against certainty, and reminding us that all these things will, one day, surrender to nothingness. As the passage unfolds, it both articulates and creates a sense of restlessness, a feeling that it will only name in its final line. For while *restles* in Middle English can signal the hopefulness of the "unceasing," it more often chimes the darker tones of the "uneasy" or the "unsettled."[7] To name the world restless is to embrace that its order and regularity are vulnerable and contingent, or even that its order *is* contingency, always subject to alteration.

As this moment in *Cleanness* might remind us, most late medieval thinkers understood the universe to be governed by a paradox.[8] Even as they proclaimed the orderliness and legibility of the cosmos, they frequently *experienced* that order as precarious and unknowable. H. H. Lamb opens his foundational study of climate history with precisely this point: "Most generations of mankind in most parts of the world have regarded the climate as an unreliable, shifting, fluctuating thing."[9] In the pages that follow, I explore several medieval literary attempts to comprehend and represent the baffling irregularity of the climate, a mutability made visible by catastrophically bad weather.

Although there is no single synonym for what we would now call "catastrophe" in Middle English, climatological abnormalities are sometimes called "wonders" (or marvels, ferlies, selcouths, prodigies). In medieval thinking, a wonder disrupts the orderliness of nature. It invites attention and it unmoors those who encounter or experience it. It raises questions about the stability and consistency of the larger order. Wonders also take us to the limits of what can be articulated or represented; they wound us. As Lorraine Daston and Katherine Park have explored, "wonders and wonder limned the cognitive boundaries between the natural and the unnatural and between the known and the unknown."[10] Characterized by their apparent singularity, wonders break from and thus imply the fragility of any larger order.[11] Yet as *exceptions* to the rule, it's a bit hard to see how or why ecological wonders such as catastrophes should be read as meaningful. How exactly can a devastating flood or a tumultuous earthquake be understood as significant for human beings, when its most immediate effect is to draw us into a place of uncertainty or unknowing?

The epistemological and representational challenges presented by ecological catastrophe are not often entertained in the relatively limited corpus of medieval disaster writing. In the handful of extant texts that attest to contemporary disasters in medieval England, most only mention unusual ecological or geological phenomena in passing.[12] Chronicle accounts provide much of the evidence we now have, but these tend toward the informational and descriptive, though they sometimes offer analysis, reflection, or even moralization. Encyclopedic and scientific texts typically speak in general terms about floods, winds, and fires rather than exploring specific instances. Practical and prognostic texts such as moon manuals and agricultural treatises (the medieval equivalents of farmers' almanacs), explain the larger ecological and cosmological effects of unusual weather that *could* happen.[13] As we have seen, sermons occasionally gesture toward contemporary disasters, seeing them as marks of the general disorder of a fallen world, punishments for sin, portents of a coming apocalypse, and prods to penance. There is even less explicit consideration of contemporary natural disasters to be found in medieval poetry, though poems frequently represent and explore the meanings of disasters in the biblical or classical past.

The rarity of poetic representation of contemporary catastrophes makes its own kind of sense. Catastrophe challenges our habits of thought and modes of representation. As David Coley has explored, even the Black Death—surely the most devastating catastrophe in a century of climatological catastrophes—is usually only referenced indirectly in English literature, though it clearly shaped the lives and values of generations of medieval people.[14] It may be, as Maurice Blanchot and others have insisted, that disaster of a certain magnitude is always nearly unrepresentable. "It is the limit of writing," Blanchot writes; "the disaster de-scribes."[15] Ecocritics such as Amitav Ghosh and Ursula K. Heise have similarly emphasized that a significant challenge of engaging climate disaster in our own moment is finding modes of representation adequate to the nearly unthinkable scale of the crisis.[16] They have suggested that we need better stories, that narrative may help us imagine the unimaginable, the unthinkable, and the contingent.[17] Scholars of poetry have also begun to show how poetic forms might offer ways into and around these epistemological and representational difficulties.[18]

Whereas chapter 3 examined how representations of biblical catastrophes explore modes of response by toggling between the cosmic and microcosmic and by exploring the stakes of compassionate witness, this chapter considers how medieval writers engage with climatological catastrophe in their own moment, focusing on how they employ poetic forms in innovative ways to navigate the paradox of nature's order and disorder, giving shape to and inviting meditation on untamable and incomprehensible forces.[19] I attend primarily to regional rather than planetary catastrophes because although the climate was indeed undergoing a tumultuous shift in the fourteenth century, medieval people, like many people now, were mainly aware of the local impacts of larger climatological changes.[20] And whereas chapter 3 explored the fraught apprehension of calamitous floods and fires in the biblical past, I here look at the challenges of comprehending and representing natural disasters in the medieval present. To put this another way, this chapter moves from myth to history, focusing largely on ecological catastrophes that actually happened. However, I am less interested in gathering data about these events than in what literary form can tell us about the difficulties of comprehending, representing, and responding to them. And so, while I gesture here toward how medieval texts seek meaning in climatological anomalies, I continue to reflect on the subtler arts these texts use to ruminate on, if never resolve, the sensory, affective, and temporal experience of ecological disaster.

Our guides in this unsettled terrain will be a small set of poets and chroniclers who attempt to represent wondrous weather and geological disasters. As they search for significance in these events, often treating them as warnings, these writers are confronted with the limits of language and meaning making in the face of catastrophe. They seek forms of expression that promise to impose order on disorder, but those forms often only underscore the extent to which disaster unmoors those who experience it. They aim to anchor disaster in time but ultimately emphasize how catastrophic time is out of joint. As they navigate these tensions, the texts this chapter considers treat ecological catastrophes as *ordinary apocalypses*. By this admittedly oxymoronic phrase, I wish to suggest both the ways in which writers attempt to fit anomalous or inassimilable ecological marvels into a cosmic *ordo*, and also how catastrophe resists such framing.[21] The climatological catastrophes I examine are apocalyptic in both our modern and the original senses of the term: they are simultaneously tragedies and midwives of new subjectivities, communities, or worlds.[22]

The medieval texts we will encounter in this chapter thus assert the experience of ecological catastrophes as unprecedented and reach for patterns, the incomprehensibility of disaster and the desire to find meaning in it, the ineffability of catastrophe and the importance of representing it. To explore these paradoxes, they experiment with many of the poetic forms that we have encountered in this book: particularly negations and inversions, jarring juxtapositions, anaphora, refrains and other echoing repetitions, shifts in scale, and inexpressibility tropes. And in so doing, they draw us into the complexities of living in, making sense of, and responding to an ecologically unpredictable world.

To explore these early experiments in writing disaster, this chapter brings poetry and historical writing into conversation, attending to accounts of three late medieval climatological and geological catastrophes: a volcanic winter, a devastating wind, and a portentous earthquake. Unlike most of the other texts I have considered in this book, the works that I examine here do not reimagine biblical narratives, though the chapter's centerpiece, the fourteenth-century dream vision *Piers Plowman*, is an intensely biblical poem, weaving biblical narratives and passages into its larger allegorical frame.[23] Instead, this chapter takes up accounts situated in the long middle of sacred time—the present. We begin with brief glance at how a thirteenth-century chronicler, Matthew Paris, employs poetic conventions when writing an account of the effects of the devastating volcanic winter of 1257 and 1258 to express the nearly inexpressible horror of the catastrophe. We then turn to poetry produced in the wake of the catastrophic second half of the fourteenth century, looking first at how ecological disaster forms the dynamic background of *Piers Plowman*, troubling the poem's certainty about the legibility of the natural world and complicating the lessons that attention to creation promises. In several moments in his poem, William Langland attempts to confront contemporary crises and catastrophes head-on, but his treatment of a destructive windstorm in 1362 suggests how a catastrophic event can "de-scribe" itself, disrupting and unsettling its audience but also catalyzing something new.[24] My final example, a lyrical account of an earthquake that shook southern England in 1382, also represents catastrophe as disruption, suggesting that what it *can* do is call those who experience it to greater attentiveness, functioning as an incitement to moral reflection and action. Taken together, these engagements with disaster reveal some of the ways that premodern writers attempted to navigate the shock of ordinary apocalypses by situating them in larger patterns, by linking the ecological and the social, and by modeling the difficult necessity of attending and responding to inexplicable, even ineffable, destruction.

Climate Catastrophe, History, and Poetic Convention

> Whatever
> contracts keep us social compel us now
> to disorder the disorder.
> CLAUDIA RANKINE, "Weather"

The most consistent sources of information about medieval natural disasters are chronicles, a genre characterized by a commitment to ordering time. Even so, their time lines are punctuated and punctured with climate catastrophes: storms strong enough to destroy church steeples, earthquakes, drought, hail, and floods.[25] Yet if they sometimes linger on the description of these events or provide a humanizing anecdote, their largely linear, teleological structure tends to emphasize the social and the political more than the environmental. In chronicles, ecological catastrophes often function as little more than the dynamic backdrops against which human history unfolds and to which it, on occasion, responds.[26] Yet sometimes a catastrophe asserts itself as an actor on the historical stage, rupturing the narrative and demanding to be reckoned with even if it can't be fully comprehended.[27] In such moments, as this section explores, some writers draw on poetic devices—intricate description, tropes, repetitions, and surprising disruptions—to approximate the cognitive and affective experiences generated by catastrophe, which we often apprehend as a unsettling mix of wonder, uncertainty, horror, and sorrow.

The challenges of representing a catastrophe of nearly unimaginable scale are evident in at least one historical treatment of what may now be the most well-known ecological catastrophe of the Middle Ages: the explosion of the Samalas volcano and the volcanic winter it produced in Europe. Sometime between May 1257 and November 1258, a massive volcano erupted in Indonesia, generating "the largest sulfur signature of any eruption in the Holocene."[28] The eruption had planetary repercussions, producing unusual environmental phenomena around the world. Thanks to the work of modern environmental historians and climate scientists, we now know that lingering atmospheric particulate matter contributed to the prolonged volcanic winter across Europe. The temporary drop of up to 2 degrees Celsius (about 3.6 degrees Fahrenheit) in temperatures led to years of agricultural disasters and famine.[29]

Although medieval chroniclers did not know the ultimate cause of these climatological changes, their accounts of the weather offer plenty of anecdotal evidence of the eruption's disquieting effects. On November 12, 1258, a total lunar eclipse was recorded in Genoa, Italy. In England, the volcanic ash seems to have contributed to several years of widespread crop failure. The thirteenth-century English Benedictine monk and chronicler Matthew Paris (ca. 1200–1259), paints a particularly grim picture of the spring of 1258:

> In this year, the north wind (Boreas) blew incessantly for several months, when April and May and the principal part of June, had passed, and scarcely were there visible any of the small and rare plants, or any shooting buds of flowers; and in consequence, but small hopes were entertained of the fruit crops. Owing to the scarcity of wheat, a very large number of poor people died; and dead

bodies were found in all directions, swollen by hunger and livid, lying by fives and sixes in pigsties, on dunghills, and in the muddy streets. Those who had houses did not dare, in their own state of need, to provide hospitality for the dying, for fear of contagion.[30]

This bleak description is only one in a series of climatological snapshots in Matthew's universal history, the *Chronica Majora*.[31] As this passage suggests, 1257 and 1258 were catastrophic years for England, especially affecting its poor. On the surface, the terrible details of Matthew's account differ little from the descriptions of famine, plague, and natural disaster that resound as dark refrains in many other late medieval chronicles. Appropriate to its chronicle form, the passage emphasizes causal relationships: because of the incessant north wind in the spring, people lost hope of fall crops; because of the "scarcity of wheat," people starved. Yet the passage also implies that such causes cannot entirely account for the horrific suffering generated by the catastrophe.

Resonating through this passage are another set of contexts that begin to suggest the challenges of narrating a disaster of this scale, as Matthew reaches for what the disaster has rendered barely visible. The imagery alone shocks. Matthew forces the reader's attention to scenes of barren land, dead bodies scattered across both muddy city streets and pastoral landscapes, and a culture of fear among the living. This is not all. Matthew approaches the challenge of communicating the effects of the volcanic winter by drawing from poetic conventions and gesturing toward the larger concept of regular seasonal change.

This catastrophic spring becomes a dark mirror of normal natural processes as Matthew subtly develops a contrast with the conventional trope of spring's regreening (*reverdie*) and its attendant values of gestation, fecundity, and hope. Popular in medieval European courtly literature of Matthew's own day, from the *Romaunt de la Rose* to early lyrics, the poetic convention of *reverdie* is perhaps most famously adopted in the next century by Geoffrey Chaucer in the opening lines to his *Canterbury Tales*, in which the sweet west winds of April "inspired hath in every holt and heeth / The tendre croppes" bringing vitality to the once dormant environment.[32] Matthew's account of the climatological and social catastrophe of this April and May subtly alludes to these poetic conventions that inspired Chaucer a century later even as it inverts them.[33] For if the *reverdie* trope celebrates spring's revivification and the enlivening force of the west wind, Matthew's description turns the convention on its head to emphasize the unnaturalness of this spring's disorder.[34] Where the earth swells with fecundity in the *reverdie*, here dead bodies swell, ripening unburied on the fields. Where the *reverdie*'s gentle west wind, Zephyrus, enlivens the world in the spring; this unseasonable, violent, and relentless north wind, Boreas, wind brings only death. Matthew's language navigates between images of excess (*plures, multitudo innumerabilis*) and poverty, failure, and scarcity (*paucis, deficiente*). It plays on the difference between what is expected and what comes as a shock, what is not seen and what takes its place. The failing world is implicitly measured by what it is *not*, as Matthew draws on literary convention and figures to turn it inside out and upside down.[35] In so doing, he reflects the lived experience of inhabiting a world riven by unspeakable violence and loss.

Yet there is more here. The very syntax of the passage mimics the all-encompassing horrors of the interlinked catastrophes. The persistent wind creeping across months is performed by the Latin's polysyndeton, which daisy-chains the three disastrous months with "ands" ("*Aprilis et Maii et Junii pars potissima*"). As Kathryn Schulz writes, *polysyndeton* means "many bindings." A rhetorical method of conjoining things or events, it is an accumulative rather than causal device. Polysyndeton, Schulz writes, gives a "long, slow, wavelike form . . . to sentences," which often "conjures a sense of awe."[36] Binding the three months into a single unit of time, Matthew thus gives syntactical shape to what Kate Rigby calls a "creeping catastrophe," an event of nearly imperceptible scale and slow progress.[37] Matthew's structure communicates both extension and growth. But, in a seeming paradox, the polysyndeton also holds the reader still, formally reproducing the suspension of hope for future growth ("*unde spes fructuum est suspensa*") that the passage soon names. The ground on which the reader stands is unsettled; we are caught in between massive, abstract forces and contradictory formal movements, between what we expect and what we experience. In this, the forms draw us into the feeling of the catastrophe, and we are suspended, caught for a moment in the process of the world's unraveling; its future is momentarily dark to us.

We might think of the landscape Matthew offers in this passage as a "dark ecology," characterized by malicious and untamable forces, both seen and unseen.[38] That Matthew can't know or articulate the ultimate cause of this catastrophe matters only insofar as his own unknowing inflects his engagement with the event's unthinkability. This brief passage highlights how forms sometimes work on a different level from semantics insofar as they might engage catastrophe's contradictory phenomenal movements and their effects—what is seen and experienced, what is apprehended if not comprehended.[39] For even if Matthew doesn't explicitly name these tensions, they are registered by the passage's use of imagery, repetition, implicit contrast, and negation, which disturb and disrupt. They temporarily draw the reader into the space of uncertainty and unknowing characteristic of experiencing a wonder, calamity, or horror beyond one's ken.[40] In so doing, these forms generate a version of what the romanticist Anahid Nersessian has called "nescience," a way of representing disaster "that shapes the uncertain experience of anticipating, living through, and remembering ecological catastrophe. It allows even evanescent changes in the world to become apprehensible as well as apprehensive—objects of experience and sources of anxiety."[41] The ecological changes marked by Matthew are similarly instantiated as ruptures and negations of the general order of things, communicated as objects of experience, felt if not fully thought or known.

The Unsettling Climes of *Piers Plowman*

> What we call nature is monstrous and mutating, strangely strange all the way down and all the way through.
> Reading the Book of Nature is momentously difficult.
> TIMOTHY MORTON, *Ecological Thought*

Such an experience of unknowing, or "nescience," is also at the heart of the fourteenth-century poem *Piers Plowman*, which recounts the allegorical journeys of its protagonist, Will, as he searches for meaning while traversing dreamscapes teeming with crisis, corruption, and catastrophe.[42] Written in the wake of both the Great Famine (1315–22) and the Black Death (beginning in the late 1340s), *Piers Plowman* emerges from and represents a world in which upheaval, profound loss, and ongoing instability are the norm.[43] It might be read as a poem about learning to live well in precarious times. In *Piers*, quotidian life is punctured by catastrophes, which turn the narrative in new directions. In this section, I focus mainly on one of these catastrophes—a devastating windstorm—to suggest that even as the poem frames catastrophic weather as punishment and warning, the catastrophe threatens to exceed this framing, suggesting the limits of meaning making of ecological wonders. If disaster "de-scribes" in *Piers Plowman*, it does so by folding the horrific exceptionality of the storm into a cosmic *ordo* and by unwriting forms or structures of living.[44] The poem's ordinary apocalypses call humans to attention, invite a reorientation to what is, and suggest the possibility of what could be.

That *Piers Plowman*'s landscapes are, on the whole, bleak ones, born of and shot through with crisis and catastrophe, is made clear on its first pages. The poem opens with imagery of the softness of English summer days, but within lines it begins to intimate that its concerns are shadowed by a darker mood.[45] In the Prologue, we find ourselves with the dreamer, Will, resting by a brook on a mild May morning, tired from wandering throughout the world looking for "wondres" (wonders).[46] Drifting asleep, he wakes to a series of dreamworlds, full of "selkouths" (wonders) and "ferlies" (marvels) of every kind. Yet these are not the fantastical marvels of romance that such introductions typically portend.[47] Instead, many of the "wondres" he encounters are ecological: some are pastoral visions of the plentitude and intricacy of creation; others are darker, apocalyptic or prophetic visions of floods, plagues, drought, and bad weather.

The dream vision itself is called a "ferly" in the poem's first few lines (Prologue 6), but when the dreamer repeats the term only sixty lines later, it will strike a more ominous tone: "Manye ferlies han fallen in a fewe yeres. / But Holy Chirche and hii holde bettre togidres, / The moost mischief on molde is mountynge up faste" (Many marvelous events have occurred in a few years. / Unless Holy Church and [the friars] hold together better, / the worst misfortune on earth is welling up quickly; Prologue 65–67).[48] Although the "ferly" of the opening lines suggests the marvelous setting of romances, these "ferlies" draw us back into the history and lived experience of the tragic landscapes of the fourteenth century, evoking the Great Famine and the Black Death, as well as clerical and social corruption.[49] As grimly prophetic passages like this might suggest, the poem's interests and shape are broadly apocalyptic, both pointing toward a catastrophic future and suggesting that ecological and meteorological wonders may serve as warnings in the present.[50]

Whether it is possible to find meaning in such "ferlies" is one of the main questions raised by the poem. In his first dream, Will surveys a field of people going about their lives. He turns to his guide, Lady Church, and asks "what may this be to meene?" (1.11) What is this to mean, indeed? It a persistent question, threaded through Will's observations of both the social and ecological landscapes and paralleled by the poem's other central concern: how does one flourish in such a frangible world? As insistent as Will's search for meaning is, the answers the poem offers to these questions are unstable. They multiply and shift over the course of the poem. Indeed, as James Simpson writes, *Piers Plowman* is a poem in which movement is "produced out of epistemological or cognitive limitations," out of moments of awe and uncertainty.[51]

Some of this uncertainty derives from the precarity of the poem's landscapes themselves. The agrarian settings of Will's first two dreams—the fair field of folk, and the half acre that must be plowed before a pilgrimage to Truth can begin—are under constant threat from famine, insurrection, and natural disaster.[52] The poem regularly reminds us of the vulnerability of the environment and institutions it depicts, often treating the land as "negatively revelatory," to use Nicolette Zeeman's term.[53] In these negative revelations, the land reveals absence, alienation, and lack. Following the plowing of the half acre and the ravaging of Hunger in passus 6, for instance, the dreamer prophesies imminent crop failure and famine:

> Ac I warne yow werkemen—wynneth whil ye mowe,
> For Hunger hiderward hasteth hym faste!
> He shal awake thorugh water, wastours to chaste;
> Er fyve yere be fulfilled swich famyn shal aryse:
> Thorugh flodes and thorugh foule wedres, fruytes shul faille. (6.319–23)

> (But I warn you, workmen, earn wages while you can
> because Hunger is hastening here quickly.
> He will wake up idle consumers with floods to chasten them;
> before five years have passed, such famine will arise.
> Because of floods and foul weather, crops will fail.)

Here ecological and climatological catastrophes—floods, foul weather, and subsequent crop failure—set into motion human tragedy: when disaster strikes and the land fails, people starve.[54] Such catastrophes were surely within living memory for some readers of *Piers Plowman*, who would have survived the Great Famine. Indeed, the prophecy here resonates in part because it has already happened. And since it has already happened, it surely could happen again. The prophecy represents catastrophe as chronic. It situates its audience in an unsettled middle space, in a place of experience but also expectation.

The prophecy also provides a glimpse of hope that it might be possible to prepare for future catastrophes. Here, natural disasters are punishments for human behavior and warnings about possible futures if such behavior continues unchecked. Ecosystemic devastation points to the need for moral transformation but also practical response. Since the promised famine will be a means of chastising those "wasters" who refuse to labor on the land, the prophecy implies, to avoid such chastisement, don't be an idle consumer, be an active worker who contributes to the larger community.[55] Even in a prophecy, the future is not entirely predetermined. Navigating the "negatively revelatory" function of ordinary apocalypses, the poem suggests, requires understanding the multiplicity of their temporalities, meanings, and outcomes.[56]

Yet, it is an earlier moment in the poem focused on another "negatively revelatory" ecological catastrophe that first moves the dreamer from attention to action.[57] In the opening five passus, which form a single dream, Will is primarily a spectator, observing the world from the fields to the court, inquiring periodically about what it all means. The fifth passus marks a new dream and a new trajectory for the poem, turning from the question of "What is false?" to "where is truth to be found?" and "How does one live well in the world?"[58]

In this dream's opening lines, the allegorical personification, Reason, preaches a sermon that treats recent plagues and storms as "ensamples" (examples):

> He preved that thise pestilences was for pure synne,
> And the south-west wynd on Saterday at even
> Was pertliche for pryde, and for no point ellis.
> Pyries and plum-trees were puffed to the erthe,
> In ensample, [segges, that ye] sholden do the bettre.
> Beches and brode okes were blowen to the grounde
> and turned upward here tail in tokenynge of drede
> That dedly synne er domesday shal fordoon hem alle. (5.13–20)

> (He showed that these plagues were caused only by sin,
> and that the southwestern wind on Saturday evening
> was clearly caused by pride, and for no other reason.
> Pear trees and plum trees were puffed to the earth,
> as an example, (men, that you) should do better.
> Beeches and broad oaks were blown to the ground
> And their roots turned upside down as a sign of dread
> That deadly sin before doomsday will destroy them all.)

At first glance, this sermon is a straightforward articulation of the "punishment paradigm": Reason characterizes both the pestilence and the storm as the result of human sin, emphasizing the anthropogenic nature of ecological catastrophe.[59] And indeed, the idea that human disorder corrupts nature's order is a through line of the poem. Yet, this reference to a particular historical catastrophe by an allegorical personification in a dream vision registers as both an ecological and a formal disturbance, temporarily blurring the line between imaginative allegory and history. Rather than describe the catastrophe, Reason "de-scribes" it, unwriting its horrific particularity and reframing it as idea, "ensample," and token. In his hands, ecological crisis becomes spiritual opportunity.

Reason's allusion to the great windstorm of 1362 appears in all three versions of the poem and provides the *terminus post quem* (latest possible date) for the A-text, usually considered the earliest version of the poem.[60] It is thus a key scene for locating *Piers Plowman* within its historical context. And it is a key scene for the narrative of the poem itself: Reason's invocation of this catastrophe sets into motion the central action of the poem—the communal move toward repentance, the pilgrimage to Truth, and the dreamer's quest to understand what it means to "do well" in a catastrophic world.

As many chronicles attest, the southwestern wind to which Reason appeals was no ordinary gust, though you may not guess that from Reason's brief account of it. The devastating gale beginning Saturday, January 15, 1362, was one of the most notable ecological disasters of the fourteenth century in England and abroad. Its fierce winds originated in the Atlantic, swept through Ireland, and destroyed English forests and cities, toppling towers and spires, including that of Norwich Cathedral. Although the death toll was surprisingly low in England and Ireland, the storm resulted in a surge of the North Sea the following day (Saint Marcellus's feast day) in the Low Countries that flooded coastlines, killed up to 25,000 people (some chronicle accounts claim mortalities of up to 100,000), and permanently swallowed more than fifty parishes in northern Europe and at least one English town (Dunwich).[61] Called the *Grote Mandrenke*, the "great drowning of humanity," this devastation has been described as "the greatest North Sea flood disaster in historical times."[62]

Unsurprisingly given the widespread destruction the storm left in its wake, when late medieval chronicles mention it, they often describe its massive scale or narrate it horrors. What chroniclers seem to be most struck by is the unprecedented, marvelous, and unspeakable nature of the storm. They attempt to communicate the ineffable horror of the devastation with particular details of its destruction. Perhaps the fullest account of the effects of the windstorm is in the fourteenth century *Chronicle of Anonymous of Canterbury*, which breathlessly recounts the storm's effects:

> Around the hour of vespers on that day, dreadful storms and whirlwinds such as had never been seen or heard before occurred in England, causing houses and buildings for the most part to come crashing to the ground, while some others, having had their roofs blown off by the force of the winds, were left in the ruined state; and fruit trees in gardens and other places, along with other trees standing in the woods and elsewhere, were wrenched from the earth by their roots with a great crash, as if the Day of Judgement were at hand, and fear and trembling gripped the people of England to such an extent that no one knew where he could safely hide, for church towers, windmills, and many dwelling-houses collapsed to the ground, although without much bodily injury.[63]

Beginning with the unprecedented nature of the storms ("such as had never been seen or heard before"), the chronicle also emphasizes its effects—structural, agricultural, and emotional. The imagery emphasizes the crashing and the collapsing of buildings and trees but then gestures toward the fear and uncertainty it generated as people discovered there was nowhere safe to shelter.

And then, perhaps to emphasize this point about the danger, the chronicle illustrates the devastation with a story of an individual's experience of the winds, recounting how when an Augustinian friar, Brother John de Sutton, had gone to close the doors against the storm, "a powerful and violent gust of wind picked him up off of the ground and hurled him through the middle of one of the windows into their garden, where—through the agency of an evil spirit, so it is believed—he was eventually left, without having been injured."[64] From this specific scene, the chronicler goes on to generalize, noting, first, that this is just one of many "extraordinary accidents" that the storm effected in London and elsewhere in England, and second, that the effects of the devastating storm lingered: "the houses and buildings which were thus destroyed by this wind remained ruined and unrepaired because of the lack of workmen." Although the storm itself did not cause great mortality in England, as the chronicler suggests, it came in the wake of the ongoing labor crises caused by the midcentury pandemics. Because there simply were not enough workers to go around, the country fell into a state of ruin. And, the chronicle implies, that ruination offers a continued witness to the strength of the storm.

Other accounts also focus on the extensive damage done to the physical landscape, to trees and buildings. Consider, for example, the following description by John of Reading:

> On the 15th day of January, the west or south wind called Affricus threw down and broke in pieces belfries, towers, trees, buildings, and other strong things, the weak things being spared, and on land, as well as by sea, irretrievably destroyed good things: there hardly remained entire a house or a tree in its course. The strength of this wind did not abate for seven days.[65]

John anthropomorphizes the wind.[66] Cataloging its victims (belfries, towers, trees, buildings), he builds a sense of loss through accumulation. And he emphasizes the material and temporal scope of the destruction. Henry Knighton's *Chronicle* (1337–96) paints a similar picture, describing the storm as "unprecedented" and its aftermath as "horrific":

> In that year on 16 Kal. February [15 January 1361] there arose a terrible and most violent storm of wind, namely upon the day and night of the feast of St Anthony, such as it was thought had never been seen in any earlier times, far beyond anything that I can tell, it flattened woods, orchards, and all kinds of trees, and tore up by their roots many more than could be believed, and destroyed churches, mills, bell-towers, walls, and houses. In London it did incalculable damage to towers, and to churches and houses.[67]

Like John of Reading, Knighton focuses primarily on the extreme violence of the winds and the ruination of the physical landscape, adopting both the inexpressibility topos and an accumulative aesthetic to suggest the horrific magnitude of the catastrophe. Knighton lists its nonhuman victims first (woods, orchards, trees) and then surveys its damage to human constructions (churches, mills, bell towers, walls, houses). This catastrophic wind is like nothing that has been seen before. The scale of its devastation strains human expression (it is "beyond anything I can tell") and comprehension (it is "more than could be believed"). The extent of the destruction is unbelievable, its damage "incalculable." Neither Knighton nor John of Reading attempts to explain the cause of the wind; they only recount its horrific physical effects.

Considered alongside these historical accounts, which describe the disaster with awe, incomprehensibility, and horror, Reason's treatment of the event registers as almost quotidian, just one of the "manye ferlies" that provide the dynamic ecological backdrop before which the poem's allegorical action unfolds. "Remember that thing that happened last Saturday night," he says. He does not succumb to the inexpressibility topos. He does not speak of the storm as unprecedented. He does not treat the wind as wondrous or even particularly exceptional. His mention of uprooted trees seems prompted more by the moral and apocalyptic potential of the image than a desire to portray the horror of its devastation, and he entirely omits the extensive ruination of human structures resulting from the storm.

Instead of emphasizing shock and awe, Reason aims to make the storm legible and morally useful. He does so by sketching out several possible meanings, gesturing toward multiple temporal contexts, and leaving other details unsaid. And in so doing, he transforms the catastrophe into an ordinary apocalypse, one that attests to cosmic order. Yet, the temporal order he suggests is multiple and complex. Reason situates the disaster within overlapping time frames: the storm is an effect of past wrongdoing, an "ensample" for present action, and a "token" of apocalypse to come.[68] Gesturing from past to present to future, this "ensample" requires reading ecological signs as temporally saturated if morally straightforward. In his account of it, the storm was caused by human pride in order to spur moral transformation and foreshadow the future destruction of all beings.

Interestingly, he does not explicitly say that *God* causes the storm to chastise pride.[69] Here, as in the prophecy about coming floods and famine in passus 6, the poem ascribes blame to people for ecological crisis rather than to divine anger, as if to imply that humans will be their own undoing. That human sin seeps into and disorders the more-than-human world is suggested by the final line's prophecy that deadly sin will destroy "hem alle." The grammatical antecedent here seems to be trees, through the passage is surely imagining a mass extinction that is human as well as arboreal. If humans don't change their ways, Reason warns, the end of all things may be nigh. For in

Reason's sermon, as in the poem more generally, nature's disorders are physical evidence of the toll human excess takes on the more-than-human world. Reason's voice here is both explanatory and prophetic, resolute in its absolute certainty about the meaning of the catastrophe.[70]

Yet such certainty about the cause and meaning of this disaster rests uneasily in a poem so invested in probing what D. Vance Smith calls "the unknowability of the ultimate causes of things."[71] And, indeed, the multiple, overlapping temporalities of his explanation belie Reason's claim to offer a straightforward account, suggesting that there remains something irreducible and unrepresentable about the catastrophe. They do not, however, make his sermon any less effective. In the hands of a preacher like Reason, a seemingly exceptional event like the Saint Maurus's Day windstorm can be understood as ordinary, part of discernible patterns. The diseases and disasters that contribute to the precarity of existence, he insists, have identifiable human causes and moral purposes and should be read as "negatively revelatory." This idea echoes across the poem. As a later passage puts it, like birds called to feed by whistling, so too, humans are called to attention and conversion by God, who "with wederes and with wondres . . . warneth us with a whistlere" (with weather and with wonders . . . warns us with a whistler; 15. 483). Reason's sermon calls attention to a ravaged landscape to encourage his audience to change their ways. For in the end, moral and social transformation is his aim.

Reason is in good company in moralizing a climatological catastrophe by seeing it as the effect of sin or a harbinger of things to come. Medieval sermons often frame ecological disasters as punishments or apocalyptic signs.[72] A sixth-century sermon by Gregory the Great that details how contemporary earthquakes, plagues, and famines were apocalyptic was included in medieval breviaries and read yearly during Advent.[73] And, as we will see in chapter 5, many Advent sermons instructed their listeners more generally to look for signs of ecosystemic collapse as portents of the coming apocalypse. Other writers and preachers moralized the Saint Maurus's Day storm. In a sermon preached on the third Sunday after Easter about a decade after the 1362 storm, Thomas Brinton similarly recalls the strong winds as a sign of God's judgment and a reminder to fear God.[74] Other accounts also situate the catastrophic storm within the "punishment paradigm." One fourteenth-century universal history comments that "it was believed by some that the misfortune was a scourging of God."[75] Another chronicle names a much more specific source of the disaster, tournaments, seeing the wind as "the wretched omens of these jousts, the harbingers of future evils."[76] In his own brief homiletic reference to the storm, Reason similarly suggests the anthropogenic nature of ecosystemic crisis and insists on the exemplarity of ecological disasters: humans inflict their brokenness on the rest of creation, and thus they need to learn to read creation's ordinary apocalypses—its storms, earthquakes, pestilences—as signs of their sin and invitations to change.

Considered within *Piers Plowman* as a whole, the exemplary, moralizing emphasis of Reason's sermon has another important context: it anticipates the exemplarist modes of reading the natural world that will be developed later in the poem. Learning to read the more-than-human world as a book of meaningful examples is, as Rebecca Davis observes, central to how the poem understands "kynde knowyng" (natural knowledge)—the idea that the created world can serve as a repository of knowledge.[77] The poem turns its full attention to the process of reading creation midway through the dreamer's journeys when Kynde (Nature) leads the dreamer to a high mountain to teach him "thorugh the wondres of this world wit for to take" (to gain understanding through the world's wonders; 11.322). The purpose of this vision of nature, Karma Lochrie writes, "is to initiate Will into wonder."[78] Will's wonder derives largely from the plentitude, diversity, and orderliness of creation. He gazes with astonishment at a regulated landscape, where each creature has its place, from "wild wormes in woods" to birds with "fleckede fetheres" (wild worms in the wodes . . . variegated feathers; 11.328-29). He immediately understands that this world and its creatures are governed by Reason.

Yet Will's reverie is fleeting. His astonished delight in ordinary wonders is met by his near immediate awareness of the *irregularity* of the human creature, who is ruled by desire more than by reason.[79] If creation retains its prelapsarian goodness, it is the human being that is disordered, a theme foreshadowed in Reason's sermon.[80] Will's realization of this reality, as Davis puts it, inaugurates the poem's crisis of "negative human exceptionalism:" the idea that the human is the locus of disorder in an otherwise orderly cosmos.[81] When the world's climatological patterns seem inconsistent and its landscapes precarious, the poem reiterates, human action is to blame. Yet attention to even the world's darker ecologies can be instructive. As Zeeman adds, medieval creation teaches doubly, through both its positive examples and its negative ones.[82] The poem insists that, be they ordinary or extraordinary, the wonders of the physical world should be examples and signs to those who know how to interpret them.[83]

Even more overwhelmed by this realization of human exceptionality and influence than he was by his awe at nature's orderliness, Will is left with a sense of disquiet and a burgeoning awareness of his own complicity in the world's disarray. As Zeeman suggests, the dreamer now experiences nature as "a site of both revelation and alienation," of knowledge and of unknowing.[84] Although Will's next allegorical guide, Imaginatif, will help him move out of his despair and return to a more positive assessment of the value of nature's lessons, some disquiet remains. The poem cannot leave behind the unease it has introduced both here and in its early attempts to find meaning in natural disasters.[85] In passus 15, another of Langland's allegorical personifications, Anima (Soul) implies that finding meaning in either ordinary or extraordinary wonders in nature might not always be easy because the world and its interpreters are both so disordered that there is now no standard against which one can measure deviation. Anima cautions Will against desiring certain sorts of knowledge by, as Davis notes, relaying the "dangerous association with curiosity."[86] To illustrate this point, Anima describes how those who once relied upon interpreting the weather or earth for their work now "fail" in their art:

> Bothe lettred and lewed beth alayed now with synne
> That no lif loveth oother, ne Oure Lord, as it semeth.
> For what thorugh werre and wikkede werkes and wederes unresonable,
> Wederwise shipmen and witty clerkes also
> Han no bileve to the lifte, ne to the loore of philosophres.
> Astronomiens alday in her art faillen,
> That whilom warned bifore what sholde bifalle after;
> Shipmen and shepherdes, that with ship and sheep wenten,
> Wisten by the walkne what sholde bitide;
> As of wedres and wyndes thei warned men ofte.
> Tiliers that tiled the erthe tolden her maistres,
> By the seed that thei sewe, what thei selle myghte,
> And what to leve and to lyve by, the lond was so trewe.
> Now failleth the folk of the flood, and of the lond bothe—
> Shepherdes and shipmen, and so do thise tilieris:
> Neither thei konneth ne knoweth oon cours bifore another.
> Astronomyens also aren at her wittes ende;
> Of that was calculed of the clemat, the contrarie thei fynde. (15.353–70)

> (Both learned and unlearned are so alloyed now with sin
> that no living being loves another, nor our Lord, it seems.
> For through war and wicked works and unreasonable weather
> weather-wise shipmen and knowledgeable clerks too
> do not trust in the sky above nor in the wisdom of philosophers.
> Astronomers fail every day in their art
> who once warned before what should happen after.
> Shipmen and shepherds that went with their ships and sheep,
> knew by the sky what would happen;
> they often warned people about weather and winds.
> Plowmen who tilled the earth, told their masters

> from the seeds that they sowed what they could expect to sell,
> and what to leave and what to live by, the land was so reliable.
> But now the people of the water and of the land both fail.
> Shepherds and shipmen, and so do these plowmen.
> They can neither understand nor interpret one pattern from another.
> Astronomers are also at their wit's end
> For what was calculated of the climate, they find to be the contrary.)

James Simpson observes how, in general, the "now-a-days (everything is going badly) topos" informs this passage, but its focus on the difficulties of environmental, meteorological, and astrological interpretation merits closer attention.[87] For this passage equivocates about the cause of this problem, neither clearly locating the fault in the disorder of the earth itself nor in its would-be interpreters. As in Reason's sermon, blame initially seems to fall on the corruption of human conscience and reason (the weathers here are "unreasonable," though other manuscripts interestingly say they are "unseasonable" or "unstable"). Yet the passage also reminds us that the world of the poem is riven with uncertainty, under constant threat of ecosystemic collapse, and that the land itself is not as "trew," or as orderly, as it should be or once was. This possibility is implied much earlier in the poem when, in the plowing of the half acre, Piers himself allows that the land itself might fail ("but if the lond faille"; 6.17). Likewise, the climate registers as "contrarie" to what the astronomers have expected of it, leaving them at the edges of understanding.[88] This universe appears to be as unreliable as are its would-be interpreters.[89]

This conflict is further manifested in the passage's structure, which works chiastically, drawing a contrast between how astronomers, shipmen, shepherds, and farmers *should* be able to read the signs of nature and their failures. These are distinctively ecological and climatological professions. They should have intimate knowledge of the workings of the physical world: of the skies, the seas, animals, plants, and the earth. Yet, the passage contrasts what they should know and their experience of unknowing, uncertainty, and failure. The poem insists that the problem here is not one of knowledge, but of love. Langland insists that the lesson to be learned is not only that human sin has reshaped people's relation to their environment but also that there is something amiss with the world itself, which is unpredictable, contrary, its patterns no longer consistent.

Thus ultimately, as this passage reminds us, for Langland, attending to the natural world offers rather ambivalent lessons. On the one hand, he implies that those observing nature should assume that nature's order is a source of spiritual knowledge and growth if one understands the creation as a book of examples.[90] Yet, on the other hand, the poem's catastrophic, disordered landscapes unsettle this assumption at every turn.[91] All is *not* right in the earth and the skies. It is not only the human creature that is broken; creation itself bears the wounds of human failure.

The Moving of This Earth

> swiche ben the customes of perturbacions, and this power they han,
> that they mai moeve a man from his place
> (*that is to seyn, fro the stabelnesse and perfeccion of his knowynge*).
> CHAUCER, *Boece*

As this chapter moves toward its close, we turn from wildfires, volcanic winters, catastrophic winds, and uncertain climatological interpretation to the unsettled earth and examine one final medieval poem about ecological disaster: a short lyric that attempts to make meaning of an earthquake that roiled England and Flanders on the afternoon of May 21, 1382.[92] Earthquakes have never been especially common in England. It's entirely possible that many fourteenth-century people may only have been familiar with them because of their appearance in biblical contexts, where, as Laura Smoller notes, earthquakes often function as "direct manifestations of God's anger," or, I would add, divine sorrow.[93] The gospel of Matthew mentions that at Jesus's death, "the earth quaked, and the rocks were rent" (27:51), an image that was reproduced and expanded in much medieval biblical literature and art. *Piers Plowman* describes how the earth trembles in sympathy for Christ's suffering on the cross: "The erthe for hevyness that he wolde suffre / Quaked as quyke thing, and al biquasshe the roche" (The earth because of heaviness that Christ suffered, / quaked as if it were a living thing and entirely squashed the rock; 18.247–48). The Chester play "The Resurrection" describes how, at the moment of Christ's death, "the wedders waxed wondrous blacke—layte, thonder—and earth beganne to quake" (the sky grew wondrously black—[with] lightning and thunder—and the earth began to quake).[94] John's Apocalypse also specifies that earthquakes would portend the Last Judgment.[95]

Chronicles and tracts sometimes draw on biblical imagery to describe the 1382 earthquake. John of Malvern writes in his continuation of Ranulf Higden's *Polychronicon*, "On the morning of this earthquake about twelve o-clock, there was a very black, cloudy, immense, and broad circle around the sun."[96] Others offer more straightforward descriptions of its effects. Knighton's *Chronicle* comments on the aftershocks of the event, noting

> an earthquake which did widespread damage in the kingdom, around the first hour after noon, on Wednesday. Then on the following Friday there was a shock

around sunrise, which did no great harm, and on Saturday a disturbance in the sea, about three o'clock in the morning, and ships in harbour were tossed by the shock.[97]

Noting the day-by-day development of the tremors, Knighton marks physical causes and effects, charting ecological disaster in terms of a linear, physical chronology, much as a historian or geologist might do today. Modern geologists now think that the epicenter of the quake was in the English Channel. Its magnitude was likely around 5.7, and it lasted for about thirty seconds. Felt throughout England, northern France, and the Low Countries, the quake especially affected Kent and London, toppling the bell tower at Canterbury Cathedral.[98]

Although a significant geological occurrence in its own right, the 1382 quake is now mainly remembered because it disrupted the Blackfriars Council, a meeting called by Archbishop Courtenay that resulted in the condemnation of twenty-four tenets of John Wyclif's teaching. Because the quake, according to one author, followed the reading of the list of Wyclif's heresies, the event is now often called the "earthquake council" (*concilium terramotus*). Perhaps unsurprisingly, both sides interpreted the tremors as signs. Wyclif and his followers understood the quake as "divine judgement" for the council's decisions.[99] Wycliffite writings also insisted that it had biblical precedent: "for þei [Blackfriars] put an heresye vpon Crist and seyntes in heueyn, wherfore þe erthe tremblide, fayland mannus voys ansueride for God, als it died in tyme of his passione" (for they put a heresy on Christ and saints in heaven, because of which the earth trembled; in the lack of human voices it answered for God, as it also did in the time of his passion).[100] Just as the earth responded to Christ's death by trembling, and in so doing proclaimed the horror that human beings did not, so too, the earth trembled for Wyclif, who becomes a figure for Christ. The friars drew a rather different analogy, explaining that the earth's violent expulsion of infected air signified the purgation of heresies from the realm. The Blackfriars thus read the quake as confirmation of the rightness of their decisions.[101]

The movements of the earth that day are also memorialized in several poems, including an English penitential lyric that, like *Piers Plowman*, treats environmental and social catastrophe as entangled. The "Earthquake poem" surveys and seeks significance in three roughly contemporaneous catastrophes: the Black Death, the 1381 Peasants' Revolt, and the 1382 quake.[102] Across its twelve stanzas, this little poem thematizes catastrophic events, understands catastrophe as a dramatic turning point, and uses forms—including anaphora, catalogues, shifts in scale, repetitions, and cliché—to convey the immediacy and horror of the catastrophe, but also its near inexpressibility. The lyric describes the effects of the three crises and explores their function as warnings, a point articulated in the alliterative refrain that such social and ecological upheavals serve as "warnyng[s] to be ware" (warnings to be mindful/aware). With the insistent ringing of this refrain and frequent sonic and syntactic repetitions, the poem circles around the catastrophes, returning the reader again and again to the world's precarity, to human responsibility, and to the necessity of appropriate response.

In the poem, upheavals—both social and environmental—are not only portents of things to come, nor simply marks of God's displeasure, but also means of God's mercy. For, in its opening stanzas, the poem pointedly remarks that these wonders and marvels are signs that God does not desire to take vengeance on his creation: "We may not sey, but ȝif we lyȝe, / That God wol vengaunce on us stele" (We cannot say, unless we lie / that God desires to take vengeance on us; 250/9–10). This insistence puts the reader in an odd position: If these crises are not divine punishments, then what exactly were they for? What do they mean? On what grounds can they be understood as merciful when their effects were so tragic?

Introducing these catastrophes in terms of God's courteousness and meekness, the opening two stanzas reframe the three uprisings (of the commons, the earthquake, and the pestilence) as the effects of human attachment to wealth rather than as punishments:

> For openly we seo with eiȝe
> This warnynges beoth wonder and feole.
> But non this wrecched worldes weole
> Maketh us live in synne and care;
> Of mony merveyles I may of mele,
> And al is warnynge to be ware. (250/11–16)

> (For openly we see with our eyes
> these warnings are both wondrous and many.
> But now this wretched world's wealth
> Makes us live in sin and care.
> I may speak of many marvels
> and all are warnings to be mindful.)

As in *Piers Plowman*, the poet here both frames disaster in terms of wonders and places blame on human disorder (the fallen world makes humans live in sin and suffering).[103] Although it may now seem counterintuitive, the poet understands the crises he details as benevolent warnings, small tragedies, ordinary apocalypses in comparison to the cataclysms that God could enact if he so desired.

The remainder of the lyric is especially interested in exploring the dynamics of human response to these crises. The fifth and sixth stanzas, which turn from the 1381 revolt (the subject of the third and fourth stanzas) to the earthquake, particularly highlight how disaster draws those who experience it into the present, shifting their values at least temporarily:

> And also whon this eorthe qwok
> Was non so proud he nas agast,
> And al his jolite forsok,
> And thou3t on God whil that hit last.
> And alsone as hit was over past,
> Men wox as uvel as thei dede are.
> Uche mon in his herte may cast,
> This was a warnyng to be ware. (251/33–40)
>
> (And when the earth quaked,
> there was no person so prideful that he was not aghast
> and entirely forsook his revels
> and thought about God while the quake lasted.
> And as soon as it had passed,
> people returned to their evils.
> Every person may know in their heart
> that this was a warning to be mindful.)

Rather than describing the earthquake or explaining it in terms of its physical effects, the poem internalizes the tremors, concatenating the feelings and thoughts it generates through a series of *and*s, which chart the cognitive and affective shifts from horror (people are "agast"), to solemnity, and finally to meditation on God. Pride and revelry fall away. Suddenly faced with its own mortality, the mind turns from this world. The anaphora of the *and*s also enacts the immediacy of the catastrophe, syntactically replicating the elongated present of the experience of the earthquake, as if all of these internal movements occur in an instant. The temporality of such a move diverges significantly from the causal models of the chronicles. The lyric uses repetition and simultaneity to begin to move toward an expression of both the subjective experience of the disaster and its significance. The experience of disaster forces the mindfulness that the refrain echoes throughout the poem. When the earth trembles, it reminds those who walk on it that they too are earth and will return to it.

But, as the poem points out, any conversion is as short-lived as the geological event itself, as evanescent as the tremors that render the ground unstable.

For with stability return the normal patterns of human existence. The following stanza reiterates this point when the poet remarks that in the astonishment and fear of finding themselves at the edges of life, "Of gold and selver thei tok non hede, / But out of ther houses ful sone thei past" (they took no heed of gold or silver, / but quickly left their homes; 251/43–44). Material possessions are rendered meaningless by the tremors, a point made only briefly before the poem rescales its perspective, from wealth to the interiors of homes, to a more panoptic view of a transformed skyline. Leaving gold and silver behind, the people escape with only their lives, as the larger physical world around them begins to crumble:

> Chaumbres, chymeneys, al to-barst,
> Chirches and castelles foule gone fare;
> Pinacles, steples, to grounde hit cast;
> And al was for warnyng to be ware. (251/45–48)
>
> (Rooms and chimneys all burst,
> churches and castles deteriorated;
> it cast pinnacles and steeples to the ground;
> and all this was a warning to be mindful.)

This rescaling is matched with sonic intensification. In this stanza, the alliteration picks up, and stresses fall on the opening syllables—an intensification of form that is characteristic of literary representations of catastrophe. The list of destroyed buildings stands in for the immensity of the loss. As the poem catalogs vast material destruction, beginning with homely domestic spaces, and then moving upward, both socially and physically, forms become more densely patterned, locking the reader in tight sonic patterns that, paradoxically, represent the material world's unpatterning. The language emphasizes the force of the quake: the rooms and chimneys explode or shatter ("to-barst"). The earthquake throws the symbols of human ambition, "pinnacles and steeples," to the ground. The poem's inventory of devastation recalls the downward movement of the *artes moriendi* tradition—all that exists will one day return to the earth from which it came.

As spectacular as this ruin may be, the poem next downscales its perspective, moving from macrocosm to microcosm to insist that the problem is not only or even primarily a ruined landscape or cosmic instability; it is that human hearts are shifting and changeable:

> The mevvyng of this eorthe iwis
> That schulde bi cuynde be ferm and stabele,

> A pure verrey toknyng hit is
> That mennes hertes ben chaungabele. (251/49–52)
>
> (The movement of the earth,
> which should, by nature, be firm and stable,
> is a true sign
> of how the human heart is changeable.)

Pivoting from horrified wonder to a desire to make meaning out of the event, the poem enacts the catastrophe as a turning, implying that the issue here is the gap between what we think the world *should be* (stable, firm, ordered, consistent) and the reality we experience, in which the cosmos reveals itself to be always in motion. Like the very soil from which humanity emerged, the individual human microcosm is unsettled and unpredictable. The poem suggests that the human heart is more mutable than we may like to imagine. We are easily moved, restless in our attentions. As Chaucer's *Boece* puts it, "swiche ben the customes of perturbacions, and this power they han, that they mai moeve a man from his place (*that is to seyn, fro the stabelnesse and perfeccion of his knowynge*)."[104] Insofar as it moves those who experience it, unsettling them, the earthquake thus carries a double significance, signaling future events and serving as a metaphor for the mutability of the human heart.

In its final stanzas, the poem swerves from the unrest within human beings to the restlessness of the collective, referencing how two other recent events—the plague and the 1381 Peasants' Revolt—also betoken the world's unsettled nature:

> The rysyng of the comuynes in londe,
> The pestilens, and the eorthe-qwake,
> Theose threo thinges, I understonde,
> Beoth tokenes of the grete vengaunce and wrake
> That schulde falle for synnes sake. (252/60–64)
>
> (The rising of the commons in the land,
> the plague, and the earthquake,
> I understand these three things
> to be tokens of the great vengeance and judgment
> that must occur because of sin.)

Shifting from feeling and experience to comprehension and explanation, the lyric reframes these three catastrophes within an apocalyptic framework, naming them as tokens of greater catastrophes to come if humans do not heed these events as opportunities for transformation. But ultimately, it is the present moment that matters most here. For the earthquake poet, these ecosystemic disruptions betray a profound failure of attention. As the poem's refrain relentlessly drums, what is lacking is awareness of human complicity in the "plyt this world is in" (plight this world is in; 252/67).

These refrains rise to a climax in the poem's final stanza, which gathers the warnings into an anaphoric litany of *be wars*:

> Be war, for I con sey no more;
> Be war, for vengaunce of trespas;
> Be war, and thenk uppon this lore;
> Be ware of this sodeyn cas.
> And ȝit be war while we have spas. (252/74–78)
>
> (Be aware, for I cannot say any more;
> Be aware, for vengeance for this trespass;
> Be aware, and think about this lesson;
> be aware of this sudden event.
> And yet, be aware, while we still have opportunity.)

Even as it moves toward a conclusion, this poetic climax retains a sense of the impossibility of fully articulating the contingent nature of life on a restless planet. Beware, the poet writes, "because I cannot say any more." Surely the poet has neither exhausted this subject matter nor come to the limits of his powers. While this may be little more than a verbal throwing up of one's hands in exasperation, the final turn to inexpressibility, to cliché (indeed, what can one say in the face of suffering, of destruction, of the world's chaos? What does this mean?), in the midst of pounding repetition, it performs the failure of language in the task of representing catastrophe. Can we do anything but resort to truism, itself a form of deep repetition but also, because of its familiarity, a source of comfort? In the end, what more is there to say than: pay attention while we still have "spas" (space, i.e., time, opportunity)?

Perhaps we should not take the poet so literally, for there apparently is indeed more to say. The poet next instructs the reader to "thenk upon this lore." While we might now read *lore* as "story," in Middle English the term is rather more multivalent, indicating instruction, narrative, or profound loss.[105]

But how do we make sense of a possible equivalence between instruction and loss? When we attend to the premodern sense of catastrophe, we are reminded that loss and instruction are often two sides of the same coin. Both are moments of change; they transform our relationship to the world and the knowledge we have of it. Yet loss can lead to new understanding, new ways of being, or new stories. For instance, in the archetypal biblical example, Adam and Eve lose their innocence in the Garden of Eden, and indeed lose Eden itself, as they "learn" from the tree of the knowledge of good and evil. This first catastrophe is a "fall," a downturn, but also the beginning of an education that sets history in motion. In one sense, all other catastrophes are mere iterations of that fundamental transition from innocence to knowledge. Twinning form and event, rupture and closure, clarification and ending, premodern catastrophes often manifest as this double-edged *lore*. And as the lyric so insistently reminds us, when we "thenk uppon this lore," when we attend deeply to precarity, disorder, and loss, we are confronted with that which will always remain somewhat inassimilable but which also presents itself to us as a moment of possible transformation. This, I think, is the essential, necessary, and difficult work of engaging with the world's ordinary apocalypses. Attending to ecological precarity, disorder, and losses provides an opportunity to look in the mirror, to accept complicity, and to move from attention to action.

In this sense, medieval texts seem to intuitively understand a point frequently made by modern environmentalists: that changes in action and policy are unlikely to happen without a shift in how we perceive the more-than-human world and our part in it. In a 2023 op-ed in the *Washington Post*, Rebecca Solnit suggests that "we need a large-scale change in perspective. To reframe climate change as an opportunity—a chance to rethink who we are and what we desire." In particular, she continues, we must reconsider what we see as "wealth," returning to its earlier, more wholistic sense of "well-being." She goes on:

> To respond to the climate crisis—a disaster on a more immense scale than anything our species has faced—we can and must summon what people facing disasters have: a sense of meaning, of deep connection and generosity, of being truly alive in the face of uncertainty. Of joy. This is the kind of abundance we need to meet the climate crisis, to make many, or even most, lives better. It is the opposite of moral injury; it is moral *beauty*. A thing we needn't acquire, because we already have it in us.[106]

The "Earthquake poem" suggests a similar point: Drawing us into places of uncertainty and unknowing, catastrophes can unmoor us, humble us, call us to attention. They can force reflection on values, on what we understand as "wealth."

The rubble of the earthquake, the ruins left by catastrophic winds, the devastation of a harvestless summer, and perhaps the climate catastrophes of our own age will surely remain somewhat inassimilable. But, contemplating them, these works suggest, reading them as warnings to "be ware" of human responsibility for ecological suffering, may well also serve as examples of how catastrophe can reorient our way of dwelling with other beings. For wonders—fair or foul—whatever else they may mean, are reminders of our fundamental vulnerability and invitations to attention, invitations to change our collective and individual way of life.

Even so, catastrophe can only ever be a "prelude to contemplation."[107] Disasters invite rather than necessitate or demand reflection. They make visible the unsettledness of a world that we frequently assume is orderly. They make immediate its frailty as well as its power. They unmoor us, shake us free of our certainties, open us to reinterpretations. They ask us to make new connections, to see the world another way. Yet ultimately, what we make of such ecological frailty and unsettledness and how we respond to it is up to us. There is nothing in a catastrophe itself that dictates either meaning or response. Perhaps, if nothing else, we contemplate our mortality, our precarity, and our vulnerability. Perhaps we are moved to respond and take action. Or, as the "Earthquake poem" warns is a common response, perhaps we just return to normal.

Ultimately, what medieval disaster writing can offer is a deeper history of the unsettledness of the world, a sense of its repetition as well as its novelty. The shock of ordinary apocalypses may always register as new and strange and disruptive, but it is only when we begin to understand catastrophe as chronic rather than acute that we may begin to take seriously the need to adapt to the real order of the world—its precarity, vulnerability, and restlessness. We need images and monuments, reminders of the untamable forces that always catch us off guard. We also need litanies, liturgies, and lists. For, ultimately, as medieval writers knew well, even the most ordinary apocalypse is never merely destructive, it's also an unveiling, an opening. And even ordinary apocalypses thus might remind us that the world's essential mutability and even precarity are also its sources of possibility and creativity.

PART III

Apocalyptic Ecologies

In the great fabric of the universe, a single slipped stitch might disclose the beginnings of the great unraveling.
    PAUL EDWARD DUTTON, "Observations on Medieval Weather"

Changing the self and changing the world [have often been] regarded as separate endeavors and viewed in either-or terms. But in the story of the Great Turning, they are recognized as mutually reinforcing and essential to one another.
    JOANNA MACY AND CHRIS JOHNSTONE, *Active Hope*

5

Fifteen Ways of Looking

Signs at the End of the World

> Presentiment—is that long Shadow—on the Lawn—
> Indicative that Suns go down—
>
> The Notice to the startled Grass
> That Darkness—is about to pass—.
> EMILY DICKINSON

Once I had a child, a redheaded boy who had been taken from his mother by the state and entrusted to my care for a time. He arrived, shell-shocked, on a June afternoon, in an apocalyptic season: the pandemic was ongoing, severe storms were devastating the Midwest, global temperatures continued to creep upward, and in southern Indiana billions of red-eyed cicadas emerged from the warming soil where they had been for the past seventeen years. Throughout May and June, they molted, fed, sang, mated, laid eggs, and died, leaving carcasses strewn across sidewalks and empty shells clutching leaves and bark. The boy was fascinated by the cicadas. In his difficult first days with me, he enjoyed little more than crushing them with the toe-edge of his sneakers.

In the evenings, when the air had begun to cool, the boy and I would sometimes walk to a nearby trail. What is now my neighborhood was once an expansive tract of farmland. Now it is a patchwork of ball fields, housing developments, and city parks, all with acres of lawn. But if you know where to look, tucked behind the community gardens and the orchard and in between the portable toilet and the compost piles, you'll find the entrance to a wooded trail. Its longest loop is only a bit more than half a mile. In the early spring, I circle it often, looking intently at the leaf cover for the first stirrings of life. When the redheaded boy arrives in midsummer, the overstory has already filled in and the ephemerals shriveled, so we look at trees and sinkholes instead.

The trail traces the edges of wide depressions where the limestone bedrock has given way to the force of water. Trunks of fallen trees bridge the leaf-filled hollows. The boy and I climb into the sinkholes, and we gawk at the wildness of the upturned roots. Deer watch warily from a distance. Not far from the trail, lines of rusty barbed wire shoot out of a sycamore's trunk like new growth.

We invariably pause by a beech on the northern end of the trail. It is broken, wounded, and so hollowed out that you can crouch in the gaping crevice in its side, look up, and see a patch of sky. Its exterior pocked with worm and woodpecker holes, its pith is soft and black. For years I assumed it was dead. One late summer day I glanced up and was astonished to see lushly leafed branches. How could it be so emptied out and yet growing? The scientific answer to such a question (that the living phloem, the tree's vascular system, is just under the protective bark; the center, sometimes called the "heartwood," need not be alive) doesn't quell my awe. Yet I love the tree for its undoing, and for its wondrously strange way of hanging on in spite of everything.

The boy loves this tree nearly as much as I do. He climbs inside it and asks me to take his picture for his mother. "Look," he says.

I snap a photo. He is bright-eyed, wearing cowboy boots, enclosed in the dark wound.

The photo reminds me of an alabaster panel from a medieval altarpiece that I've long loved (figure 5.1). It too is an image of an apocalyptic season, though you probably wouldn't guess that at first glance. In it, human and avian figures gaze off in all directions, captured in an instant of astonishment. Bulbous trees twist around and enclose the figures, pocked with bloody dew. A tiny owl peers out from a hollow. At the base, white flowers bloom against the green. A depiction of one of the signs of the apocalypse, the panel displays the entangled fates of humans, birds, and flora in the final days. "Look," its wide-eyed figures seem to say.

Years before the boy and I would walk the trail and gawk at the tree or before I would encounter the alabaster panel, I spent a summer in York participating in a seminar. One July afternoon, the instructor led us into All Saints North Street, a parish church with some of the best-preserved medieval glass in England. The sun fell through the heavily leaded windows, tinting the floor with deep reds and blues. In one window, Anne teaches the child Mary to read. In another, figures tend to the poor and sick and neglected, modeling the Corporal Works of Mercy. But my gaze flitted past those scenes to land on a window that was less immediately legible (figure 5.2). Wilder and more abstract, its frames are filled with trees, leaning, overturned, with rocks tumbling. In one panel, vicious fish rise from an unsettled sea. In another, figures crouch in caves, peering out. Others I couldn't make heads nor tails of.[1] At the margins of some of the scenes, small figures gesture toward the chaos.

I looked with awe and incomprehension.

I would later learn that the window, like the alabaster panel, depicts the ecological tremors of a dying world: the Fifteen Signs of Doomsday.[2] The fifteen catastrophes imagined in this popular apocalyptic tradition range from

FIGURE 5.1. The Fifth Sign of the Last Judgment (ca. 1430–75). Panel, painted and gilded alabaster. Given by Dr. W. L. Hildburgh (acc. no. A.118-1946). Photograph © Victoria and Albert Museum.

FIGURE 5.2. Fifteen Signs of the Last Judgment (ca. 1410). All Saints Church, North Street, York, UK. Photograph by Steven Rozenski.

those that may seem to anticipate the precarity of our own ecological situation—oceans rise, the earth is shaken by quakes and burned by fires, animals suffer, cities are laid waste—to phenomena that now seem more fantastic: blood sits like dew on trees and grass, fish rise out of the sea and roar, birds huddle together mourning, and, in the final days, humans run around as if mad, unable to understand what is happening to the world or to speak. The Fifteen Signs tradition asks us to look attentively at ecosystemic undoing as a series of stages. It asks us to contemplate the process of how, to use William Butler Yeats's phrase, "things fall apart": ecologies, buildings, animals, communities, even human cognition.[3] The Fifteen Signs narrate this day-by-day collapse of the ordered universe into a disordered one, which finally disintegrates into a second chaos from which a new heaven and earth can be born. It represents "the great unraveling" of the tapestry of creation.[4]

Although many apocalyptic images depict a final ecosystemic undoing, they often represent the end of the world through symbol and enigma; if we are to understand anything about the revelation they depict, it is that things are not quite what they seem. Yet even a casual glance at any of the hundreds of visual and verbal representations of the Fifteen Signs suggests that this motif is different. The Fifteen Signs depict this-worldly phenomena—the movements of water, rocks, trees, mountains, stars, fish, birds—and in a surprisingly literal way, treating environmental marvels as portents, physical events that foreshadow future events, rather than as symbols or allegories, which signify something other than what they are.[5] For instance, the rising and receding of the sea (the first and second signs) surely would have called to mind the biblical flood, but the motif neither names this typology nor ascribes any symbolic import to these watery catastrophes. The signs simply foreshadow another event. Indeed, in only a handful of the hundreds of appearances of the Fifteen Signs are the natural disasters they catalog explicitly moralized or analyzed.[6]

The signs are also rather less interested than we might expect in the toll that these catastrophes take on human beings, who are present primarily as witnesses.[7] Instead, the motif trains the gaze on the more-than-human world, representing ecosystemic collapse with little explanation. In so doing, the Fifteen Signs positions its audience as proleptic observers, encouraging sustained imagination of scenes of future suffering (a point of view modeled in the donor portraits at the base of the Fifteen Signs window). "Look at all the ways the world can end," the motif says. It invites us to locate ourselves as both proximate to and outside these scenes, both experiencing them in the now and imagining them as yet to come, a position not unlike the one we occupy when scrolling through scenes of disaster on our cell phones or watching disaster movies.[8]

And not unlike contemporary accounts of the signs of climate change, the Fifteen Signs typically circulate as a list.[9] Consider, for example, the opening lines of a Middle English lyric found in Oxford, Bodleian Library, MS Laud Misc. 622:

> Þe first day þe Cee schal arise & as a wal stonde
> Wel heiȝer by xl feet þan any hil in þis londe.
> Þat oþer dai, it schal so lowe aliȝt þat vnneþe men schul it se,
> Alle þe fissches þe þrid day abouen þe water schull be,
> & so reuly a cri ȝiuen þat all men schullen haue fere.
> Þe fierþe day, water schal brenne as þeiȝ it coles were;
> Þe v^{te} day, schal euerych tre blede dropes of blood.
> Þe vj^{te} day, schull castels & houses fall, all þat euer stood.
> Þe vij^{te} day, stones schull fiȝtt; Þe viij þe erþe quake
> Þe ix^e day, all hilles spreden abrod & al þe werld euen make
> Þe x day, men schul renne about as þai wode were,
> As wilde bestes holes to seche to hide hem inne for fere.[10]

> (The first day, the sea shall rise and stand like a wall,
> more than forty feet higher than any hil in this land.
> The second day, it shall fall so low that people will not be able to see it.
> All the fishes on the third day shall be above the water
> and cry so pitifully that all people will be afraid.
> The fourth day, water shall burn as if it were coals.
> The fifth day, every tree will bleed drops of blood.
> The sixth day, all the castles and houses that ever stood shall fall.
> The seventh day, stones will fight; the eighth, the earth will quake.
> The ninth day, all the hills will disintegrate, and the world become level.
> The tenth day, human beings will run around as if they have gone mad,
> like wild beasts seeking holes to hide in because of fear.)

Like most textual treatments of the motif, this lyric simply lists the coming calamities. The lyric's list calls attention to particular losses and also, by gathering these losses, invites a God's-eye view of the suffering cosmos. Relying on the power of accretion, lists of the Fifteen Signs pile catastrophe on catastrophe in quick succession. In so doing, they aim to elicit both fear and pity. But, unlike the scenes of biblical catastrophes we considered in chapter 3, which also develop sympathetic witness by focusing the readerly gaze on scenes of suffering, the Fifteen Signs motif almost never acknowledges its audience in order to offer scripts for devotional response. Its implicit invitation seems only to be: look![11]

And in looking at fallen trees, rising seas, and suffering animals, representations of the Fifteen Signs invite us to contemplate both the inevitability and the ultimate unknowability of an apocalyptic future. Where other apocalyptic motifs often imply that external forms must be seen *through*, the Fifteen Signs tradition depicts wonders to be looked *at*, that demand apprehension but remain opaque and resistant to full comprehension.[12] The motif throws into relief the epistemological paradoxes at the heart of the apocalyptic imagination—that observation and comprehension are not always coincident; that there may be a fundamental fissure between imagination and understanding; but also that imagination itself may well be the best tool we have in preparing for a future that is fundamentally unknowable and unrepresentable. The motif encourages us to attend to the more-than-human world not only because of what it teaches us about ourselves but also because it, too, suffers, and because that suffering has inherent value and significance. And thus, in inviting sustained attention to scenes of a wounded world, the Fifteen Signs advocate compassionate witness and the work of care as the most suitable responses both to the suffering they depict and to its inscrutability.[13]

If you have read the previous chapters of this book, you will not be surprised that I meditate here on how the motif's catalog of catastrophes can facilitate sympathetic imagination of what I have called "apocalyptic ecologies" to encourage its audience to imagine new ways of being in the world.[14] Some of the fifteen signs may feel prescient to us inhabitants of the Anthropocene, for the language of apocalyptic signs continues to shape our sense of expectation and urgency. And we too find ourselves in the middle, in a position of anticipation, uncertainty, and imagination when it comes to conceptualizing possible futures. We too can be prone to read the Book of Nature as a doomsday book. Many of us understand the images that increasingly populate our news cycle of a world parched, on fire, and under water as portents of even greater catastrophes to come. We may share a sense that our impending doom is self-inflicted, even if we reach for economic or social causes rather than moral ones.[15] And we also proliferate doomsday scenarios to try to communicate the urgent need for conversion and reformation of our destructive habits and relations with the world and one another. Apocalypse, Lawrence Buell writes, remains "the single most powerful master metaphor that the contemporary environmental imagination has at its disposal."[16]

Yet premodern ways of imagining apocalypse are rarely part of the current dialogue about ecological catastrophe, even though modern environmental rhetoric often evokes apocalypse.[17] I suspect that this is largely because they are often assumed to be too different—too religious, too anthropocentric, too unconcerned with the fate of nonhuman beings. Because premodern texts frequently emphasize a final divinely ordained destruction of the earth, ecocritical work has often dismissed them as either inherently uninterested in the devastation of the environment or as an active source of that degeneration. However, this chapter argues that medieval texts often tell a more complex story than these modern narratives allow. Care is as central to the Fifteen Signs as is terror; and care, the motif suggests, begins with witness, with attentive *looking* at a dying world.

Attending to its association of attention with care, I read the Fifteen Signs as a cosmic *ars moriendi*. This interpretation returns us to our beginning. Just as the practice of imagining one's inevitable death encourages reflection on what makes for a good life, so too, imagining the earth's inevitable end can bring into greater focus what is valuable in the present.[18] The Fifteen Signs motif throws into relief how medieval thinking about the physical cosmos is interested in the status and responsibilities of human beings in a world that is fundamentally ephemeral, in which both individual and cosmic death are givens. Further, this catalog of catastrophes suggests how one might tell a story about ecological impermanence that both mourns losses and acknowledges that imagining dark futures might spur greater compassion in the present.

After providing a brief overview of the origins of this motif, I focus on how its paradox of apocalyptic knowing and unknowing runs through Middle English texts. I turn to sermons and poetry to consider how the motif encourages environmental watchfulness, moves human experience from the center to the margins, heightens the scenes' pathos, and emphasizes the humbling inscrutability of apocalyptic ecologies. Yet, significantly, unknowing is not the end of the story: many medieval treatments of the Fifteen Signs pair the apocalyptic motif with depictions of Christ's *ostentatio vulnerum*, the display of his wounds, and the Corporal Works of Mercy. In so doing, they urge care for a wounded world, reminding us that although death—both our own and our world's—remains nearly unthinkable to us, the practice of attempting to envision it may well encourage humility, awareness of the suffering of others, compassionate action, and the work of care.

Roots and Branches

> The trees are coming into leaf
> Like something almost being said;
> The recent buds relax and spread,
> Their greenness is a kind of grief.
> PHILLIP LARKIN, "The Trees"

That the coming apocalypse will be marked by ecological collapse might seem a particularly modern notion.[19] But the popularity of the Fifteen Signs motif reminds us that people have long imagined the end of the world as an environmental event and thus have also long interpreted ecosystemic disasters as portents of that end.[20] By the late Middle Ages, the Fifteen Signs were found in hundreds of Latin texts and in many vernacular languages and in many visual media. The specifics of the motif's development remain rather murky, but most scholars tend to agree that it derives from biblical and apocryphal traditions, first appears in the early Middle Ages as short enumerative lists of six or seven signs (probably in an Insular context), and expands into the full fifteen-sign tradition by the mid-eleventh century. From there, versions proliferate in Latin and many vernacular languages well into the Renaissance, after which the motif largely disappears.

The belief that the natural world is the canary in the eschatological coal mine has deep biblical roots. So, too, does one of the central paradoxes of the Fifteen Signs (and of Christian eschatology in general): that even though there will be ecological evidence of the approach of the end, no one will know the hour or the day. This tension between what the Book of Nature reveals and conceals runs through the Fifteen Signs motif and appears in several of the motif's apparent biblical sources, including the Gospel according to Matthew, where Jesus suggests in a sermon that the final days will be presaged by cosmological signs and wonders: "Wheresoever the body shall be, there shall the eagles also be gathered together. And immediately after the tribulation of those days, the sun shall be darkened and the moon shall not give her light, and the stars shall fall from heaven, and the powers of heaven shall be moved: And then shall appear the sign of the Son of man in heaven: and then shall all tribes of the earth mourn" (Matthew 24:28–30). Though there is no single biblical source of the Fifteen Signs motif, this passage contains several of the signs: the gathering of birds, the falling of the stars, and the darkening of the sun all recur in late medieval treatments of the motif. This passage also gestures toward the uncertainty of accurately reading natural phenomena as portents; several verses later, the gospel follows its projections with the caution that "of that day and hour no one knows" (Matthew 24:36). Other gospel passages provide additional cosmological signs while also querying their legibility.[21] An analogous scene in the Gospel according to Luke similarly mentions "signs in the sun, and in the moon, and in the stars; and upon the earth distress of nations," and adds watery portents, including "the confusion of the roaring of the sea and of the waves," and describes "men withering away for fear, and expectation of what shall come upon the whole world" (Luke 21:25–27). Ecological portents of the Last Days also can be found in the Hebrew scriptures and pseudepigrapha. Ezekiel details several cataclysmic phenomena, relating how an earthquake will make fish, birds, animals, and people tremble in fear (esp. Ezekiel 38:19–20). Esdras describes a series of natural omens such as bleeding trees, sounding stones, ruined landscapes, and fire (4 Esdras 5–7).[22] John's Apocalypse draws on some of this earlier imagery, prophesying an earthquake as well as the darkening of the sun, a bloody moon, stars falling from heaven, and humans hiding "in the dens and in the rocks of mountains" alongside its more symbolic depictions of the End (Apocalypse 6:12–16). Although these biblical portents were not always understood literally by medieval exegetes, they are at the root of what will become a long tradition of reading anomalies in the natural world as signs of the coming catastrophe.

Early theologians continued to interpret natural disasters as warnings of the world's imminent end. Groups of environmental calamities believed to precede the Last Judgment appear in patristic writings, which draw both from biblical and sibylline traditions.[23] Yet it is not until the fourth and fifth centuries that we begin to find enumerated lists of portents. Most influentially, the fifth-century *Apocalypse of Thomas*, an apocryphal letter from Jesus to the doubting disciple, outlines a sequence of eschatological cataclysms that will occur during the six or seven days before the end of the world.[24] According to the letter, each day before the Final Judgment, great voices will sound from the heavens and will be followed by clouds that rain blood, thunder, and lightning; earthquakes that destroy both idols and cities; massive fires; and ultimately darkness covering the earth. In this vision of the seven-day de-creation of the world, God will speak the cosmos *out* of being in much the same way as God spoke it into existence.

The *Apocalypse of Thomas* and other eschatological texts found ready audiences in the following centuries, as extreme weather and changes in the macroclimate generated a good deal of theological and ecclesiastical reflection on whether nature's anomalies could be interpreted as apocalyptic portents.[25] And it seems to have influenced the production of other lists of six or seven doomsday signs that began to appear in Insular sermons and poetry by the tenth century.[26] Though some of these early sequences anticipate portents in the later fifteen-sign tradition—including thunderous noise, bloody rain, earthquakes, falling stars, and human flight to caves—these lists are rather more spiritualizing, representing the earth and heavens as gearing up for a cosmic battle.[27] Yet rather than emphasizing the supernatural aspects of the signs, as the motif develops in the eleventh and twelfth centuries, it grounds the portents even more firmly in the natural world. These centuries mark a critical transformation in the motif's form (it expands from six or seven to fifteen signs), a surge in its popularity, and growing ambivalence about both the authority of the tradition and the legibility of natural portents more generally.[28]

If the earliest sets of signs parallel the six-day destruction of the cosmos with its six-day creation, the expanded fifteen-sign tradition instead links the Second Coming of Christ with his First Coming.[29] The first datable instances of the full motif are in mid-eleventh-century letters by Peter Damian (d. 1072/3), but the version found in the *Historia scholastica* of Peter Comestor (d. 1178) was perhaps even more influential.[30] Although they include slightly different signs and orderings, all three of these Latin branches (Pseudo-Bede, Damian, and Comestor) attribute the list of signs to an earlier, now unknown and likely apocryphal, work supposedly cited by Jerome, *In annalibus Hebraeorum*.[31] Yet even medieval authors expressed doubt about the legitimacy of this lost ancient source. Thomas Aquinas, for instance, questions both the validity of interpreting natural signs as portents and the attribution of the Fifteen Signs tradition to Jerome, noting that they "are not asserted by him; he merely says that he found them written in the annals of the Jews: and, indeed, they contain very little likelihood."[32] Shortly thereafter, he concedes that although the gospels indicate that there will be signs, it will not be easy to recognize them as such. One scholar has called this paradoxical idea that there will be portents of the end, but that no one will know the hour or the day, the apocalyptic "uncertainty principle."[33] Thus, even as the motif begins to spread in theological texts, many questions remained about both its authenticity and its reliability—how does one know if a natural disaster has any greater meaning? To what extent is it even possible to predict the end of the world by attending to environmental abnormalities?

The other major branch of the motif is less interested in such questions. Unlike the three Latin branches, the vernacular Anglo-Norman branch, which is found first in a poem following the mid-twelfth-century play *Jeu d'Adam* (*Play of Adam*; in Tours, Bibliothèque municipale, MS 927), is rather more interested in using the motif as a tool for conversion. This branch seems to originate in a sibylline tradition and differs significantly from the Latin branches in the nature of the signs, their sequencing, and their meaning.[34] Although several of the signs are similar to those of the Latin branches, the Anglo-Norman signs are, on the whole, described much more fully and include chilling details that emphasize the pathos of the surreal scenes they depict. Unlike the Latin versions, this branch also consistently writes human experience into the apocalyptic cataclysms. On the first day, for example, as the skies pour down bloodred rain, unborn children cry from their mothers' wombs, praying not to be birthed into the dying world. During the final days, according to this branch, the earth's disruption extends to heaven and hell: angels and disciples kneel before God, afraid and calling for mercy; demons come out of hell and pray that God let them back into heaven. And, whereas the Latin branches tend to conclude with resurrection of the dead, many texts in this version look forward to the Final Judgment, describing how Jesus displays his wounds and separates the good and bad souls based on their love and bodily care (or lack thereof) for both neighbors and stranger. As we will see, the Anglo-Norman branch will exert a powerful influence on the Middle English poetic tradition, but in Old English and later medieval English prose texts, the Latin branches largely determine the signs and their ordering.[35]

The uncertainties surrounding environmental interpretation that are inherent in the Latin tradition are given even greater focus in what is perhaps the most influential appearance of the motif: Jacobus de Voragine's *Legenda aurea* (*The Golden Legend*, ca. 1260), which conflates Damian and Comestor's versions and associates the signs with Advent.[36] Inclusion in the *Legenda*'s opening section, "De adventu Domini," most likely ensured the motif's wide dissemination in late medieval Europe. Like many of its predecessors, the *Legenda*'s representation of the Fifteen Signs is essentially an apocalyptic set piece, a numbered list embedded in a longer discussion of the causes and effects of Christ's coming. After rehearsing a series of biblical passages containing portents of the Second Coming (Luke 21, Matthew 24, and Apocalypse 21), Jacobus lists the Fifteen Signs:

> Jerome finds Fifteen Signs preceding the Judgment but does not say whether they will be continuous or intermittent. On the first day the sea will rise forty cubits above the tops of the mountains, standing in place like a wall. Only on the second day will it come down and be almost invisible. On the third day the sea beasts will come out above the surface and will roar to the heavens, and God alone will understand their bellowing. On the fourth day the sea and waters will burn up. On the fifth day the trees and grasses will exude a bloody dew; also on this fifth day, as others assert, all the birds in the sky will gather together in the fields, each species in its place, not feeding or drinking but frightened by the imminent coming.[37]

On its surface, the passage offers a straightforward, day-by-day list, but a closer look reveals it to be rife with equivocations, some of which derive from the *Legenda*'s attempt to reconcile the differences in the earlier versions of the motif. The description careens between confident assertions of what will certainly happen and suggestions of the ambiguities inherent in this list of portents: Will the signs be "continuous or intermittent"? What does the bellowing of the fish mean? Jacobus also acknowledges that there already appear to be conflicting accounts of the fifth day: some say that the vegetation will bleed, others say that the birds will gather.[38] Simultaneously evoking a linear narrative and questioning it, the *Legenda* invites doubt as well as belief. Some such moments of ambivalence had appeared in the earlier Latin sources, but the *Legenda* highlights the inscrutability that will come to characterize most subsequent English treatments of the tradition, which emphasize the fundamental incomprehensibility of the final days to their human observers.

Herein lies one of the central paradoxes of the motif: the list of ecological portents seems to promise knowledge, but the signs themselves undermine human certainty at every turn. What can one discover about the apocalypse based on these signs? Perhaps only that human beings will not be able to readily identify environmental abnormalities as apocalyptic portents when they encounter them. Further, the *Legenda* suggests, though this is a story *for* humans, it is not exclusively or even primarily *about* humans. The *Legenda*'s list is strikingly indifferent to the effect of these ecological disasters on people, who remain marginal here, witnesses rather than participants. People don't make an appearance until midway through the catalog of signs (sign seven), and the *Legenda*'s first mention of them marks their obliviousness to the catastrophic events: when the world's rocks collide and break, "no man will hear the sound, only God" ("nescietque homo sonum illum, sed tantum Deus").

Ultimately, human beings will be neither unaffected by nor able to ignore these apocalyptic ecologies. For, as the *Legenda*'s treatment of the motif makes clear, ecological chaos has social as well as environmental effects: in the final days of the sequence, "men will come out of the caves and go about as if demented, unable to speak to each other."[39] As the physical world wanes, human rationality, language, and the markers of civilization disintegrate as well. Yet, strikingly, the *Legenda* neither laments the future decline nor explicitly invokes it in the service of moral chastisement. Instead, the *Legenda* straightforwardly narrates the cataclysmic events of the final days of the world as moments of environmental and social disorder, many of which lie beyond human comprehension, analysis, and even articulation.

See the Fig Tree

>soon there were
>eight or nine
>people gathered beneath
>the tree looking into
>it like a
>constellation pointing
>*do you see it*
>ROSS GAY, "To the Fig Tree on 9th and Christian"

The *Legenda*'s version of the signs, with all of its uncertainty and paradox, was massively influential because it was commonly used as a resource for preachers.

And, one of the main ways that this motif circulated was through vernacular sermons. As we saw in chapter 4, preachers found in apocalyptic ecologies both warnings about moral disorder and a powerful opportunity to represent future ecosystemic crises as events that demanded present reflection and response. In this section I consider again how some late medieval English sermons imply that environmental disorder might be anthropogenic, the effect of human disorder. Yet the apocalyptic sermons that include the Fifteen Signs tend to minimize such moralizing and instead encourage listeners to practice watchfulness and witness, to notice where the world is sick, wounded, or suffering and consider it as potentially meaningful, even if the meaning or moral import remains difficult to discern.[40]

The coming Judgment and the need for repentance were commonplaces of medieval sermons, and preachers seem to have often pointed out that the world was already permeated with symptoms of its sickness and imminent end.[41] Yet, such sermons tend to emphasize social corruption more than ecological cataclysm and blame that corruption and catastrophe on human sin. For instance, in his treatment of the Last Things in a 1388 sermon, Thomas Wimbledon writes that the first sign to summon humanity to the universal Judgment will be the world's sickness ("þe worldis sykenesse"), which is manifested by the cooling of charity ("charites acoldynge"), as the love of neighbor grows faint.[42] For Wimbledon, although the nonhuman world might experience its effects, both the source of, and the remedy for, the world's sickness are to be found in the human failure to love their neighbors. Ecosystemic disorder is thus, as we have considered throughout this book, caused by human behavior.

Given the hortatory emphasis of many sermons, one might expect those that include the Fifteen Signs to punctuate their lists of disasters with moral injunctions, as we saw in Reason's sermon about the Saint Maurus's Day windstorm in *Piers Plowman*.[43] Instead, late medieval sermons cleave closely to the *Legenda*'s descriptive mode and Advent setting. Using Jesus's First Coming as an occasion for urging preparation for his return, late medieval sermons almost always communicate the signs as a straightforward list, emphasize their predictive function, and avoid suggesting that either their cause or their meaning is easily accessible, though some Advent sermons bookend the list with reminders of the need to prepare for the coming Judgment.[44]

The ecological focus of the Fifteen Signs fits neatly within these sermons, which typically open with the biblical parable of the fig tree, wherein Jesus tells his disciples to look to the natural world for portents of the final days. "See the fig tree and all trees," Jesus says, "when they send forth their fruit, you know that summer is nigh. So also, when you shall see these things come to pass, know the kingdom of God is at hand" (Luke 21.29–31). Taking this example as their theme, Advent sermons often imply that understanding the predictive order of the natural world can help one notice and recognize the significance of any disorder in it. These sermons take the scripture's example of ecological processes literally, suggesting that the end days might be discerned by carefully watching for environmental change—attending to the fig tree and other trees toppled by strong winds, to the seas, to rocks, and to animals.[45] A fifteenth-century sermon explains: "The vnderstonyng of this gospel, after þe litteral sens and seyng of docturs, is to vnderstonde of the mervels and wounders that schall fall before the commyng of Criste at the dredful day of dome" (The understanding of this gospel, following the literal sense and writings of doctors, is to understand the marvels and wonders that will occur before the coming of Christ at the dreadful day of doom).[46] Although the "mervels and wounders" that will portend the earth's final days are, as a dramatic version of the motif repeatedly puts it, "agaynste kinde" (unnatural), these sermons suggest that nature's process offers a helpful analogy for how ruptures in that process should be read.[47] Creation will proclaim its end, in part, by falling into disorder. And thus, ecological and cosmological marvels demand attention precisely because they seem to be *un*natural, to diverge from or disrupt the order of nature.[48]

In sermons, the Fifteen Signs' representation of nature's disorder, decline, and deformation—its moments of apparent unnaturalness—is primarily a call to sympathetic witness, a stance implied by the gospel passage itself. As one Middle English sermon translates part of the day's scripture (Luke 21:25–28):

> Tokens schall be in þe sonne and þe moone and in þe sterris, in the erthe, overleyng the pepill for confusion of the sowne of the see and the floddis. . . . And when these þingis ben begon to be made, beholde ȝe and reyse ȝe ȝour heddis, for ȝowre redempcion is nyȝe.[49]

> (There shall be tokens in the sun and the moon and in the stars and in the earth, overwhelming the people because of the confusion of the noise of the sea and the floods. . . . And when these things have begun to occur, behold and raise your heads, for your redemption is nigh.)

This passage invites environmental watchfulness and expectation. After all, "when these þingis ben begon to be made" could be now, or if not now, then soon. And the response to the cosmological signs promoted here is not only, as we might expect, fear and trembling, but also active, even optimistic, witness. "Behold," the passage insists.

Referencing the same passage, the sermon for the second Sunday in Advent in the Northern Homily Cycle, an early fourteenth-century series of rhyming gospel homilies, offers a less optimistic image of witness, framing the list of the Fifteen Signs within a larger discussion of the effect of the wounded world on those who will experience its death throes during the Final Days:

> "Takning," [Jesus] said "sal be don
> Bathe in the son, and in the mon,
> And in the sternes al biden;
> And folc sal thol wandreth and ten,
> For folc sal duin for din of se,
> And for baret that than sal be.
> Over al this werd bes rednes,
> Wandreth and uglines."[50]

> ("Signs," (Jesus) said, "shall appear
> both in the sun and in the moon
> and in the stars all together;
> and people shall suffer misery and pain,
> for people shall die because of the din of the sea
> and because of the struggle that shall then take place.
> Over all of this world will be redness,
> misery, and ugliness.")

In this abbreviated list of portents, which precede the sermon's full rehearsal of the Fifteen Signs motif, disorder manifests itself in the heavens and on earth. Human suffering and sorrow ("folc sal thol wandreth") are directly related to the future pain ("wandreth") and deformation ("uglines") of the created order.[51] As if bleeding, the world is covered with "rednes." Imagining the wounded, suffering body of the world here becomes an opportunity for moral injunction: Jesus preaches about the tokens of the end, the sermon later notes, to teach people "For to forsak this werdes winne, / Ful of wrechedhed and sinne, / For Christ sais us hou it sal end" (to forsake this world's pleasure, / full of wretchedness and sin, / for Christ tells us how it will end).[52] After this didactic preface, however, the preacher recounts the parable of the fig tree and then runs through the list of the Fifteen Signs.

Given this moralizing frame, it comes as a bit of a surprise that the sermon's treatment of the signs themselves is straightforwardly catalogic and descriptive. For instance, although the preacher characterizes the crying of the fish on the third day as "rueful" (pitiful), the descriptions of the following three days contain little affective or moral commentary:

> The ferthe day freis water and se
> Sal bren als fir and glouand be.
> The fift day sal greses and tres

> Suet blodi deu that grisli bes.
> The sexte day sal doun falle
> Werdes werks, bathe tours and halle.⁵³

> (The fourth day, fresh water and the sea
> shall burn like fire and glowing be.
> The fifth day, grasses and trees
> will sweat bloody dew that will be horrible.
> The sixth day, the world's works,
> both towers and halls, shall fall down.)

The affective power of the signs here derives from the mode of their representation. Free of the sorts of explanatory interjections or textual analysis found elsewhere in the sermon, the Fifteen Signs passage communicates the horrific scale of the catastrophe through its accumulative aesthetic: imagery, repetition, and accretion. It piles up concrete details with enumerative syntax, nominal pairings (fresh water and sea, grass and trees, towers and halls), couplets, and occasional alliteration. Both fresh and salt water glow as if on fire. Grass and trees drip blood. Human constructions collapse.⁵⁴ Painting a vivid picture of a catastrophic future, the sermon implies, may be as effective a goad to conversion as is explicit moralizing.

Similarly appealing to the apocalyptic imagination, later prose Advent sermons also insert the motif as a set piece, rarely elaborating on the descriptions of the signs but rather allowing the accumulation of calamities to generate both horror and sympathy. Preachers do, however, sometimes use prefatory material to draw focus to specific elements of the motif.⁵⁵ For instance, in his *Festial*, a fifteenth-century sermon cycle organized by feast days, John Mirk translates the *Legenda*'s entire catalog of the Fifteen Signs from Latin to Middle English, only adding the occasional phrase to heighten rhetorically the motif's affective impact.⁵⁶ That Mirk seems "quite satisfied to render the Signs in full, without any comment," strikes at least one modern reader as "disappointing."⁵⁷ Yet Mirk's framing of the motif is telling: rather than prefacing the list of signs with the biblical parable of the fig tree, he instead bookends the catastrophic scenes with images of wounded bodies. Immediately before the motif, he comments that "ryght as a knyght schowuet þe wondes þat he hadde in batel" (just as a knight displays the wounds that he won in battle), so too, the sins of human beings will be on display in the last days, for honor or for shame.⁵⁸ And directly after rehearsing the fifteenth sign, Mirk says that "Þen schal Iesu Crist... schewe hys wondes, fresch and new bledyng" (then shall Jesus Christ... show his wounds, fresh and newly bleeding).⁵⁹ The *ostentatio vulnerum* (the display of wounds) frames the catalog of creation's suffering.

Whereas human wounds might serve as physical evidence of past battles, Mirk emphasizes that the environmental wounds foretold by the Fifteen Signs offer evidence of even more horrific suffering in the future. Mirk writes:

> The secunde coming of Crist to þe dom schal be so cruel, fereful and orribul þat þer schal come byfore fyftene tokenes of gret drede, so þat, by þe euedens of þe tokenes komyng byfore, a mon may knowe in party þe grete horribylyte and drede þat schal come at þe dom aftur.
>
> (The second coming of Christ to judgment shall be so cruel, frightening, and horrible that there shall come before fifteen tokens of great dread, so that, by the evidence of these tokens that come before, a man may partly know the great horribleness and dread that shall come afterward at the judgment.)[60]

Highlighting the horrors of the Second Coming, Mirk's description of the signs emphasizes future events (with the repeated "schal"). Yet it also invites his listeners to enter the space between the "byfore" and "aftur," reminding them that disasters are not the end but signs of it, mere glimpses of what is to come. The knowledge provided by the signs must remain partial, not entirely accessible to those listening to the sermon and attempting to imagine a catastrophic future. Indeed, Mirk seems to know that the real function of the apocalyptic imagination lies in its present efficacy in building a sense of urgency in his listeners. The signs here locate their audience in a liminal temporality, between the first and second Advents, in the "now" of the hearing and also the "not-yet" of the apocalypse.

As in the *Legenda* and other contemporary Advent sermons, Mirk's brief introduction to the motif is followed simply by a listing of the signs, with small nods toward the difficulty they will present to human comprehension. Mirk notes that on the third day "alle þe see-swyn and gloppes of þis see schul stondyn on þe see and makyn a roryng and a noyse so hydewys þat no mon may telle hyt but God" (all of the sea-swine and the sea monsters shall stand on the sea and make a roaring and noise so hideous that no human may speak it, only God).[61] On the seventh day, he writes, the stones and rocks "schal vchon breken oþer and bete togedur wyth a hydewys noyse, þe whech noyse God hymself schal know and vndurstond" (shall each break the other and beat together with a hideous noise, a noise which God himself shall know and understand).[62] The noisiness of the nonhuman world is met by human silence. Mirk represents human beings as voiceless, ineffectual observers of the ecological collapse who on the tenth day go mad and lose their ability to speak. Another contemporary sermon, which offers an especially violent depiction of the signs, elaborates on this theme, adding that humans cannot speak *because of* "the woundres [wonders] that they schall see then."[63] I doubt that the semantic echo of wonders with wounds would have been lost on the early audience—wonders here *are* wounds.[64] The motif depicts the dying world as injured, disordered, and broken, and renders humans inhabiting it as the passive observers of its suffering. Confronted by ecological changes that they will apprehend but not be able to comprehend, these sermons portray human beings as witnesses of the environmental and social devastation in the final days, suffering with the rest of the created world. This is precisely the reason, some of these sermons will add, that the devout should pursue works of mercy in the present, attending to the suffering of those around them.

Bleeding Branches

Try to praise the mutilated world
ADAM ZAGAJEWSKI, "Try to Praise the Mutilated World"

The call to imagine a nonhuman world that is wounded, bleeding, and sick and to proleptically *feel* creation's suffering is articulated even more powerfully in the lyric tradition of the Fifteen Signs.[65] Whereas Middle English sermons tend not to elaborate on the basic list of portents provided by the *Legenda* but rather allow the larger homiletic context to shape their meaning and reception, poetic treatments often expand the descriptions of the cataclysmic scenes, heightening their pathos with more extended snapshots of the suffering of the more-than-human world. These poems explore how, as the lyric following the twelfth-century Anglo-Norman drama *Le Mystère d'Adam* solemnly reflects, the whole world will be unified in suffering in the final days: "All things will be in sadness."[66] In these poems, green trees drip blood, wondrous fish rise up from the sea, birds and beasts gather and wail, rocks fight, unborn children plead that they not be born into the dying world. And as this section will explore, in these poems, the tradition's commitment to representing the hiddenness of meaning, the depth of the suffering of the nonhuman world, and the marginal status of the human in apocalyptic ecologies comes into even greater focus.

There is far more variation among the poetic than the homiletic corpus. Poetic treatments of the signs appear in dozens of fourteenth- and fifteenth-century English manuscripts. In longer moral poems and in plays, including the *Prick of Conscience* and the Chester "Prophets of Antichrist," or interpolated in copies of the *South English Legendary*, the Middle English translation of Robert Grosseteste's *Chasteau d'Amour*, and *Dives and Pauper*, the signs tend to follow the catalog of the *Legenda* branch.[67] The early fourteenth-century *Cursor Mundi*, one of the earliest Middle English verse treatments of the signs, is the exception here; it reflects the Anglo-Norman tradition.[68] Interestingly, many of the numerous shorter, stand-alone English lyrics also originate in the Anglo-Norman branch, though they frequently order the signs differently and incorporate signs from other versions.[69]

Poems deriving from both branches inherit the Fifteen Signs motif's central themes and paradoxes, and especially its conflicting emphases on revelation and incomprehensibility and its commitment to depicting the shared vulnerability of all beings. For instance, "Quindecim signa," a popular Middle English lyric from the Anglo-Norman branch, opens with a prayer asking for help before the loss of understanding and language: "Kyng of grace, & ful o pyte, / Lord of heuyn, I-blyssyd þou be! / Haue mercy on vs, we the beseche, / Or we lese our wytt & speche!" (King of Grace and full of pity, Lord of Heaven, blessed may you be! Have mercy on us, we beseech you, before we lose our wit and speech.)[70] Because the final days will render humans silent, this preface implies, one must speak, pray, and care while one still can. As we have begun to see, such articulations about the loss or inefficacy of human understanding and language are at the heart of this tradition, which often seems more interested in communicating the limits of human knowledge than it is in providing an interpretive guide for unnatural phenomena.

Since there was some disagreement about whether the end would come with clear warning signals, poetic treatments of the signs, like contemporaneous sermons, often tried to navigate this paradox of knowing and not knowing, of anticipation and surprise. For instance, in its account of the Day of Doom and its portents, which occupies its fifth book, the *Prick of Conscience* stresses not only that no person shall be certain what time Christ will come to judgment ("sal na man certayn be / What tyme Crist sal come til þe dome") but also that people should not even try to determine the date; rather, we should all make ourselves ready ("Ne we suld noght yherne it to lere, / Ne witte wether it be ferre or nerer. / Bot we suld mak us redy alle").[71] Such warnings appear only lines before description of the various sorts of portents that might be expected to foreshadow the Doom, including the Fifteen Signs. Though this juxtaposition sends a rather mixed message, what is most certain about the end, the *Prick* suggests, is how difficult it will be to understand it as such.

The poetic tradition particularly emphasizes the inscrutability of apocalyptic ecologies when characterizing the suffering of the nonhuman world. Long before we hear of human pain and confusion, the motif invites us to imagine fish, birds, and beasts gathering and mourning. In the *Prick of Conscience*'s treatment of the fourth sign (the roaring or moaning of the sea creatures), the poet describes both how wondrous this sight is and how impossible it is for human witnesses to grasp the meaning out of it:

>Þe fierth day, sal swilk a wonder be
>Þe mast wonderful fishes of þe se
>Sal com to-gyder and mak swilk roryng
>Þat it sal be hydus til mans heryng.
>But what þat roryng sal signify,
>Na man may whit, bot God almighty.[72]
>
>(The fourth day, such a wonder shall occur:
>the most wonderful fish of the sea
>will come together and make such a roaring
>that it will be hideous to human hearing.
>But what that roaring will signify,
>no person may know, only God almighty.)

The *Prick*'s portrayal of this scene emphasizes the terrible awe it generates: the fish are "mast wonderful," and their "hydus" roaring is also a wonder. The dark underbelly of wonder here is horror, for to characterize the roaring as "hideous" is to emphasize less the unpleasantness of the sound than the affective response it generates.[73] But the passage also suggests that although the fishes' roaring is meaningful, its significance lies beyond the comprehension of human beings, who can only apprehend it, experiencing it affectively. "The deliberate representation of the ultimate unfathomability of animals to human understanding," Karl Steel writes of this motif, "breaks sharply with the anthropocentrism of nearly all medieval engagements with animals, where they appear for humans almost always as interpretable signs."[74] Insofar as they are resistant to being the site of human meaning making, these suffering animals offer a humbling rejoinder to any belief that the nonhuman world is valuable only when it supplies human needs. This movement of the human to the margins is not limited to the motif's representation of animal suffering: the opacity of climatological and ecological signs is almost a refrain. Human beings see and hear the suffering of the world; God alone understands it.

This emphasis on human witness characterizes John Lydgate's early fifteenth-century treatment of the motif in his lyric "The Fifftene Toknys aforn the Doom," which also invites sustained attention to the suffering of the more-than-human world, repeatedly disavows the possibility of discovering the meaning of the signs, and explores the disintegration of environmental, social, and mental ecologies.[75] Throughout the lyric, Lydgate emphasizes the role of human beings as witnesses, punctuating each stanza with comments about what people will see and hear. On the first day, for instance, the seas rise forty cubits "in euery mannys sight" (in every man's sight; 118/8). On the fifth day, the vegetation appears "bloody dewed to the sight" (bloody-dewed to the sight; 118/20). On the ninth day, "men shal seen" (people will see) the mountains leveled to dust (119/47). On other days they hear the cries of creatures and the crashing of rocks. In this, Lydgate rarely veers far from the descriptive mode of the tradition, providing little elaboration on the list on signs and virtually no moralization or interpretation of them (this is a rather unusual mode for Lydgate, whose poetic hallmark is amplification). His few additions and expansions insist on the importance of apprehending the signs even as he stresses the essential hiddenness of their meaning.

For all its emphasis on witness, Lydgate's lyric suggests that there remains something inaccessible in the scenes of more-than-human suffering he details. As in the *Prick of Conscience*, Lydgate's treatment of the motif describes how after the oceans have risen and then receded, birds, beasts, and fish tremble and cry out to the heavens:

> Wilde beestys vpon the flood Rorende,
> The thridde day herd on mount and pleyn,
> Foul, beest and fyssh, shal tremble in certeyn,
> Compleynyng in ther hydous moone
> Vp the skyes; this noyse nat maad in veyne,
> For what they mene, God shal knowe alloone. (118/11–16)

> (On the third day, wild beasts roaring on the flood
> will be heard on mountains and plains;
> birds, beasts, and fish shall certainly tremble,
> complaining with hideous moans
> skyward. This noise is not made in vain:
> for what they mean, God alone will know.)

Here Lydgate imagines the effect of the end times on environmental and animal ecologies. From the sea to the mountains, plains, and skies, all of creation cries out in a cacophony of lament. Yet even though this noise might not be comprehensible to human ears, the poem adds that it is no "vain din." There is purpose and meaning to the animal noise, but it remains opaque to its human witnesses. Thus, while acknowledging human presence, the poem situates human beings first as observers rather than active participants and, in so doing, implies that the world has a value outside human appreciation or use.

Later in the lyric, Lydgate characterizes animals as both signs of the eschaton and victims of it, imagining them gathering in shared suffering. Just as the birds, beasts, and fish on the third day all complain in a unified "hideous moan," on the fifth day, when trees are covered with a bloody dew, birds will take flight "as they were echoon of assent" (as if they were all in agreement; 118/22). And, when the stars fall from the heavens on the twelfth day:

> beestys alle shal comyn in presence
> With-Inne a feeld, and of verray drede
> Nouthir Ete nor drynke for noon Indigence,
> But krye, and howle, and dar hemsilf nat fede. (119–20/69–72)
>
> beasts shall all come together
> in a field, and out of true dread
> neither eat nor drink despite their hunger,
> but rather cry and howl and do not dare to feed themselves.

Fear again draws the animals into a fellowship of suffering and gives them voices to lament their pain.[76] Even so, to their human witnesses, Lydgate insists, the meaning of their howls and cries registers as little more than noise, communicating only the animals' fear of and vulnerability to catastrophes that they, too, feel but cannot understand.

The din of the animals, that unintelligible noise that is "nat maad in veyn," echoes throughout the poem's apocalyptic landscapes. For the animals are not alone: the movement of stones will generate a racket of dreadful "hurtling noyse," and one, too, that escapes human meaning making. On the seventh day, when the rocky depths of the world shift, break, and crash, Lydgate comments that no person shall know openly what all these things mean, those hidden secrets, nor interpret the tokens privately, except God alone in his high majesty.[77] Despite the human desire for knowledge, the meaning of nature's disorder remains beyond human jurisdiction; Lydgate insists that the signs are hidden, private, secret, their significance interpretable only by God.

Yet if Lydgate suggests that human witnesses will experience but not understand this lithic catastrophe, in other versions of the Latin branch of the motif following the *Legenda*, humans are not even granted the privilege of hearing the noises of the physical world. In the fifteenth-century Chester play "Antichrist's Prophets," for example, when the fish rise from the sea to "yell and rore so hideouslye... only God shall heare."[78] And when the stones break their stony fellowship, rising up against each other on the seventh day, "both rocke and stonne / shall breake asunder and fight as fonne [foes]. / The sound thereof shall here [hear] no man, / But onlye God almight."[79] The clashing battles of the anthropomorphized rocks go unheard by human ears. Strikingly, locating people at the margins rather than the center of the created world, these poetic treatments of the motif suggests that people will be only partially aware of or able to comprehend what is happening in the nonhuman world, though they, too, will be affected by ecological collapse.

It is not only the animal and lithic world that will suffer conflict and destruction; the apocalyptic ecologies of the poem soon extend to the social and cultural worlds of human beings. Although he initially focuses on the more-than-human world, Lydgate also uses the motif to imagine the end of human communities, suggesting that whereas the cataclysms will draw animals together in shared suffering, it will force humans apart, rupturing their cultural productions and personal bonds. The first objects destroyed are human constructions: on the sixth day, houses, castles, and towns made of lime and stone ("touns maad of lym and stone"; 118/26) are wrecked by fire and water until all is destroyed and gone ("al be wast and spent"; 118/30). Several days later, human understanding and community deteriorate as people emerge from the caves in which they have sought shelter. They run about as if they are drunk or frantic. Unable to acknowledge the kinship of other human beings, they ultimately succumb to silence and isolation:

> And renne abrood lyk drounke men þat Ravys,
> Or as they weren frentyk, outhir wood,
> Dedly pale, and devoyde of blood;
> Nat speke a word Oon vnto anothir,
> As witles peple of resoun and of mood,
> No queyntaunce maad, brothir vnto brothir. (119/51–56)

> (And run around like drunk men that rave,
> or as if they were frantic, or insane,
> deadly pale and devoid of blood,
> one person will not speak a word to another,
> [but behave] like witless people of reason and affect,
> nor recognize acquaintances, brother unto brother.)

Having lost both reason and recognition of other beings, humans descend into madness. The *Prick of Conscience* similarly describes the human remnant wandering around "als wode men, þat na witt can, / And nane sal spek til other þan" (as crazy men, that are witless; and none shall speak to another then).[80] Another lyric of the period characterizes human beings as increasingly animalistic: "Þe x. day, men schul renne aboute; as þai wode were, / as wilde bestes holes to seche; to hide hem inne for fere" (the tenth day, men will run about, as if they were crazy, to seek holes like wild beasts, where they can hide themselves out of fear).[81] As this simile might suggest, as human connection breaks down, an interspecies kinship of sorts develops between humans and animals during these final days: animals cry out like humans and humans lose rationality and behave increasingly like animals. Like death, the poem suggests, disaster can be an ontological leveler, a point made literal by Lydgate's lines on the seventh sign, which note that when the earth is shaken by a quake, neither "man nor beeste on ther feet shal stonde" (man nor beast will stand on their feet; 119/44).

As Ellen Rentz comments, these later signs speak to "a devastating societal breakdown. Amid the rubble, people will find themselves profoundly isolated from one another."[82] In a sense, the signs that come after this will be superfluous. The people who remain to witness them, incapable of understanding or responding to them, reminding us that even though the tradition evokes images of an inevitable future, it is fundamentally intended for those who experience it in the present, inviting them to proleptically witness the unthinkable by imagining scenes of nonhuman suffering. What matters, the Fifteen Signs emphasize time and again, is attending to the suffering and transience of the world in such a way as to generate compassion and response.

Working Mercy in a Wounded World

> Seeing, then, that all these things shall be dissolved,
> what manner of persons ought you to be?
> AUGUSTINE, *De civitate Dei* 20.24

If the apocalyptic devastation of the Fifteen Signs resists directly linking creaturely suffering with moral judgment, if it insists both on the power of imagination and on partial knowledge, if it situates human beings largely outside the scenes it depicts, what type of response does it want of its audience?[83] For many patristic and medieval theologians and writers, the point of imagining apocalyptic ecologies was to encourage renunciation and relinquishment: earthly ruin, catastrophe, and social and ecological decay are the world's reminders *not* to love it, reminders to look beyond the mutability of the physical realm to the stability of the spiritual one. And yet, although renunciation of the material realm may be the dominant medieval response to the ephemerality of all created things, as I think the Fifteen Signs motif can remind us, it is not the only one. Some versions of the Fifteen Signs employ a different emphasis: after facilitating sympathetic witness through their enumerative lists, they invite their audience to redirect that gaze to their own time, where they will also find suffering and opportunities to practice the work of compassion and *caritas*. Confronting the inevitability of ecological catastrophe, imagining its terrors, and coming to terms with our inability to fully understand it, this tradition implies, might help teach us how to die, which is, of course, to teach us how to live.

The question, then, posed by the Fifteen Signs is that raised by Augustine in the epigraph that opens this section. Quoting 2 Peter 3:10–11 in his discussion of the signs of the apocalypse in *The City of God*, he asks, "Seeing, then, that all these things shall be dissolved, what manner of persons ought you to be?"[84] But how exactly does a tradition that is usually little more than a descriptive list and that largely evades exegesis answer such a question? On the one hand, as we have seen, sermons often frame the motif with moral injunctions, directing listeners to live in such a way as to be ready for the coming judgment. On the other, as in Mirk's homiletic framing of the Fifteen Signs with images of wounds, many of the treatments of the motif, and especially those in the Anglo-Norman branch, link Jesus's wounded body with a wounded world.[85] In these contexts, Jesus's *ostentatio vulnerum* directs attention to the physical signs of his suffering. His body, like the wounded world, is riven and bloody—a parallel, as I have already suggested, that is drawn by a number of treatments of the motif. For instance, the "Ffiftene Toknes" lyric I mentioned in this chapter's introduction immediately follows its catalog of environmental catastrophes, which include a depiction of how every tree will bleed drops of blood ("euerych tre blede dropes of blood"; 92/9) with an image of Christ's return as judge "with his bledyng wound" (93/27). By pairing the tokens of doomsday with the tokens of Jesus's Passion, the poem aligns Jesus's suffering with the suffering of the world. Just as the poem has directed its reader to gaze imaginatively on signs of the future woundedness of the world, so too, Jesus displays his wounds, the signs of his own past suffering, implying his identification with the pains that have preceded his return.

Following the Fifteen Signs and Jesus's *ostentatio vulnerum* in many of these texts is another popular apocalyptic motif, the Corporal Works of Mercy, which also uses a list to emphasize the importance of caring for suffering human bodies in the present world. Drawn largely from the story of the separation of the sheep and the goats in the Final Judgment in Matthew 25, this motif was a catechetical commonplace by the late Middle Ages, painting an apocalyptic picture of the "Son of Man" in majesty, dividing the saved and the damned souls based on their care for the bodily needs of those around them. Jesus commends the virtuous souls: "For I was hungry, and you gave me to eat; I was thirsty, and you gave me to drink; I was a stranger, and you took me in: Naked, and you covered me: sick, and you visited me: I was in prison, and you came to me" (Matthew 25:35–36). When the saved souls object, saying they have done none of these things, Jesus explains that whenever they have cared for the bodily needs of another person, they have cared, unknowingly, for him.

The Corporal Works of Mercy frequently accompany the *ostentatio vulnerum* and the Fifteen Signs in medieval literature and art.[86] In "Ffiftene Toknes," for example, Jesus's display of his wounds is followed by an admonition:

> Oure lord wil schewe his bitter woundes; And Sigge, "Man! For þe,
> Look what ich haue ysuffred; what hastow suffred for me?"
> Mest he wil vnderstonde þere: þe vii merciful dedes:

Who þat haþ hem here ydo; as he with his mouþ sede,
Þe hungri forto fede; & schride þe cloþles,
Ofte goo to sek men; & herberew þe housles,
Þe dede forto bury; þe bounden to vnbynde,
Þai þat þise on erþe loueden; þere hii schullen it fynde. (93/34–42)

(Our Lord will display his bitter wounds and say, "Man,
look what I have suffered for you! What have you suffered for me?"
Mostly by this he will mean the seven works of mercy
and whoever has done them here, as he said with his mouth:
to feed the hungry, and to clothe the naked,
to visit the sick often, to house the homeless,
to bury the dead, to free the prisoner.
They that did these things on earth; there they should find it.)[87]

As Eamon Duffy writes of the treatment of this motif in the York Judgment play, in this juxtaposition of Christ's wounds with the Works of Mercy, the "*ostentatio vulnerum* is also an *ostentatio pauperum*: the wounds of Christ are the sufferings of the poor, the outcast, and the unfortunate."[88] Yet when the display of the wounds and the Corporal Works follow the Fifteen Signs, the analogy extends further: the display of Christ's wounds mirrors the wounded creation, the vulnerability and suffering of the seas, trees, rocks, and animals in the final days.

Fittingly, not far from the Fifteen Signs window at All Saints North Street was a window dedicated to the Corporal Works of Mercy, donated to the parish by Nicholas Blackburn around the same time that the window depicting the Fifteen Signs was installed. Ellen Rentz has observed that these windows work in tandem, together offering "a practical guide for turning from fear to worship."[89] Unlike the images of the Fifteen Signs window, which mainly lack human figures, the six panels representing the Corporal Works are packed with people who are actively engaged in compassionate care rather than simply witnessing the suffering around them; in these panels, Blackburn feeds the hungry, cares for prisoners in shackles, pours water into the vessels of the thirsty, gives clothes to the naked, and visits the sick. To be sure, situated in the context of the terrors of the Fifteen Signs, the exhortation to pursue the acts of bodily mercy may well have registered as threat or coercion. As Blackburn's self-insertion into the altruistic scenes of the All Saints' Corporal Works window suggests, admonitions to practice the work of bodily care may also have been driven more by the desire for individual salvation than by any concern for collective flourishing. Even so, it seems to me that when following the Fifteen Signs, a tradition that focuses in such a sustained way on the physical deterioration and misery of the world, on its cries of suffering and its bleeding wounds, the injunction to care for the bodily needs of one's suffering neighbor takes on new power and urgency. What can be done to prepare for the inevitable death of the world? Attend to the suffering now, this tradition suggests.[90] Look around and you will see where there is a need for attention and care.

When paired with the Corporal Works of Mercy, the Fifteen Signs motif also suggests that if the problem of responding to catastrophe is one of its overwhelming scale, then one possible response is to see the universal as an invitation to particularity, the future as a call to attend to the present. Writing of the representation of doomsday in the York Corpus Christi cycle, Ryan McDermott similarly calls attention to how the medieval apocalyptic imagination more generally emphasizes "that this is my last chance to love before the end. In representing the time at which it is too late to love, it holds out the present moment as the time in which to love."[91] Although the Fifteen Signs motif's appeal to care is fundamentally anthropocentric, it emphasizes that the things that will matter in the final days—as language, knowledge, and matter deteriorate or are destroyed—are suffering, the need for compassionate engagement, and the work of bodily care, for both neighbor and stranger.

Ultimately, the model of care encouraged by this tradition is more palliative than preventative. I am not proposing that medieval texts such as the Fifteen Signs that imagined apocalyptic ecologies advocated for environmental conservation, offered a nonanthropocentric account of the created order, articulated a sense of human responsibility for the earth or its animals, or even expressed real desire to stall or prevent the future degradation of the physical world. Whereas modern environmentalists often proclaim that "there is no planet B," for medieval Christians, the end of the world was not an end at all. Medieval providential thinking about the inevitable apocalypse was fundamentally optimistic, seeing the cataclysms of the last days as a necessary if painful means of cleansing the cosmos, the death pangs that usher in a new heaven and a new earth. To put this another way, many medieval texts urge their audiences to embrace the coming catastrophe rather than accept responsibility for it or work to avert it. Yet, for all the blindnesses of medieval apocalyptic thinking, a tradition like the Fifteen Signs also reminds us that one way to prepare for a nearly unthinkable future is to try to imagine it in all of its nearly incomprehensible horror, attending to all the beings that ecological cataclysm will affect, and look for ways to practice the work of care now.

Imaginative representations of environmental apocalypse have become even more widespread and urgent in the Anthropocene than they were in the late medieval contexts this chapter has surveyed, though they continue to use many of the same devices to communicate the urgency of the situation. For instance, Al Gore opened his September 2019 op-ed on climate change in the *New York Times* with a catalog of environmental catastrophes: "Hurricanes are developing, monster fires ignite and burn on every continent but Antarctica, ice is melting in large amounts there and in Greenland, and accelerating sea-level rise now threatens low-lying cities and island nations. Tropical diseases are spreading to higher latitudes. Cities face drinking water shortages. The ocean is becoming warmer and more acidic, destroying coral reefs and endangering fish populations."[92] Rising seas, hurricanes, fires, melting ice, and disease, he implies, are portents of the devastation bound to come if human beings and governments do not change their exploitative habits. And, his rhetoric suggests, lists of ecological horrors such as these may be the best means we have to begin to articulate climate change, a concept that can feel abstract and that exists on a scale almost too massive to be comprehended.

Whereas Gore, like medieval preachers, treats ongoing disasters as portents and urges conversion, much other recent writing on climate change focuses on imaginative predictions of future catastrophe. In the summer of 2015, an article published in the *New Yorker* by Kathryn Schulz outlined in eloquent, apocalyptic detail the imminent threat of a catastrophic earthquake and tsunami in the Pacific Northwest in the coming century. After narrating an ominous tale of oceans rising, receding, returning to normal, of the works of civilization tumbling, of floods and fires, the essay concludes only with a lament for how unprepared the region is for this type of ecological catastrophe, noting how "the brevity of our lives breeds a kind of temporal parochialism—an ignorance or an indifference to those planetary gears which turn more slowly than our own." The author comments that our failure to take the threat seriously is "no longer a problem of information. . . . Where we stumble is in conjuring up grim futures in a way that helps to avert them."[93] That same year, Roy Scranton's provocative meditation, *Learning to Die in the Anthropocene*, painted a similar picture. Opening with apocalyptic description, its book jacket proclaimed: "Our world is changing. Rising seas, spiking temperatures, and extreme weather imperil . . . civilization itself."[94] Given the helplessness of our ecological situation, Scranton argues that humans are left only to consider how best to live as a species that is facing its own imminent death. Since "we cannot escape our fate," he writes, "our future will depend on our ability to confront it not with panic, outrage, or denial, but with patience, reflection, and love."[95] Attending to our future extinction, Scranton suggests, should encourage us to reflect both on what it means to be human and to "cultivate understanding [of] the intimate, necessary connection of all things to each other."[96]

As these modern authors suggest, ultimately, questions of attention and care are questions of solidarity and kin making, of hanging on and "staying with the trouble." Such ecological solidarity, James Bridle writes, is a "product of imagination as well as action." Yet the "active, practical care" that solidarity asks of us "resists certitude and conclusions. Rather, this kind of solidarity with the more-than-human world consists in listening and working with, in mitigating, repairing, restoring and engendering new possibilities through collaboration and consensus."[97] Or, as Donna Haraway puts it, "The task is to make kin in lines of inventive connection as a practice of learning to live and die well with each other in a thick present."[98] Could it be that this solidarity begins with the solidarity of shared suffering? Of dwelling within precarious times?

Although clearly it is not a thing to be wished for, witnessing catastrophe—imaginatively or not—can shift our values, inviting us to develop a sense of connection with and care for those we dwell among. Implicit in medieval representations of the Fifteen Signs is a belief in the power of literature and art to help people meditate on ecological precarity, and in so doing to nudge an audience toward response.[99] Medieval Christians did not share our world's optimism about the ability of human ingenuity to engineer a way out of the final destruction, and we may not share medieval optimism about a new earth that will follow the destruction of this one. Yet, as the Fifteen Signs suggest, the practice of ecological attention, then as now, invites both meditation on the ephemerality of all things and on how to more generously care for the world that we still have.

"Consider the fig tree," the verse commands. I consider the beech instead. When I think of what attention and care might look like at the end of the world, I think of my garden, but also of the boy and the beech tree and the ephemerals that line the forest path each spring.

After the boy has left, I circle the trail alone. I picture him among the trees, wrapped in the beech trunk, peering up through the opening. "Look," he is saying. I stop to contemplate the beech's hollow wound and note how the tree still clings to its papery leaves. They flicker high above me, catching the last light of day, cradling the bony branches. Ghostly reminders of a long-lost summer. Unlike most hardwoods, American beeches don't entirely discard their foliage in the fall but rather hold on to it through a process called *marcescens*, a term that comes from the Latin *marcescere* ("to fade"). Particularly in young trees, the leaves hang on until spring, when they are released to make space for new growth. Scientists don't know exactly why some trees do this. Perhaps their rattling and sourness protects the tree's branches and bark and buds against hungry deer. Or perhaps, some observers suggest, it is a kind of arboreal mutual aid: maybe in their hanging on, they are providing shelter for birds and other small critters. I prefer this image of ecosystemic, cross-species care, even as I feel the bittersweetness of the coppery leaves on a gray winter afternoon; even as I listen to how they rustle alone in the silence. These tokens of warmer days are strangely untimely, out of sync. They will let go and fall to the ground in the spring just as the ephemerals begin to emerge. If they are signs of anything, I think, it is of resilience, of hanging on in a winter-barren world, of waiting until the new thing emerges.

EPILOGUE

Learning to Love

Ecological Attention and the Work of Care

> Let us love the country of here below. It is real.
> It offers resistance to love.
> SIMONE WEIL, *Waiting for God*

Once in a class on environmental literature, I invited a local writer to speak with my students about some of his essays. We asked him how to move from appreciation of nature to activism. "Love," he said. "Advocacy for a place or a species is always born of love for it." I've been mulling over this truism for several years now. While I hope my love of the world is evident throughout, it is not lost on me that neither love nor attention always results in care and that the ecologies that we inhabit (and that we, in fact, *are*) are often far from lovable. The work of loving and caring for the world can be difficult indeed.

Ecological catastrophes both large and small remind us that the world is "red in tooth and claw," obdurate, filled with a horrific fecundity, with pests, parasites, viruses, poisonous plants, noxious gases, and dangerous forces—strong storms, rising waters, tornadoes, wildfires—and in bed with death. We often experience the world in which we dwell to be precarious, chock-full of dangers, uncertainties, and wondrously strange. It is quite reasonable to question the environmentalist's dictum of world love. After all, why should we love a world that suffers and dies and that inflicts suffering and death on all its creatures? Why should we feel beholden to a world that does not seem always to return the favor? A world in which our well-being seems threatened by forces beyond our control, as massive as hurricanes that sweep up the coastlines, fires that decimate woodlands, or earthquakes that level cities, and as microscopic as deadly viruses that pass unseen between us?[1] To posit such questions, this book has suggested, is not only to acknowledge the world's "dark ecologies" but also accept our responsibility for those institutional and ecological harms we have created or contributed to.

Yet "world love" remains a key aspect both of environmentalist discourse and of many of the biblical traditions this book has considered, even as it is inevitably shot through with a sense of disquiet or distrust. It is at the heart of what may be the most quoted scriptural text of our own time: "For God so loved the world" (John 3:16). But this apparently world-affirming statement is followed by an undermining command in one of the epistles: "Do not love the world or anything in the world . . . [for] the world is passing away" (1 John 2:15). In both texts, the Greek word translated "world" is *kosmos*, the universe or whole order of creation.[2] On the one hand, the passages suggest that the cosmos is an object of divine delight (as the York Creation play so ecstatically performs). On the other hand, human beings are commanded *not* to love that cosmos, and certainly not to become too attached to it (as we saw in some versions of "Erthe toc of Erthe"). In the aporia created by these passages, we are invited into the tensions we have considered on almost every page of this book: between what is ephemeral and what is lasting, between wonder and horror, between comprehension and incomprehension, between anthropocentric values and ecocentric ones, between love for the world and contempt for it. As we have seen, medieval biblical literature often raises but rarely resolves these tensions.

These tensions shape and are equally urgent in our own moment, though they manifest differently in the Anthropocene, an age in which our responsibility for climatic instability is evident everywhere. As we navigate the seemingly constant catastrophe, the ongoing apocalypse caused by modern consumptive habits, many of us find ourselves asking, as Barry Lopez does in one of his last essays, if it is "still possible to face the gathering darkness and say to the physical earth, and to all its creatures, including ourselves, fiercely and without embarrassment, I love you, and to embrace fearlessly the burning world."[3] How does one love a dying world in all of its wonder, delight, and horror? Should we spend our love on this? What do we risk when we refuse to do so, when we turn away?

I have suggested throughout that there is an urgency to our love of the dying. We often love things and people with a special ferocity when we are drawn into the orbit of their suffering, when their death is imminent, when we are shocked into awareness of their absence. Tinged with anticipatory grief, this love holds the beloved more tenderly and works more passionately for both healing and comfort. It aims to make the most of the time that remains, all while hoping for and working toward a different outcome. We don't love the burning world *only* because it is burning, but its flames ignite our awareness of our love. They move us to care.

Yet, as we have seen throughout this book, in medieval religious writing, the relationship between care and world love can be fraught. This ambivalence is particularly evident in the apocalyptic finale of the fourteenth-century allegorical dream vision *Piers Plowman*, which depicts a crisis of care in a time of catastrophe.[4] At the beginning of the poem's final dream, we find ourselves in a richly allegorized agrarian landscape not entirely unlike the fields in the poem's opening scenes. But now, rather than watching laborers ready the land for planting, the dreamer, Will, observes as Antichrist destroys the soil and crops. Laying waste to the once-cultivated fields, he takes the form, as Eleanor Johnson points out, of "ecosystemic collapse."[5] To defend against Antichrist, Conscience cries out to Kynde (nature/God) for help as he and his followers retreat into the Barn of Unity (variously signifying a fortress, a grainery, and the church). But when Kynde emerges from the planets, he comes as catastrophe, afflicting people with a vast range of diseases and ailments, from coughs and toothaches to heart attacks and plague. These "foragers of Kynde" decimate the living and create a culture of fear. Those that remain now fear Kynde, crying out, "Help! Here cometh Kynde / With Deeth that is dredful, to undo us alle!" (Help! Here comes Kynde / with Death, who is dreadful, to kill us all; 20.88–89). This is nature as "dark ecology." Kynde here is cosmic, apocalyptic, providential, a retributive agent of God. It is a bringer of death rather than a giver of life.

Even the dreamer is affected by Kynde's arrival. As A. C. Spearing notes, the poem aligns the "last days of the world" with "the last days of the dreamer's life," offering us a parallel cosmic and microcosmic *ars moriendi*.[6] When the dreamer, Will, crosses paths with this dark Kynde, he begins to feel his life slipping away. He calls out to Kynde to save him "out of care" (out of suffering, 20.201). But instead, Kynde tells him to head to the Barn of Unity and learn some craft. When Will asks what "craft" one should learn, Kynde replies:

> "Lerne to love," quod Kynde, "and leef alle othere."
> (WILL:) "How shal I come to catel so, to clothe me and to feede?"
> (KYNDE:) "And thow love lelly, lakke shal thee never
> Weede ne worldly mete, while thi lif lasteth." (20.207–10)

> (Kynde replied, "Learn to love and forsake everything else."
> "How then shall I sustain myself with clothing or food?"
> "If you faithfully love, you shall never lack
> clothing or food while your life lasts.")

Part of learning to die, this passage implies, is learning to love well. Kynde figures love as a "craft," a skill that must be learned and cultivated, and perhaps especially in the midst of a burning world. Will's immediate concern is for his own material well-being, but Kynde redirects him by inviting him into community, implying that life in the Barn of Unity is characterized by mutual aid.

This is not the first time that the poem has associated attention to Kynde with a hermeneutic of love or suggested that some loves require leaving something else behind.[7] For instance, in the vision of middle earth, Kynde led the dreamer to a mountaintop to teach him how to love the creator through "eche a creature" (every creature; 10.326).[8] There Will learns by entering into dialogue with Kynde. And here, again, at the apparent end of the world, Kynde distills one of the larger lessons of the poem: learning to love is a rigorous practice; it is a reiterative process; it requires beginning again; it requires failing, acknowledging one's error, and starting anew. Indeed, the command "learn" may be the most important part of Kynde's advice. Importantly, though this advice comes in the midst of apocalypse, this is not the end of the story. Calling the dreamer into the Barn of Unity, Conscience suggests that because apocalyptic ecologies generate care (suffering), they render visible the pressing need for relinquishment and ever-new forms of community.

However, as the remainder of the poem explores, neither of these needs is easily met. The very idea of what it means to *care* itself is troubled. The poem seems to know, as Maggie Nelson writes of another context, that "care, too, is an economy, with limits and breaking points."[9] And it is these breaking points that emerge in the apocalyptic final lines of *Piers Plowman*. The dreamer largely disappears from the narrative after receiving his instructions from Kynde, and the poem turns its focus to the friars, whom Conscience also admonishes to learn to love. After admitting them into the Barn of Unity, Conscience tells them that they will never suffer "lakke" if they "leve logic; and learneth for to lovye" (forsake the study of logic and learn to love; 20.249–50). He then suggests that if they desire a "cure" (a Middle English word implying attention, responsibility, spiritual care, but also an ecclesiastical office, as in a curate), they will find it by attending to Kynde, which teaches the measure and order of the cosmos (20.253).[10]

This moment is, I believe, the first time in which the poem brings "cure/care" into the mix, notably shortly after we have witnessed a side of Kynde we have not seen before, where it is less as aligned with a generative cosmic order than with apocalyptic destruction, senescence, and death. What, then, does the poem suggest care means in a burning, dying world? To be sure, the "cure" that the friars desire is a curacy, a position that often came with property that would give these covetous friars some economic stability, freeing them from the perpetual need created by their profession of poverty. Yet, etymologically, a curate's main responsibility is care (usually in the form of *cura pastoralis*, the pastoral care of souls). Conscience's invitation implicitly asks them to trade in one type of care/cure for another, their desire for a curacy for the hard labor of caring.

It's striking that most of *Piers Plowman*'s uses of the terms *cure* and *curator* appear in the final two passus of the B-text.[11] Forms of *cure* appear nine times in this apocalyptic conclusion. Forms of *care* appear three times in this passus. What these appearances make visible is the doubleness of care. In the Middle Ages, much like now, *care* is semantically ambivalent: it can be both cause and remedy, both suffering and a response to suffering. In Latin, *cura* means either "suffering, pain, distress" *or* "attention, responsibility, devotion." The Middle English *care*, on the other hand, is slightly less ambivalent. Deriving from the Old English noun *cearu*, its primary meaning is negative (suffering), though the *Middle English Dictionary* suggests that is also used to indicate the more positive idea of responsibility.[12] Though they have slightly different emphases and different etymological roots, the Middle English *cure* and *care* both carry the conflicting meanings into the vernacular. Thus, "caring about" is related to but differs from "caring for" or "having cares."

In its repetition of the language of "cure" and "care," the final, apocalyptic scenes ultimately play out a profound failure of care, particularly by the friars, who seek to be curators (carers), but only because of how it will personally benefit them.[13] They care when it pays to care; they are reluctant to share in others' cares. Even so, until the very final lines, Conscience hopes for change, opening the Barn of Unity to those who claim that they can commit to the work of care, even when their history suggests otherwise. This openness leads to a shockingly risky, and ultimately unwise, act of welcome. The figure of Conscience offers hospitality to "Sir Penetrans Domus" (20.340), a friar representing the coming apocalypse, whose "moral valence is unambiguously negative" but whose welcome reflects the poem's continued hope for reform and renewal even as the structures meant to sustain collective flourishing are disintegrating.[14] Ultimately, Conscience's act of welcome, itself an embodiment of care, leads to a breakdown of Unity: the friar corrupts the community from within.

As Conscience reckons with this devastating failure, the poem's final lines circle back to its opening, suggesting a new beginning enacted not in the safety that refuges or fortresses might offer against the manifold apocalyptic threats but rather in outward movement, change, and seeking, in leaving behind the stability of the past for the possibility of something better.[15] Conscience ends the poem by making himself vulnerable as a pilgrim heading out into the wide world, echoing the poem's opening lines in which we found Will traveling "wide in this world wondres to here" (widely in the world to hear wonders; Prologue 4). Yet in the poem's final scene, Will's search for wonders has been replaced by Conscience's cries for Grace. In this circularity, we are reminded that the poem doesn't narrate *the* apocalypse, but rather *an* apocalypse, or, to be more precise, apocalypses: crises of care that may also be moments of revelation. The poem stages a moment of potentiality, urging reform as necessary for survival. Yet though that reform fails, partly because of a failure of care, hope is not entirely lost. Its final lines show *Piers Plowman*, in effect, beginning again, opening up into possibilities that are both like and unlike what has come before.[16] And it is beginning again, that the poem suggests hope for different futures might still be found.

Several years after his visit to my class, the nature writer left an envelope of cosmos seeds in my mailbox on campus, gleaned from his garden at the end of the summer. I had admired the lanky flowers with their feathery leaves and explosions of orange petals and wondered out loud that the deer didn't seem to bother them. Discovering the seeds in my box months later, I am moved that he remembered my offhand comment. When I look up the planting instructions, I make note of their scientific name: *Cosmos sulphureus*. Very loosely translated: burning world.[17] I delight in them, and, inspired by his gift, I begin to gather seeds from my zinnias, echinacea, and mammoth sunflowers. I scoop them out of my squash and peppers. I dry them and pinch them into tiny envelopes for safekeeping and then distribute the packets to friends and family in the dead of winter. Next spring, when the ephemerals begin to bloom in the woods, I will return the remaining seeds to the soil in my garden alongside the cosmos seeds and the tiny kale and mustard starts that my father brings me each spring.

Sharing seeds is surely not what my course visitor meant when he spoke of world love as the first step toward action on its behalf. Or perhaps it's exactly what he meant. Though small, it is a work of learning to love the world through attention, care, and participation in its "fayre processe." Caring for a garden and becoming beholden to the land on which I live have taught me the necessity of collaborating with the more-than-human world and about our shared transience. I don't know how to ground my thinking about ecological suffering and care without thinking about my neighbors, the people and animals and plants and objects with whom I dwell; without thinking about the redheaded child and my garden and the beech tree; without thinking about the karst topography under my feet, the students I learn with in cinder block classrooms, the towns drowned just south of my home to provide the water I drink, the trash I drag to the curb on Sundays, the rewilded farmland west of town, the industrial feedlots to the south, those without homes who seek shelter in the wooded areas of city parks, and the hawks and squirrels and deer with whom I share this place. I also don't know how to think about the future without attending to the present and listening to the past. I am convinced that learning to see the cosmic and the microcosmic, the universal and the particular, the then and the now as coextensive, as so many of the texts I have considered in this book do, will be an important part of moving forward with hope and care in our ecologically precarious world.

Even so, I am far from immune to that creeping cynicism that insists that a local focus in an age of global catastrophe is a denial of or naivete about the political. I sometimes think that the only legitimate response is systemic critique, political action, and perhaps even physical destruction and disruption.[18] These are necessary responses, for today, as in the Middle Ages, ecological precarity is a political, social, and economic problem, a problem of resource management. Yet from this perspective, to emphasize that it is also a problem of attention and to advocate care for the most proximate can look like accommodation at best, or the self-soothing of the privileged at worst. It can look like an embrace of the Voltairean dictum, "Il faut cultiver notre jardin" (one must tend one's own garden), rejecting the suffering of a larger world in favor of private retreat. It can, but it doesn't have to. I like my colleague Ross Gay's response to the suggestion that tending one's garden is a privilege unavailable to many. He asks: "What would happen if we acknowledged that none of this is privilege, but rather it is as it should and *could* be? And what if we figured out, together, in a million different ways, how to make it so? Or to say it another way, rather than cursing the darkness, what if we planted some seeds?"[19]

This is what many of biblical texts I've considered in this book do. They plant seeds. They do so in part by inviting us to attend to suffering and transience, both human and more-than-human. But they also do so by using the formal affordances of literature to encourage us to see the cosmic and microcosmic, the political and personal, and the past, present, and future as coextensive.[20] Their use of lists and repetitions and sustained descriptions help slow us down and attend to process, ask us to bear witness to figures we might not otherwise notice, emphasize interconnection, and remind us of how the particular can also be the universal. They suggest that reclaiming attention and care may also be potent modes of dissent and disruption.[21] For care is a commitment to living *as if* we were already enmeshed and full participants in networks of mutual flourishing, to living as if strangers were already kin, as if the local were (as it is) the planetary. I cling to the hope that the more we do so collectively, the more likely it is that we can bring a new world into being.

Acknowledgments

I wrote most of this book in southern Indiana, on the ancestral homelands of the Miami, Delaware, Potawatomi, and Shawnee people. I recognize them as past, present, and future caretakers of this land.

To this land and place which has nurtured my mind, spirit, and body; to the limestone substrate on which I live, to the old-growth and repaired forests all around me, to the fawns that race through the woods, the raccoon family in the decaying trunk, the nuthatches and finches and titmice that make their home so close to mine. Thank you.

To Robyn Bartlett and Becky Davis, who read every word of this book, some words several times, who offered both encouragement and consistently good advice. This book is so much better because of the care and attention you have given to it over the past several years. Thank you.

To my colleagues and students at Indiana University. How lucky I was to find an academic home with you in Bloomington. And especially to Patty Ingham, who always sharpens my thinking; Karma Lochrie, for good questions and old-time jams; Joey McMullen, Liz Hebbard, and Penelope Anderson, for camaraderie. To the Creative Ecologies for Just Futures research group, who inspire me with their commitment to environmental justice. To all in the IU English department who assisted me at critical points, particularly Joshua Pontillo and Zac Engledow for help with research and editing; and to Lisa LaPlante, Bev Hankins, Robin Noakes, and Kayla Pointer for administrative support. And to all my students, who are so often my teachers. Thank you all.

To all those friends and colleagues who read all or part of this manuscript or talked with me about it and offered such generous and incisive feedback: Will Revere, Jenny Sisk, Neil and Emily Dhingra, Evelyn Reynolds, Arthur Bahr, Bruce Holsinger, Scott Russell Sanders, Christoph Irmscher, Byron

Santangelo, Rob Womack, Ingrid Nelson, Barbara Lehr, Maggie Gilchrist, Alyce Miller, Ellen Stenstrom, and Donna Eder. Thank you.

To Charles Marsh and my cohort in the Virginia Project on Lived Theology, who first encouraged me to write about how my story intersects with the religious works I study. Thank you.

To the institutions that have given me the gift of time to write, particularly the IU College Arts and Humanities Institute, and those that offered me the chance to think with you about these ideas: The Newberry Library, Purdue University, the University of Michigan, the University of Virginia, Rutgers University, Yale University, UC Irvine, UNC Asheville, and the IU Medieval Studies Institute. Thank you.

To Randy Petilos, Nathan Petrie, and Lindsy Rice at the University of Chicago Press for helping this book find its way into the world. And to Lori Meek Schuldt for eagle-eyed edits. Thank you.

To my coven, Jenny Adams, Elisabeth Andrews, and Tristra Newyear-Yeager, who inspire me with your brilliance and your big hearts and who challenge me to take risks. And to Hazel and Maddy, whose creaturely companionship over two decades has brought such joy. Thank you.

Most of all to my family, but especially to my father and my late mother, who taught me the names of wildflowers and constellations, how to care for injured wildlife, how to "stay with the trouble" in all sorts of ways, and that such mundane work of attention and care and welcome can be potent, if quiet, ways of remaking the world.

Thank you.

Bloomington, IN
March 2024

Notes

Sources are cited in short form in the notes. For full source citations, see the bibliography.

Introduction

Opening epigraph attributed to Alan of Lille in a thirteenth-century manuscript, "Omnis Mundi Creatura," in Alan of Lille, *Literary Works*, 544–45. Throughout I have made some slight changes to Winthrop Wetherbee's translations.

1. For additional examples, see Job 14:12; James 1:10, 11; 1 Peter 1:24. All English translations from the Bible are from *The Holy Bible: The Douay-Rheims Version*.
2. Nemo, *Job and the Excess of Evil*, 17.
3. Wilson, *English Lyrics in John of Grimestone's Preaching Book*, 26.
4. There is a vast corpus of scholarship on the idea that nature is like a book or a mirror. For representative recent studies focused on late medieval English literature, see Robertson, *Nature Speaks*, esp. 60–64; R. Davis, *"Piers Plowman" and the Books of Nature*; and R. Davis, "Book of Nature." Many scholars have been dismissive of this convention. Steven Epstein sees the phrase "reading the book of nature" as a "banality" that has "incited a vast literature of baffled synthesis and conjecture" (*Medieval Discovery of Nature*, 8).
5. "The swelling sea closes in the harbor / and day ends in evening" (Alan of Lille, "Book of Creation," pp. 546–47, lines 35–36).
6. Both Grimestone and Alan's lyrics are representative examples of the massive medieval genre of mortality or transience lyrics. For an overview of medieval English lyrics about death, see, most influentially, Woolf, *English Religious Lyric*, esp. chaps. 3 and 9.
7. Alan of Lille, "Book of Creation," pp. 544–45, lines 8–9.
8. I borrow the phrase "more-than-human" from D. Abram, *Spell of the Sensuous*, but my thinking on the "more-ness" of this world is also indebted to Bridle, *Ways of Being*.
9. Muir, *My First Summer in the Sierra*, 110. The term *ecology* is a nineteenth-century invention, first used in the German naturalist Ernst Haeckel's 1866 book *Generelle Morphologie der Organismen*. My use of the plural, *ecologies*, is intended to suggest the overlapping networks of relationship we move within and between. It is indebted to the work of Félix Guattari, who writes

of the postmodern "ethico-aesthetic aegis of an ecosophy: social ecology, mental ecology, and environmental ecology" (*Three Ecologies*, 41).

10. There is a huge corpus of scholarship on apocalypse as both a mode and a genre in ancient, medieval, and modern contexts. For useful overviews, see Garrard, *Ecocriticism*, 93–116; and Emmerson and McGinn, *Apocalypse in the Middle Ages*.

11. On medieval attitudes toward natural disasters, see Epstein, *Medieval Discovery of Nature*, 148–84, and the essays in Bjork, *Catastrophes and the Apocalyptic*. That "catastrophes and crises are exceptions, disruptions of order" is a commonplace of modern disaster studies (Meiner and Veel, *Cultural Life of Catastrophes and Crises*, 1).

12. In this doubleness, *apocalypse* is much like *catastrophe*, which originated as a dramatic term used to describe a disruption or turn that brings order or moves toward a conclusion. See Gayk and Reynolds, "Forms of Catastrophe," 1–2. To be sure, as history shows, the apocalyptic can function either as a tool of resistance (often to political power or larger social orders) or as a means of reinforcing the status quo.

13. My thinking about the relation of catastrophe to hope and possibility is indebted to Rebecca Solnit's work on disaster in *A Paradise Built in Hell*, but also to Donna Haraway's *Staying with the Trouble*. It is important to both writers that catastrophe *invites* responsibility and care rather than obligating such responses. Catastrophe offers a moment of clarity and potentiality rather than any defined mandate. For other approaches by medievalists to dwelling within a catastrophe world, see Cohen and Duckert, "Introduction: Eleven Principles," 1–26; and Coley, "Failure," 183–95.

14. By focusing on imaginative adaptation of biblical texts, this book contributes to and draws from the small field of criticism on medieval vernacular biblical literature, though my methods and overall focus differ significantly from most previous studies, which tend to emphasize influence and source study. For foundational studies, see D. Fowler, *Bible in Middle English Literature*; Morey, *Book and Verse*; and Besserman, *Biblical Paradigms*. For an overview of the English tradition, see Lawton, "Englishing the Bible." Most recently, in *Middle English Biblical Poetry* (2021), Hume offers a thoughtful reading of the romance and domestic themes of late medieval biblical literature. Von Contzen and Goodblatt's 2020 collection of essays, *Enacting the Bible*, overviews biblical texts in dramatic performance. Old English literary criticism has offered a far livelier discussion of biblical reception, adaptation, and innovation. See, for instance, Zacher, *Rewriting the Old Testament*. On the Latin tradition, see Lapidge, "Versifying the Bible," 11–40.

15. The foundational study of the "adventurousness" of fourteenth-century English religious writing is N. Watson, "Censorship and Cultural Change."

16. On medieval ideas of materiality as simultaneously subject to both "survival and decay, meaning and meaninglessness," see Bynum, *Christian Materiality*, 286.

17. For a reflection on how "the sheer pace of change playing out right now is making it harder for us to maintain our myth of a stable planet," see E. Fitzgerald, "Stability Fantasy."

18. Cohen and Duckert, *Veer Ecology*, is similarly focused on ecological dynamism and possibility. On the need for scientific models that can better account for ecological, geological, and climatological uncertainty, see Carslaw et al., "Climate Models Are Uncertain."

19. Gregory the Great quoted by McGinn, *Visions of the End*, 63.

20. Morton, *Ecological Thought*, 161.

21. For foundational discussions, see Bill McKibben's 1989 manifesto about the impacts of climate change, *The End of Nature*; an early ecofeminist account, Carolyn Merchant's *The Death of Nature* (1979), which associated the end of a feminized nature with the rise of mechanistic, scientific

NOTES TO PAGES 6–13

thinking in the seventeenth century; and more recently, Jedidiah Purdy's *After Nature* (2015), which insists that it is no longer possible to think of nature as existing apart from human influence.

22. On the significance of medieval death culture and the *ars moriendi*, see especially Appleford, *Learning to Die in London*; and D. Smith, *Arts of Dying*.

23. For another ecological reading of the medieval micro- and macrocosm relationship, see Robertson, "Scaling Nature." Any ecological hermeneutic must also navigate multiple scales, attending to the minutiae that contribute to systemic eutrophy.

24. Scranton, *Learning to Die*, 20–21. Scranton's approach both here and in his next book, (*We're Doomed, So Now What?*), has frequently been critiqued as passive and fatalistic, as in Andreas Malm's recent discussion in *How to Blow Up a Pipeline*, but I think such readings miss Scranton's central point: that "learning to die" may lead to learning to live in new, transformative way.

25. Scranton, *Learning to Die*, 92.

26. Scranton references the medieval *ars moriendi* and the medieval transience lyric "Erthe toc of Erthe."

27. Many people in the United States have outsourced much of this final caregiving, as Atul Gawande explores so beautifully in his book, *Being Mortal*.

28. Gilbert, *Living Death*, 1.

29. On these more practical *ars moriendi* manuals, see Appleford, *Learning to Die in London*.

30. Bruster and Rasmussen, *Everyman and Mankind*, line 119.

31. D. Smith, *Arts of Dying*, 1–2.

32. For influential considerations of the difficulty of thinking or representing the catastrophe of climate change, see Ghosh, *Great Derangement*; Heise, "Science Fiction and the Time Scales of the Anthropocene"; and Nixon, *Slow Violence*.

33. *Mankind*, in Bruster and Rasmussen, *Everyman and Mankind*, p. 91, line 31.

34. White, "Historical Roots," 1205.

35. White, "Historical Roots," 1205.

36. White, "Historical Roots," 1205.

37. See Glotfelty and Fromm, *Ecocriticism Reader*. More recently, it has been excerpted for McKibben, *American Earth*, 405–12.

38. For a concise discussion of the essay's legacy, see Jenkins, "After Lynn White." There are several dedicated scholarly journals to this subfield, including the *Journal for the Study of Religion, Nature, and Culture*.

39. White himself later qualified his claims in a follow-up article, suggesting that not all strands of interpreting the Genesis narrative support his provocative thesis. See White, "Continuing the Conversation," 55–65. The original essay has been critiqued from a variety of disciplinary perspectives. For an early response, see Feenstra, "Christian Impact on Ecology." For representative reassessments of and challenges to this essay, see LeVasseur and Peterson, *Religion and Ecological Crisis*; Hoffman, *Environmental History of Medieval Europe*, 87–91; and C. Abram, *Evergreen Ash*, 26–28.

40. Morton, *Ecological Thought*, 27.

41. Kimmerer, *Braiding Sweetgrass*, 7.

42. Lochrie, *Nowhere in the Middle Ages*, 2.

43. Francis, *Laudato si'*.

44. There has been a significant amount of ecocritical scholarship of Middle English texts since 2009. Earlier studies often focused on the representation of nature, landscape, and environment. For foundational studies, see Douglass, "Ecocriticism and Middle English Literature"; Stanbury, "EcoChaucer"; Rudd, *Greenery*; Hanawalt and Kiser, *Engaging with Nature*.

45. More recent ecocriticism has employed object-oriented or new materialist methodologies to reconsider the agency or vitality of the nonhuman world. See, for example, Dinshaw, "Ecology," 347–62; and Cohen, *Stone*. Vin Nardizzi offers a useful overview of the field up to 2012 in "Medieval Ecocriticism."

46. Many scholars, most of them not medievalists, imply that there is a single medieval model of human relations with the natural world and often imagine it as a rather idealized pastoralism. On this point, see Robertson's discussion of C. S. Lewis's *The Discarded Image*, which establishes the language of the medieval model, in *Nature Speaks*, 4–8. For representative studies positing a single medieval model, see R. Watson, *Back to Nature*. Carolyn Merchant's influential study of women, nature, and the scientific revolution also saw medieval nature as "a kindly and caring motherly provider" that was cast off in favor of a mechanistic and male cosmos (*Death of Nature*, 6). A number of Merchant's assumptions about the medieval past continue to shape contemporary ecofeminist studies. See, for instance, Plumwood, *Feminism and the Mastery of Nature*.

47. Le Goff, *Medieval Imagination*, 5. An approach to ecological attention that has inspired much of my thinking is Christie, *Blue Sapphire of the Mind*. My approach is also indebted to Lawrence Buell's foundational work, *Environmental Imagination*. The opening epigraph for this section is from Stafford, *Oregon Message*, 24.

48. In this approach, I join recent studies focused on later fields that explore how poets engaged larger climatological and geological changes. See, most powerfully, Nersessian, *Calamity Form*; and Menely, *Climate and the Making of Worlds*.

49. I see them as offering imaginative, performative, affective "scripts" in the sense that Sarah McNamer has explored. See McNamer, "Feeling." On literature, genre, and "form of life," see I. Nelson and Gayk, "Genre as Form of Life."

50. Leopold, "The Land Ethic," in *Sand County Almanac*, 201–14; and Morton, *Ecological Thought*.

51. Haraway, *Staying with the Trouble*.

52. My thinking about textual ecologies is indebted to Myra Seaman's *Objects of Affection*.

53. For a recent volume that similarly invites its contributors to practice *emplacement* of their analyses of premodern literature, see Nardizzi and Werth, *Premodern Ecologies*.

54. Hartman, "Tea and Totality," 58. My method here is not "presentist" but rather multisynchronist. I attempt to acknowledge the "thickness" of time (following Catherine Brown, "In the Middle"), to encounter texts in their multiple *nows*, of their production, their various reception, and my own encounter with them. For another influential model, see Dinshaw, *How Soon Is Now?*

55. For a more sustained meditation on the dynamics of the "we" in a medieval text, see my essay: Gayk, "'A comon light': Julian of Norwich's Participatory Prose."

56. M. Nelson, *On Freedom*, 10–11.

57. The opening epigraph for this section is from MacFarlane, *Underland*, 16.

58. I borrow the idea of future hauntings from the introduction to Tsing et al., *Arts of Living on a Damaged Planet: Ghosts*.

Excursus: A Brief History of Medieval Climate Change

1. Aberth, *From the Brink of the Apocalypse*, 6. See also Bowlus, "Ecological Crises." For a picture of the major ecosystemic challenges facing late medieval people (land shortage, climate change, food scarcity, contagion, pollution), see Johnson, *Waste and the Wasters*, esp. 11–36.

2. *Middle English Dictionary* (hereafter cited as *MED*), s.v. "climat" and s.v. "clime," accessed May 3, 2023. For medieval climate maps, see Langeslag, "Weathering the Storm," 76–91.

3. *Oxford English Dictionary*, online edition (hereafter cited as *OED*), s.v. "Climate Change," accessed May 3, 2023, https://www.oed.com/search/dictionary/?scope=Entries&q=climate+change.

4. Fagan, *Little Ice Age*, xii.

5. Fagan, *Little Ice Age*, xiii.

6. Behringer, *Cultural History of Climate*, vii. Neither Behringer nor I are suggesting a model of climate determinism by noting how climatic disorder often has larger social, economic, and political implications. For a helpful overview, see also Aberth, *Environmental History*.

7. The classic study of climate history is Lamb, *Climate, History, and the Modern World*, 172ff, though there have been several recent surveys, including Behringer, *Cultural History of Climate*, and the final chapters of Hoffman, *Environmental History of Medieval Europe*.

8. On the period's widespread deforestation, see M. Williams, *Deforesting the Earth*, esp. 87–117.

9. Rosen, *Third Horseman*. Until recently, most scientific studies of the medieval climate anomaly focused on Europe, but researchers have begun to show the global effects of preindustrial climate change. See, for instance, Lüning et al., "Medieval Climate Anomaly in South America," which demonstrates widespread warming and glacial retreat in South America.

10. For more information about the relation of NAO to climate variability today, see Lindsey and Dahman, "Climate Variability." Negative NAO leads to cold conditions in northern Europe and warmer conditions in southern Europe and the Mediterranean. Importantly, the last several decades have been marked by a high NAO, which seems to be caused by anthropogenic global warming. For an extended discussion of the NAO's influence on the Little Ice Age (from which my brief overview is derived), see Fagan, *Little Ice Age*, 23–28.

11. Johnson, *Waste and the Wasters*, 4–5.

12. Quoted in Fagan, *Little Ice Age*, 29.

13. Behringer, *Cultural History of Climate*, 101.

14. Jordan, *Great Famine*, 7. See also Behringer, *Cultural History of Climate*, 104–5.

15. Trokelowe, *Annates*.

16. Rosen, *Third Horseman*, 133. Johnson, *Waste and the Wasters*, 18.

17. Dean, "The Simonie," lines 1–5.

18. Mitchell, *Becoming Human*, 41. For an extended treatment of medieval understandings of the human impact on ecosystems, see Johnson, *Waste and the Wasters*.

19. Johnson, *Waste and Wasters*, 36.

20. Rosen, *Third Horseman*, 100.

21. Coley, *Death and the Pearl Maiden*.

22. *The Second Shepherds' Play*, in Cawley and Stevens, *Towneley Plays*, p. 129, lines 79–87.

23. Cohen, "Drown," 248.

24. *Mum and the Sothsegger*, lines 1727–39, in Dean, *Richard the Redeless and Mum and the Sothsegger*.

Chapter One

1. Harrison, *Gardens*, 19.

2. Stevens, "Sunday Morning," in *Collected Poems*, 69.

3. Wilner, "A Moralized Nature," in *The Girl with Bees in Her Hair*, 46.

4. *The Creation*, in Beadle, *The York Plays*, 58/170. Hereafter, all references to the York Plays will be to this edition and cited parenthetically by page and line in the text. All translations are my own.

5. Wikipedia, s.v. "Origin of Death," accessed October 19, 2022, https://en.wikipedia.org/wiki/Origin_of_Death.

6. This command is the subject of the debate between Eve and the serpent in Genesis 3. See also Romans 6:25a: "For the wages of sin is death."

7. Augustine is particularly occupied with the dynamics of change and mortality in the physical world and the "struggle for life" as part of the prelapsarian ecological condition. He even suggests that human bodies may have been mortal before the Fall since they needed physical food to sustain them. See Augustine, *Literal Meaning of Genesis*, vol. 1, bk. 3 (esp. pp. 76–92). For an adjacent but confessionally motivated assessment of the "unfallen" creation, see Garvey, *God's Good Earth*, which argues that prelapsarian biological transience was a mainstream idea among premodern theologians, but fails to account for the fact that the world's corruption in the Fall was a commonplace of popular writing produced throughout the Middle Ages. In "De Natura," Warnez offers some useful qualifications of Garvey's rather one-sided argument, surveying the long history of patristic and scholastic writing on prelapsarian death and "natural evil." Neither of these treatments accounts for the witness offered by vernacular literature, which provides even more variation than the Latin theological tradition.

8. Bynum, *Christian Materiality*, 34–35.

9. For a very helpful overview of medieval theological approaches to prelapsarian animal and plant death, see Minnis, *From Eden to Eternity*, esp. 140ff.

10. For instance, in a pair of essays, "Natura Ridens" and "Natura Lachrymosa," John Fleming notes that the word *nature* "could invoke two radically different moral universes. One world of nature was stamped with the perfection of paradise, and in it, humankind lorded it over an unendingly varied and fascinating animal and material creation which God himself had declared to be 'good, very good.' Of the other, the emblem was death, often referred to by the moralists simply as man's 'debt to nature.' A physically and morally corrupt human race lived out its brief and brutish life in warfare with a hostile and treacherous natural world" (Fleming, *Man and Nature*, 1). Neither of these options, though, accords with many of the hexameral treatments of prelapsarian creation.

11. One intermediary view is explored by Sara Ritchey, who argues that from the twelfth century onward, many religious writers argued for the "re-creation" of the world through the incarnation of Christ. See Ritchey, *Holy Matter*.

12. White, "Historical Roots." For an extended discussion of White's influential thesis, see my introduction, 10–13. For a similar view of the relation of humans to the natural world, see Thomas, *Man and the Natural World*, esp. 17–29.

13. Although there are two "creation stories" in Genesis, medieval *hexamera* tend to treat them as a single narrative. As Siewers notes, Genesis's creation narrative is "on its own terms an extraordinarily Earth-focused text within pre-Scholastic traditions" ("Ecopoetics of Creation," 56).

14. For helpful meditations on gardens and care, see Harrison, *Gardens*, 1–13.

15. Foucault, "Of Other Spaces."

16. For an overview of the how paradise often took the form of a sacred garden in ancient religions, see Delumeau, *History of Paradise*. On Eden as the paradigmatic enclosed garden, see Rudd, *Greenery*, 165–206; Harrison, *Gardens*, 1–24; and McClean, *Medieval English Gardens*, 13.

NOTES TO PAGES 32–35

17. Take, for example, three recent studies of the affordances of gardens in late medieval literature. In *The Island Garden* (2012), Lynn Staley argues that medieval writers use the trope of the island garden to articulate anxieties about national identity. In *Shaping the Archive* (2017), Sarah Novacich explores how the garden, and Eden in particular, offer medieval thinkers a space for thinking the compilation of the archive. Most recently, in *The Enclosed Garden* (2021), Liz Herbert McAvoy explores how medieval enclosed gardens function as a space for expression of and resistance to the patriarchal narratives that structure much medieval religious thinking.

18. Biblical scholars have long advised that we might read passages such as Genesis 1–3 as prophetic rather than descriptive. For instance, John Rogerson argues that Genesis 1 "is not a mandate for human exploitation of the world; it is a critique of the actual state of human behavior" ("Creation Stories," 27). Such ideals have been put into practice by ecological initiatives and groups (many of which are named some version of "Eden"). Note, for instance, the Eden Project, a tourist destination in Cornwall that features a series of geodesic domes representing different biomes. It hosted the G7 in 2021 and welcomes millions of visitors each year, aiming to give them an experience of a sustainable ecology (https://www.edenproject.com/). For a critique of this "recovery narrative," see my brief discussion in chapter 2 of this book and Merchant, *Reinventing Eden*.

19. Minnis, *From Eden to Eternity*, 1. Minnis is interested primarily in how Latin scholastics and John Wyclif represented Eden, whereas I am more interested in its depiction in vernacular contexts that suggest lay reception.

20. Stewart, "Garden Agon," 111.

21. Novacich, *Shaping the Archive*, 41; and Howes, *Chaucer's Gardens*, 16–22.

22. On the "virtuality" of dance, a concept applicable to other forms of embodied performance, see Chaganti, *Strange Footing*, 6–13.

23. Though we might now identify this biological script as DNA, medieval texts would have seen the script as the *virtu* of divine word and order.

24. The term is explicitly applied to drama in the Banns to *The Croxton Play of the Sacrament*, where the second Vexillator calls the play "this lytell processe." See Sebastian, *Croxton Play of the Sacrament*, line 75. "Processe" is also closely related to "procession," a practice with which many medieval plays are closely associated (as in the *corpus Christi* processions that gave rise to some of the cycle plays).

25. *OED*, s.v. "process."

26. Ronda, "Mourning and Melancholia in the Anthropocene." As Ronda suggests, rhythm is central to other literary analyses that bring together the formal and the social. I want to suggest further that rhythm also brings together the formal and ecological. For key studies, see LeFebvre, *Rhythmanalysis*; and Levine, *Forms*, esp. 49–81.

27. For similar readings of medieval play scripts as sites of potentiality and virtuality, see Gayk, "Idiot Psalms"; Sergi, *Practical Cues and Social Spectacle*; and Chaganti, *Strange Footing*.

28. On the timing and location of the day, see Beadle, "York Corpus Christi Play"; and Twycross, "Forget the 4.30 am Start."

29. There are surprisingly few scholarly studies of Middle English creation plays. For some discussion, see James, "Paradise, Pleasure, and Desire"; Walker, "'In the Beginning . . .'"; Novacich, chap. 1 of *Imagining the Archive*; Black, "The Time of the Tree"; and G. Williams, Merrylees, and Richmond, "Producing 'The Creation' and 'The Fall of Man.'"

30. Although the cycle begins with the Barker's "Fall of the Angels," I have not included it in this list since it only touches on the events in the opening chapters of Genesis.

31. This format and length have posed some challenges for modern revivals of this play. On how they were managed in a 2006 production, see Biebly, "Creation of the World to the Fifth Day."

32. For a discussion of York's representation of creation by divine word in the cycle's first play, "The Creation of the Angels and the Fall of Lucifer," see Walker, "'In the Beginning ...,'" 36–43.

33. Vernacular texts also employ similar imagery. *Cursor Mundi*, for instance, describes God as a very clever wright who is not only an expert builder but also able to make his own materials. See Morris, *Cursor Mundi*, Trinity Manuscript, 27/331–36. All subsequent quotations to *Cursor Mundi* are to this text and manuscript, and numerals refer to page and line numbers of this edition. For a brief but useful introduction to the manuscripts and contents of *Cursor Mundi*, see Morey, *Book and Verse*, 99–107.

34. By *poiēsis* (ποίησις), I simply mean an act of bringing something new into being, though my understanding here is also aligned with the Heideggerian sense of revealing or "bringing forth." For Heidegger, the "unfolding of the natural world, the unaided blossoming of nature, is *itself* a process of *poiesis*. Indeed it is *poiesis* 'in the highest sense.'" See Wheeler, "Martin Heidegger."

35. *MED*, s.v. "fayre."

36. On creation ex nihilo from both scholastic and Lacanian perspectives, see Ingham, *Medieval New*, esp. 42–47.

37. For a helpful study of temporality in medieval drama that offers some discussion of the multiple temporalities of creation plays, see Black, *Play Time*.

38. Compare also the two-line description offered by the Towneley Creation play, "Out of the erth herbys shal spryng, / Trees to florish and frute furth bring" (Cawley and Stevens, *Towneley Plays*, 4/43–44).

39. Fein, "Twelve-Line Stanza Forms."

40. Similar stanzaic structures appear in other late medieval biblical paraphrase and liturgical literature, suggesting that it may have been seen as an appropriate high-style vernacular form, appropriate for sacred texts and performances. Fein notes similar twelve-line stanza plays in the York Cycle, including the plays of Abraham and Isaac, Moses and Pharoah, the Transfiguration, the Raising of Lazarus, and the Last Supper. Perhaps the most famous version of this stanza in Middle English verse is *Pearl*.

41. For a compelling discussion of medieval ideas of innovation and repetition, see Ingham, *Medieval New*, esp. 1–18.

42. King, *York Mystery Cycle*, 56.

43. John Chrysostom makes a similar point regarding the divine creation of animals: "God's blessing and the form of words, 'Increase and multiply,' bestowed on them life and permanence" (*Homilies on Genesis*, 98–99).

44. Lumiansky and Mills, *Chester Mystery Cycle*, 14–15/33–38. Citations for the Chester cycle refer to page and line numbers of this edition.

45. Compare also the analogous passage from the *Middle English Metrical Paraphrase of the Old Testament*:

> He bad that yt suld spryng and sprede
> Herbys and treyse with wod and wand
> and sed to saw when thei wer dede,
> So that new suld up spryng

there sted forto restoyre
And flours and frutt forto furth bryng.

(He bade that it should spring and spread
herbs and trees with wood and branches
and seed to sow when they were dead
So that new [ones] should spring up
in their place in order to restore
and bring forth flowers and fruit.)

See Livingston, *Middle English Metrical Paraphrase*, lines 90–95.

46. For a consideration of the formal affordances of botanical "virtue" in an early modern context, see Rosenberg, *Botanical Poetics*, esp. chap. 2.

47. Ambrose, *Hexameron, Paradise, and Cain and Abel*, 92.

48. In the *History of the Patriarchs* (a Middle English translation of portions of Comestor's popular biblical summary), the author frequently draws on the language of ornament to describe creation, noting, for instance that the stars and planets were ordained to "ornament" the heavens (Taguchi, *The History of the Patriarks*, 14).

49. Imagining the creation of the world as occurring in the spring was a commonplace in the period. For instance, in his hexameral commentary on this passage, which was included in the *Glossa Ordinaria*, Bede comments on this seasonal identification in the scriptural source (Bede, *On Genesis*, 79).

50. Pearsall and Salter, *Landscapes and Seasons*, 58.

51. Rudd, *Greenery*, 166.

52. Writing of the Cornish creation play, Daisy Black similarly notes the complexity of representing the temporality of creation: "Narratives depicting the beginning of the world necessarily negotiate a slippery path between God's eternal divinity and the temporality constituted in the act of creation" ("Time of the Tree," 66).

53. *MED*, s.v. "shulen," meaning 3a. *Willen* is rather more complicated since it can function both as a regular verb (expressing delight, desire, or obligation) and as modal auxiliary. For the latter usage, which I am persuaded is the main use in this play, see *MED*, s.v. "willen," meaning 9.

54. This is not to suggest that patristic and medieval theologians had nothing to say about *utilitas*, but rather that some representations of the prehuman world, such as the York Creation, do not frame their delight in the world's beauty in terms of utility. As Minnis writes, for many theologians, the "true *utilitas* of creation" lies in its ability to teach and nourish humans, but that the mortal creation is ultimately "dispensable" and to be transcended (*From Eden to Eternity*, 150–51).

55. Basil, *Hexaemeron* 5.4–5.

56. Ambrose, *Hexameron* 3.38–39. There are, to be sure, many hexameral accounts that insist that the primary value of the more-than-human world is in its utility for humans. For an overview of this issue with an excellent survey of patristic hexameral accounts, see Warnez, "De Natura."

57. Chrysostom, "Homily 7," in *Homilies on Genesis*, 98–99.

58. Grosseteste, *On the Six Days of Creation* 4.30.5 (p. 157).

59. Cohen, "Love of Life," 39.

60. For an extended discussion of animal death and suffering in Eden, see Minnis, *From Eden to Eternity*, 140–52. On Genesis's depiction of human-animal relations in Eden, also see Steel, *How Not to Make a Human*, 7–8; and Alexander, *Saints and Animals*, 128. For the epigraph that opens this section, see Dillard, *Pilgrim at Tinker Creek*, 162.

61. Morris, *Cursor Mundi*, 47, 49/683–94.

62. For an extended discussion of the richness of Kinde and kinds in the Middle Ages, see R. Davis, *"Piers Plowman" and the Books of Nature*. As Davis shows here and elsewhere, the "Vision of Kinde" in *Piers Plowman* emphasizes the goodness and justice of animal relations and the exceptionality of the human.

63. Minnis, *From Eden to Eternity*, 16.

64. Chaucer, "Former Age," in *Riverside Chaucer*, 650–52. For a discussion of how Golden Age narratives shaped the medieval imagination of Eden, see chapter two of this book.

65. Augustine, *The Literal Meaning of Genesis*, vol. 1, 3.16.25 (p. 92).

66. Aquinas, *Summa Theologiae*, 1a, qu. 96, art. 1 (vol. 13, pp.122–25).

67. Basil, *Hexaemeron* 9.2.

68. Much of this work focuses on talking birds, esp. in Chaucer and lyrics. See, for instance, Kordecki, *Ecofeminist Subjectivities*; and Leach, *Sung Birds*.

69. Langland, *Vision of Piers Plowman*, passus 11, lines 344–61. Strikingly, as my epilogue will consider, in *Piers*, Kinde is not only the catalyst of life, as this passage suggests, but also the bringer of death.

70. For a representative example, see the lengthy discussion in Grosseteste, *On the Six Days of Creation*, 7.2-11 (pp. 204–209).

71. *MED*, s.v. "beli" (n); "bale" is a common alternate spelling.

72. Minnis, *From Eden to Eternity*, 141.

73. For an engaging treatment of medieval practices mirroring this divine blessing, see Rivard, *Blessing the World*.

74. See, for instance, Bede, *Hexameron*, which sees the first humans as immortal creatures but also worries over the fact that they take in fleshly nourishment like mortal creatures (*On Genesis* 1.29–30 [p. 95]).

75. *MED*, s.v. "skil."

76. For an overview of medieval theological understandings of prelapsarian dominion, see Minnis, *From Eden to Eternity*, 84–98. As Minnis observes, hexameral writings went to great lengths to try to explain how human beings could have had dominion over the tiniest animals and insects (88).

77. Lumiansky and Mills, *Chester Mystery Cycle*, 20/177–78.

78. Cawley and Stevens, *Towneley Plays*, 8/165–73.

79. Morris, *Cursor Mundi*, 47/677–83.

80. Livingston, *Middle English Metrical Paraphrase*, lines 125–28.

81. On human exceptionalism, see R. Davis, "'Save man allone.'"

82. See, by way of contrast, Minnis's discussion of John Wyclif's treatise on creation: "The helplessness of mankind was not a feature of his first creation, but a punishment for his transgression" (*From Eden to Eternity*, 14). One could also read these passages as protolapsarian, as anticipating the Fall. See Wyclif, *De statu innocencie*, 500–505.

83. Ecologically minded theologians and religious studies scholars have long observed the importance of the earthy kinship asserted by the opening chapters of Genesis. See especially the work of Ellen Davis, including her essay "Land as Kin."

84. On this idea, see Palti, "Bound Earth."

85. Donne quotation from Donne, *Divine Poems*, p. 13, lines 1–2.

86. Alaimo, *Bodily Natures*, 2.

87. Morton, *Ecological Thought*, 109.

88. Macy, *World as Lover, World as Self.*

89. For a reading of premodern subjectivity that pushes back against such dualisms by arguing for premodern "porous" subjectivities, see Taylor, *Sources of the Self.*

90. Emerson, "Nature," 36.

91. Alan of Lille, *De planctu naturae*, 6.11, in *Literary Works*, 76–77.

92. Robertson, "Scaling Nature."

93. Morris, *Cursor Mundi*, 39/543–52.

94. Higden, *Polychronicon*, vol. 2, bk. 2, chap. 1 (p. 183). Cf. the description of the eight parts of Adam in the Wheatley Manuscript *Adam Book*, in Day, *Wheatley Manuscript*, 77.

95. Aristotle, *De Anima* 3.1.412a20–21. For a helpful overview of Aristotle's hylomorphism, see Shields, "Aristotle's Psychology." On hylomorphism and late medieval conversations about matter, see Robertson, "Medieval Materialism," esp. 110–12.

96. On the substantial makeup of human beings, see also Mitchell, *Becoming Human*, esp. chap. 1, "Being Born."

97. On this trope, see especially Robertson, *Nature Speaks*, 55–60. For an earlier but influential study, see Chenu's *Nature, Man, and Society*, which examines how twelfth-century cosmology explored the dual nature of the human: "Man encompasses an antinomy—he is seen as simultaneously an image of the world (as philosophy would have it) and an image of God (as Genesis declares)" (33).

98. Robertson, "Scaling Nature," 610.

99. Robertson, "Scaling Nature," 624.

100. There are multiple versions of this poem, all are which are edited in Murray, *Erthe Upon Erthe*. For a lengthy ecocritical reading of this poem, see also Rudd, *Greenery*, 21–26. For a brief discussion of this poem's representation of human beings as earth "bound," see Palti, "Bound Earth," 31–32. For a general overview of the poem, see Woolf, *English Religious Lyric*, 84–85.

101. Gray, *Themes and Images*, 197–98.

102. On the polysemous nature of earth, see also Cohen and Elkins-Tanton, *Earth*. See also the useful discussion of this poem in Novacich, *Shaping the Archive*, 30–31.

103. D. Smith, "Medieval Forma," 74. This argument is taken up at greater length in "Unearthly Earth, Mortuary Lyric," in D. Smith, *Arts of Dying*.

104. D. Smith, "Medieval Forma," 75 and 77.

105. Woolf, *English Religious Lyric*, 85. One might also read it as an example of Agambenian "bare life."

106. See Rudd, "Thinking through Earth," 146; and Rudd, *Greenery*, 23–24.

107. Cambridge University Library, MS Ii.4.9, edited in Murray, *Erthe Upon Erthe*, pp. 57–58, lines 11–14.

108. I. Nelson, "Form's Practice," 47.

109. For the texts of all the versions, see Murray, ed., *Erthe Upon Erthe.*

110. Berry, "The Body and the Earth."

111. For information about recent performances, see the York Mystery Plays website, https://www.yorkmysteryplays.co.uk/. Several scholars have studied the modern revival; see especially Beckwith, *Signifying God*, esp. 161–90; and the essays in M. Rogerson, *York Mystery Plays.*

112. York Museum Gardens, "About St Mary's Abbey." For discussion of using the St. Mary's ruins as a setting for the drama as they function as "technologies of remembrance," throwing into relief larger issues of cultural nostalgia and memory, see Beckwith, *Signifying God*, 9–16.

113. On using ruins as landscape features, see Woodword, *In Ruins.*

114. Ramsey, "Dustsceawung."
115. Thompson, *Northern Homily Cycle*, prologue, line 14.
116. Julian of Norwich, *Writings of Julian of Norwich*, chap. 53, lines 36–37 (p. 295).
117. Harrison, *Gardens*, 19.
118. My thinking here on "dark ecologies" is inspired both by the theoretical work of Timothy Morton, who penned this phrase, and Annie Dillard, whose works embody the horrific wonder of dark ecologies so beautifully. See especially Morton, *Dark Ecology*, and Dillard, *Pilgrim at Tinker Creek*.
119. Harrison, *Gardens*, 12.

Chapter Two

1. As Timothy Morton and others have noted, Darwin's "struggle for existence" is often misunderstood; rather, "existence is coexistence, or, as Darwin puts it, 'adaptation'" (Morton, *Ecological Thought*, 60).
2. For a useful survey of the Irenean (negative) and the Augustinian (positive) views of the integrity of the postlapsarian world, see Warnez, "De Natura." Also see Fleming, "Natura Ridens; Natura Lachrymosa."
3. A Middle English translation of Robert Grosseteste's Anglo-Norman allegory *Le Château d'Amour* (*The Castle of Love*), edited as "The King and His Four Daughters," in Shuffleton, *Codex Ashmole 61*, lines 167–72.
4. By "care," I here mean primarily "suffering" (*MED*, s.v. "care"; deriving from the Old English "cearu") but also "help/concern" (deriving from the Latin "cura"). I will discuss this distinction later in this book.
5. Julian of Norwich, *Writings of Julian of Norwich*, chap. 10, line 46 (p. 161). This is the first of several repetitions of this phrase throughout the long text of Julian's *Revelations*.
6. "King and His Four Daughters," in Shuffleton, *Codex Ashmole 61*, line 164.
7. Dean, *World Grown Old*, 54. Sarah Ritchey offers an important counterargument to this declensionist reading in her study of how some medieval thinkers imagined the "re-creation" of the world in Christ's incarnation, death, and resurrection. See Ritchey, *Holy Matter*.
8. For an overview of the two main stories of decline and progress (which doesn't take the medieval witness fully into account), see Merchant, *Reinventing Eden*; Merchant, *Columbia Guide to American Environmental History*, 206.
9. Joni Mitchell, "Big Yellow Taxi," on *Ladies of the Canyon*, Reprise Records, 1970.
10. For instance, Ursula Heise summarizes the concept of declensionism as follows: "modern society has degraded a natural world that used to be beautiful, harmonious, and self-sustaining" (*Imagining Extinction*, 7). Other scholars, such as Geraldine Heng, have noted premodern industrial production (*Global Middle Ages*, 9–11).
11. Merchant observes that this narrative "of recovery functioned as ideology and legitimation for settlement of the New World, while capitalism, science, and technology provided the means of transforming the material world" ("Reinventing Eden," 137).
12. Nicola Masciandaro similarity explores the way in which medieval origin narratives function either as primitivist/declensionist or progressive, though his work focuses on the valuation of labor rather than ecological engagement. See Masciandaro, *Voice of the Hammer*, esp. 68–69.
13. For a thorough study of these interrelated tropes, see Dean, *World Grown Old*.

14. Dean, *World Grown Old*, 2.

15. These works are not technically elegies (a form) but rather elegiac (a mode). As scholars of elegy often note, it operates more commonly as a mode than a form, embracing narrative as well as lyric works. For a useful overview, see Kennedy, *Elegy*. The elegiac works this chapter considers could be further classified as "pastoral elegies," since they tend to lament the absence of a lost ecological harmony. On pastoral elegy, see the discussion of Edenic pastoralism in L. Buell, *Environmental Imagination*, esp. chap. 1, "Pastoral Ideology," 31–35. On the elegiac tendencies of pastoral more generally, see R. Williams, *Country and City*.

16. My thinking on the ordering effects of the refrain is indebted to Deleuze and Guattari, *A Thousand Plateaus*, especially chapter 11, "Of the Refrain."

17. Dean, *World Grown Old*, 31.

18. On medieval temporality and historiography, see Jahner, Steiner, and Tyler, introduction to *Medieval Historical Writing*; and Galloway, "Writing History in England." Older but still influential studies include Patrides, *The Phoenix and the Ladder* (1964), and, on the repetitions of sacred time, see, most influentially, Auerbach, "Figura," in *Scenes from the Drama of European Literature*, 11–76.

19. Minnis, *From Eden to Eternity*, 11.

20. The opening epigraph for this section is from Chaucer, *Boece*, bk. 2, metrum 5. All subsequent quotations from Chaucer's works are taken from Chaucer, *Riverside Chaucer*, and are noted parenthetically by page and line number in the body of the text.

21. See esp. Fyler, "Love and the Declining World."

22. The concept of "primitivism" as an idealization of rustic simplicity dates only to the 1860s; see *OED*, s.v. "primitivism." For an excellent study of medieval primitivism as it relates to labor and production, see Masciandaro, *Voice of the Hammer*, esp. chap. 2. On the depiction of "primitive peoples" elsewhere in the world, see Steel, "Fourteenth-Century Ecology," 186–99.

23. As I noted previously, most modern environmental declensionist narratives also see the development of industry and technology as a force of ecological decline. On this point, see esp. Merchant, *Reinventing Eden*.

24. In his work on American pastoralism, Leo Marx writes that nostalgia for a lost Edenic garden is predicated on the rise of the machine; see Marx, *Machine in the Garden*.

25. Stanbury, "Multilingual Lists," 36. For a subtle account of the ambivalence of this critique that suggests Chaucer's main interest is in ignorance, see Galloway, "Chaucer's 'Former Age' and the Fourteenth-Century Anthropology of Craft." For a reading of Chaucer's poem as an instance of late medieval primitivism that is less invested in the lyric's irony, see Stock, "Past and Present."

26. As Patricia Clare Ingham has explored, this is not the only moment of "revolutionary pastoral" in Chaucer's corpus; the opening of the Wife of Bath's tale also suggests the "utopian power of pastoral's emotive claim on the real" as the Wife juxtaposes an enchanted absorption in the world with its consumption and colonization (Ingham, "Pastoral Histories," 35).

27. For an early study that makes these points, see Schmidt, "Chaucer and the Golden Age."

28. Masciandaro, *Voice of the Hammer*, 103.

29. As Galloway writes on the poem's treatment of primitivist ignorance, Chaucer's version of the narrative "offers an essentially secular view of the mechanism of historical change" ("Chaucer's 'Former Age,'" 537).

30. Steel, "Fourteenth-Century Ecology," 190.

31. For a consideration of the way the lyric idealizes an early kinship with animals, see Steel, "Fourteenth-Century Ecology," 190–92.

32. Murdoch and Tasiolas, *Apocryphal Lives of Adam and Eve*, p. 67, lines 91–92. All subsequent quotations from the *Canticum* and the Auchinleck *Life* are taken from this edition and are noted parenthetically by page and line number.

33. These three medieval technologies, White suggested, revolutionized agriculture in the Middle Ages and may have had some effect on other social dynamics. White's technological determinism has had many critics, but his attention to the possible social effects of these devices is also very suggestive. For some responses, see Worthen, "Influence of Lynn White Jr.'s Technology and Social Change"; and for White's book on the topic, see White, *Medieval Technology and Social Change*. For another brief critique, see the opening pages of Ingham, *Medieval New*.

34. Masciandaro, *Voice of the Hammer*, 96.

35. For the frequency of this phrase in postplague literature, see Wenzel, "Pestilence in Middle English Literature," 133.

36. I read this literature as "nostalgic" in the earliest sense of the term: the Greek roots suggest *nostalgia* is "homecoming pain," the suffering of exile from or desire to return to one's home. See *OED*, s.v. "nostalgia": "ancient Greek νόστος return home (see *nostos* n.) + -αλγία -algia (pain)."

37. Scholars have long noted that the play's realism and colloquial dialogue draw its biblical speakers into the late medieval world. The classic study of the contemporaneity of the vernacular is Auerbach's *Mimesis*, 142–51, but also see Fassler, "Representations of Time."

38. Justice, "Authority of Ritual."

39. The stage direction immediately before this lament reads: "*Hic respiciat Adam paradisum et ambas manus suas elevabit contra eum et caput pie inclinans dicet*" (*Here Adam should look back toward Paradise and raise both his hands toward it, and bowing his head devoutly say:*). All citations to "The Play of Adam" are from the edition and translation by Carol Symes in C. Fitzgerald and Sebastian, *Broadview Anthology of Medieval Drama*. The edition is based on Aebischer, *Le Mystère d'Adam*.

40. Higden, *Polychronicon*, vol 2, bk. 2. chap. 4 (p. 219).

41. King, *York Mystery Cycle*, 56. Woolf also notes the surprising expansion of this scene but calls attention to its particularly "beautiful lines of lyric lament" (*English Mystery Plays*, 120).

42. *MED*, s.v. "werken." For a useful discussion of Middle English words for labor and work, see Masciandaro, *Voice of the Hammer*, esp. 11–22. As scholars long noted, the York plays often thematize labor since the plays were staged by York's guilds. For a comparative study of the social contexts of the York and Chester cycles, see Rice and Pappano, *Civic Cycles*.

43. For a discussion of the tensions inherent in ideas of human creation/work, see Ingham, *Medieval New*, esp. 23–47.

44. As Minnis notes, many medieval commentaries suggested that Adam and Eve would have labored in Eden as well, cultivating and caring for the garden (*From Eden to Eternity*, 125).

45. *MED*, s.v. "trauel." See also Masciandaro, *Voice of the Hammer*, 14–15. *Travail* is the term used to describe the subjective experience of labor resulting from the Adamic curse in the Wycliffite translation of Genesis 3:17: "cursid is the erthe in thi werk; in traueyls thow shalt ete of it alle the daies of thi lijf" (*Holy Bible [. . .] by John Wycliffe*).

46. For a related discussion of "unsignified vocalizations," see Lears, *World of Echo*. One could also read this turn toward the nonrepresentational as an element of the fall of language, as Jager explores in *Tempter's Voice*.

47. For a reading of the earthiness of Adam in this play and the larger tradition, see chapter 1, "Being Earth," esp. 48–52.

48. Both the original Cornish text and the modern English translation are from *The Ancient Cornish Drama*, edited and translated by Edwin Norris, with subsequent citations referring to page and line numbers of this edition. Revisions to or divergences from this translation will be noted using italics.

49. The Cornish plays are extant in one medieval manuscript—Oxford, Bodleian Library MS Bodley 791—and two later copies: Oxford, Bodleian MSS 28556–28557, and Wales, Peniarth MS 428E. For brief introductions to the plays, see Scherb, "Cornish *Ordinalia*"; and Murdoch, "Cornish Medieval Drama."

50. *Ancient Cornish Drama*, 28/372–78.

51. Original Cornish text:

> Gas adam the'th egery.

(*Ancient Cornish Drama*, 28/382)

52. Original Cornish text:

> Kee kymmer myns a vynny
> Adam a'n beis ol adro
> Thy'so ef a veyth besy
> Hag ahanes a theffo

(*Ancient Cornish Drama*, 30/404–406).

53. "war an beys meystry" (*Ancient Cornish Drama*, 30/409).

54. "Adam a ol the drevas / an degves ran thy'mmo gas / wheth in atal the kesky" (*Ancient Cornish Drama*, 32/425–27). The idea of a tithe first appears in Genesis 14:18–20 when Abraham gives 10 percent of his possessions to Melchizedek after winning a battle. The author of the *Ordinalia* backdates this practice and gives it a divine primogeniture in imagining that God commands the tithe himself shortly after Adam and Eve are expelled from the Garden.

55. For a discussion of the major medieval English discourses of "waste," see Johnson, *Waste and the Wasters*; Johnson, "Poetics of Waste."

56. Milton, *Paradise Lost*, in *Complete Poems and Major Prose*, 648–49. All citations of *Paradise Lost* are from this edition.

57. Woolf, *English Mystery Plays*, 125.

58. These parabiblical legends date from the earliest days of Christianity. See "Life of Adam and Eve," vol. 2:249–95. For a wide-ranging treatment of the early reception of the story of Adam and Eve, see Greenblatt, *Rise and Fall of Adam and Eve*, esp. chap. 4, "The Life of Adam and Eve."

59. For an overview of the development of these stories and comments on the questions that seem to have inspired them, see Murdoch, *Apocryphal Adam and Eve in Medieval Europe*, esp. vii–ix; and Greenblatt, *Rise and Fall of Adam and Eve*, 64–74.

60. Michael Stone identifies seventy-three manuscripts of the Latin *Vita*; see Stone, *History of the Literature of Adam and Eve*, 25–30. The Middle English corpus includes five distinct versions of the legend in both poetry and prose. The most complete account of the Middle English versions is available in Murdoch, *Apocryphal Adam and Eve in Medieval Europe*, chap. 3. Also relevant are Murdoch, *Adam's Grace*; and Murdoch, *Medieval Popular Bible*, esp. 42–69.

61. These two Middle English verse versions of the legend have been edited in Murdoch and Tasioulas, *Apocryphal Lives of Adam and Eve*. The prose versions include the "Life of Adam and Eve" in Day, *Wheatley Manuscript*, 76–100; "Þe lyff of Adam and Eve," in the Vernon Manuscript,

in Horstmann, *Sammlung altenglischer Legenden*; and various lives of Adam included in copies of the *Legenda Aurea*. See Jacobi a Voragine, *Legenda aurea*.

62. Dean, "Domestic and Material Culture," 27–28.

63. See especially Dean, "Domestic and Material Culture," but also, more recently, Hume, "Auchinleck Adam and Eve," 36–51; Hume, *Middle English Biblical Poetry*, 59–92; and McAvoy, *Enclosed Garden*, esp. chap. 1, "Out of Eden: Framing Eve."

64. Murdoch and Tasioulas, *Apocryphal Lives of Adam and Eve*, 66/40, 46–48.

65. Horstmann, *Sammlung altenglischer Legenden*, p. 222, lines 37–39.

66. Dean, "Domestic and Material Culture," 30–31.

67. Murdoch and Tasioulas, *Apocryphal Lives of Adam and Eve*, 43/152–60.

68. "Þe lyff of Adam and Eue," in Horstmann, *Sammlung altenglischer Legenden*, p. 222, line 45. Cf. Day, *Wheatley Manuscript*, 81/19–21.

69. "lyff of Adam and Eue," in Horstmann, *Sammlung altenglischer Legenden*, p. 222, line 44–45.

70. Day, *Wheatley Manuscript*, 82/10–19.

71. Cited in Warnez, "De Natura," 961.

72. Day, *Wheatley Manuscript*, 82/22–26.

73. Murdoch and Tasioulas, *Apocryphal Lives of Adam and Eve*, 70/173–77.

74. Murdoch and Tasioulas, *Apocryphal Lives of Adam and Eve*, 70/200–205.

75. The strange detail that Eve is "green as grass" is drawn directly from the *Vita*'s "Et tunc exiuit Eua de aqua et caro eius uiridis erat sicut herba de frigoribus aque" (131.10–11).

76. See the notes to Murdoch and Tasioulas, *Apocryphal Lives of Adam and Eve*, 113.

77. Dean, "Domestic and Material Culture," 36. It is also a common way of describing a morbidly pale and livid body in late medieval writing; *MED*, s.v. "grene."

78. Murdoch and Tasioulas, *Apocryphal Lives of Adam and Eve*, 48/325–26, 329–34.

79. Murdoch and Tasioulas, *Apocryphal Lives of Adam and Eve*, 45/219–21. On penance in the larger *Vita Adae* tradition, see Murdoch, *Adam's Grace*, 41–49.

80. On the shaping force of typological interpretation on medieval literature and art, see Emmerson, "*Figura* and the Medieval Typological Imagination." The foundational study is Auerback's long essay, "Figura."

81. Dean, "Domestic and Material Culture," 27.

82. I borrow the idea of future hauntings from Tsing et al., *Arts of Living on a Damaged Planet*, which observes how "anthropogenic landscapes are also haunted by imagined futures. We are willing to turn things into rubble, destroy atmospheres, sell out companion species in exchange for dreamworlds of progress" (G2).

83. Stewart, *On Longing*, 2.

84. The most complete treatment of the Fall and its repercussions in Julian's *Revelations* is the Parable of the Lord and Servant in chapter 51; see Julian of Norwich, *Writings of Julian of Norwich*, 273–89.

85. There are many theological exceptions to this rule, though—for example, the American social gospel in the early twentieth century, the social justice work of the Quakers, and liberation theology.

86. Kimmerer, *Braiding Sweetgrass*, 20.

87. Ingham, *Medieval New*, 196.

88. Morton, "Dark Ecology of Elegy," 253. On elegy and closure see, Sacks, *English Elegy*, esp. chap. 1.

89. R. Williams, *Country and City*.

90. The idea of "climate repentance" has recently been taken up by some modern interfaith groups, which have sought to acknowledge that a change of heart and acknowledgement of guilt are important steps toward climate action for many religious communities. See, for instance, the work of the global interfaith alliance, which convened for a ritual of repentance at the UN climate conference COP 27 in November 2022: Climate Repentance, "10 Spiritual Principles and Ceremony of Repentance."

91. Heise, *Imagining Extinction*, 12.

92. Harrison, *Gardens*, 10.

93. Tsing et al., *Arts of Living on a Damaged Planet*, G7.

Excursus: On Plague, Precedent, and the Punishment Paradigm

Opening epigraph from "Eurydice on History" in Graham, *Swarm: Poems*, 108.

1. Cohen, "Drown," 246.

2. Isidore, *Etymologies*, 283.

3. For a useful discussion of these historical comparisons, see Patterson et al., "Societal Impacts of Pandemics."

4. For an overview of religious and secular responses to the "lessons" of the pandemic, see Pew Research Center, "What Lessons Do Americans See for Humanity in the Pandemic?"

5. Mangum, "Pandemic as God's Judgement."

6. Wenzel, "Pestilence and Middle English Literature," in *Black Death*, 133.

7. For an innovative study of how medieval doctors made use of their firsthand observations of the Black Death, see Aberth, *Doctoring the Black Death*. For an Italian example of medieval sermons attributing ecological and climatological catastrophes to sin, see Hanska, "Catastrophe Sermons." The homiletic poems in London, British Library, Cotton MS Nero A. x, offer other examples of late medieval apocalyptic sermons, though these focus more on biblical examples of catastrophe than incidents of that period. For a recent argument about how the catastrophe of the plague forms the backdrop of these poems, see Coley, *Death and the Pearl Maiden*.

8. Foot, "Plenty, Portents, and Plague," 32.

9. *MED*, s.v. "plage"; cf. *MED*, s.v. "vengeaunce" and s.v. "wound."

10. Chaucer, *Book of the Duchess*, in *Riverside Chaucer*, 345/1206-7. As the note to the *Riverside Chaucer* explains, "the connection between *dismal* and the *ten woundes of Egypte* is complex" (975).

11. Livingston, *Middle English Metrical Paraphrase*, lines 1717–18.

12. On the Exodus as an analogy for medieval understandings of disaster, see Johnson, *Waste and the Wasters*, 38–40. For an article that questions the "medieval" equation of natural disaster and divine punishment, see Rohr, "Man and Natural Disaster."

13. Quoted in Horrox, *Black Death*, 35.

14. Horrox, *Black Death*, 66–67; Original is in Venables, *Chronicon Abbatiae de Parco Ludae*, 38–39.

15. "Sed verum hec pestilencia particularis aliaque infortunia accidunt hiis diebus. Illi qui talia ascribunt ceteris planetis et constellacionibus, non peccatis, dicant quails planeta regnauit tempore Noe, quando exceptis octo animabus Deus totum mundum per diluuium submergebat, nisi planeta malicie et peccati." Sermon 70, "Vigilate," in Devlin, *Sermons of Thomas Brinton*, 2:323. Translation comes from Horrox, *Black Death*, 145. On the tension between scientific and

religious explanations of the plague that this passage suggests, see Smoller, "Of Earthquakes, Hail, Frogs, and Geography."

16. Translation provided in Horrox, *Black Death*, 193.
17. Horrox, *Black Death*, 35.
18. Rigby, *Dancing with Disaster*, 3.
19. For a consideration of this relationship in Gower's *Confessio Amantis*, see Mitchell, *Becoming Human*, 41–43.
20. Bjork, *Catastrophes and the Apocalyptic*, 1. See also O'Mathúna "Christian Theology and Disasters."
21. Larger debates about ecological causation were already well underway in the schools by the thirteenth century, emerging from the Aristotelian distinction between primary and secondary causation, but given that my focus here is on popular biblical literature, these important debates are outside the scope of this book.
22. Rigby, *Dancing with Disaster*, 5. As Smoller argues, the naturalization of disaster/apocalypse had already begun in the wake of Aristotelian learning in late medieval Europe, though understanding of disasters as punishment or portents remained a dominant mode of interpretation ("Of Earthquakes, Hail, Frogs, and Geography," 156–87).
23. Rigby, *Dancing with Disaster*, 4, 6.
24. Cronon, "Trouble with Wilderness."
25. Recent climate science has challenged the Enlightenment model as well, providing a powerful framework for understanding how human agency shapes geological and ecological change, aiming to break down the nature-culture dualism inscribed within so much modern thinking.
26. Rigby, *Dancing with Disaster*, 6.
27. In my use of *nonmodern* here, I'm thinking of not only premodern European traditions but also other global and Indigenous traditions not shaped by the particular form of modernity that arose with the Enlightenment in the West.

Chapter Three

1. Sanders, "On Loan from the Sundance Sea," in *Conservationist Manifesto*, 119. My reflections here are also inspired by Sanders's essay "After the Flood," in *Staying Put*.
2. Until these settlers arrived and displaced the Indigenous peoples inhabiting the karst landscapes of southern Indiana, these were the ancestral homelands of the Miami, Delaware, Potawatomi, and Shawnee peoples.
3. See Mordoh, "Portrait of a Lost Community."
4. On the too-muchness of the barrage of images of climatological catastrophes and the simple problem that we "just aren't paying a whole lot of attention anymore," see Nordhaus and Shellenberger, "Apocalypse Fatigue."
5. Rigby, *Dancing with Disaster*, 3. For a more extended discussion of how medieval biblical literature adopts and transforms this paradigm, see the excursus preceding this chapter, "On Plague, Precedent, and the Punishment Paradigm."
6. For an excellent survey of the state of the field up to 2017, see the review essay by Crocker, "Medieval Affects Now." Crocker also observes that much of the early study of medieval emotions focused on "affective piety." For a recent overview, see the outstanding Wikipedia entry on the subject: Wikipedia, s.v. "Affective Piety," last modified December 3, 2023, 00:42,

https://en.wikipedia.org/wiki/Affective_piety. A key monograph is McNamer, *Affective Meditation*. For a recent set of essays on medieval affect in less explicitly religious contexts, see Burger and Crocker, *Medieval Affect, Feeling and Emotion*, esp. the introduction.

7. Some recent work on the history of emotions has attended to the distance of "transhistorical feelings," as Louise D'Arcens considers in several essays, including the introduction to a special issue of *Exemplaria* (with Andrew Lynch) on "Feeling for the Premodern," 183–90; and D'Arcens, "Feeling Medieval."

8. Stanbury, *Seeing the Gawain-Poet*, 2; and Coley, *Death and the Pearl Maiden*.

9. See especially Cohen, "Drown"; and Cohen, "Response: Into the Storm." Cohen and Yates's book *Noah's Arkive* explores these issues in much greater depth.

10. Nixon, *Slow Violence*, 116.

11. Nixon, *Slow Violence*, 15–16.

12. On the "long pedigree" of the iconography of suffering, see Sontag, *Regarding the Pain of Others*, 40. My thinking in this chapter about observing suffering from a distance is also indebted to Mary Favret's stunning book *War at a Distance*.

13. In his short book *Shipwreck with Spectator*, Hans Blumenberg explores the history of reading Lucretius's shipwreck metaphor (see esp. 26). See also the discussion of this scene and of Blumenberg's reading in Passannante, *Catastrophizing*, 11.

14. Cited in Blumenberg, *Shipwreck with Spectator*, 36.

15. Peter of Limoges, *Moral Treatise on the Eye*, 110.

16. Newhauser, "Toward a History of Human Curiosity," 563.

17. Ingham, *Medieval New*, esp. 9–12, quotation at 11.

18. Sontag, *Regarding the Pain of Others*, 42.

19. Perhaps the best example of this universalizing is Margery Kempe's tendency to *see* Christ in ordinary people and objects—mothers with babies, beautiful men, statues—in the *Book of Margery Kempe*. *Piers Plowman* also offers an extended example of how the poor serve as images of Christ (11.180–245). See Gibson on "the incarnational aesthetic" in *Theater of Devotion*, esp. chap. 1.

20. Nixon, *Slow Violence*, 15. As Rae Greiner reminds us, "emotions elicited by art, responsive to representations, are no less authentic than those inspired by experienced events" (*Sympathetic Realism*, 3). There have been many studies of *how* literature and art generate empathy, sympathy, or compassion, though this field has been most thoroughly explored in relation to fiction, and especially the novel. See Greiner, *Sympathetic Realism*; and Keen, *Empathy and the Novel*.

21. Nixon, *Slow Violence*, 14.

22. Luke 17:26–31: "And as it came to pass in the days of Noe, so shall it be also in the days of the Son of man. They did eat and drink, they married wives, and were given in marriage, until the day that Noe entered into the ark: and the flood came and destroyed them all. Likewise as it came to pass, in the days of Lot: they did eat and drink, they bought and sold, they planted and built. And in the day that Lot went out of Sodom, it rained fire and brimstone from heaven, and destroyed them all. Even thus shall it be in the day when the Son of man shall be revealed."

23. 2 Peter 2:5–6: God "spared not the original world, but preserved Noe, the eighth person, the preacher of justice, bringing in the flood upon the world of the ungodly. And reducing the cities of the Sodomites, and of the Gomorrhites, into ashes, condemned them to be overthrown, making them an example to those that should after act wickedly."

24. As Evelyn Reynolds and I explore, the movement between such dyads is a common element of catastrophic forms. See Gayk and Reynolds, "Forms of Catastrophe."

25. As Lecklider points out, the *Cleanness* poet conflates Matthew and Luke's accounts of this parable in a unique way (*Cleanness: Structure and Meaning*, 35).

26. Although scholars have sometimes seen this poem as uneven in its structure (Condren writes that *Cleanness* "seems to ramble eclectically through three random stories"; *Numerical Universe*, 74), many others have observed the poet's nuanced development of the poem's major themes.

27. *Cleanness* has never been a critical darling. It is a challenging read, both because its Middle English dialect can be difficult for modern audiences and because its moralizing and brutality can be hard to stomach. Grim and dour, the poem depicts a God who is easily angered and prone to destruction; it imagines that destruction in what one scholar has called "elaborately realistic detail" (Spearing, *Gawain-Poet*, 46, 60).

28. Stanbury, *Seeing the Gawain-Poet*, 2.

29. Coley observes that the poems engage this trauma subtly (*Death and the Pearl Maiden*, 7), and thus his argument is necessarily speculative, though I find it largely compelling.

30. Coley, *Death and the Pearl Maiden*, 31.

31. *MED*, s.v. "wrake." For the nominal, "wreck," the *OED* simply provides: "something that has been wrecked or destroyed." While I will be focusing on the physical act of destruction, the poem's emphasis on "wrake" could also be seen as part of the "pattern of judgment," as suggested by Morse's reading of the poem in *Pattern of Judgment*.

32. *Sir Gawain and the Green Knight*, in *Poems of the Pearl Manuscript*, 16. All subsequent references to poems in this volume (including *Cleanness*) will be cited parenthetically in the text by page and line number.

33. The foregoing citations are representative examples; other references to *wrake* appear in lines 302, 570, 718, 1143, and 1808.

34. This timeline differs from other accounts of the duration of the fall, which more typically describe it as seven to nine days. See Morey, "Fall in Particulate," 92–94.

35. This is a point increasingly made by anthropologists and other disaster theorists interested in what emerges in the ruins of ecological catastrophe. See, for instance, Tsing, *Mushroom at the End of the World*.

36. Translation is from Jacobus de Voragine, *The Golden Legend*, 2:205. Cf. the description of friars as swarming in hell like bees out of a hive, which can be found in the prologue to Chaucer's "Summoner's Tale," in *Riverside Chaucer*, 128/1693–96.

37. For examples, see Lecklinder, *Cleanness: Structure and Meaning*, 65. James Morey observes that particulate images seem to be limited to vernacular writing; see his insightful essay "The Fall in Particulate." Cf. the thirteenth-century *Middle English Fall and Passion*, which also compares the angels falling over the course of seven days and nights to falling snow (in Turville-Petre, *Kildare Manuscript*).

38. Morey, "Fall in Particulate," 93.

39. Milton, *Paradise Lost*, bk. 1, lines 302–3.

40. For this reading of the syntax and poetics, see Bahr, "Finding the Forms of *Cleanness*," 465.

41. Spearing, *Gawain-Poet*, 66.

42. For an engaging overview of the Flood story, from its origins to its reception, see Cohn, *Noah's Flood*. For an insightful study of how early modern writers found in the Flood narrative a way of thinking about the scientific and theological dynamics of ecological decline, see Barnett, *After the Flood*, esp. 1–19.

43. The modern twentieth-century fundamentalist fascination has resulted, among many other things, in a supposedly accurate reproduction of the Ark at the Ark Encounter, a theme park in Ken-

tucky run by the organization Answers in Genesis (https://arkencounter.com/). On earlier fascination with the dimensions and logistics of ark building, see Cohen and Yates, *Noah's Arkive*, esp. chap. 4.

44. Arngart, *Middle English Genesis and Exodus*, pp. 68–69, lines 581–88.

45. The "undede" of the original may here simply mean "undead" or alive, but as the *Middle English Dictionary* suggests, it could also originate in the Latin *unda*, for waves or undulations. *MED*, s.v. "unded"; Cf. *MED*, s.v. "undede."

46. Livingston, *Middle English Metrical Paraphrase*, lines 319–20.

47. Capgrave, *John Capgrave's Abbreviation of Cronicles*, p. 18, lines 15–20. Compare the treatment in Trevisa's Middle English translation of Ranulph Higden's *Polychronicon*, which focuses on the wondrous construction of the ark, which is interpreted allegorically. It limits description of the flood itself to the following: "oure Lorde sent reyne vppon erþe. And so þe flood was imade, and occupied þe erþe wel ny3h a 3ere. De water of þe flood passede fiftene cubites aboue þe hisest hilles" (*Polychronicon*, bk. 2, chap. 5 [p. 237]).

48. It may be, as Horrall and others have argued, that *Cursor Mundi*'s description of the Flood is a source for *Cleanness*'s depiction, though it seems more likely to me and to recent critics, such as Ad Putter, that both texts are relying on a similar source rather than in direct relation to each other. For discussion of sources, see Horrall, "*Cleanness* and *Cursor Mundi*"; Putter, "Sources and Backgrounds"; and Putter, "*Cleanness* and the Tradition of Medieval Versification."

49. *De diluvio mundi* is included in Avitus, *Avit de Vienne*.

50. For brief discussion and the complete passage in both Latin and English, see Lecklider, *Cleanness*, 104–6. For the text of Avitus, *De diluvio mundi*, see *Patrologia Latina* (hereafter cited as *PL*) 59.352–53. Ad Putter argues that Lecklider overstates the influence of Avitus on the poem and suggests instead that the *Cleanness* poet was drawing from a range of contemporary biblical literature and commonplaces. See Putter, "*Cleanness* and the Tradition of Medieval Versification."

51. Interestingly, the other homiletic poem in Cotton Nero A.x also offers an extended description of a sea storm, see *Patience*, lines 133–54. For some discussion about the relation of human and nature in the poem, see Palti, "Bound Earth."

52. As Lecklider notes, "most writers exempted the fish from destruction" (*Cleanness: Structure and Meaning*, 96).

53. On this point, see Jacobs, "Alliterative Storms in Middle English."

54. Morris, *Cursor Mundi*, Trinity MS, p. 111, lines 1762–77. All subsequent quotations of *Cursor Mundi* are from this text and manuscript and refer to its page and line numbers.

55. See, for instance, Jesus says, "ne is more sorwe to se" in "Men rent me on rode," in Davies, *Medieval English Lyrics*, p. 116, line 15.

56. On the particular vulnerability of the poor, see, Nixon, *Slow Violence*.

57. The poet's unsettling fascination with the fear and despair of the submerged is echoed in the other homiletic poem in *Cleanness*'s manuscript, *Patience*, a retelling of the story of Jonah that also tells a tale of divine destruction by way of stormy weather. As in *Cleanness*, the poet elaborates on the storm description, painting the movement of the waters as both divine judgment and exploring what it feels like to be submerged. Encountered alongside *Cleanness*, *Patience* registers as a counternarrative, a story in which divine mercy remains possible and which represents suffering but also the potential of escape. For powerful readings of the place of ecology, sanctuary, and enclosure in this poem, see Palti, "Bound Earth"; and Allen, "'As mote in at a munster dor': Sanctuary and Love of This World."

58. As Stanbury discusses, this move from the general to the particular and back again is a central part of the poet's visualizing mode and process of "focalization" (*Seeing the Gawain-Poet*, 3–4).

59. For a similar reading, see Cohen and Yates, *Noah's Arkive*, 93–94.
60. Morse, *Pattern of Judgement*, 156.
61. Spearing, *Gawain-Poet*, 67.
62. Wallace, "*Cleanness* and the Terms of Terror," 93.
63. Johnson, "Horrific Visions of the Host," 162.
64. Putter, "Sources and Backgrounds," 147. Offering another approach, Stanbury considers the poem's commitment to exploring the challenge of correctly interpreting (and responding to) what we see (Stanbury, *Seeing the Gawain-Poet*).
65. "Al to late! al to late! / Wanne the bere is ate gate," See "Wanne mine eyhnen misten," in Davies, *Medieval English Lyrics*, p. 75, lines 13–14.
66. The illustrator of *Cleanness*, however, omits the submerged bodies in his depiction of the scene, focusing on Noah and his family's attention to the carnivorous fish swimming below the ark (British Library, Cotton Nero A.x, fol. 60r).
67. Though God does mourn creating humanity in Genesis 6.6, this emphasis on God's remorse for the destruction is an addition by the *Cleanness* poet. Genesis 8:21 only notes that when God smells the burning sacrifice, he decides never to curse the earth again.
68. Most Middle English biblical paraphrases, adaptations, and histories skip over this story entirely. As I will discuss in the next section, the episode also appears in *Cursor Mundi* (lines 2764-916), though the poem does not include a description of the catastrophe itself. The destruction is also briefly mentioned in the Middle English *Genesis and Exodus*, which describes the "wreche" as "hardere" than that inflicted by the flood (see lines 1108–19) and in Kalen, *A Middle English Metrical Paraphrase of the Old Testament*, vol. 1, lines 553–636.
69. For a sensitive discussion of the poetic mastery of this passage, see Spearing, *Gawain-Poet*, 67–69.
70. "Apocalypse of Thomas" in Elliott, *Apocryphal New Testament*, 645–51. For further discussion of this and other possible sources of this passage, see Lecklider, *Cleanness*, 143–44.
71. This could also be read in a rather different way: as the dying people crying out that Christ might have pity on them.
72. Haraway, *Staying with the Trouble*, 1.
73. As Utley shows in "One Hundred and Three Names," the wife was given a name as early as the second century.
74. Interestingly, while the Hebrew scriptures say virtually nothing of Noah's wife, the Koran links her with Lot's wife as examples of unbelievers: "God sets forth an example to those who disbelieve: the wife of Noah and the wife of Lot, they were both under two of Our righteous servants, but they acted treacherously towards them so they availed them naught against God, and it was said: Enter both the fire with those who enter" (*Qur'an*, Sura 66 [At-Tahrim], ayat 10).
75. It may be that the legend of Noah's wife was still developing when *Cursor Mundi* was written, for the poem does offer a more general account of how Noah's relatives mock him when he is building the ark, asking him why he is so afraid of nothing (lines 1729–44).
76. For an overview of this apocryphal tradition, see Kolve, *Chaucer and the Imagery of Narrative*, 199–210. On the Newcastle play, see Normington, "'Have here a Drink full good.'"
77. This would be play no. 4, "Noah"; see Sugano, *N-Town Plays*.
78. For early studies that emphasize the typology of the episode, see Woolf, *English Mystery Plays*, esp. 136–45; and Kolve, *Play Called Corpus Christi*, 67–72.
79. There is a large critical discourse about Noah's wife, with recent studies focusing on her rebellion as resistance, and earlier studies focusing on typology, the comic elements of her

NOTES TO PAGES 132–143

domestic brawls with Noah, and the gendered dynamics of the play's domestic violence. See for instance, Woolf, *English Mystery Plays*, 136–44; Kolve, *Corpus Christi*, 146–51; Mill, "Noah's Wife Again"; Tolmie, "Mrs. Noah and Didactic Abuses"; and Novacich, *Shaping the Archive*, 66.

80. Tolmie, "Mrs. Noah and Didactic Abuses," 11, 14.

81. In Middle English, *rokke* can mean either "rock" or "distaff" (*MED*, s.v. "rokke"). Scholars usually read or gloss this reference as "distaff" to emphasize the wife's labor; although this seems like the most likely reading to me as well, I see no contextual reason why it couldn't also mean "rock."

82. Kolve, *Corpus Christi*, 150; Novacich, *Shaping the Archive*, 92.

83. Kolve, *Corpus Christi*, 150.

84. Kolve notes that Augustine connects the second day of creation and the second age of humanity in *De Genesi contra Manichaeos* (*Corpus Christi*, 151).

85. Haraway, *Staying with the Trouble*, 4.

86. Kiser, "Animals in Chester's *Noah's Flood*," 23.

87. Kiser, "Animals in Chester's *Noah's Flood*," 27.

88. Kiser, "Animals in Chester's *Noah's Flood*," 29.

89. Only the Cornish *Ordinalia* allows other characters to doubt the justice of God's plan or express empathy for the loss. In the Cornish play, Noah himself displays both horror at God's plan and kinship with those who will die. "Since though wilt kill every one," he says to God, "except only my people and me, / Kill us with them as well." ("aban vynnyth pup huny / lathe ol an nor vys-ma / sav vnsel ov tus hammy / lath ny ganse mage ta.") *Ancient Cornish Drama*, 73/969, 971–72.

90. Tolmie, "Mrs. Noah and Didactic Abuses," 12.

91. Novacich, *Shaping the Archive*, 102.

92. Birkholz, "Mapping Medieval Utopia," 608.

93. On the gendered associations of compassion, see McNamer, *Affective Meditation*, esp. 119–49.

94. Diaz, "Of Course She Looked Back," in *When My Brother Was an Aztec*, 88.

95. Livingston, *Middle English Metrical Paraphrase*, lines 605–10.

96. *MED*, s.v. "simple" entry 4b.

97. Stanbury, *Seeing the Gawain-Poet*, 2.

98. *MED*, s. v. "blishen." Both the *MED* and the *OED* suggest that the term is rooted in a rosy radiance.

99. Cf. the description of the shining ring "þat bere blusschande bemeȝ as þe bryȝt sunne" in *Sir Gawain and the Green Knight*, line 1817.

100. Coley, *Death and the Pearl Maiden*, 35.

101. *MED*, s.v. "bāle n.(1)."

102. *MED*, s.v. "fain."

103. I am grateful to Jenny Sisk for suggesting this second alternative.

104. Coley, *Death and the Pearl Maiden*, 35.

105. In addition to figure 3.2, see also the depiction in the Peterborough Psalter, Koninklijke Bibliotheek van België, ms. 9961-62, f. 12v, where she is particularly ghostly.

106. Interestingly, Lot's wife is not the only mineral maiden in the manuscript. Elsewhere in *Cleanness*'s manuscript one finds both visual and poetic depictions of the Pearl Maiden. *Cleanness* immediately follows *Pearl* in Cotton Nero A.x. Scholars have often noted points of commonality between these two texts but have paid the most attention to their shared lexicon of purity and filth.

107. See also H. Martin, "Forgetting Lot's Wife."
108. Stanbury, "In God's Sight," 112.
109. Coley develops this point in some detail; see *Death and the Pearl Maiden*, 38–40.
110. Anderson, "Lucy Hutchinson's Sodom," 253.
111. Birkholz, "Mapping Medieval Utopia," 606.
112. Birkholz, "Mapping Medieval Utopia," 605.
113. Diaz, "Of Course She Looked Back," 88–89.
114. For a development of this point, see Novacich, *Shaping the Archive*, 66.
115. As Coley writes, *Cleanness* both reveals "a tangle of broken bodies and bricks" and "also focuses upon the few who emerge from their biblical calamities to negotiate such losses," including Noah and Abraham (*Death and the Pearl Maiden*, 30).
116. Although Mandeville's *Travels* has long been considered the *Cleanness* poet's source for this imagery, Putter notes that many contemporary biblical paraphrases conclude with an account of the geography and geology of the Dead Sea ("*Cleanness* and the Tradition of Medieval Versification," 182–83).
117. Spearing, *Gawain-Poet*, 68.
118. Tsing, *Mushroom at the End of the World*.
119. *MED*, s.v. "saun-de-ver(e)." Interestingly, this line from *Cleanness* is the only nonmedicinal used mentioned in references provided by the *MED*.
120. Nissenbaum, "Utilization of Dead Sea Asphalt"; Nissenbaum, "Dead Sea—An Economic Resource."
121. See, for example, Nissenbaum, Aizenshtat, and Goldberg, "Floating Asphalt Blocks of the Dead Sea."
122. My overview of this geological history is from Neev and Emery, *Destruction of Sodom, Gomorrah, and Jericho*; and also Harris, *Destruction of Sodom: A Scientific Commentary*.
123. Haraway, *Staying with the Trouble*, 35.
124. *MED*, s.v. "bihōlden v."; See also "behold" in *OED*, which notes that it derives from the English Old English *bihaldan* (West Saxon *behealdan*) and that only the English senses of the term apply it to watching or looking.
125. For useful introductions to medieval optical theory, see Biernoff, *Sight and Embodiment*; and Akbari, *Seeing through the Veil*.

Chapter Four

Opening epigraph from Langland, *Vision of Piers Plowman*, 15.483. Unless otherwise noted, subsequent quotations to *Piers Plowman* are to the B-text and will be noted parenthetically by passus and line number in the text.

1. Z. Smith, "Elegy for a Country's Seasons."
2. On the dynamics of climatological catastrophizing, see Morton, *Hyperobjects*, 99; and Passannante, *Catastrophizing*, esp. 238.
3. In an insightful analysis of Chaucer's *Complaint of Mars*, Kara Gaston similarly explores how attention to celestial movements can function as a useful analogue for reading. See Gaston, "Forms and Celestial Motion." For a critique of drawing analogies between reading poetry and reading ecological systems, see Chua and Garrard, "Ecopoetics and the Myth of Motivated Form," 30–44.
4. The very term *seasonal* speaks to how ingrained those expectations of atmospheric and geological order are. For an investigation of medieval literary explorations of "season," see

Pearsall and Salter, *Landscapes and Seasons*, esp. chap. 5, "The Landscape of the Seasons." On the tension between the expectation of seasonal regularity and the experience of weather variance, see also the introduction to Lawrence-Mathers, *Medieval Meteorology*, esp. vii. For a more contemporary take on this issue, see E. Fitzgerald, "Stability Fantasy."

5. Although there has been relatively little scholarship on medieval representations of weather, the inaugural issue of the journal *Medieval Ecocriticisms* is devoted to this topic. See especially the introduction: Warren, "Medieval Weather," 1–10.

6. I am not alone in identifying a dark undercurrent in this passage; nearly fifty years ago, Pearsall and Salter also commented on the "pain" it relates (*Landscapes and Seasons*, 130). In a sense, the passage encourages counterfactual thinking of the very sort that continues to characterize some modern responses to climatological anomalies. For a related approach to the relation of climatic observation and causation, see Hannart et al., "Causal Counterfactual Theory."

7. Strikingly, the only use of the term with a positive valence that the *Middle English Dictionary* provides is this passage in *Cleanness*. See *MED*, s.v. "restles."

8. There are many scholarly treatments of this tension; see, for instance, see the introduction to Clarke and Claydon, *God's Bounty*; Sarah Foot's essay in that volume, "Plenty, Portents, and Plague"; Bartlett, *Natural and Supernatural*; and Robertson, *Nature Speaks*. For discussion of how this paradox was "resolved" by medieval thinkers such as Boethius by attributing both order and disruption of order to a divine intelligence, see Pearsall and Salter, *Landscapes and Seasons*, 126.

9. Lamb, *Climate, History, and the Modern World*, 1.

10. Daston and Park, *Wonders and the Order of Nature*, 20. For a discussion of medieval wonders more generally, see Bynum, "Wonder." On the relationship of wonder to wounds, see also Fradenburg, "Simply Marvelous," esp. 19.

11. On wonders and "unlikeness," see Daston and Park, *Wonders and the Order of Nature*, 33.

12. For two studies that focus on medieval European disaster literature, see Rohr, "Writing a Catastrophe"; and Rohr, "Man and Natural Disaster."

13. I am grateful to Michael Johnston for his suggestion that I look at prognostics. While they are largely outside the limited scope of this chapter, they represent an important area for future investigation of how medieval writers "read" the weather. See, for instance, Taavitsainen, *Middle English Lunaries*. Middle English prognostics also often appear among historical texts and poems, as in the commonplace book of John Colyn (London, British Library Harley MS 2252).

14. Coley, *Death and the Pearl Maiden*, 4.

15. Blanchot, *Writing of the Disaster*, 7.

16. For representative examples, see Ghosh, who in *The Great Derangement* prioritizes fiction but questions the value of realism; and Heise, who considers how "literary forms—the novel above all—might be able to accommodate the spatial scale and cultural heterogeneity of an entire planet," and asks, "If the Anthropocene indeed calls for a scaling-up of the imagination, how might that imagination translate into narrative?" (in "Science Fiction and the Time Scales of the Anthropocene," at 276 and 297). See also Nixon, *Slow Violence*, 3.

17. The roots of this emphasis on the affordances of fiction may well lie in Fredric Jameson's foundational work in *The Political Unconscious*, which argues for the centrality of the narrative mode in apprehending "a social order in the process of penetration and subversion, reorganization and rationalization" (148).

18. See most powerfully, Anahid Nersessian's work on nineteenth-century poetry in *The Calamity Form*.

19. In this approach, my thinking has been inspired and informed by Nersessian's work. Moreover, because I, like Nersessian, understand forms to be embedded in and produced by particular historical contexts, my account of literary attempts to communicate catastrophe in the Middle Ages necessarily differ from hers in some significant ways. For another approach to the central modes of the "poetry of disaster" and what it can do, see Cooley, "Poetry of Disaster."

20. For a brief discussion of the medieval warm period and subsequent cooling, see the excursus "A Brief History of Medieval Climate Change" following the introduction in this book.

21. I thus use *apocalypse* here in its broadest sense, though many of the phenomena I discuss also carry an explicitly eschatological sense. For a brilliant discussion of how apocalypticism is fundamentally concerned with spatial and temporal order, holding "together the revelation of order and the eruption of chaos," see Rhodes, "Apocalyptic Aesthetics."

22. For consideration of the term *catastrophe* in a premodern context as well as an exploration of the forms afforded by premodern catastrophe, see Gayk and Reynolds, "Forms of Catastrophe." For a useful study of climatological variance as understood through the developing medieval science of meteorology that considers questions of predictability and prognostication, see Lawrence-Mathers, *Medieval Meteorology*.

23. Some scholars have even suggested that the poem "offers itself to us as scripture," reading the poem as a "conscious imitation of biblical prophecy" or apocalypse. See, most influentially, Bloomfield, *"Piers Plowman" as a Fourteenth-Century Apocalypse*.

24. Blanchot, *Writing of the Disaster*, 7.

25. Britton's *Meteorological Chronology* offers a riveting compilation of passages focused on extreme weather in medieval chronicles to 1450.

26. For a recent collection of essays that offer a reassessment of the diversity and complexity of medieval historical writing, see Jahner, Steiner, and Tyler, *Medieval Historical Writing*.

27. Smoller, "Of Earthquakes, Hail, Frogs, and Geography," 156–87, esp. 173.

28. Brooke, *Climate Change and the Course of Global History*, 382; Oppenheimer, "Ice Core and Palaeoclimatic Evidence"; and Oppenheimer, *Eruptions that Shook the World*, 261.

29. For an insightful historical assessment of the impact of this volcano on English climate, crop yields, and the famine of 1258, see Campbell, "Global Climates."

30. This English translation is largely from *Matthew Paris's English History*, 3:280, though I have made a number of small changes to emphasize certain formal elements more apparent in the Latin original. The Latin text is from Paris, *Chronica majora*: "Ipso quoque anno, Borea per plures menses continue flante, cum jam Aprilis et Maii et Junii pars potissima pertransierant, vix flosculi rari et parvi cum paucis germinibus pullulantibus apparuerunt, unde spes fructuum est suspensa. Defi[ci]ente insuper annona, pauperum multitudo innumerabilis mortua est. Et inventa sunt passim eorum corpora tumida prae fame et liventia, quina vel sena in porcariis, sterquiliniis, et lutosis plateis, in semetipsis morticina miserabiliter tabefacta. Nec ausi sunt, qui domos habebant, perituros propter tabem et contagia infirmorum in suam propriam inediam hospitari" (vol 7, p. 690).

31. For a recent overview of Matthew Paris's work and contribution to English historical writing, see Weiler, "Historical Writing in Medieval Britain," 319–38.

32. Chaucer, "General Prologue" to *Canterbury Tales* in *Riverside Chaucer*, p. 23, lines 6–7. For a reading of Chaucer's lines that sees them as "protesting too much," see Johnson, *Waste and the Wasters*, 26–27.

33. The range of Matthew's literary learning in particular has long been acknowledged. See, for example, Marshall, "Thirteenth-Century Culture."

34. Some fifteenth-century poets make a similar move, emphasizing the darkening days of autumn and winter in a clear reversal of the trope of the *reverdie*. Compare, for example, the opening lines of Thomas Hoccleve's *Series*.

35. Such contrasts are not unlike the formal moves that also shape texts on the expulsion from Eden. See chapter 2 for an extended discussion.

36. Schulz, *Lost & Found*, 202–3.

37. Rigby, *Dancing with Disaster*, 52.

38. For an extended discussion of the dynamics of "dark ecology," see Morton, *Dark Ecology*.

39. Judith Butler offers a helpful discussion of the difference between the apprehension and the recognition of horror and suffering; see Butler, *Frames of War*, 4–5.

40. For three rather different approaches to the potency of wonders and the dynamics of the responses they elicit, see Bynum, "Wonder"; Fradenburg, "Simply Marvelous"; and Karnes, "Wonders in the Medieval Imagination."

41. Nersessian, "Two Gardens," 311. Nersessian develops the concept of nescience in much greater detail in *Calamity Form*, esp. 3–4.

42. For a reading of *Piers Plowman* that focuses on unknowing and apophasis, see D. Smith, "Negative Langland." See also Zeeman, *"Piers Plowman" and the Medieval Discourse of Desire*.

43. On the devastation of the Great Famine in general, see Jordan, *Great Famine*. For a foundational discussion of famine in *Piers Plowman*, see Frank, "'Hungry Gap,' Crop Failure, and Famine."

44. My argument, though differently focused, is very much in line with Nicolette Zeeman's points about how the forms or modes of allegory in this poem disrupt. See Zeeman, *Arts of Disruption*.

45. As Pearsall and Salter note, those commonplaces of summer quickly give way to "'wo in wynter-tyme," for the poor who fill the pages of the poem are particularly subject to the weather: "yit wynter for hem worse, for wete-shodde thei gange, / A-fyrst sore and afyngred." See Pearsall and Salter, *Landscapes and Seasons*, 133. Pearsall and Salter quote the following from the B-text of *Piers Plowman*: 14.112, 164–65; 17.226–226; and from the C-text: 10.78; 13.192; and 16.292.

46. On the poem's exploration of wonders, see Lochrie, *Nowhere in the Middle Ages*, esp. chap. 4.

47. James Simpson reads the Prologue's promise of marvels as misleading, suggesting that the poem itself quickly "deflates" the generic expectations its allusions to "fairy" raise (*Piers Plowman: Introduction to B-text*, 8).

48. For consideration of how the spectacle of social diversity functions as a "ferli" in the prologue of the poem, see Lochrie, *Nowhere in the Middle Ages*, 136–39.

49. Noting this shift from the opening lines of the Prologue, Andrew Galloway observes that "'ferly' always has instability in its movement between alluring and sinister senses" (*Prologue-Passus 4*, 84).

50. Langland's combination of revelatory dream vision, social critique, and prophecy has long been acknowledged as "apocalyptic" or "prophetic." The classic study is Bloomfield, *"Piers Plowman" as a Fourteenth-Century Apocalypse*. For other representative studies, see Bertz, "Prophecy and Apocalypse"; Hanna, "Reading Prophecy/Reading Piers"; Adams, "Some Versions of Apocalypse"; Emmerson, "The Prophetic, the Apocalyptic, and the Study of Medieval Literature"; and Emmerson, "'Yernen to Rede Redels?' *Piers Plowman* and Prophecy."

51. Simpson, "From Reason to Affective Knowledge," 2. D. Vance Smith also argues that the poem's mode is one of negation, undermining the definitions it offers, in "Negative Langland."

52. There has been a good deal of work on the nature of these threats, but for an insightful study that brings together the ecological, social, and political dynamics of the threat, see the recent dissertation by William Rhodes, "Ecology of Reform," esp. the introduction and chap. 1. For another approach to the engagement of agrarian crises in these apparently pastoral scenes, see Little, *Transforming Work*.

53. Zeeman, *"Piers Plowman" and the Medieval Discourse of Desire*, 158, 187ff.

54. For a thorough overview of critical approaches to prophecy and the apocalyptic in the poem through 1993, see Emmerson, "'Yernen to Rede Redels?' *Piers Plowman* and Prophecy." This passage, which concludes with enigmatic signs, has never been convincingly explained, though Bloomfield ultimately takes the lines as portents of "a new or final apocalyptic age" (*"Piers Plowman" as a Fourteenth-Century Apocalypse*, 211–12n 42). Emmerson sees it not as "eschatological prophecy," but as "comments on contemporary events" ("Yernen," 40). Not all prophetic moments in the poem invoke ecological or climatological portents. Compare, for instance, Conscience's prophecy at 3.325–30.

55. For a recent version of this reading and an extended treatment of the poem's treatment of "wasters," see Johnson, *Waste and the Wasters*, 21–23.

56. This idea is related to the poem's larger method, which, as David Aers writes, is one of "restless argument. Multimodal, dramatic, lyrical and adventurous, [the poem] moves by exploring a range of positions and their consequences" and "is committed to disrupting narratives" (Aers, *Beyond Reformation?* 98–99).

57. Zeeman, *"Piers Plowman" and the Medieval Discourse of Desire*, 158, 187ff.

58. My synthesis of these opening passus and their governing questions is indebted to James Simpson's helpful *Piers Plowman: Introduction to B-text*.

59. On the "punishment paradigm," see the excursus "On Plague, Precedent, and the Punishment Paradigm" at the beginning of part 2 in this book; see also Rigby, *Dancing with Disaster*.

60. On this dating, see Bennett, "The Date of the A-Text of *Piers Plowman*." The analogous passages in the other versions are A.5.13–20 and C.5.115–122.

61. Lamb and Frydendahl, *Historic Storms*, 16–17. See also I. Gram-Jensen, *Sea Floods*.

62. Lamb and Frydendahl, *Historic Storms*, 20. For brief comment on this storm surge, see Fagan, *Little Ice Age*, 65–66.

63. Given-Wilson and Scott-Stokes, *Chronicon Anonymi Cantuariensis*, 118–19.

64. In the original Latin: "uentus superuenit magnus et terribilis eleuans eum de terra et transuiexit eum per medium unius fenestre usque in gardinum eorium, et ibidem per malum, ut creditor, spiritum est super quondam absque lesione dismissus." Given-Wilson and Scott-Stokes, *Chronicon Anonymi Cantuariensis*, 118–19.

65. Translated in Britton, *Meteorological Chronology*, 144. In the original Latin: "xv die Januarii, ventus zephyrus sive auster, affricus, pessimus campanilia, turres, arbores, aedificia, alia que fortia prostravit et contrivit in frustra, debilibus parcendo, et tam in terra quam in mari bona consumpsit irrecuperabilia; vix in suo cursu domos aut arbores, quas prae montibus attingere poterat, aliquas reliquit integras. Nec quievit a flatu forti septem diebus ac noctibus contiguis." John of Reading, *Chronica Johannis de Reading*, 150–51.

66. Other historical accounts, such as the *Chronicon Angliae* (1329–88), also particularly emphasize that the winds toppled "strong and durable things" (Britton, *Meteorological Chronology*, 144).

67. G. Martin, *Knighton's Chronicle*, 184–85, which also provides the original Latin: "Ventus horribilis. Eodem anno. xvi. kalendas Februarii, scilicet in die et nocte Sancti Antonii, orta

est horribilis et nimis ualida tempestas uentorum, qualem nunquam retroactis temporibus non creditur a plebe fuisse uisam. Nam ultra quam dici potest boscos, pomeria, et omne genus arborum prostrauit et multas ultra quam crederet cum radicibus euertit. Ecclesias, molendina, campanilia, muros, domos dilapidauit. Apud Londonias mala innumera de campanilibus et aliis domibus et ecclesiis exercuit."

68. On ecological catastrophes as moral indictments, see Smoller, "Of Earthquakes, Hail, Frogs, and Geography," 156–87. Discussions of natural portents as divine punishments appear in English catechetical texts of that time, for instance, the discussion of portents in Barnum, *Dives and Pauper*, 1:147–48.

69. Though some have questioned the apocalypticism of Reason's sermon, scholars have also tended to see it as a paradigmatic example of the punishment paradigm. For instance, Emmerson suggests that this passage does not "establish a systematic reckoning of future events based on natural portents or other tokens. Instead, it seems more interested in using 'prophecies' to reproach sinful society in the present" ("'Yernen to Rede Redels?' *Piers Plowman* and Prophecy," 41). For a discussion of trees here and throughout the poem, see Allor, "Propping the Tree of Charity."

70. Most scholarly treatments of this scene have not been troubled by the conflict between Reason's certainty and his explanation of these crises, seeing the storm as an effect of God's anger. In *Pestilence in Medieval and Early Modern English Literature*, for instance, Byron Lee Grigsby explains the passage by noting, "For Langland, both the pestilence and the storm are a representation of God's anger with man, and Langland believes it is his job to interpret the meaning of these events" (103). In *Waste and the Wasters*, Eleanor Johnson similarly sees evidence of an "irate" biblical God in this passage (21–22).

71. D. Smith, "Negative Langland," 56.

72. For several discussions of medieval apocalyptic preaching that draw on contemporary catastrophes, see Mertens et al., *Last Judgement in Medieval Preaching*.

73. Bjork, introduction to *Catastrophes and the Apocalyptic*, ix.

74. "Secundo nos excitat ad timorem Dei excellencia diuine pietatis, que in finali iudicio male iudicata reiudicat et scrutatur. Si timor fuit magnus nobis Anglicis paucis annis elapsis vidisse per ventum arbusta erui, domos opprimi, pinnacula et ecclesias dirui, et in pestilencia homines ad vesperam sanos in mane sepeliri, quomodo in iudicio non erit maior timor quando Arescent homines pre timore que superuenient vniuerso orbi." Quoted in Devlin, *Sermons of Thomas Brinton*, 1:184.

75. Translated in Britton, *Meteorological Chronology*, 144.

76. Given-Wilson and Scott-Stokes, *Chronicon Anonymi Cantuariensis*, 118–19.

77. R. Davis, *"Piers Plowman" and the Books of Nature*, chap. 4. On "kynde knowyng," also see Karnes, *Imagination, Meditation, and Cognition*, chap. 5; and Steiner, *Reading Piers Plowman*, 111–12, 131–37.

78. Lochrie, *Nowhere in the Middle Ages*, 161.

79. For comments on this "sense of unease" and alienation, see Rudd, *Greenery*, 195; and Zeeman, *"Piers Plowman" and the Medieval Discourse of Desire*, 164–87.

80. This point is echoed in Reason's citation of Genesis 1:31 slightly later in the passage (11.396): "Et vidit Deus cunta que fecerat, et errant valde bona" (And God saw all things he had made, and they were very good).

81. R. Davis, *"Piers Plowman" and the Books of Nature*, 159. Davis adopts this phrase from Shannon, "Eight Animals in Shakespeare," 477.

82. Zeeman, *"Piers Plowman" and the Medieval Discourse of Desire*, 187–95.

83. The poem's exploration of how to interpret nature's ordinary wonders has been the subject of several recent studies. See, most importantly, R. Davis, *"Piers Plowman" and the Books of Nature*, chap. 3; Lochrie, *Nowhere in the Middle Ages*, chap. 4; and Rudd, *Greenery*, 185–200.

84. Zeeman, *"Piers Plowman" and the Medieval Discourse of Desire*, 111.

85. See 12.216–21. Rather than seeking causes, Imaginatif insists that the more appropriate question is "What is nature for?" His answer is a relatively straightforward one (if entirely anthropocentric): nature is *exemplary*, it has a use for humans insofar as it provides examples for action. On the Latin sources of this exemplarism, see R. Davis, *"Piers Plowman" and the Books of Nature*, chap. 4. For another approach to Langland's exemplarism, see Clopper, "Songs of Rechelesnesse," 105.

86. R. Davis, *"Piers Plowman" and the Books of Nature*, 175.

87. Simpson, *Piers Plowman: Introduction to B-text*, 176.

88. Some manuscripts substitute "element" for "climat," though the latter makes slightly more sense in the context. See the 15.371 at the Piers Plowman Electronic Archive (http://piers.chass.ncsu.edu/) for alternate readings.

89. For a similar treatment in the "*Piers Plowman* tradition" of the difficulty of climatological interpretation that offers reflection on professional knowledge and wonder, see also the passage from *Mum and the Sothsegger* cited in this book's first excursus, "A Brief History of Medieval Climate Change," taken from Dean, *Richard the Redeless and Mum and the Sothsegger*, lines 1727–39.

90. R. Davis, *"Piers Plowman" and the Books of Nature*, 163.

91. Davis also notes that the poem includes a more skeptical vision of nature throughout, commenting in the book's introduction that "Langland's expansive conception of *kynde* describes a *via positiva*, an advisedly optimistic account of natural capacity that persists alongside the poem's darker expressions of doubt and deficiency in the natural realm" (*"Piers Plowman" and the Books of Nature*, 9).

92. The poem is found in the Vernon MS (Oxford, Bodleian Library MS Eng. Poet. a.1) and British Library Additional MS 22,283, fol. 132. I use the version that has been edited in T. Wright, *Political poems and songs*, 250–52. Other editions include; Horstmann and Furnivall, *Minor Poems of the Vernon Manuscript*, 719–21; and Carleton Brown, *Religious Lyrics of the XIVth Century*, 186–88. On this quake, see Mallet, *On the Facts of Earthquake*. The opening epigraph for this section is from Chaucer, *Boece*, in *Riverside Chaucer*, p. 407, lines 49–53. An abbreviated version of this section also appears in "Forms of Catastrophe," which I wrote with Evelyn Reynolds, though most of the readings that follow are my own.

93. Smoller cites a range of biblical passages, including Isaiah 29:6–7, Matthew 27:51, Acts 16:26, and Revelation 6:12, 8:5, 11:13, 11:19, and 16:18, as well as the gospel accounts of the signs of the judgment. See Smoller, "Of Earthquakes, Hail, Frogs, and Geography," 163–64.

94. "The Resurrection," in Lumiansky and Mills, *Chester Mystery Cycle*, 340/38–39.

95. Revelation 16:18: "And there were lightnings, and voices, and thunders, and there was a great earthquake, such an one as never had been since men were upon the earth, such an earthquake, so great."

96. Cited and translated in Britton, *Meteorological Chronology*, 148.

97. G. Martin, *Knighton's Chronicle*, 242–43, which also provides the original Latin: "xii. kalendas Junii terre motus generalis mala multa faciens in regno quasi prima hora post nonam feria quarta. Item die Veneris sequenti quasi in ortu solis, terre motus non multum nocens. Sabbato sequenti aque motus quasi hora tercia mane. Naues uacillabant in portubus ab aque motu."

NOTES TO PAGES 172–187

98. This information is drawn from de Boer and Sanders, *Earthquakes in Human History*, 67–68, though its ultimate source remains unclear. See also the brief mention by Musson, "British Earthquakes," 323.

99. Aston, "Wyclif and the Vernacular," 282.

100. Hudson, *Selections from English Wycliffite Writings*, 18. For discussion of this passage in relation to Wyclif's comments about the earthquake in his *Trialogus*, see Aston, "Wyclif and the Vernacular," 281–82.

101. For this account of the council and earthquake, see Shirley, *Fasciculi Zizaniorum*, 272–73: "Sed tamen eodem die, hora quasi secunda post meridiem, factus est terrremotus per totam Angliam. Unde quidam de suffraganeis et aliis volebant totum negotium dimisisse; sed vir fortis zelans pro Dei ecclesia Willelmus Cantuariensis eos confortavit, monens ut in causa ecclesiae desides non essent. Et revera terrremotus praetendebat purgationem regni ab haeresibus. Sicut enim in terrae visceribus includuntur aer et spiritus infecti, et egrediuntur in terrremotum; et sic terra depuratur, sed non absque magna violentia; sic ante erant multae haereses inclusae in cordibus reproborum; sed per condemnationem regnum fuit depuratum, sed non absque taedio et motione magna."

102. All subsequent references to the "Earthquake poem" are from the edition found in T. Wright, *Political poems and songs*, pp. 250–52, and are cited parenthetically by line number in the body of the text. A Latin lyric of that time also takes up these three catastrophes; see "On the Council of London, 1382," in T. Wright, *Political poems and songs*, 253–63. For a discussion of this poem (which is also known by its incipit: "Heu, quanta desolatio"), see Kerby-Fulton, *Books under Suspicion*, esp. 164–87.

103. Curtis Gruenler briefly considers this poem in the context of the enigmatic prophecies in *Piers Plowman* (Gruenler, *"Piers Plowman" and the Poetics of Enigma*, 123).

104. Chaucer, *Boece*, in *Riverside Chaucer*, 407/49–53.

105. *MED*, s.v. "lore."

106. Solnit, "What if Climate Change Meant Not Doom but Abundance?"

107. Daston and Park, *Wonders and the Order of Nature*, 14.

Chapter Five

1. I offer a more thorough consideration of the visual treatments of the motif in Gayk, "Present of Future Things." For an especially thorough discussion of this window, see Powell, "Text and Image in the *Pricke of Conscience* Window." Other recent studies include Rentz, *Imagining the Parish*, 122–48; Stevenson, *Performance, Cognitive Theory, and Devotional Culture*, 71–76; and Rozenski, "A Light to Lighten the Gentiles," 285–308. On the donors and the window more generally, see Gee, "Painted Glass." For discussions of this motif in relation to apocalyptic imagery in England more generally, see Davidson, "End of the World in Medieval Art and Drama" and "Signs of Doomsday in Drama and Art."

2. The most complete survey of the textual tradition remains Heist, *Fifteen Signs before Doomsday*, though Daniela Wagner has recently offered an updated treatment of the motif with special attention to its visual contexts in *Die Fünfzehn Zeichen*. For another version of my argument with much fuller contexts and references, see Gayk, "Apocalyptic Ecologies."

3. Yeats, "Second Coming," in *Collected Poems*, 187.

4. Dutton, "Observations on Medieval Weather," 175.

5. Temporal orientation is central to the distinction between types of signs or tokens that I am drawing here: symbols and allegories may signify a person, abstraction, or event in the

past, present, or future; portents foreshadow something that is going to happen in the future. In emphasizing the relation of two "historical" or literal (albeit imagined) events, portents signify much like medieval typology. As opposed to symbolic signification, where "at least one of the two elements is a pure sign," as Erich Auerbach succinctly explains, in typology or "a figural relation[,] both the signifying and the signified facts are real and concrete historical events" ("Typological Symbolism," 5–6). For another perspective on how portents were understood "not as symbols but as signs," see Daston and Park, *Wonders and the Order of Nature*, 51–52.

6. For an excellent study of how seemingly apocalyptic phenomena were typically understood as moral indictments, see Smoller, "Of Earthquakes, Hail, Frogs, and Geography." Notable exceptions to the motif's general avoidance of the punishment paradigm include an Old English version found in London, British Library, Cotton MS Vespasian D. xiv (at fols. 102r–103v), and some of the poems in the Anglo-Norman tradition of the motif, discussed briefly later in this chapter. On scholastic approaches, see Lerner, "Sign Theory."

7. The major exceptions here are the handful of extant alabaster panels, which focus on human response.

8. For my more developed discussion of the proleptic temporality of this motif, see Gayk, "Present of Future Things."

9. See, for instance, the list offered by the US Geological Survey, "What Are Some of the Signs of Climate Change?" The list includes rising sea levels, melting polar ice caps, increasingly strong tropical storms, and longer and more extended droughts worldwide.

10. Davy, "Ffiftene toknes," p. 92, lines 3–14.

11. On affective meditation, reading, and the devotional gaze, see especially McNamer, *Affective Meditation*.

12. In this, apocalypse functioned for medieval people, I would suggest, like Timothy Morton's "hyperobject"; see Morton, *Hyperobjects*, 12. A number of scholars have pointed out that the resistance to comprehension is a definitional feature of medieval wonders. See, for example, Daston and Park, *Wonders and the Order of Nature*; and Bynum, "Wonder."

13. My understanding of the hortatory uses of the Fifteen Signs is thus very much in line with James Palmer's point that early medieval apocalyptic thinking "is a powerful part of reform discourse about how to best to direct people—individually and collectively—towards a better life on earth" (*Apocalypse in the Early Middle Ages*, 3). On the relationship between the prophetic and the apocalyptic, see Emmerson, "The Prophetic, the Apocalyptic, and the Study of Medieval Literature." 45.

14. For additional discussion of this phrase, see the introduction, esp. pages 4–6.

15. The idea of the "Book of Nature" was a commonplace in the late Middle Ages, but a number of texts also imagine the end of the world in bookish terms: *The Apocalypse of Thomas* (and a number of Old English texts that draw from it, such as the Blickling Homilies) depict the end of the world as the folding up of a book.

16. L. Buell, *Environmental Imagination*, 285.

17. Studies of environmental apocalypticism sometimes open with but rarely linger long on premodern contexts and instead focus their readings on modern texts and contexts. For example, see F. Buell, *From Apocalypse to Way of Life*; and Garrard, "Apocalypse," in his *Ecocriticism*, 93–116. Conversely, studies of medieval apocalypse and natural disaster rarely approach calamity from the perspective of environmental history or ecocriticism. Robert Bjork's collection, *Catastrophes and the Apocalyptic*, for instance, contains several chapters on historical calamities interpreted as omens of apocalypse, though none approaches the topic from the vantage point

NOTES TO PAGES 190–192

of ecocriticism or environmental history. There are notable exceptions. For a recent ecocritical study of medieval apocalyptic catastrophe, see C. Abram, *Evergreen Ash*. On some of the ways in which discourses of modern ecocatastrophe have inherited premodern rhetorical modes, see also Kate Rigby's discussion of the Black Death in *Dancing with Disaster*.

18. Association of the Fifteen Signs with the late medieval *ars moriendi* also takes material form. For discussion, see Driver, "Picturing the Apocalypse," 65.

19. Source of the epigraph that opens this section is Larkin, "The Trees," in *Collected Poems*, 166.

20. The size of this archive and its diversity has made the motif a particularly challenging object of study. Perhaps unsurprisingly, since Heist's landmark 1952 survey of the motif, the overwhelming majority of treatments of it have focused on uncovering and describing new witnesses, tracing the motif's sources, classifying its major branches, and determining its influence on literature and art. There are many studies of the European traditions. On insular examples, see Giliberto, "Fifteen Signs before Doomsday in Cotton Vespasian D. xiv"; Hawk, "Fifteen Signs before Judgment"; Steel, "Woofing and Weeping"; and Steel, *How to Make a Human*, 225–32.

21. For similar sentiments in the epistles, see 1 Thessalonians 5:1–3; 2 Thessalonians 2:1–12; 2 Peter 3:1–11.

22. As William Heist notes, some early scholars saw the portents in Esdras as the most likely source of the Fifteen Signs motif, though he concludes that he doesn't find these passages "sufficiently close to justify our accepting them as [the motif's] immediate source" (Heist, *Fifteen Signs before Doomsday*, 53).

23. For an overview of patristic and early medieval treatments of eschatological signs with a special focus on apocalyptic temporality, see Markus, "Living within Sight of the End," 23–34. For third- and fourth-century descriptions of eschatological portents, see Augustine's incorporation of a sibylline acrostic in *De civitate Dei* 18.23; and Lactantius, *Divinae Institutiones* 7.16–17. Giliberto suggests the third-century *Liber de consummatione mundi* as the earliest patristic work describing some of the signs: "Fifteen Signs of Doomsday of the First Riustring Manuscript," 132.

24. See Heist, *Fifteen Signs before Doomsday*, 33–34, 62–72. For the *Apocalypse of Thomas*, see Elliott, *Apocryphal New Testament*, 645–51. The relation of the seven-sign tradition to the tradition of the fifteen signs remains disputed, though it has been little remarked upon since Heist's 1952 overview. For some discussion, see Gatch, "Two Uses of Apocrypha," 380.

25. Representative discussions of these changes by environmental historians include Palmer, "Climates of Crisis"; McCormick, Dutton, and Mayewski, "Volcanoes and Climate Forcing"; and Dutton, "Observations on Medieval Weather." On the understanding of such events as portents, see Foot, "Plenty, Portents, and Plague," 25–32.

26. Wright, "Apocalypse of Thomas: Some New Latin Texts," 41–51. See also Biggs and Wright, "Apocalypse of Thomas," 71–72.

27. Giliberto, "Fifteen Signs Cotton Vespasion D. xiv," 290. Cf. Heist, *Fifteen Signs before Doomsday*, 52.

28. Much about the motif's evolution remains uncertain, but it seems likely that the longer versions developed in response to or concurrence with chiliastic predictions and expectations, and perhaps also in tandem with the "discovery of nature" in the schools. For the broader, European contexts of millenarianism, apocalypticism, and prophesy in this period, see, for example, Landes, "Fear of an Apocalyptic Year 1000"; Palmer, *Apocalypse in the Early Middle Ages*; Cohn, *Pursuit of the Millennium*; Landes, *Heaven on Earth*. On the twelfth-century "discovery of nature," see Chenu, *Nature, Man, and Society*; and, more recently, Robertson, *Nature Speaks*, esp. 39–124.

29. This association with Advent may first appear in the Pseudo-Bedan *Collectanea*, which may also be the earliest extant Latin version of the complete fifteen-sign tradition. The Fifteen Signs are part 2, nos. 356–71; see Pseudo-Bede, *Collectanea*, 178–79.

30. *Die Briefe des Petrus Damiani*, ed. Reindel, MGH Briefe d. dt. Kaiserzeit 4.1–4, 4.3:20–23, 29–31; Comestor, *Historia scholastica*, PL 198:1049–722, at 1611A–B (chapter 141). For a brief description and discussion of the Comestor branch of the tradition, see Heist, *Fifteen Signs before Doomsday*, 24–26. For transcriptions of several of the Latin source texts and a number of vernacular versions, see the appendix to J. Fowler, "Fifteen Last Days," 323–37.

31. Some scholars have begun to entertain the possibility that the motif does, in fact, derive from an as-yet-undiscovered ancient text (Stone, *Signs of the Judgment*, 13–15). See also the brief discussion in McNamara, "(Fifteen) Signs before Doomsday," 230–31.

32. "Signa vero quae Hieronymus ponit, non asserit, sed in annalibus Judaeorum se e reperisse scripta dicit." Aquinas, *Commentarius in quartum librum sententiarum magistri Petri Lombardi*, ed. Mandonnet, distinct. XLVIII, q. 1, a. 4 (p. 1090).

33. Lerner, "Refreshment of the Saints," 103.

34. Heist terms this branch the "French" branch. I use "Anglo-Norman" instead to characterize the English examples of the motif that seem to derive from the poem found with the *Play of Adam*. On the sibylline tradition in Old English writing, see Biggs, "Sibylline Oracles (*Versus sibyllae de iudicio*)," 17–19. For a brief introduction and overview, see Heist, *Fifteen Signs before Doomsday*, 23–31. For a discussion of extant examples of the French branch and several full transcriptions, see Mantou, "Le thème des 'Quinze signes.'" On the possibility that the text of the Fifteen Signs following the *Ordo representatio Ade* in Tours, Bibliothèque municipale, MS 927 may have been intended as part of the play, see Fassler, "Representations of Time," 99. On the relationship of this text to other French versions of the signs, see Heist, *Fifteen Signs before Doomsday*, 176–77.

35. Several versions of the Fifteen Signs appear in Latin and Old English. As Giliberto has discussed, the earliest vernacular example of the full Fifteen Signs motif appears in the twelfth-century Old English homiletic codex, London, British Library, Cotton MS Vespasian D. xiv (at fols. 102r–103v); see Giliberto, "Fifteen Signs Cotton Vespasion D. xiv," 293–95. See also Warner, *Early English Homilies*, 89; and Heist, *Fifteen Signs before Doomsday*, 125–27. For additional consideration of the influence of the motif on Old English poetry, such as *Judgment Day I*, see Hawk, "Fifteen Signs before Judgment."

36. On the influence of the *Legenda* in the dissemination of the motif and an argument for a separate *Legenda* branch of the tradition, see Sandison, "'Quindecim signa ante iudicium.'"

37. Translation is from Jacobus de Voragine, *Golden Legend*, 1:8. The Latin reads: "Hieronymus autem in annalibus Hebraeorum invenit XV signa praecedentia judicium. Sed utrum continue futura sint an interpolatim, non expressit. Prima die eriget se mare XL cubitus super altitudinem montium stans in loco quasi murus. Secunda die tantum descendet ut vix videri possit. Tertia die marinae belluae apparentes super mare dabunt rugitus usque ad coelom et earum mugitus solus Deus intelliget. Quarta ardebit mare et aqua. Quinta arbores et herbae dabunt rorem sanguineum: in hac etiam quita die, ut alii asserunt, omnia volatilia coeli con gregabuntur in campis, unumquodque genus in ordine suo, non gustantia, nec bibentia, sed vicinum adventum judicis formidantia." The Latin text has been edited in Jacobi a Voragine, *Legenda aurea*, 6–7. Jacobus is following Comestor's *Historia scholastica* (with some additions from Damien).

38. Here the *Legenda* combines the Damien and Comestor versions of the fifth day.

39. "exibunt homines de cavernis et ibunt velut amentes nec mutuo sibi loqui poterit" (Jacobi a Voragine, *Legenda aurea*, 8).

NOTES TO PAGES 196–199

40. Gay, "To the Fig Tree on 9th and Christian," in *Catalog of Unabashed Gratitude*, 3.

41. The proleptic nature of present decay and corruption of the world is a very old homiletic theme and one exemplified by Gregory the Great's Homilies on Ezekiel, but it is also evident in many a vernacular sermon, such as the Old English Blickling Homily 10 on the end of the world (Morris, *Blickling Homilies*, 106–15). As these sermons suggest, invocation of this trope is usually part of a plea to renounce the world and its pleasures while there is still time. For discussion of the treatment of the Last Judgment and its various portents in sermons, see Mertens et al, *Last Judgement in Medieval Preaching*.

42. Wimbledon, *Wimbledon's Sermon: Redde Rationem Villicationes Tue*, 109–10. See the brief discussion of the apocalyptic imagery of this portion of Wimbledon's sermons in Emmerson, "Apocalyptic Themes and Imagery," 405–6.

43. I have come across only one English homiletic treatment of the signs that includes moralizing or inculpatory interpolations, a sermon in the twelfth-century Old English homiletic codex, London, British Library, Cotton MS Vespasian D. xiv (at fols. 102r–103v). On the fifth day, for instance, when the flora sweat blood, the passage explains that the plants will do so because sinful people stepped on them and the trees because the sinful profited from them and their fruits ("for þy þaet þa synfulle maen heo traeden, & þa treowwen, for þan þe þa synfulle haefden freome of heom & of heroa waestmen"). See Warner, *Early English Homilies*, 90. For discussion of this unique sermon with text and translations, see Giliberto, "Fifteen Signs Cotton Vespasian D. xiv."

44. Although they tend to avoid explicit moralization when rehearsing the motif itself, I would not go quite as far as Veronica O'Mara does in claiming that sermons with the signs describe "the Doom as an event rather than as a potential shaper of events and influence on behaviour" (O'Mara, "'Go 3e curselynges, to euerelasting fier': Doomsday in Middle English Prose Sermons," 283). See also O'Mara, "Last Judgement in Middle English Prose Sermons," 27–29.

45. There were, however, some preachers who chose to focus their sermons on this reading on a more allegorical interpretation of the signs of the end. See, for example, the sermon for the "Second Sunday in Advent," in Cigman, *Lollard Sermons*, 13–30, which offers an exegesis of apocalyptic portents in general rather than of the Fifteen Signs.

46. "Dominica IIa, in Aduentu domini," lines 19–21, in Morrison, *Late Fifteenth-Century Dominical Sermon Cycle*, 1:11.

47. "Antichrist's Prophets," in Lumiansky and Mills, *Chester Mystery Cycle*, 405/270.

48. On the way in which wonders disrupt the apparent order of nature, see Daston and Park, *Wonders and the Order of Nature*. Although, as Laura Smoller has considered, many late medieval thinkers were interested in distinguishing between the natural and divine causality of apocalyptic signs, vernacular treatments of the Fifteen Signs are not troubled by such distinctions, which are ultimately irrelevant to the larger aims of communicating the motif ("Of Earthquakes, Hail, Frogs, and Geography," 157–58).

49. Morrison, *Late Fifteenth-Century Dominical Sermon Cycle*, 1:11.

50. "Homily 2," in Thompson, *Northern Homily Cycle*, lines 5–12.

51. *MED*, s.v. "wandrawe": "A state of misery, wretchedness; also, an affliction, a pain."

52. "Homily 2," lines 43–45.

53. "Homily 2," lines 121–26.

54. The English list is followed by a second list of the signs in Latin that is rather more affectively oriented, emphasizing the confusion, horror, and grief these cosmological phenomena will prompt. Compare, for example, the Latin treatment of the fifth sign, "Rorem sanguineum

quinto deducet ab herbis / Horror et arboribus lacrimis perfusus acerbis" (lines 159–60), with the Middle English, "The fift day sal greses and tres / Suet blodi deu that grisli bes" (lines 123–24). The Latin version of the signs, an interpolated comment notes, should be omitted when the preacher is reading the sermon to English laypeople ("Isti versus omittantur a lectore quando legit Anglicum coram laycis"). For the Latin version of the signs, see "Homily 2," lines 147–83.

55. Interpolated phrases of human response or moral exhortation are much more characteristic of the Anglo-Norman versions than those of the Latin branch.

56. Mirk notes in his prologue that "I haue drawe this tretis owt of *Legenda Aurea* wyth more adding to." See Powell, *John Mirk's "Festial,"* 1:3. Subsequent quotations from Mirk's *Festial* are from this edition and will be cited by page and line number.

57. O'Mara, "'Go, ȝe curselynges,'" 282–83.

58. Powell, *Mirk's "Festial,"* 4/41–42.

59. Powell, *Mirk's "Festial,"* 5/81.

60. Powell, *Mirk's "Festial,"* 5/49–52. A popular fifteenth-century revision of this sermon entirely omits the introductory material, as well as many of the articulations of uncertainty or ambiguity included in the *Festial*. See Powell, *Advent and Nativity Sermons*, 71–73.

61. Powell, *Mirk's "Festial,"* 5/58–59.

62. Powell, *Mirk's "Festial,"* 5/65–66.

63. Morrison, *Late Fifteenth-Century Dominical Sermon Cycle*, 14/76–77.

64. Although the two words do not seem to be etymologically linked, their similarity can be traced back to the Old English "wund" (wound) and "wundor" (wonder). See *MED*, s.v. "wound" and s.v. "wonder."

65. Davy, "Ffiftene toknes," p. 92, line 9: "Schal euerych tre blede dropes of blood." Cf. the seven-sign lyric, "In a thestri stude Y stod," line 55, in Fein, Raybin, and Ziolkowski, *Complete Harley 2253*.

66. "Tote rien serra en tristesce" (Aebischer, *Le Mystère d'Adam*, line 1150).

67. As Bengt Lindström has noted, the signs are sometimes interpolated into copies of longer works rather than integrated into the tradition as a whole. For instance, the signs are inserted into the Glasgow manuscript of *Dives and Pauper*, in chapter 16 of the section devoted to the eighth commandment (Lindström, "Two Descriptions of the Signs"). For the interpolation in the Oxford, Bodleian Library, Additional MS B. 107 copy of *Chasteau d'Amour*, see Horstmann and Furnivall, *Minor Poems of the Vernon MS.*, 394, 403–6; see also Heist, *Fifteen Signs before Doomsday*, 145.

68. Morris, *Cursor Mundi*, lines 22428–710.

69. For Heist's list of many of the manuscripts containing these Middle English lyrics, see *Fifteen Signs before Doomsday*, 178–79. The most popular of these lyrics, by the evidence of extant manuscripts, is the 268-line poem "Quindecim signa," also known by its incipit as "King of grace and full of pity" (Digital Index of Middle English Verse [hereafter cited as DIMEV], no. 300; and in Furnivall, *Hymns to the Virgin and Christ*, 118–25). Subsequent references to the "Quindecim signa" are to the page and line numbers of this edition.

70. "Quindecim signa," 118/1–4.

71. Rolle, *Pricke of Conscience*, 131/4819–20 and 127/4663–65. This and subsequent references are to page and line numbers of the Morris-edited version.

72. Rolle, *Pricke of Conscience*, 129–130/4770–75.

73. *MED*, s.v. "hidǒus."

74. Steel, "Woofing and Weeping," 190.

NOTES TO PAGES 203–209

75. Lydgate, "Fifftene Toknys," in *Minor Poems of John Lydgate*, 117–20. Subsequent references to page and line numbers are cited parenthetically in the text.

76. The tradition does not speak in a single voice on the meaning of the animal cries. The Anglo-Norman branch typically denies any meaning to the beasts' cries, as one poem puts it (lines 141–46, in Varnhagen, "Zu mittelenglischen gedichten," 537):

> þat of speche be dombe
> Upward schall ther hedys tombe
> And calle to god on ther wyse.
> So sore þen schall þem agryse,
> And wolden crye, yf they couthe,
> Yf they myght speke with mouthe.

> (those animals unable to speak,
> shall lift their heads up,
> and call to God, each in their way.
> So terribly they will shudder
> and would cry, if they knew how,
> if they might speak with their mouths.)

77. Lydgate, "Fifftene Toknys," 119/36–40:

> no man shal knowe Opynly
> What al thyng menyth, the hyd previte
> Nor enpowne the toknys secrely
> But God alloone in his hih maieste.

78. Lumiansky and Mills, *Chester Mystery Cycle*, 405/279–80.

79. Lumiansky and Mills, *Chester Mystery Cycle*, 406/301–304.

80. Rolle, *Pricke of Conscience*, 130/4800–4801.

81. Davy, "Ffiftene toknes," 92/13–14.

82. Rentz, *Imagining the Parish*, 132.

83. "His omnibus pereuntibus quales oportet esse uos?" Augustine, *De civitate Dei*, 20.24, line 32, in Dombart and Kalb edition.

84. Augustine, *De civitate Dei* 20.24, line 32.

85. The lyrics in the Anglo-Norman branch very often follow the Fifteen Signs with the *ostentatio vulnerum* and the Works of Mercy. See, for example, "Quindecim signa" in Furnivall, *Hymns to the Virgin and Christ*, 118–25; and the treatment of the signs in Morris, *Cursor Mundi*, 4:1283–99.

86. For a brief overview of the Corporal Works of Mercy, see Duffy, *Stripping of the Altars*, 357–62. On the Works of Mercy in All Saints, North Street, York, see Rentz, *Imagining the Parish*, 138–43.

87. This final "it" is ambiguous, though likely refers to heaven or salvation. Likewise, although "loueden" could mean "love" or "praise," here it more likely indicates embodied action or consent, see *MED*, s.v. "lŏven v.(2)." Also, this passage interestingly provides only six of the seven works of mercy, omitting giving water to the thirsty.

88. Duffy, *Stripping of the Altars*, 248.

89. Rentz, *Imagining the Parish*, 137. On this window, also see Varnam, *Church as Sacred Space*, 221–23.

90. This association of signs of the ecological decline with advocacy for the poor and forgotten has increasingly become commonplace among recent intersectional work on environmental justice. Pope Francis, in his 2015 papal encyclical *Laudato si'*, offered an impassioned call for a recommitment to the idea of "integral ecologies," advocating an ethic of care based on the interconnectedness of all things that results in "a refusal to turn reality into an object simply to be used and controlled." His 2023 addendum to this encyclical, *Laudate Deum*, goes even further in condemning "excessive anthropocentrism." Rob Nixon and authors of many other recent ecocritical works have also drawn attention to how ecological catastrophe has significant social and personal repercussions, inordinately affecting the poor. See Nixon, *Slow Violence*.

91. McDermott, *Tropologies*, 368.

92. Gore, "Climate Crisis Is the Battle of Our Time."

93. Schulz, "Really Big One."

94. Scranton, *Learning to Die*, back cover.

95. Scranton, *Learning to Die*, 27.

96. Scranton, *Learning to Die*, 117.

97. Bridle, *Ways of Being*, 280.

98. Haraway, *Staying with the Trouble*, 297.

99. Recent studies have lamented our failure to properly imagine the scale of future catastrophe; see, for example, Ghosh, who notes that the climate crisis is a crisis "of the imagination" (*Great Derangement*, 9).

Epilogue

1. For another approach to these same questions, see Scott, "Love," 377–91.

2. As environmentally oriented theologians have often pointed out, the term in the Septuagint is *kosmos*—a word for the entirety of the physical creation, the universe as a whole. It is a term that includes but is not exclusive to human beings.

3. Lopez, "Love in a Time of Terror," in *Embrace Fearlessly*, 122.

4. On the apocalypticism of the final passus, see Kerby-Fulton, *Reformist Apocalypticism*; Bloomfield, *"Piers Plowman" as a Fourteenth Century Apocalypse*.

5. Johnson, *Waste and the Wasters*, 99.

6. Spearing, *Medieval Dream Poetry*, 159. On this point, also see D. Smith, *Arts of Dying*, 135.

7. See also the Samaritan's teaching on the communal and ethical aspects of "kyndness" in 17.250ff.

8. For instance, Will's earlier desires to "look and learn" (8.57) and also his desire for kynde knowing. The phrase also connects to the idea of the "lawe of love." For discussion of these issues, see R. Davis, *"Piers Plowman" and the Books of Nature*, chap. 4.

9. M. Nelson, *On Freedom*, 53.

10. *MED*, s.v. "cure." For a classic overview of the meanings of care, see Reich, "History of the Notion of Care."

11. Of the five appearances of *cure* (n) in the B-text, three appear in 20 (lines, 233, 237, and 253). The verbal form, *curen*, only appears once, in 20.326. The term *curatour* is more spread out in the poem, but of its eleven appearances, five are in passus 19 and 20. For the full list, see Wittig, *Piers Plowman Concordance*, 155. The term *care* appears more frequently in the poem. In its nominal form, *care*, it makes eleven appearances in the B-text, including 20.165, 201. It appears as a verb four times, including 19.381 and 20.150. See Wittig, *Piers Plowman Concordance*, 117–18.

12. *MED*, s.v. "care."

13. This indifference of the friars might be linked to the poem's larger thematization of narratives of failure, as Nicolette Zeeman discusses in *Piers Plowman and the Medieval Discourse of Desire*, esp. 282–83. On the poem's negations and failures, see also D. Smith, "Negative Langland."

14. Sisk, "Langland's Ethical Imaginary."

15. See Allen, *Uncertain Refuge*; see also Cohen and Yates's work on the danger of constructing arks in *Noah's Arkive*.

16. On the poem's consistent return to beginnings, see D. Smith, *Book of the Incipit*.

17. Yes, I've taken a bit of poetic license here. Technically, *sulphureus* indicates the flowers' yellow-orange color, but the *Oxford English Dictionary* suggests its close figurative association with fire and flames. *OED*, s.v. "sulfureous."

18. See, for instance, the opening chapters of Malm, *How to Blow Up a Pipeline*.

19. For a powerful elaboration of these points and others, see Gay, "We Kin," in *Inciting Joy*, 28–42, quoted at 35.

20. Johnson makes a similar point in *Waste and the Wasters*, 7.

21. For an accessible book that brings "the attention economy" into conversation with environmental concerns, see Odell, *How to Do Nothing*.

Abbreviations

CCSL Corpus Christianorum Series Latina
DIMEV Digital Index of Middle English Verse
EETS The Early English Text Society
MED *Middle English Dictionary*
OED *Oxford English Dictionary*
PL *Patrologia Latina*
TEAMS Teaching Association for Medieval Studies

Bibliography

Aberth, John. *Doctoring the Black Death: Medieval Europe's Medical Response to Plague.* Lanham, MD: Rowman & Littlefield, 2021.
———. *An Environmental History of the Middle Ages.* New York: Routledge, 2013.
———. *From the Brink of the Apocalypse: Confronting Famine, War, Plague, and Death in the Later Middle Ages.* New York: Routledge, 2001.
Abram, Christopher. *Evergreen Ash: Ecology and Catastrophe in Old Norse Myth and Literature.* Charlottesville: University of Virginia Press, 2019.
Abram, David. *The Spell of the Sensuous: Perception and Language in a More-than-Human World.* New York: Vintage Books, 1996.
Adams, Robert. "Some Versions of Apocalypse: Learned and Popular Eschatology in *Piers Plowman*." In *The Popular Literature of Medieval England*, edited by Thomas J. Heffernan, 194–236. Knoxville: University of Tennessee Press, 1985.
Aebischer, Paul, ed. *Le Mystère d'Adam, Ordo representacionis Ade.* Textes Littéraires Français 9. Geneva: Librairie Droz, 1964.
Aers, David. *Beyond Reformation? An Essay on William Langland's Piers Plowman and the End of Constantinian Christianity.* Notre Dame, IN: University of Notre Dame Press, 2015.
Akbari, Suzanne Conklin. *Seeing through the Veil: Optical Theory and Medieval Allegory.* Toronto: University of Toronto Press, 2004.
Alaimo, Stacy. *Bodily Natures: Science, Environment, and the Material World.* Bloomington: Indiana University Press, 2010.
Alan of Lille. *Literary Works: Alan of Lille.* Edited and translated by Winthrop Wetherbee. Dumbarton Oaks Medieval Library 22. Cambridge, MA: Harvard University Press, 2013.
Alexander, Dominic. *Saints and Animals in the Middle Ages.* Woodbridge, UK: Boydell Press, 2008.
Allen, Elizabeth. "'As mote in at a munster dor': Sanctuary and Love of This World." *Philological Quarterly* 87, no. 1 (2008): 105–33.
———. *Uncertain Refuge: Sanctuary in the Literature of Medieval England.* Philadelphia: University of Pennsylvania Press, 2021.
Allor, Danielle. "Propping the Tree of Charity: Allegory and Salvation History in *Piers Plowman*." *Yearbook of Langland Studies* 35 (2021): 29–59.

Ambrose. *Hexameron, Paradise, and Cain and Abel*. Translated by John J. Savage. Washington, DC: Catholic University of America Press, 1961.

The Ancient Cornish Drama. Edited and translated by Edwin Norris. Oxford: Oxford University Press, 1859.

Anderson, Penelope. "Lucy Hutchinson's Sodom and the Backward Glance of Feminist Queer Temporality." *Seventeenth Century* 30, no. 2 (2015): 249–64.

Appleford, Amy. *Learning to Die in London: 1380-1540*. Philadelphia: University of Pennsylvania Press, 2015.

Aquinas, Thomas. *Commentarius in quartum librum sententiarum magistri Petri Lombardi*. Edited by P. Mandonnet. 2 vols. Paris: Lethielleux, 1929.

———. *Summa Theologiae*. Edited and translated by the Blackfriars. 60 vols. New York: McGraw Hill, 1963.

Aston, Margaret. "Wyclif and the Vernacular." In *From Ockham to Wyclif*, edited by Anne Hudson and Michael Wilks, 281–330. Woodbridge, UK: Boydell & Brewer, 1987.

Auerbach, Erich. "Figura." In *Scenes from the Drama of European Literature*, 11–76. Minneapolis: University of Minnesota Press, 1984.

———. *Mimesis*. Translated by Willard R. Trask. Princeton, NJ: Princeton University Press, 1953.

———. "Typological Symbolism in Medieval Literature." *Yale French Studies* 9 (1952): 3–10.

Augustine. *De civitate Dei*. Edited by Bernhard Dombart and Alfons Kalb. CCSL 48. Turnhout, Belgium: Brepols, 1955.

———. *The Literal Meaning of Genesis*. 2 vols. Translated by John Hammond Taylor. New York: Newman Press, 1982.

Avitus. *Avit de Vienne: Histoire spirituelle*. Edited by N. Ilecquet-Noti, Sources Chretiennes. 2 vols. Paris: CERF, 1999–2005.

Bahr, Arthur. "Finding the Forms of *Cleanness*." *Studies in Philology* 110, no. 3 (2013): 459–82.

Barnett, Lydia. *After the Flood: Imagining the Global Environment in Early Modern Europe*. Baltimore: Johns Hopkins University Press, 2019.

Barnum, Priscilla Heath, ed. *Dives and Pauper*. 2 vols. EETS o.s. 275, 280, 323. London: Oxford University Press, 1976–2004.

Bartlett, Robert. *The Natural and Supernatural in the Middle Ages*. Cambridge: Cambridge University Press, 2008.

Beadle, Richard. "The York Corpus Christi Play." In *The Cambridge Companion to Medieval English Theatre*, edited by Richard Beadle and Alan J. Fletcher, 99–124. Cambridge: Cambridge University Press, 2008.

———, ed. *The York Plays*. London: Edward Arnold, 1982.

Beckwith, Sarah. *Signifying God: Social Relation and Symbolic Act in the York Corpus Christi Plays*. Chicago: University of Chicago Press, 2001.

Bede. *On Genesis*. Translated by Calvin B. Kendall. Liverpool: Liverpool University Press, 2008.

Behringer, Wolfgang. *A Cultural History of Climate*. Translated by Patrick Camiller. Cambridge: Polity Press, 2010.

Bennett, J. A. W. "The Date of the A-Text of *Piers Plowman*." *PMLA* 58, no. 2 (1943): 566–72.

Berry, Wendell. "The Body and the Earth." *Psychoanalytic Review* 81 (1994): 125–70.

———. "A Native Hill." In *Art of the Commonplace*, edited by Norman Wirzba, 3–31. Berkeley, CA: Counterpoint Press, 2003.

Bertz, Douglas. "Prophecy and Apocalypse in Langland's *Piers Plowman*, B-Text, Passus XVI to XIX." *Journal of English and Germanic Philology* 84, no. 3 (1985): 313–28.
Besserman, Lawrence. *Biblical Paradigms in Medieval English Literature*. London: Routledge, 2012.
Biebly, Steve. "Creation of the World to the Fifth Day—The Wagon." In M. Rogerson, *York Mystery Plays*, 132–34.
Biernoff, Susannah. *Sight and Embodiment*. New York: Palgrave Macmillan, 2002.
Biggs, Frederick M. "Sibylline Oracles (*Versus sibyllae de iudicio*)." In Biggs, *Sources of Anglo-Saxon Literary Culture*, 18–19.
———, ed. *Sources of Anglo-Saxon Literary Culture: The Apocrypha*. Instrumenta Anglistica Mediaevalia 1. Kalamazoo, MI: Medieval Institute Publications, 2007.
Biggs, Frederick M., and Charles D. Wright. "Apocalypse of Thomas." In Biggs, *Sources of Anglo-Saxon Literary Culture*, 71.
Birkholz, Daniel. "Mapping Medieval Utopia: Exercises in Restraint." *Journal of Medieval and Early Modern Studies* 36, no. 3 (2006): 585–618.
Bjork, Robert E., ed. *Catastrophes and the Apocalyptic in the Middle Ages and the Renaissance*. Turnhout, Belgium: Brepols, 2019.
Black, Daisy. *Play Time: Gender, Anti-Semitism and Temporality in Medieval Biblical Drama*. Manchester: University of Manchester Press, 2021.
———. "The Time of the Tree: Returning to Eden after the Fall in the Cornish *Creacion of the World*." *Medieval Feminist Forum* 50, no. 1 (2014): 61–89.
Blanchot, Maurice. *The Writing of the Disaster*. Translated by Ann Smock. Lincoln: University of Nebraska, 1995.
Bloomfield, Morton W. *"Piers Plowman" as a Fourteenth Century Apocalypse*. New Brunswick, NJ: Rutgers University Press, 1961.
Blumenberg, Hans. *Shipwreck with Spectator: Paradigm of a Metaphor for Existence*. Translated by Steven Rendall. Cambridge, MA: MIT Press, 1997.
Bowlus, Charles. "Ecological Crises in Fourteenth Century Europe." In *Historical Ecology: Essays on Environment and Social Change*, edited by Lester J. Bilsky, 86–99. Port Washington, NY: Kennikat Press, 1980.
Bridle, James. *Ways of Being: Animals, Plants, Machines: The Search for a Planetary Intelligence*. New York: Farrar, Straus and Giroux, 2022.
Britton, C. E. *A Meteorological Chronology to A.D. 1450*. London: Meteorological Office, 1937.
Brooke, John. *Climate Change and the Course of Global History*. Columbus: Ohio State University Press, 2014.
Brown, Carleton, ed. *Religious Lyrics of the XIVth Century*. Oxford: Clarendon, 1924.
Brown, Catherine. "In the Middle." *Journal of Medieval and Early Modern Studies* 30, no. 3 (2000): 547–74.
Bruster, Douglas, and Eric Rasmussen, eds. *Everyman and Mankind*. London: Methuen Drama, 2009.
Buell, Frederick. *From Apocalypse to Way of Life: Environmental Crisis in the American Century*. New York: Routledge, 2003.
Buell, Lawrence. *The Environmental Imagination: Thoreau, Nature Writing, and the Formation of American Culture*. Cambridge, MA: Harvard University Press, 1995.
Burger, Glenn D., and Holly A. Crocker. *Medieval Affect, Feeling and Emotion*. Cambridge: Cambridge University Press, 2019.
Butler, Judith. *Frames of War: When Is Life Grievable?* New York: Verso, 2016.

Bynum, Caroline Walker. *Christian Materiality: An Essay on Religion in Late Medieval Europe.* New York: Zone Books, 2011.

———. "Wonder." *American Historical Review* 102, no. 1 (1997): 1–26.

Campbell, Bruce M. S. "Global Climates, the 1257 Mega-Eruption of Samalas Volcano, Indonesia, and the English Food Crisis of 1258." *Transactions of the RHS* 27 (2017): 87–121.

Capgrave, John. *John Capgrave's Abbreviation of Chronicles.* Edited by P. J. Lucas EETS o.s. 285. Oxford: Oxford University Press, 1983.

Carslaw, K. S., L. A. Lee, L. A. Regayre, and J. S. Johnson. "Climate Models Are Uncertain, but We Can Do Something about It." *Eos*, February 26, 2018. https://eos.org/opinions/climate-models-are-uncertain-but-we-can-do-something-about-it.

Carson, Rachel. *Silent Spring.* New York: Mariner Books, 2002.

Cawley, A. C., and Martin Stevens, eds. *The Towneley Plays.* EETS s.s. 13–14. Oxford: Oxford University Press, 1994.

Chaganti, Seeta. *Strange Footing: Poetic Form and Dance in the Late Middle Ages.* Chicago: University of Chicago Press, 2018.

Chaucer, Geoffrey. *The Riverside Chaucer.* Edited by Larry Benson. New York: Houghton Mifflin, 1987.

Chenu, M. D. *Nature, Man, and Society in the Twelfth Century: Essays on New Theological Perspectives in the Latin West.* Edited and translated by Jerome Taylor and Lester K. Little. Chicago: University of Chicago Press, 1968.

Christie, Douglas E. *Blue Sapphire of the Mind: Notes for a Contemplative Ecology.* Oxford: Oxford University Press, 2012.

Chrysostom, John. *Homilies on Genesis.* Translated by Robert C. Hill. Washington, DC: Catholic University of America Press, 1985.

Chua, Rina Garcia, and Greg Garrard. "Ecopoetics and the Myth of Motivated Form." In *Close Reading the Anthropocene*, edited by Helena Fader. New York: Routledge, 2021.

Cigman, Gloria, ed. *Lollard Sermons.* EETS o.s. 294. Oxford: Oxford University Press, 1989.

Clarke, Peter, and Tony Claydon, eds. *God's Bounty? The Churches and the Natural World.* Studies in Church History 46. Woodbridge, UK: Boydell & Brewer, 2010.

Cleanness. In *The Poems of the Pearl Manuscript: Pearl, Cleanness, Patience, Sir Gawain and the Green Knight*, edited by Malcolm Andrew and Ronald Waldron. Exeter: University of Exeter Press, 2007.

Climate Repentance. "10 Spiritual Principles and Repentance Ceremony." Accessed February 13, 2024. https://climaterepentance.com/.

Clopper, Lawrence M. *"Songs of Rechelesnesse": Langland and the Franciscans.* Ann Arbor: University of Michigan Press, 1998.

Cohen, Jeffrey Jerome. "Drown." In Cohen and Duckert, *Veer Ecology*, 246–67.

———. "The Love of Life: Reading *Sir Gawain and the Green Knight* Close to Home." In Nardizzi and Werth, *Premodern Ecologies in the Modern Literary Imagination*, 25–58.

———. "Response: Into the Storm." *Early Modern Culture* 13 (2018): 149–51.

———. *Stone: An Ecology of the Inhuman.* Minneapolis: University of Minnesota Press, 2015.

Cohen, Jeffrey Jerome, and Lowell Duckert. "Introduction: Eleven Principles of the Elements." In *Elemental Ecocriticism: Thinking with Earth, Air, Water, and Fire*, edited by Jeffrey Jerome Cohen and Lowell Duckert, 1–26. Minneapolis: University of Minnesota Press, 2015.

Cohen, Jeffrey Jerome, and Lowell Duckert, eds. *Veer Ecology: A Companion for Environmental Thinking.* Minneapolis: University of Minnesota Press, 2017.

Cohen, Jeffrey Jerome, and Linda T. Elkins-Tanton. *Earth.* New York: Bloomsbury Academic, 2017.

Cohen, Jeffrey Jerome, and Julian Yates. *Noah's Arkive*. Minneapolis: University of Minnesota Press, 2023.

Cohn, Norman. *Noah's Flood: The Genesis Story in Western Thought*. New Haven, CT: Yale University Press, 1996.

———. *The Pursuit of the Millennium: Revolutionary Millenarians and Mystical Anarchists of the Middle Ages*. New York: Oxford University Press, 1970.

Coley, David. *Death and the Pearl Maiden: Plague, Poetry, England*. Columbus: Ohio State University Press, 2019.

———. "Failure." In Nardizzi and Werth, *Premodern Ecologies in the Modern Literary Imagination*, 183–95.

Comestor, Peter. *Historia scholastica*. PL 198:1049–722.

Condren, Edward. *The Numerical Universe of the Gawain-Pearl Poet: Beyond Phi*. Gainesville: University of Florida Press, 2002.

Cooley, Nicole. "The Poetry of Disaster." poets.org. February 20, 2014. https://poets.org/text/poetry-disaster.

Crocker, Holly A. "Medieval Affects Now." *Exemplaria* 29, no. 1 (2017): 82–98.

Cronon, William. "The Trouble with Wilderness: Or, Getting Back to the Wrong Nature." *Environmental History* 1, no. 1 (1996): 7–28.

———, ed. *Uncommon Ground: Rethinking the Human Place in Nature*. New York: W. W. Norton, 1996.

D'Arcens, Louise. "Feeling Medieval: Mood and Transhistorical Empathy in Justin Kurzel's *Macbeth*." *Screening the Past* 4 (2016). http://www.screeningthepast.com/2016/10/feeling-medieval-mood-and-transhistorical-empathy-in-justin-kurzels-macbeth/.

D'Arcens, Louise, and Andrew Lynch. "Feeling for the Premodern." In "Feeling for the Premodern," special issue, *Exemplaria* 30, no. 3 (2018): 183–90.

Daston, Lorraine, and Katharine Park. *Wonders and the Order of Nature, 1150–1750*. New York: MIT Press, 1998.

Davidson, Clifford. "The End of the World in Medieval Art and Drama." *Michigan Academician* 5 (1972): 257–63.

———. "The Signs of Doomsday in Drama and Art." *Historical Reflections / Réflexions Historiques* 26, no. 2 (2000): 223–45.

Davies, R. T., ed. *Medieval English Lyrics: A Critical Anthology*. London: Northwestern University Press, 1964.

Davis, Ellen. "Land as Kin: Renewing the Imagination," in *Rooted and Grounded: Essays on Land and Christian Discipleship*, edited by Ryan D. Harker, and Janeen Bertsche Johnson, 3–24. Eugene, OR: Wipf and Stock Publishers, 2016.

Davis, Rebecca. "The Book of Nature." In *Nature and Literary Studies*, edited by Peter Remien and Scott Slovic. Cambridge Critical Concepts Series. Cambridge: Cambridge University Press, 2022.

———. *"Piers Plowman" and the Books of Nature*. Oxford: Oxford University Press, 2016.

———. "'Save man allone': Human Exceptionality in *Piers Plowman* and the Exemplarist Tradition." In *Medieval Latin and Middle English Literature*, edited by Christopher Cannon and Maura Nolan, 41–64. Cambridge: D. S. Brewer, 2011.

Davy, Adam. "Ffiftene toknes." In *Adam Davy's Five Dreams about Edward II; The Life of St. Alexius; Solomon's Book of Wisdom; St. Jeremie's Fifteen Tokens before Doomsday; The Lamentacion of Souls. Edited from the Laud MS. 622 in the Bodleian Library*, edited by F. J. Furnivall. EETS o.s. 69. London: Oxford University Press, 1878.

Day, Mabel, ed. *The Wheatley Manuscript*. EETS o.s. 21. London: Oxford University Press, 1921.
Dean, James M. "Domestic and Material Culture in the Middle English Adam Books." *Studies in Philology* 107, no. 1 (2010): 25–47.
———, ed. *Richard the Redeless and Mum and the Sothsegger*. TEAMS Middle English Texts Series. Kalamazoo, MI: Medieval Institute Publications, 2000. https://d.lib.rochester.edu/teams/text/dean-richard-the-redeless-and-mum-and-the-sothsegger-mum-and-the-sothsegger.
———, ed. "The Simonie." In *Middle English Political Writings*. TEAMS Middle English Texts Series. Kalamazoo, MI: Medieval Institute Publications, 1996. https://d.lib.rochester.edu/teams/text/dean-medieval-english-political-writings-simonie.
———. *The World Grown Old in Later Medieval Literature*. Cambridge, MA: Medieval Academy of America, 1997.
de Boer, Jelle Zeilinga, and Donald Theodore Sanders. *Earthquakes in Human History: The Far-Reaching Effects of Seismic Disruptions*. Princeton, NJ: Princeton University Press, 2005.
Deleuze, Gilles, and Félix Guattari. *A Thousand Plateaus: Capitalism and Schizophrenia*. Translated by Brian Massumi. Minneapolis: University of Minnesota, 1987.
Delumeau, Jean. *History of Paradise: The Garden of Eden in Myth and Tradition*. Translated by Matthew O'Connell. Chicago: University of Illinois Press, 2000.
Devlin, Mary Aquinas, ed. *The Sermons of Thomas Brinton, Bishop of Rochester (1373–1389)*. Camden Third Series 85–86.2 vols. London: Offices of the Royal Historical Society, 1954.
Diaz, Natalie. *When My Brother Was an Aztec*. Port Townsend, WA: Copper Canyon Press, 2012.
Dickinson, Emily. *Final Harvest: Emily Dickinson's Poems*. Edited by Thomas H. Johnson. Boston; Little, Brown, 1961.
Dillard, Annie. *Pilgrim at Tinker Creek*. New York: Harper Perennial, 1998.
Dinshaw, Carolyn. "Ecology." In *A Handbook of Middle English Studies*, edited by Marion Turner, 347–62. West Sussex, UK: Wiley-Blackwell, 2013.
———. *How Soon Is Now? Medieval Texts, Amateur Readers, and the Queerness of Time*. Durham, NC: Duke University Press, 2012.
Donne, John. *The Divine Poems*. Edited by Helen Gardner. Oxford: Oxford University Press, 2000.
Douglass, Rebekah M. "Ecocriticism and Middle English Literature." *Studies in Medievalism* 10 (1998): 136–63.
Driver, Martha. "Picturing the Apocalypse in the Printed Books of Hours." In Morgan, *Prophecy, Apocalypse, and the Day of Doom*, 52–67.
Duffy, Eamon. *The Stripping of the Altars: Traditional Religion in England, c. 1400–c. 1580*. New Haven, CT: Yale University Press, 1992.
Dungy, Camille. "this beginning may have always meant this end." *Poetry*, April 2018. https://www.poetryfoundation.org/poetrymagazine/poems/146230/this-beginning-may-have-always-meant-this-end.
Dutton, Paul Edward. "Observations on Medieval Weather in General, Bloody Rain in Particular." In *The Long Morning of Medieval Europe: New Directions in Early Medieval Studies*, edited by Jennifer R. Davis and Michael McCormick, 167–80. Aldershot, UK: Ashgate, 2008.
Elliott, J. K., trans. *The Apocryphal New Testament: A Collection of Apocryphal Christian Literature in an English Translation*. Oxford: Oxford University Press, 1993.
Emerson, Ralph Waldo. "Nature." In *Nature and Selected Essays*, edited by Larzer Ziff, 36. New York: Penguin Classics, 2003.

Emmerson, Richard Kenneth. "Apocalyptic Themes and Imagery in Medieval and Renaissance Literature." In *The Encyclopedia of Apocalypticism*, edited by Bernard McGinn, 402–44. Vol. 2 of *Apocalypticism in Western History and Culture*. 2nd ed. New York: Continuum, 2000.

———. "*Figura* and the Medieval Typological Imagination." In *Typology and English Medieval Literature*, edited by Hugh T. Keenan, 7–42. New York: AMS Press, 1992.

———. "The Prophetic, the Apocalyptic, and the Study of Medieval Literature." In *Poetic Prophecy in Western Literature*, edited by Jan Wojcik and Raymond-Jean Frontain, 40–54. London: Fairleigh Dickinson University Press, 1984.

———. "'Yernen to Rede Redels?' *Piers Plowman* and Prophecy." *Yearbook of Langland Studies* 7 (1993): 27–76.

Emmerson, Richard Kenneth, and Bernard McGinn, eds. *The Apocalypse in the Middle Ages*. Ithaca, NY: Cornell University Press, 1992.

Epstein, Steven. *The Medieval Discovery of Nature*. Cambridge: Cambridge University Press, 2012.

Fagan, Brian M. *The Little Ice Age: How Climate Made History, 1300–1850*. New York: Basic Books, 2000.

Fassler, Margot. "Representations of Time in 'Ordo representacionis Ade.'" *Yale French Studies* (1991): 97–113.

Favret, Mary. *War at a Distance: Romanticism and the Making of Modern Wartime*. Princeton, NJ: Princeton University Press, 2010.

Feenstra, Ernest S. "Christian Impact on Ecology." *Science* 156 (1967): 737.

Fein, Susanna. "Twelve-Line Stanza Forms in Middle English and the Date of *Pearl*." *Speculum* 72, no. 2 (1997): 367–98.

Fein, Susanna, David Raybin, and Jan Ziolkowski, eds. and trans. *The Complete Harley 2253 Manuscript*. Kalamazoo, MI: Medieval Institute University, 2014.

Fitzgerald, Christina, and John T. Sebastian, eds. *The Broadview Anthology of Medieval Drama*. Peterborough, ON: Broadview Press, 2013.

Fitzgerald, Emmett. "The Stability Fantasy." *Orion Magazine*, August 2021. https://orionmagazine.org/article/the-stability-fantasy/.

Fleming, John V. "Natura Ridens; Natura Lachrymosa." In *Man and Nature in the Middle Ages*, edited by Robert G. Benson and Susan J. Ridyard, 1–36. Sewanee, TN: University of the South Press, 1995.

Foot, Sarah. "Plenty, Portents, and Plague: Ecclesiastical Readings of the Natural World in Early Medieval Europe." In Clarke and Claydon, *God's Bounty?* 15–41.

Foucault, Michel. "Of Other Spaces." Translated by Jay Miskowiec. *Diacritics* 16, no. 1 (October 1984): 22–27.

Fowler, David. *The Bible in Middle English Literature*. Seattle: University of Washington Press, 1984.

Fowler, J. T. "The Fifteen Last Days of the World in Medieval Art and Literature." *Yorkshire Archaeological Journal* 23 (1915): 313–37.

Fradenburg, L. O. Aranye. "Simply Marvelous." *Studies in the Age of Chaucer* 26, no. 4 (2006): 1–27.

Francis. *Laudate Deum*. Vatican City: Vatican Press, 2023.

———. *Laudato si'*. Vatican City: Vatican Press, 2015.

Frank, Robert Worth, Jr. "The 'Hungry Gap,' Crop Failure, and Famine: The Fourteenth-Century Agricultural Crisis and *Piers Plowman*." *Yearbook of Langland Studies* 4 (1990): 87–104.

Frost, Robert. "The Oven Bird." In *Mountain Interval*, 27. New York: Henry Holt, 1916.

Furnivall, Frederick, ed. *Hymns to the Virgin and Christ, The Parliament of Devils, and Other Religious Poems, Chiefly from the Archbishop of Canterbury's Lambeth MS. No. 853*. 1867. Facsimile of the first edition. Millwood, NY: Krause Reprint, 1990.

Fyler, John. "Love and the Declining World: Ovid, Genesis, and Chaucer." *Mediaevalia* 13, no. 1 (1987): 295–307.

Galloway, Andrew. "Chaucer's 'Former Age' and the Fourteenth-Century Anthropology of Craft: The Social Logic of a Premodernist Lyric." *English Literary History* 63, no. 3 (1996): 535–54.

———. *C Prologue-Passus 4; B Prologue-Passus 4; A Prologue-Passus 4*. Vol. 1, *The Penn Commentary on "Piers Plowman."* Philadelphia: University of Pennsylvania Press, 2006.

———. "Writing History in England." In Wallace, *Cambridge History of Medieval English Literature*, 255–83.

Garrard, Greg. *Ecocriticism*. 2nd ed. London: Routledge, 2012.

Garvey, Jon. *God's Good Earth: The Case for an Unfallen Creation*. Eugene, OR: Wipf and Stock, 2019.

Gaston, Kara. "Forms and Celestial Motion in Chaucer's *Complaint of Mars*." *PMLA* 133, no. 2 (2018): 282–95.

Gatch, Milton McCormick. "Two Uses of Apocrypha in Old English Homilies." *Church History* 33, no. 4 (1964): 379–91.

Gawande, Atul. *Being Mortal: Medicine and What Matters in the End*. New York: Metropolitan, 2017.

Gay, Ross. *Catalog of Unabashed Gratitude*. Pittsburgh: Pitt Poetry Series, 2015.

———. *Inciting Joy: Essays*. Chapel Hill, NC: Algonquin Books, 2022.

Gayk, Shannon. "'A comon light': Julian of Norwich's Participatory Prose." In *Oxford Handbook of Middle English Prose*, edited by Emily Steiner and Sebastian Sobecki. Oxford: Oxford University Press, forthcoming.

———. "Apocalyptic Ecologies: Eschatology, the Ethics of Care, and the Fifteen Signs of the Doom in Early England," *Speculum* 96, no. 1 (January 2021): 1-37.

———. "Idiot Psalms: Sound, Style, and the Performance of the Literary in the Towneley Shepherds' Plays." In Meyer-Lee and Sanok, *Medieval Literary*, 119–40.

———. "The Present of Future Things: Medieval Media and the Signs of the End of the World." In *Alabaster Sculpture in Medieval England: A Reassessment*, edited by Jessica Brantley, Elizabeth Teviotdale, and Stephen Perkinson, 229–60. Kalamazoo, MI: Medieval Institute Publications, 2021.

Gayk, Shannon, and Evelyn Reynolds. "Forms of Catastrophe." *Journal of Medieval and Early Modern Studies* 52, no. 1 (2022): 1–16.

Gee, E. A. "The Painted Glass of All Saints' Church, North Street, York." *Archaeologia* 102 (1969): 151–202.

Ghosh, Amitav. *The Great Derangement: Climate Change and the Unthinkable*. Chicago: University of Chicago Press, 2016.

Gibson, Gail. *The Theater of Devotion: East Anglian Drama and Society in the Late Middle Ages*. Chicago: University of Chicago Press, 1989.

Gilbert, Jane. *Living Death in Medieval French and English Literature*. Cambridge: Cambridge University Press, 2011.

Giliberto, Concetta. "The Fifteen Signs before Doomsday in Cotton Vespasian D. xiv: Role and Contextualisation." In *Practice in Learning: The Transfer of Encyclopaedic Knowledge in the

Early Middle Ages, edited by Rolf H. Bremmer Jr. and Kees Dekker, 285–309. Storehouses of Wholesome Learning 2. Paris: Peeters Publishers, 2010.

———. "The Fifteen Signs of Doomsday of the First Riustring Manuscript." In *Advances in Old Frisian Philology*, edited by Rolf H. Bremmer Jr., Stephen Laker, and Oebele Vries, 129–52. Amsterdam: Brill, 2007.

Given-Wilson, Chris, and Charity Scott-Stokes, eds. and trans. *Chronicon Anonymi Cantuariensis: The Chronicle of Anonymous of Canterbury 1346–1365*. Oxford: Clarendon, 2008.

Glotfelty, Cheryll, and Harold Fromm, eds. *The Ecocriticism Reader: Landmarks in Literary Ecology*. Athens: University of Georgia, 1996.

Gore, Al. "The Climate Crisis Is the Battle of Our Time, and We Can Win." *New York Times*, September 20, 2019. https://www.nytimes.com/2019/09/20/opinion/al-gore-climate-change.html.

Graham, Jorie. *Swarm: Poems*. New York: Ecco Press, 2000.

Gram-Jensen, I. *Sea Floods: Contributions to the Climatic History of Denmark*. Copenhagen: Danish Meteorological Institute, 1985.

Gray, Douglas. *Themes and Images in the Medieval English Religious Lyric*. London: Routledge & Kegan Paul, 1972.

Greenblatt, Stephen. *The Rise and Fall of Adam and Eve*. New York: Norton, 2017.

Greiner, Rae. *Sympathetic Realism in Nineteenth-Century British Fiction*. Baltimore: Johns Hopkins University Press, 2012.

Grisby, Byron Lee. *Pestilence in Medieval and Early Modern English Literature*. New York: Routledge, 2004.

Grosseteste, Robert. *On the Six Days of Creation: A Translation of the Hexaëmeron*. Translated by C. F. J. Martin. Oxford: Oxford University Press, 1996.

Gruenler, Curtis. *"Piers Plowman" and the Poetics of Enigma: Riddles, Rhetoric, and Theology*. Notre Dame, IN: University of Notre Dame Press, 2017.

Guattari, Felix. *The Three Ecologies*. Translated by Ian Pindar and Paul Sutton. London: Athlone Press, 2000.

Haeckel, Ernst. *Generelle Morphologie der Organismen: Allgemeine Grundzüge der organischen Formen-Wissenshaft, mechanisch begründet durch die von Charles Darwin*. Berlin: G. Reimer, 1866.

Hanawalt, Barbara A., and Lisa J. Kiser, eds. *Engaging with Nature: Essays on the Natural World in Medieval and Early Modern Europe*. Notre Dame, IN: University of Notre Dame Press, 2008.

Hanna, Ralph, III. "Reading Prophecy/Reading Piers." *Yearbook of Langland Studies* 12 (1998): 153–57.

Hannart, A., J. Pearl, F. E. L. Otto, P. Naveau, and M. Ghil. "Causal Counterfactual Theory for the Attribution of Weather and Climate Related Events." *Bulletin of the American Meteorological Society* 97, no. 1 (2016): 99–110.

Hanska, Jussi. "Catastrophe Sermons and Apocalyptic Expectations: Eudes de Châteauroux and the Earthquake of 1269 in Viterbo." In Mertens et al., *The Last Judgement in Medieval Preaching*, 117–34.

Haraway, Donna. *Staying with the Trouble: Making Kin in the Chthulucene*. Durham, NC: Duke University Press, 2016.

Harris, Graham. *The Destruction of Sodom: A Scientific Commentary*. Oxford: Lutterworth Press, 2015.

Harrison, Robert Pogue. *Gardens: An Essay on the Human Condition*. Chicago: University of Chicago Press, 2008.

Hartman, Geoffrey H. "Tea and Totality." In *Minor Prophecies: The Literary Essay in the Culture Wars*. Cambridge, MA: Harvard University Press, 1991.

Hawk, Brandon W. "The Fifteen Signs before Judgment in Anglo-Saxon England: A Reassessment." *Journal of English and Germanic Philology* 117, no. 4 (2018): 443–57.

Heise, Ursula K. *Imagining Extinction: The Cultural Meanings of Endangered Species*. Chicago: University of Chicago Press, 2016.

———. "Science Fiction and the Time Scales of the Anthropocene." *English Literary History* 86, no. 2 (2019): 275–304.

Heist, William W. *The Fifteen Signs before Doomsday*. East Lansing: Michigan State College Press, 1952.

Heng, Geraldine. *The Global Middle Ages: An Introduction*. Cambridge: Cambridge University Press, 2021.

Higden, Ranulf. *Polychronicon Ranulfi Higden Monachi Cestrensis; Together with the English Translations of John Trevisa and of an Unknown Writer of the Fifteenth Century*. Edited by C. Babington and Joseph Rawson Lumby. 9 vols. Cambridge: Cambridge University Press, 1874.

Hoffman, Richard C. *An Environmental History of Medieval Europe*. Cambridge: Cambridge University Press, 2014.

Hogan, Linda. *Solar Storms*. New York: Simon and Schuster, 1995.

The Holy Bible, Containing the Old and New Testaments, with the Apocryphal Books, in the Earliest versions Made from the Latin Vulgate by John Wycliffe and his Followers. Edited by Rev. Josiah Forshall. 4 vols. Oxford: Oxford University Press, 1850.

The Holy Bible: The Douay-Rheims Version. Baltimore, 1899.

Horrall, Sarah. "*Cleanness* and *Cursor Mundi*." *English Language Notes* 22, no. 3 (1985): 6–11.

Horrox, Rosemary, ed. and trans. *The Black Death*. Manchester Medieval Sources Series. Manchester: Manchester University Press, 1994.

Horstmann, Carl, ed. *Sammlung altenglischer Legenden*. Heilbronn: Henninger, 1878.

Horstmann, Carl, and Frederick James Furnivall, eds. *The Minor Poems of the Vernon MS*. Vol. 1. London: K. Paul, Trench, Trübner, 1892.

Howes, Laura. *Chaucer's Gardens and the Language of Convention*. Gainesville: University of Florida Press, 1997.

Hudson, Anne, ed. *Selections from English Wycliffite Writings*. New York: University of Toronto Press, 1997.

Hume, Cathy. "The Auchinleck Adam and Eve: An Exemplary Family Story." In *The Auchinleck Manuscript: New Perspectives*, edited by Susanna Fein, 36–51. Woodbridge, UK: York Medieval Press, 2016.

———. *Middle English Biblical Poetry: Romance, Audience, and Tradition*. Cambridge: D. S. Brewer, 2021.

Ingham, Patricia Clare. *The Medieval New: Ambivalence in an Age of Innovation*. Philadelphia: University of Pennsylvania Press, 2015.

———. "Pastoral Histories: Utopia, Conquest, and the Wife of Bath's Tale." *Texas Studies in Literature and Language* 42, no. 1 (2002): 34–46.

Isidore of Seville. *The Etymologies of Isidore of Seville*. Translated by Stephen A. Barney. New York: Cambridge University Press, 2010.

Jacobi a Voragine. *Legenda aurea: Vulgo Historia lombardica dicta*. Edited by Johann Georg Theodor Grässe. 3rd ed. Breslau, 1890. Facsimile of the first edition. Osnabrück, Ger.: Otto Zeller Verlag, 1965.

Jacobus de Voragine. *The Golden Legend: Readings on the Saints.* 2 vols. Translated by William Granger Ryan. Princeton, NJ: Princeton University Press, 1993.
Jacobs, Nicholas. "Alliterative Storms in Middle English." *Speculum* 47, no. 4 (1972): 695–719.
Jager, Stephen. *The Tempter's Voice: Language and the Fall in Medieval Literature.* Ithaca, NY: Cornell University Press, 1994.
Jahner, Jennifer, Emily Steiner, and Elizabeth M. Tyler, eds. *Medieval Historical Writing: Britain and Ireland, 500–1500.* Cambridge: Cambridge University Press, 2019.
James, Sarah. "Paradise, Pleasure, and Desire: Edenic Delight in Some Late-Medieval Dramatic Fragments." *Literature & Theology* 32, no. 1 (2018): 53–68.
Jameson, Fredric. *The Political Unconscious: Narrative as a Socially Symbolic Act.* Ithaca, NY: Cornell University Press, 1981.
Jenkins, Willis. "After Lynn White: Religious Ethics and Environmental Problems." *Journal of Religious Ethics* 37, no. 2 (2009): 283–309.
John of Reading. *Chronica Johannis de Reading et anonymi Cantuariensis, 1346–1367.* Edited by James Tait and Stephen Birchington. Manchester: Manchester University Press, 1914.
Johnson, Eleanor. "Horrific Visions of the Host: A Meditation of Genre." *Exemplaria* 27, no. 1–2 (2015): 150–66.
———. "The Poetics of Waste: Middle English Ecocriticism." *PMLA* 127, no. 3 (2012): 460–76.
———. *Waste and the Wasters: Poetry and Ecosystemic Thought in Medieval England.* Chicago: University of Chicago Press, 2023.
Jordan, William Chester. *The Great Famine: Northern Europe in the Early Fourteenth Century.* Princeton, NJ: Princeton University Press, 1996.
Julian of Norwich. *The Writings of Julian of Norwich: A Vision Showed to a Devout Woman and A Revelation of Love.* Edited by Nicholas Watson and Jacqueline Jenkins. State College: Pennsylvania State University Press, 2006.
Justice, Steven. "The Authority of Ritual in the *Jeu d'Adam*." *Speculum* 62, no. 4 (1987): 851–64.
Kalen, Herbert, ed. *A Middle English Metrical Paraphrase of the Old Testament.* Gothenburg, Swed.: Elanders, 1923.
Karnes, Michelle. *Imagination, Meditation, and Cognition in the Middle Ages.* Chicago: University of Chicago Press, 2011.
———. "Wonders in the Medieval Imagination." *Speculum* 90, no. 2 (2015): 327–65.
Keen, Suzanne. *Empathy and the Novel.* Oxford: Oxford University Press, 2007.
Kennedy, David. *Elegy.* The New Critical Idiom. New York: Routledge, 2008.
Kerby-Fulton, Kathryn. *Books under Suspicion: Censorship and Tolerance of Revelatory Writing in Late Medieval England.* Notre Dame, IN: University of Notre Dame Press, 2006.
———. *Reformist Apocalypticism and "Piers Plowman."* Cambridge: Cambridge University Press, 1990.
Kimmerer, Robin Wall. *Braiding Sweetgrass: Indigenous Wisdom, Scientific Knowledge, and the Teachings of Plants.* Minneapolis: Milkweed, 2013.
King, Pamela A. *The York Mystery Cycle and the Worship of the City.* Cambridge: D. S. Brewer, 2006.
Kiser, Lisa. "The Animals in Chester's *Noah's Flood*." *Early Theatre* 14, no. 1 (2011): 15–44.
Kolve, V. A. *Chaucer and the Imagery of Narrative: The First Five Canterbury Tales.* Stanford, CA: Stanford University Press, 1984.
———. *The Play Called Corpus Christi.* Stanford, CA: Stanford University Press, 1966.
Kordecki, Lesley. *Ecofeminist Subjectivities: Chaucer's Talking Birds.* New York: Palgrave, 2011.

Lactantius. *Divinae Institutiones*. Edited by Samuel Brandt. Corpus Scriptorum Ecclesiasticorum Latinorum 19. Prague: F. Tempsky, 1891.

Lamb, Hubert H. *Climate, History, and the Modern World*. London: Methuen, 1982.

Lamb, Hubert H., and Knud Frydendahl. *Historic Storms of the North Sea, British Isles and Northwest Europe*. Cambridge: Cambridge University Press, 1991.

Landes, Richard. "The Fear of an Apocalyptic Year 1000: Augustinian Historiography, Medieval and Modern." *Speculum* 75, no. 1 (2000): 97–145.

———. *Heaven on Earth: The Varieties of Millennial Experience*. Oxford: Oxford University Press, 2011.

Langeslag, P. S. "Weathering the Storm: Adverse Climates in Medieval Literature." In *Climate and Literature*, edited by Adeline Johns-Putra, 76–91. Cambridge: Cambridge University Press, 2019.

Langland, William. *The Vision of Piers Plowman: A Critical Edition of the B-text Based on Trinity College Cambridge MS B.15.17*. Edited by A. V. C. Schmidt. 2nd ed. London: Everyman, 1995.

Lapidge, Michael. "Versifying the Bible in the Middle Ages." In *The Text in the Community: Essays on Medieval Works, Manuscripts, Authors, and Readers*, edited by Jill Mann and Maura Nolan, 11–40. South Bend, IN: University of Notre Dame Press, 2006.

Larkin, Phillip. *The Collected Poems*. Edited by Anthony Thwaite. New York: Faber, 1993.

Lawrence-Mathers, Anne. *Medieval Meteorology: Forecasting the Weather from Aristotle to the Almanac*. Cambridge: Cambridge University Press, 2020.

Lawton, David. "Englishing the Bible, 1066–1549." In Wallace, *Cambridge History of Medieval English Literature*, 454–82.

Leach, Elizabeth Eva. *Sung Birds: Music, Nature, and Poetry in the Later Middle Ages*. Ithaca, NY: Cornell University Press, 2007.

Lears, Adin E. *World of Echo: Noise and Knowing in Late Medieval England*. Ithaca, NY: Cornell University Press, 2020.

Lecklider, Jane K. *Cleanness: Structure and Meaning*. Woodbridge, UK. D. S. Brewer, 1997.

LeFebvre, Henri. *Rhythmanalysis: Space Time and Everyday Life*. Translated by Stuart Elden and Gerald Moore. London: Bloomsbury, 2004.

Le Goff, Jacques. *The Medieval Imagination*. Translated by Arthur Goldhammer. Chicago: University of Chicago Press, 1985.

Leopold, Aldo. *A Sand County Almanac and Sketches Here and There*. New York: Oxford University Press, 1989.

Lerner, Robert. "Refreshment of the Saints: The Time after Antichrist as a Station for Earthly Progress in Medieval Thought." *Traditio* 32 (1976): 97–144.

———. "Sign Theory: Some Scholastic Encounters with 'The Fifteen Signs before the Day of Judgement.'" *Journal of Ecclesiastical History* 73, no. 4 (2022): 720–36.

LeVasseur, Todd, and Anna Peterson, eds. *Religion and Ecological Crisis: The "Lynn White Thesis" at Fifty*. Routledge Studies in Religion 50. New York: Routledge, 2017.

Levine, Caroline. *Forms: Whole, Rhythm, Hierarchy, Network*. Princeton, NJ: Princeton University Press, 2015.

"The Life of Adam and Eve." Translated by M. D. Johnson. In *The Old Testament Pseudepigrapha*. Edited by James H. Charlesworth. 2 vols. London: Darton, Longman and Todd, 1985.

Lindsey, Rebecca, and Luann Dahlman. "Climate Variability: North Atlantic Oscillation." Climate.gov. August 30, 2009. https://www.climate.gov/news-features/understanding-climate/climate-variability-north-atlantic-oscillation.

Lindström. Bengt. "Two Descriptions of the Signs before the Last Judgement." *Studia Neophilologica* 48, no. 2 (1976): 307–11.

Little, Katherine. *Transforming Work: Early Modern Pastoral and Late Medieval Poetry*. Notre Dame, IN: University of Notre Dame Press, 2013.

Livingston, Michael, ed. *Middle English Metrical Paraphrase of the Old Testament*. Kalamazoo, MI: Medieval Institute Publications, 2011.

Lochrie, Karma. *Nowhere in the Middle Ages*. Philadelphia: University of Pennsylvania Press, 2016.

Lopez, Barry. *Embrace Fearlessly the Burning World: Essays*. New York: Random House, 2022.

Lumiansky, R. M., and David Mills, eds. *The Chester Mystery Cycle*. EETS s.s. 3. London: Oxford University Press, 1974–86.

Lüning, Sebastian, Mariusz Gałka, Florencia Paula Bamonte, Felipe García Rodríguez, and Fritz Vahrenholt, "The Medieval Climate Anomaly in South America." *Quaternary International* 508 (2019): 70–87.

Lydgate, John. *The Minor Poems of John Lydgate: Edited from All Available MSS., with an Attempt to Establish the Lydgate Canon*. Edited by Henry Noble MacCracken, EETS e.s. 107. London: Oxford University Press, 1911.

MacFarlane, Robert. *Underland: A Deep Time Journey*. New York: W. W. Norton, 2019.

Macy, Joanna. *World as Lover, World as Self: Courage for Global Justice and Ecological Renewal*. New York: Penguin, 1991.

Macy, Joanna, and Chris Johnstone. *Active Hope: How to Face the Mess We Are in without Going Crazy*. Novato, CA: New World Library, 2012.

Mallet, R. *On the Facts of Earthquake Phaenomena: A Catalogue of known Earthquakes*. London: Reports of the British Association for the Advancement of Science, 1854.

Malm, Andreas. *How to Blow Up a Pipeline: Learning to Fight in a World on Fire*. London: Verso, 2021.

Mangum, Todd. "The Pandemic as God's Judgement." *Christianity Today*, May 15, 2020. https://www.christianitytoday.com/ct/2020/may-web-only/pandemic-as-gods-judgment.html.

Mantou, Reine. "Le thème des 'Quinze signes du jugement dernier' dans la tradition française." *Revue belge de philologie et d'histoire* 45, no. 3 (1967): 827–42.

Markus, Robert. "Living within Sight of the End." In *Time in the Medieval World*, edited by Chris Humphrey and W. M. Ormrod, 23–34. Rochester, NY: York Medieval Press, 2001.

Marshall, Miriam Helene. "Thirteenth-Century Culture as Illustrated by Matthew Paris." *Speculum* 14, no. 4 (1939): 465–77.

Martin, G. H., ed. and trans. *Knighton's Chronicle, 1337–1396*. Oxford: Clarendon Press, 1995.

Martin, Harries. "Forgetting Lot's Wife: Artaud, Spectatorship, and Catastrophe." *Yale Journal of Criticism* 11, no. 1 (1998): 221–38.

Marx, Leo. *The Machine in the Garden: Technology and the Pastoral Ideal in America*. Oxford: Oxford University Press, 1964.

Masciandaro, Nicola. *The Voice of the Hammer: The Meaning of Work in Middle English Literature*. Notre Dame, IN: University of Notre Dame Press, 2007.

McAvoy, Liz Herbert. *The Enclosed Garden in the Medieval Religious Imaginary*. Cambridge: Boydell & Brewer, 2021.

McClean, Teresa. *Medieval English Gardens*. Mineola, NY: Dover, 1980.

McCormick, Michael, Paul Edward Dutton, and Paul A. Mayewski. "Volcanoes and Climate Forcing of Carolingian Europe, A.D. 750–950." *Speculum* 82, no. 4 (2007): 865–95.

McDermott, Ryan. *Tropologies: Ethics and Invention in England, c. 1350–1600*. Notre Dame, IN: University of Notre Dame Press, 2016.

McGinn, Bernard, ed. *The Encyclopedia of Apocalypticism*. Vol. 2, *Apocalypticism in Western History and Culture*. New York: Continuum, 1998.

———. *Visions of the End: Apocalyptic Traditions in the Middle Ages*. Vol. 96 of *Records of Civilization, Sources and Studies*. New York: Columbia University Press, 1979.

McKibben, Bill, ed. *American Earth: Environmental Writing since Thoreau*. New York: Penguin, 2008.

———. *The End of Nature*. New York: Random House, 1989.

McNamara, Martin. "The (Fifteen) Signs before Doomsday in Irish Tradition." *Warszawskie Studia Teologiczne* 20, no. 2 (2007): 222–54.

McNamer, Sarah. *Affective Meditation and the Invention of Medieval Compassion*. Philadelphia: University of Pennsylvania Press, 2010.

———. "Feeling." In *Middle English: Oxford Twenty-First Century Approaches to Literature*, edited by Paul Strohm, 241–57. Oxford: Oxford University Press, 2007.

Meiner, Carsten, and Kristin Veel, eds. *The Cultural Life of Catastrophes and Crises*. Berlin: De Gruyter, 2012.

Menely, Tobias. *Climate and the Making of Worlds: Toward a Geohistorical Poetics*. Chicago: University of Chicago Press, 2021.

Merchant, Carolyn. *The Columbia Guide to American Environmental History*. New York: Columbia University Press, 2002.

———. *The Death of Nature: Women, Ecology, and the Scientific Revolution*. New York: HarperCollins, 1990. First published 1979.

———. *Reinventing Eden: The Fate of Nature in Western Culture*. New York: Taylor and Francis, 2013.

———. "Reinventing Eden: Western Culture as a Recovery Narrative." In *Uncommon Ground: Rethinking the Human Place in Nature*, edited by William Cronon, 132–59. New York: W. W. Norton, 1996.

Mertens, Thom, Maria Sherwood-Smith, Michael Mecklenburg, and Hans-Jochen Schiewer, eds. *The Last Judgement in Medieval Preaching*. Turnhout, Belgium: Brepols, 2013.

Meyer-Lee, Robert J., and Catherine Sanok, eds. *The Medieval Literary: Beyond Form*. Woodbridge, UK: D. S. Brewer, 2018.

Middle English Dictionary. Online edition. Middle English Compendium. Data last refreshed December 2023. https://quod.lib.umich.edu/m/middle-english-dictionary/dictionary.

Mill, Anna Jean. "Noah's Wife Again." *PMLA* 56, no. 3 (1941): 613–26.

Milton, John. *Paradise Lost*. In *Complete Poems and Major Prose*, edited by Merritt Y. Hughes. New York: Macmillan, 1985.

Minnis, Alastair. *From Eden to Eternity: Creations of Paradise in the Later Middle Ages*. Philadelphia: University of Pennsylvania Press, 2016.

Mitchell, J. Allan. *Becoming Human: The Matter of the Medieval Child*. Minneapolis: University of Minnesota Press, 2014.

Mordoh, Alice. "Portrait of a Lost Community: A Folklife Study of the Salt Creek Valley of South Central Indiana and the Effects of Community Displacement Following Formation of the Monroe Reservoir." PhD diss., Indiana University, 1986.

Morey, James H. *Book and Verse: A Guide to Middle English Biblical Literature*. Urbana: University of Illinois Press, 2000.

———. "The Fall in Particulate." *Yearbook of Langland Studies* 5 (1991): 91–97.

Morgan, Nigel, ed. *Prophecy, Apocalypse, and the Day of Doom: Proceedings of the 2000 Harlaxton Symposium*. Harlaxton Medieval Studies New Series 12. Lincolnshire, UK: Shaun Tyas, 2004.

Morris, Richard, ed. and trans. *The Blickling Homilies*. EETS o.s. 73. London: N. Trübner, 1880.

———, ed. *Cursor Mundi (The Course of the World): A Northumbrian Poem of the XIVth Century in Four Versions*. EETS o.s. 57, 59, 62, 66. London: K. Paul, Trench, Trübner, 1874–93.

Morrison, Stephen, ed. *A Late Fifteenth-Century Dominical Sermon Cycle: Edited from Bodleian Library MS E Musaeo 180 and Other Manuscripts*. 2 vols. EETS o.s. 337–38. Oxford: Oxford University Press, 2012.

Morse, Charlotte. *The Pattern of Judgment in the Queste and Cleanness*. Columbia: University of Missouri Press, 1978.

Morton, Timothy. *Dark Ecology: For a Logic of Future Coexistence*. New York: Columbia University Press, 2018.

———. "The Dark Ecology of Elegy." In *The Oxford Handbook of the Elegy*, edited by Karen Weisman, 251–70. Oxford: Oxford University Press, 2010.

———. *The Ecological Thought*. Cambridge, MA: Harvard University Press, 2010.

———. *Hyperobjects: Philosophy and Ecology after the End of the World*. Minneapolis: University of Minnesota Press, 2013.

Muir, John. *My First Summer in the Sierra*. Boston: Houghton Mifflin, 1911.

Murdoch, Brian, ed. *Adam's Grace: Fall and Redemption in Medieval Literature*. Cambridge: D. S. Brewer, 2000.

———. *The Apocryphal Adam and Eve in Medieval Europe: Vernacular Translation and Adaptations of the Vita Adae et Evae*. Oxford: Oxford University Press, 2009.

———. "The Cornish Medieval Drama." In *The Cambridge Companion to Medieval English Theatre*, edited by Richard Beadle, 211–39. Cambridge: Cambridge University Press, 1994.

———. *The Medieval Popular Bible: Expansions of Genesis in the Middle Ages*. Cambridge: D. S. Brewer, 2003.

Murdoch, Brian, and J. A. Tasioulas, eds. *The Apocryphal Lives of Adam and Eve*. Exeter: University of Exeter Press, 2002.

Murray, Hilda M. R., ed. *The Middle English Poem Erthe Upon Erthe: Printed from Twenty-Four Manuscripts*. EETS o.s. 141. Oxford: Oxford University Press, 1911.

Musson, R. M. W. "British Earthquakes." *Proceedings of the Geologists' Association* 118, no. 4 (2007): 305–37.

Nardizzi, Vin. "Medieval Ecocriticism." *Postmedieval* 4 (2013): 112–23.

Nardizzi, Vin, and Tiffany Jo Werth, eds. *Premodern Ecologies in the Modern Literary Imagination*. Toronto: University of Toronto Press, 2019.

Neev, David, and K. O. Emery. *The Destruction of Sodom, Gomorrah, and Jericho: Geological, Climatological, and Archaeological Background*. Oxford: Oxford University Press, 1995.

Nelson, Ingrid. "Form's Practice: Lyrics, Grammars, and the Medieval Idea of the Literary." In Meyer-Lee and Sanok, *Medieval Literary*, 35–60.

Nelson, Ingrid, and Shannon Gayk. "Genre as Form of Life." *Exemplaria* 27, no. 1 (2015): 3–17.

Nelson, Maggie. *On Freedom: Four Songs of Care and Constraint*. Minneapolis: Grey Wolf Press, 2021.

Nemo, Phillipe. *Job and the Excess of Evil*. Pittsburgh: Duquesne University Press, 1998.

Nersessian, Anahid. *The Calamity Form: On Poetry and Social Life*. Chicago: University of Chicago Press, 2020.

———. "Two Gardens: An Experiment in Calamity Form." *Modern Language Quarterly* 74, no. 3 (2013): 307–29.

Newhauser, Richard. "Toward a History of Human Curiosity." *Deutsche Vierteljahrsschrift für Literaturwissenschaft und Geistesgeschichte* 56, no. 4 (1982): 559–75.

Nissenbaum, A. "The Dead Sea—An Economic Resource for 10,000 Years." *Saline Lakes* 5 (1993): 127–41.

———. "Utilization of Dead Sea Asphalt through History." *Reviews in Chemical Engineering* 9, no. 3–4 (1993): 365–83.

Nissenbaum, A., Z. Aizenshtat, and M. Goldberg. "The Floating Asphalt Blocks of the Dead Sea." *Physics and Chemistry of the Earth* 12 (1980): 157–61.

Nixon, Rob. *Slow Violence and the Environmentalism of the Poor*. Cambridge, MA: Harvard University Press, 2011.

Nordhaus, Ted, and Michael Shellenberger. "Apocalypse Fatigue: Losing the Public on Climate Change." E360. November 16, 2009. Yale School of the Environment. https://e360.yale.edu/features/apocalypse_fatigue_losing_the_public_on_climate_change.

Normington, Katie. " 'Have here a Drink full good': A Comparative Analysis of Staging Temptation in the Newcastle Noah Play." In *Staging Scripture: Biblical Drama, 1350–1600*, edited by Peter Happé and Wim Hüsken, 166–81. Leiden, Neth.: Brill, 2016.

Novacich, Sarah. *Shaping the Archive in Late Medieval England: History, Poetry, and Performance*. Cambridge: Cambridge University Press, 2017.

Odell, Jenny. *How to Do Nothing: Resisting the Attention Economy*. New York: Melville House, 2019.

O'Mara, Veronica. " 'Go 3e curselynges, to euerelasting fier': Doomsday in Middle English Prose Sermons." In Morgan, *Prophecy, Apocalypse, and the Day of Doom*, 277–91.

———. "The Last Judgement in Medieval English Prose Sermons: An Overview." In Mertens et al., *Last Judgement in Medieval Preaching*, 19–41.

O'Mathúna, Dónal P. "Christian Theology and Disasters: Where Is God in All This?" In *Disasters: Core Concepts and Ethical Theories*, edited by Dónal P. O'Mathúna, Vilius Dranseika, and Bert Gordijn. Cham, Switz.: SpringerOpen, 2018. https://doi.org/10.1007/978-3-319-92722-0.

Oppenheimer, Clive. *Eruptions that Shook the World*. Cambridge: Cambridge University Press, 2011.

———. "Ice Core and Palaeoclimatic Evidence for the Timing and Nature of the Great Mid-Thirteenth Century Volcanic Eruption." *International Journal of Climatology* 23 (2003): 417–26.

Palmer, James T. *The Apocalypse in the Early Middle Ages*. Cambridge: Cambridge University Press, 2014.

———. "Climates of Crisis: Apocalypse, Nature, and Rhetoric in the Early Medieval World," *Viator* 48, no. 2 (2017): 1–20.

Palti, Kathleen. "The Bound Earth in *Patience* and Other Middle English Poetry." *ISLE: Interdisciplinary Studies in Literature and Environment* 20, no. 1 (2013): 31–51.

Paris, Matthew. *Chronica majora*. Edited by H. R. Luard. Rolls Series 57,7 vols. London, 1883.

———. *Matthew Paris's English History: From the Year 1235 to 1273*. Translated by J. A. Giles. 3 vols. London: G. Bell, 1889–93.

Passannante, Gerard. *Catastrophizing: Materialism and the Making of Disaster*. Chicago: University of Chicago Press, 2019.

Patrides, C. A. *The Phoenix and the Ladder: The Rise and Decline of the Christian View of History*. Berkeley: University of California Press, 1964.

Patterson, Grace E., K. Marie McIntyre, Helen E. Clough, and Jonathan Rushton. "Societal Impacts of Pandemics: Comparing COVID-19 with History to Focus Our Response." *Frontiers in Public Health* 9 (April 11, 2021). https://doi.org/10.3389/fpubh.2021.630449.

Pearsall, Derek, and Elizabeth Salter. *Landscapes and Seasons of the Medieval World*. Toronto: University of Toronto Press, 1973.

Peter of Limoges. *The Moral Treatise on the Eye*. Edited and translated by Richard Newhauser. Toronto: Pontifical Institute of Medieval Studies, 2012.

Pew Research Center. "What Lessons Do Americans See for Humanity in the Pandemic?" October 8, 2020. https://www.pewforum.org/essay/what-lessons-do-americans-see-for-humanity-in-the-pandemic/.

Plumwood, Val. *Feminism and the Mastery of Nature*. London: Routledge, 1993.

Popa, Maya C. "Letter to Noah's Wife." Poets.org. https://poets.org/poem/letter-noahs-wife. Originally published September 30, 2019, in Poem-a-Day by the Academy of American Poets.

Powell, Susan. "All Saints' Church, North Street, York: Text and Image in the *Pricke of Conscience* Window." In Morgan, *Prophecy, Apocalypse, and the Day of Doom*, 292–316.

Powell, Susan, ed. *The Advent and Nativity Sermons from a Fifteenth-Century Revision of John Mirk's Festial: Ed. from B.L. MSS Harley 2247, Royal 18 B XXV, and Gloucester Cathedral Library 22*. Middle English Texts 13. Heidelberg: C. Winter, 1981.

———, ed. *John Mirk's "Festial": Edited from British Library MS Cotton Claudius A.II*. 2 vols. EETS o.s. 334–35. Oxford: Oxford University Press, 2009–11.

Pseudo-Bede. *Collectanea Pseudo-Bedae*. Edited by Martha Bayless and Michael Lapidge. Scriptores Latini Hiberniae 14. Dublin: School of Celtic Studies, Dublin Institute for Advanced Studies, 1998.

Purdy, Jedediah. *After Nature: A Politics for the Anthropocene*. Cambridge, MA: Harvard University Press, 2015.

Putter, Ad. "*Cleanness* and the Tradition of Medieval Versification." In *Medieval Alliterative Poetry*, edited by John A. Burrow and Hoyt N. Duggan, 166–84. Dublin, Ireland: Four Courts Press, 2010.

———. "Sources and Backgrounds for Descriptions of the Flood in Medieval and Renaissance Literature." *Studies in Philology* 94 (1997): 137–59.

Ramsey, M. K. "Dustsceawung: Texting the Dead in the Old English Elegies." In *Laments for the Lost in Medieval Literature*, edited by Jane Tolmie and M. J. Toswell, 45–66. Turnhout, Belgium: Brepols, 2010.

Rankine, Claudia. "Weather." *New York Times*, June 15, 2020. https://www.nytimes.com/2020/06/15/books/review/claudia-rankine-weather-poem-coronavirus.html.

Reich, Warren. "History of the Notion of Care." In *Encyclopedia of Bioethics*, vol. 5, edited by Warren Thomas Reich, 319–33. New York: Simon & Schuster Macmillan, 1995.

Rentz, Ellen K. *Imagining the Parish in Late Medieval England*. Columbus: Ohio State University Press, 2015.

Rhodes, William. "The Apocalyptic Aesthetics of the List: Form and Political Economy in *Wynnere and Wastoure*." *Journal of Medieval and Early Modern Studies* 52, no. 1 (2022): 119–45.

———. "The Ecology of Reform: Land and Labor from *Piers Plowman* to Edmund Spenser." PhD diss., University of Virginia, 2015.

Rice, Nicole, and Margaret Aziza Pappano. *The Civic Cycles: Artisan Drama and Identity in Premodern England*. Notre Dame, IN: University of Notre Dame Press, 2015.

Rich, Adrienne. *Diving into the Wreck: Poems 1971–1972*. New York: W. W. Norton, 1973.

Rigby, Kate. *Dancing with Disaster: Environmental Histories, Narratives, and Ethics for Perilous Times*. Charlottesville: University of Virginia Press, 2015.

Ritchey, Sarah. *Holy Matter: Changing Perceptions of the Material World in Late Medieval Christianity*. Ithaca, NY: Cornell University Press, 2014.

Rivard, Derek. *Blessing the World: Ritual and Lay Piety in Medieval Religion*. Washington, DC: Catholic University Press, 2008.

Robertson, Kellie. "Medieval Materialism: A Manifesto." *Exemplaria* 22, no. 2 (2010): 99–118.

———. *Nature Speaks: Medieval Literature and Aristotelian Philosophy*. Philadelphia: University of Pennsylvania Press, 2017.

———. "Scaling Nature: Microcosm and Macrocosm in Later Medieval Thought." *Journal of Medieval and Early Modern Studies* 49, no. 3 (2019): 624–25.

Rogerson, John. "The Creation Stories: Their Ecological Potential and Problems." In *Ecological Hermeneutics: Biblical, Historical, and Theological Perspectives*, edited by David G. Horrell, Cherryl Hunt, Christopher Southgate, and Francesca Stavrakopoulou. London: Bloomsbury Publishing, 2010.

Rogerson, Margaret. *The York Mystery Plays: Performance in the City*. Woodbridge, UK: Boydell & Brewer, 2011.

Rohr, Christian. "Man and Natural Disaster in the Late Middle Ages: The Earthquake in Carinthia and Northern Italy on 25 January 1348 and Its Perception." *Environment and History* 9, no. 2 (May 2003): 127–49.

———. "Writing a Catastrophe: Describing and Constructing Disaster Perception in Narrative Sources from the Late Middle Ages." *Historical Social Research / Historische Sozialforschung* 32, no. 3 (2007): 88–102.

Rolle de Hampole, Richard. *The Pricke of Conscience (Stimulus Conscientiae): A Northumbrian Poem*. Edited by Richard Morris. Berlin: A. Asher, 1863.

Ronda, Margaret. "Mourning and Melancholia in the Anthropocene." Post45. June 10, 2013. https://post45.org/2013/06/mourning-and-melancholia-in-the-anthropocene/.

Rosen, William. *The Third Horseman: Climate Change and the Great Famine of the Fourteenth Century*. New York: Viking, 2014.

Rosenberg, Jessica. *Botanical Poetics: Early Modern Plant Books and the Husbandry of Print*. Philadelphia: University of Pennsylvania Press, 2022.

Rozenski, Steven. "A Light to Lighten the Gentiles: Stained Glass, the Prick of Conscience, and Theological Double Vision in All Saints (North Street), York." In *Devotional Interaction in Medieval England and Its Afterlives*, edited by Elisa A. Foster, Julia Perratore, and Steven Rozenski, 285–308. Art and Material Culture in Medieval and Renaissance Europe 12. Leiden, Neth.: Brill, 2018.

Rudd, Gillian. *Greenery: Ecocritical Readings of Late Medieval English Literature*. Manchester: Manchester University Press, 2007.

———. "Thinking through Earth in Langland's *Piers Plowman* and the Harley lyric 'Erthe toc of Erthe.'" *Ecotheology* 8, no. 2 (2003): 137–49.

Sacks, Peter M. *The English Elegy: Studies in the Genre from Spenser to Yeats*. Baltimore: Johns Hopkins University Press, 1985.

Sanders, Scott Russell. *A Conservationist Manifesto*. Bloomington: Indiana University Press, 2009.

———. *Staying Put: Making a Home in a Restless World*. Boston: Beacon Press, 1993.

Sandison, H. E. "'Quindecim signa ante iudicium': A Contribution to the History of the Latin Versions of the Legend." *Archiv für das Studium der neueren Sprachen und Literaturen* 124 (1910): 72–82.

Scherb, Victor. "Cornish Ordinalia." In *The Oxford Encyclopedia of British Literature*, edited by David Kastan, 74–76. Oxford: Oxford University Press, 2006.

Schmidt, A. V. C. "Chaucer and the Golden Age." *Essays in Criticism* 26 (1976): 99–115.
Schulz, Kathryn. *Lost & Found: Reflections on Grief, Gratitude, and Happiness.* New York: Random House, 2022.
———. "The Really Big One." *New Yorker*, July 13, 2015. http://www.newyorker.com/magazine/2015/07/20/the-really-big-one.
Scott, Rebecca R. "Love." In Cohen and Duckert, *Veer Ecology*, 377–91.
Scranton, Roy. *Learning to Die in the Anthropocene: Reflections on the End of a Civilization.* San Francisco: City Lights Books, 2015.
———. *We're Doomed: Now What? Reflections on War and Climate Change.* New York: Soho Press, 2018.
Seaman, Myra. *Objects of Affection: The Book and the Household in Late Medieval England.* Manchester: Manchester University Press, 2021.
Sebastian, John, ed. *The Croxton Play of the Sacrament.* Kalamazoo, MI: Medieval Institute Publications, 2012.
Sergi, Matthew. *Practical Cues and Social Spectacle in the Chester Mystery Plays.* Chicago: University of Chicago Press, 2020.
Shannon, Laurie. "The Eight Animals in Shakespeare, or, Before the Human." *PMLA* 124, no. 2 (2009): 472–79.
Shields, Christopher. "Aristotle's Psychology: Hylomorphism in General." In *Stanford Encyclopedia of Philosophy*, Stanford University, 1997–. Article published January 11, 2000; last modified October 12, 2020. https://plato.stanford.edu/entries/aristotle-psychology/#HyloGene.
Shirley, Walter Waddington, ed. *Fasciculi Zizaniorum magistri Johannis Wyclif cum tritico / Ascribed to Thomas Netter of Walden.* Rolls Series. London: Longman, Brown, Green, Longman, & Roberts, 1858.
Shuffleton, George, ed. *Codex Ashmole 61.* Kalamazoo, MI: Medieval Institute Publications, 2008.
Siewers, Alfred Kentigern. "The Ecopoetics of Creation: Genesis LXX 1–3." In *Reimagining Nature: Environmental Humanities and Ecosemiotics*, edited by Alfred Kentigern Siewers, 45–78. Lewisburg, PA: Bucknell University Press, 2014.
Simpson, James. "From Reason to Affective Knowledge: Modes of Thought and Poetic Form in *Piers Plowman*." *Medium Aevum* 55, no. 1 (1986): 1–23.
———. *Piers Plowman: An Introduction to the B-text.* London: Longman, 1990.
Sir Gawain and the Green Knight. In *The Poems of the Pearl Manuscript: Pearl, Cleanness, Patience, Sir Gawain and the Green Knight*, edited by Malcolm Andrew and Ronald Waldron. Exeter: University of Exeter Press, 2007.
Sisk, Jennifer. "Langland's Ethical Imaginary: Refuge and Risk in 'Piers bern.'" *Exemplaria* 34, no. 3 (2022): 233–39.
Smith, D. Vance. *Arts of Dying: Literature and Finitude in Medieval England.* Chicago: University of Chicago Press, 2020.
———. *Book of the Incipit: Beginnings in the Fourteenth Century.* Minneapolis: University of Minnesota Press, 2001.
———. "Medieval Forma: The Logic of the Work." In *Reading for Form*, edited by Susan J. Wolfson and Marshall Brown. Seattle: University of Washington Press, 2006.
———. "Negative Langland." *Yearbook of Langland Studies* 23 (2009): 33–59.
Smith, Zadie. "Elegy for a Country's Seasons." *New York Review*, April 3, 2014.
Smoller, Laura A. "Of Earthquakes, Hail, Frogs, and Geography: Plague and the Investigation of Apocalypse in the Later Middle Ages." In *Last Things: Death and the Apocalypse in the*

Middle Ages, edited by Caroline Walker Bynum and Paul Freeman, 156–87. Philadelphia: University of Pennsylvania Press, 2000.

Solnit, Rebecca. *A Paradise Built in Hell: The Extraordinary Communities That Arise in Disaster*. New York: Penguin, 2010.

———. "What if Climate Change Meant Not Doom but Abundance?" *Washington Post*, March 15, 2023. https://www.washingtonpost.com/opinions/2023/03/15/rebecca-solnit-climate-change-wealth-abundance.

Sontag, Susan. *Regarding the Pain of Others*. New York: Picador, 2003.

Spahr, Juliana. "Gentle Now, Don't Add to Heartache." In *well then there now*, 123–33. Boston: Black Sparrow Press, 2011.

Spearing, A. C. *The Gawain-Poet: A Critical Study*. Cambridge: Cambridge University Press, 1970.

———. *Medieval Dream Poetry*. Cambridge: Cambridge University Press, 1976.

Stafford, William. *An Oregon Message: Poems*. New York: Harper and Row, 1987.

Staley, Lynn. *The Island Garden: England's Language of Nation from Gildas to Marvell*. Notre Dame, IN: University of Notre Dame Press, 2012.

Stanbury, Sarah. "EcoChaucer: Green Ethics and Medieval Nature." *Chaucer Review* 39, no.1 (2004): 1–16.

———. "In God's Sight: Vision and Sacred History in *Purity*." In *Text and Matter: New Critical Perspectives on the Pearl-Poet*, edited by Robert J. Blanch. Albany: Whitston Publishing, 1991.

———. "Multilingual Lists and Chaucer's 'The Former Age.'" In *The Art of Vision: Ekphrasis in Medieval Literature and Culture*, edited by Andrew James Johnston, Ethan Knapp, and Margitta Rouse, 36–54. Columbus: Ohio State University Press, 2015.

———. *Seeing the Gawain-Poet: Description and the Art of Perception*. Philadelphia: University of Pennsylvania Press, 1991.

Steel, Karl. "A Fourteenth-Century Ecology: 'The Former Age' with Dindimus." In *Rethinking Chaucerian Beasts*, edited by Carolynn Van Dyke, 186–99. New York: Palgrave Macmillan, 2012.

———. *How Not to Make a Human: Pets, Feral Children, Worms, Sky Burial, Oysters*. Minneapolis: University of Minnesota Press, 2019.

———. *How to Make a Human: Animals and Violence in the Middle Ages*. Columbus: Ohio State University Press, 2011.

———. "Woofing and Weeping with Animals in the Last Days." *Postmedieval* 1 (2010): 187–93.

Steiner, Emily. *Reading "Piers Plowman."* Cambridge: Cambridge University Press, 2013.

Stevens, Wallace. "Sunday Morning." In *Collected Poems*. New York: Vintage, 1923.

Stevenson, Jill. *Performance, Cognitive Theory, and Devotional Culture: Sensual Piety in Late Medieval York*. New York: Palgrave 2010.

Stewart, Susan. "Garden Agon." *Representations* 62 (1998): 111–43.

———. *On Longing: Narratives of the Miniature, the Gigantic, the Souvenir, the Collection*. Durham, NC: Duke University Press, 1993.

Stock, Lorraine. "Past and Present in Chaucer's 'The Former Age': Boethian Translation or Late Medieval Primitivism." *Carmina Philosophiae: A Journal of the International Boethius Society* 2 (1993): 1–37.

Stone, Michael E. *A History of the Literature of Adam and Eve*. Atlanta: Scholars Press, 1992.

———, ed. *Signs of the Judgment, Onomastica Sacra, and the Generations from Adam*. University of Pennsylvania Armenian Texts and Studies 3. Chico, CA: Scholars Press, 1981.

Sugano, Douglas, ed. *The N-Town Plays*. Rochester, NY: Medieval Institute Publications, 2007.

Taavitsainen, Irma. *Middle English Lunaries: A Study of the Genre*. Helsinki: Société Néophilologique, 1988.

Taguchi, Mayumi, ed. *The History of the Patriarks*. Heidelberg: Heidelberg Universitätsverlag, 2010.

Taylor, Charles. *Sources of the Self: The Making of the Modern Identity*. Cambridge, MA: Harvard University Press, 1989.

Thomas, Keith. *Man and the Natural World: A History of the Modern Sensibility*. New York: Pantheon Books, 1983.

Thompson, Anne B., ed. *The Northern Homily Cycle*. Kalamazoo, MI: Medieval Institute Publications, 2008.

Tolmie, Jane. "Mrs. Noah and Didactic Abuses." *Early Theater* 5, no.1 (2002): 11–35.

Trokelowe, Johannes de. *Annales*. Edited by H. T. Riley. Rolls Series 28, pp. 92–95. London, 1866. Translated by Brian Tierney for Fordham University, Internet Medieval Source Book, January 1996, https://sourcebooks.fordham.edu/source/famin1315a.asp.

Tsing, Anna Lowenhaupt. *The Mushroom at the End of the World: On the Possibility of Life in Capitalist Ruins*. Princeton, NJ: Princeton University Press, 2015.

Tsing, Anna Lowenhaupt, Heather Swanson, Elaine Gan, and Nils Bubandt. *Arts of Living on a Damaged Planet: Ghosts and Monsters of the Anthropocene*. 3rd ed. Minneapolis: University of Minnesota Press, 2017.

Turville-Petre, Thorlac, ed. *The Poems of the Kildare Manuscript*. EETS o.s. 345. Oxford: Oxford University Press, 2015.

Twycross, Meg. "Forget the 4.30 am Start: Recovering a Palimpsest in the York Ordo Paginarum." *Medieval English Theater* 25 (2003): 98–152.

US Geological Survey. "What Are Some of the Signs of Climate Change?" Accessed February 23, 2024. https://www.usgs.gov/faqs/what-are-some-signs-climate-change.

Utley, Francis Lee. "The One Hundred and Three Names of Noah's Wife." *Speculum* 16, no. 4 (1941): 426–52.

Varnam, Laura. *The Church as Sacred Space in Middle English Literature and Culture*. Manchester: Manchester University Press, 2018.

Varnhagen, Hermann. "Zu mittelenglischen gedichten. X: Zu den 'Signa ante Judicium.'" *Anglia* 3 (1880): 533–51.

Venables, Edmund, ed. *Chronicon abbatiae de Parco Ludae: The Chronicle of Louth Park Abbey*. Horncastle, UK: Lincolnshire Record Society, 1891.

Von Contzen, Eva, and Chanita Goodblatt, eds. *Enacting the Bible in Medieval and Early Modern Drama*. Manchester: Manchester University Press, 2022.

Wagner, Daniela. *Die Fünfzehn Zeichen vor dem Jüngsten Gericht: Spätmittelalterliche Bildkonzepte für das Seelenheil*. Berlin: Dietrich Reimer Verlag, 2016.

Walker, Greg. "'In the Beginning...': Performing the Creation in the York Corpus Christi Plays." In *The Oxford Handbook of Tudor Drama*, edited by Thomas Betteridge and Greg Walker, 36–54. Oxford: Oxford University Press, 2012.

Wallace, David. *The Cambridge History of Medieval English Literature*. Cambridge: Cambridge University Press, 1999.

———. "*Cleanness* and the Terms of Terror." In *Text and Matter: New Critical Perspectives of the Pearl-Poet*, edited by Edward Wilson, 93–104. Oxford: Oxford University Press, 1994.

Warner, Rubie D.-N. ed. *Early English Homilies: From the Twelfth Century MS. Vesp. D. XIV*, EETS o.s. 152. London: Kegan Paul, Trench, Trübner, 1917.

Warnez, Matthew T. "De Natura: The Church Fathers on Creation's Fallenness." *Nova et Vetera* 19, no. 3 (2021): 933–78.
Warren, Michael. "Medieval Weather: An Introduction." *Medieval Ecocriticisms* 1, no. 1 (2021): 1–10.
Watson, Nicholas. "Censorship and Cultural Change in Late-Medieval England: Vernacular Theology, the Oxford Translation Debate, and Arundel's Constitutions of 1409." *Speculum* 70, no. 4 (1995): 822–64.
Watson, Robert. *Back to Nature: The Green and the Real in the Late Renaissance.* Philadelphia: University of Pennsylvania Press, 2006.
Weil, Simone. *Waiting for God.* New York: Putnam, 1951.
Weiler, Bjorn. "Historical Writing in Medieval Britain: The Case of Matthew Paris." In Jahner, Steiner, and Tyler, *Medieval Historical Writing*, 319–38.
Wenzel, Siegfried. "Pestilence and Middle English Literature: Friar Grimestone's Poems on Death." In *The Black Death: The Impact of the Fourteenth-Century Plague*, edited by Daniel Williman, 131–59. Binghamton, NY: Center for Medieval & Early Renaissance Studies, 1982.
Wheeler, Michael. "Martin Heidegger." In *Stanford Encyclopedia of Philosophy*, Stanford University, 1997–. Article published October 12, 2011. https://plato.stanford.edu/entries/heidegger/.
White, Lynn. "Continuing the Conversation." In *Western Man and Environmental Ethics: Attitudes Toward Nature and Technology*, edited by Ian Barbour, 55–65. Reading, MA: Addison-Wesley, 1973.
———. "The Historical Roots of Our Ecologic Crisis." *Science* 155 (1967): 1203–7.
———. *Medieval Technology and Social Change.* London: Oxford University Press, 1962.
Williams, Gweno, John Merrylees, and David Richmond. "Producing 'The Creation' and 'The Fall of Man' in 21st Century York." In M. Rogerson, *York Mystery Plays*, 145–55.
Williams, Michael. *Deforesting the Earth: From Prehistory to Global Crisis.* Chicago: University of Chicago Press, 2003.
Williams, Raymond. *The Country and the City.* Oxford: Oxford University Press, 1973.
Wilner, Eleanor. *The Girl with Bees in Her Hair.* Port Townsend, WA: Cooper Canyon, 2004.
Wilson, Edward. *A Descriptive Index of the English Lyrics in John of Grimestone's Preaching Book.* Medium Ævum Monographs 2. Oxford: Basil Blackwell, 1973.
Wimbledon, Thomas. *Wimbledon's Sermon: Redde Rationem Villicationes Tue; A Middle English Sermon of the Fourteenth Century.* Edited by Ione Kemp Knight. Pittsburgh: Duquesne University Press, 1967.
Wittig, Joseph. *"Piers Plowman": Concordance.* London: Athlone Press, 2001.
Woodword, Christopher. *In Ruins: A Journey through History, Art, and Literature.* New York: Vintage Books, 2001.
Woolf, Rosemary. *The English Mystery Plays.* Berkeley: University of California Press, 1972.
———. *The English Religious Lyric in the Middle Ages.* Oxford: Clarendon Press, 1968.
Worthen, Shana. "The Influence of Lynn White Jr.'s *Technology and Social Change.*" *History Compass* 7, no. 4 (2009): 1201–17.
Wright, Charles D. "The Apocalypse of Thomas: Some New Latin Texts and their Significance for the Old English Versions." In *Apocryphal Texts and Traditions in Anglo-Saxon England*, edited by Kathryn Powell and Donald Scragg, 27–64. Publications of the Manchester Centre for Anglo-Saxon Studies 2. Woodbridge, UK: Boydell & Brewer, 2003.

Wright, Thomas, ed. *Political poems and songs relating to English history, composed during the period from the accession of Edw. III. to that of Ric. III.* London: Longman, Green, Longman, & Roberts, 1861.

Wyclif, John. *Tractatus de statu innocencie*. Edited by Johann Loserth and J. D. Matthew. Wyclif Society 23. London: C. K. Paul, 1922.

Yeats, William Butler. "The Second Coming." In *The Collected Poems of W. B. Yeats*, edited by Richard J. Finneran. New York: Macmillan, 1991. First published 1989.

York Museum Gardens. "About St Mary's Abbey." Accessed February 9, 2024. https://www.yorkmuseumgardens.org.uk/about/st-marys-abbey/.

Zacher, Samantha. *Rewriting the Old Testament in Anglo-Saxon Verse: Becoming the Chosen People*. London: Bloomsbury Academic, 2014.

Zagajewski, Adam. "Try to Praise the Mutilated World." In *Without End*, translated by Clare Cavanagh, 60. New York: Farrar, Straus and Giroux, 2003.

Zeeman, Nicolette. *The Arts of Disruption: Allegory and "Piers Plowman."* Oxford: Oxford University Press, 2020.

———. *"Piers Plowman" and the Medieval Discourse of Desire*. Cambridge: Cambridge University Press, 2006.

Index

Aberth, John, 19, 226, 227, 239
Adam, 30, 42; creation of, 48–52; as earth, 48–49, 54–55, 57; life after Expulsion, 63, 69, 72–86; penance of, 84–86
Adam Books, 69, 81–89. *See also* Auchinleck *Life of Adam*; *Canticum de Creatione*; *Life of Adam and Eve* (*Vita Adae et Euae*)
Advent, 200, 256n29; sermons for, 167, 194, 196–98
affective piety, 105, 107, 240
agriculture, 21–22, 24, 67
Alaimo, Stacy, 53–54
Alan of Lille, 1, 3–4, 53–54
Ambrose of Milan, 40–42, 85
Anglo-Norman literature, 72–73, 193–94, 201–2
animals: on ark, 133–35; in last days, 202–6; postlapsarian condition of, 61, 84–86; predation, 44–45, 61–62, 92; prelapsarian condition of, 41–47; suffering/lamenting of, 46–47, 84–86, 120–24, 202–6, 259n76
Anthropocene, 19, 103, 189, 210–11, 215
anthropocentrism, 11, 91, 189, 210, 215, 252n85
anthropomorphism, 56, 165, 205
antithesis, 63, 65, 68–69, 71–74, 87, 109, 158–59, 170
apocalypse: definition of, 4–6, 155, 224n12; as end of world, 6, 10, 166, 193; as "hyperobject," 254n12; as metaphor, 189; as presaged by ecosystemic collapse, 167, 187–91, 195, 210; as quotidian, 151–55, 166, 178–79, 215; as revelatory event, 90, 155, 160–68, 176–77, 218–19; signs of, 167, 184–207; temporality of, 16, 161, 200, 248n21, 255n23. *See also* Fifteen Signs of Doomsday (motif)
Apocalypse of John. *See* Bible: Apocalypse (Revelation)
Apocalypse of Thomas, 129, 192, 254n15

apocalypticism, in modern world, 98, 183, 189, 210–11
apocryphal texts, 10, 66, 81–88, 191–93
Aquinas, Thomas: on animals, 44–45; on the Fifteen Signs, 193
Aristotle, 55, 233n95
ark (of Noah), 100, 106, 113, 115–17, 123–24, 131–37, 241n22; reproduction of, 242n43
ars moriendi, 6–9, 58, 175, 195, 216
attention, 4–9, 13–15, 62, 104–8, 119, 130, 142–44, 149, 162, 167–68, 176–79, 188–90, 203, 208–12, 214–20
Auchinleck *Life of Adam*, 82, 87. *See also* Adam Books
Augustine (saint), 44, 106, 207
Avitus, *De diluvio mundi*, 115

Basil (saint), 41, 46
beholdenness. *See* responsibility
Berry, Wendell, 58
Bible: Genesis, 12, 30–32, 35–36, 39, 42, 50–51, 57, 63, 81, 109, 114, 126, 130–31, 140, 153, 228n6; Exodus, 99–100, 239n12; Job, 2, 223n1; Psalms, 2; Isaiah, 2, 252n93; Jeremiah, 23; Esdras, 192; Ezekiel, 99–100, 191–92; Daniel, 109; Jonah, 109, 243n57; Matthew, 109, 171, 191, 194, 208; Luke, 2, 108, 131, 191, 194, 197; Romans, 85, 228n6; 2 Peter, 108, 207; Apocalypse (Revelation), 171, 192, 194, 252n93, 252n95
birds, 32, 45–47, 59, 83, 92, 167, 213; on ark, 115, 134; in Eden, 45–47, 50–52; at end of world, 184, 187, 191, 194, 204–5; mourning of, 86–87, 187, 204; predation, 61–62; song of, 8, 11, 61; as threat, 83
Black Death, 5, 24, 98–100, 109, 154, 161, 172, 239n7. *See also* plague
Blanchot, Maurice, 154

INDEX

Boethius, 66–67
Book of Nature, 3–4, 6, 191, 223n4, 254n15; as doomsday book, 189
Brinton, Thomas, 99, 167
bubonic plague. *See* Black Death
Buddhism, 7, 53
Buell, Lawrence, 189, 226n47, 235n15, 254nn16–17
Bynum, Caroline Walker, 31, 224n16, 228n8, 247n10, 249n40, 254n12

Canticum de Creatione, 69, 82–87, 236n32. *See also* Adam Books
Capgrave, John, 115, 243n47
Carson, Rachel, 11
cats, 9, 45, 60, 222
Chaganti, Seeta, 229n22, 229n27
Chaucer, Geoffrey: *Boece*, 66–67, 171; *The Book of the Duchess*, 99; *Canterbury Tales*, 158; "The Former Age," 66–71
Chester Mystery Cycle, plays of: "The Creation," 39, 50; "Noah's Flood," 131, 133–36; "The Resurrection," 171; "Prophets of Antichrist," 201, 205
chronicles, 154–55; on Great Flood, 115; on natural disasters, 22–23, 157–60, 164–67, 171–72; on plague, 99. *See also* Matthew Paris
Chrysostom, John, 42, 230n43, 231n57
Cleanness (poem), 105, 109, 152–53; on destruction of Sodom, 126–29; on Great Flood, 113, 115–17, 119–26, 136; on Lot's Wife, 131, 140–44; wreckage in, 109–13, 146–48
climate, premodern definition of, 19–21
climate change, 8–9, 24, 149, 188; anthropogenic, 19–20, 104, 178, 211; denial, 10. *See also* Anthropocene
Cohen, Jeffrey Jerome, 25, 43, 97, 105, 224n13, 224n18, 226n45, 231n51, 233n102
Coley, David, 24, 105, 109, 142–43, 154, 239n7, 245n115
Comestor, Peter, 193–94, 231n48
consumption, 25, 69, 81, 235n26
contemptus mundi, 9, 89
contrast. *See* antithesis; form, literary
Corporal Works of Mercy, 184, 190, 208–10, 259n86
cosmology, 9–12, 30–32, 35–36
COVID-19, 59, 72, 97–98, 183
Cronon, William, 101
Croxton Play of the Sacrament, The, 229n24
cura, 106–7, 217–18, 234n4, 260n11
curiosity (*curiositas*), 106–7, 119, 122, 124, 130, 141–44, 149, 169
Cursor Mundi, 105; on apocalyptic signs, 259n85; on creation and Eden, 43, 230n33; on Great Flood, 108, 115, 117–19, 122–24, 142–43, 243n48; on the human body, 54–55; on human dominion, 50–51

dark ecology, 6, 77, 159, 216, 234n118
Davis, Rebecca, 168–69, 221, 223n4, 232n62, 252n83, 252n85, 252n91, 260n8
Dead Sea, 127, 146–48, 246n116
death: from catastrophe, 23–24, 72, 98, 103, 121–24, 136, 149, 158–59, 164–65, 198; of Christ, 171–72, 234n7; lyrics about, 1–4, 56–58, 124, 223n6; in/of nature, 1–6, 29–31, 34, 59–61, 124, 206, 214–15; as object of contemplation, 1–3, 6–8, 52, 58, 174, 179, 190, 210–11; personified, 8, 216–17; in post-lapsarian world, 63, 66, 228n5; in prelapsarian world, 30–31, 34–36, 39–49, 228n7, 228n9. *See also ars moriendi*
declensionism, 63–68, 71, 89–91, 97, 234n7, 234n10, 234n12, 235n23. *See also* primitivism
deforestation, 5, 21, 91, 103, 227n8
Diaz, Natalie, 139, 145
Dickinson, Emily, 183
dilation. *See* form, literary: amplification (*amplificatio*)
Dillard, Annie, 43, 234n118
disturbance, ecological: the Fall as, 62, 65–66, 81; natural disasters as, 163, 172; as site of emergence, 89–91, 104, 147
Dives and Pauper, 201, 251n68, 258n67
dominion, 11, 32, 41, 50–52, 59, 63–64, 69, 80–81, 91, 232n76
Donne, John, 53
Doom, the. *See* Judgment, Last
drought, 5, 6, 24, 152, 157, 161, 254n9

earth, 9, 23; as antagonistic, 77–81; as cursed/wounded, 62–64, 75, 83–84, 171; destruction of, 189–90, 197; exploitation of, 11, 24, 32, 51, 68–69, 229n18; humans as, 31, 34, 48–57, 78; new, 210, 212; personified, 78–81, 171; as soil, 4, 29–30, 40–42, 58–59, 91; as world, 19, 27, 37–42, 51, 62, 75, 101, 115–16, 129, 153, 215. *See also* "Erþe toc of Erþe" (lyric)
"Earthquake poem," 171–79
earthquakes, 17, 22, 24, 100, 129, 153, 156–57, 167–68, 171–76, 187, 188, 191–92, 206, 211, 214
ecocriticism, 12–13, 33, 53, 225n44
ecology, definition of, 4, 14
Eden, Garden of, 30–34, 67, 177, 228n16; animals in, 43–47; death in, 30–31, 34, 43–48; as *locus amoenus*, 40; in modern imagination, 229n18; nostalgia for, 72–74, 81, 83–84
environmentalism, 9–12, 64, 90–91, 178, 210, 214–15
ephemerals, 1–2, 5, 183, 212–13, 219
"Erþe toc of Erþe" (lyric), 56–58
eschatology, 10–12, 117, 190–92. *See also* apocalypse
Eve, 30–31, 42–43, 48, 63, 69, 72, 74–75, 79–83, 86–88, 138, 177, 228n6
Everyman (play), 8
Exodus. *See under* Bible

INDEX

Fagan, Brian, 20
Fall, the, 30–32, 43–44, 52, 62–67, 79–81, 88–89, 228n7
famine, 21, 23–24, 67, 157–58, 161–62, 166–67. *See also* Great Famine
"Ffiftene Toknes" (poem), 188, 208–9
Fifteen Signs of Doomsday (motif), 117, 184–212
fires, 22; that destroy Sodom, 100, 126–28, 139, 142, 146, 241nn22–23; in Last Judgment, 138, 187, 192, 199, 206; in modern world, 98, 104, 151–52, 211
fish: crying, 86, 184, 188, 191–92, 194, 198, 202–5; in Great Flood, 115–16, 243n52, 244n66; human dominion over, 50–51, 76; prelapsarian, 43–45, 48
Fleming, John, 228n10
floods, 97, 104, 105–6, 162, 197, 211; Great Flood, 99–100, 104–8, 113–26, 130–38, 146. *See also Grote Mandrenke*
form, literary: alliteration, 38, 40, 74, 128, 142, 175, 199; amplification (*amplificatio*), 14, 33, 35, 57–58, 74, 116, 204; anaphora, 70, 118, 155, 172, 174, 177; catalogs and lists, 14, 17, 23, 33–34, 70, 99–100, 118, 133, 147–48, 189, 207–8, 211, 220; exclamation (*ecphonesis*), 63, 65, 71, 77; refrain, 63, 65–66, 110, 155, 173–74, 177, 235n16; repetition, 34, 38, 56–58, 63, 65–66, 74–77, 81, 88–90, 111, 152, 159, 173–74, 177, 199, 218
Francis (pope), 12, 260n90
Francis of Assisi (saint), 12

gardens, 1, 8, 16, 29–33, 35, 40, 58–60, 164–65, 183, 212, 219, 220. *See also* Eden, Garden of
Gay, Ross, 195, 220
Genesis. *See under* Bible
Golden Age, 21, 44, 65–67. *See also* Chaucer, Geoffrey: "The Former Age"
Golden Legend, The (*Legenda aurea*), 112, 194–95, 200–201, 205
Graham, Jorie, 97
Great Famine, 22–24, 160–62, 249n43
Gregory the Great, 99–100, 167
Grosseteste, Robert, 42, 201
Grote Mandrenke, 164

Haraway, Donna, 14, 130, 133, 149, 212, 224n13
Harrison, Robert Pogue, 29, 60, 90
Heise, Ursula K., 90, 154, 234n10, 247n16
hexameron(a), 31–32, 40–47, 48, 56, 228n13, 231n56, 232n76
Historia scholastica, 193–94, 256n30
Hogan, Linda, 95
homilies. *See* sermons
hunger, 23, 80, 84, 158, 205; personified, 24, 162. *See also* famine

Indiana, 1, 15, 60, 91–93, 103–4, 151, 221, 240n2
Ingham, Patricia Clare, 90, 107, 230n36, 230n41, 235n26, 236n33, 236n43
Isidore of Seville, 66, 97

Jerome, 193–94
Jesus: baptism of, 88; sayings of, 2, 131, 191, 198; wounded body of, 118, 194, 199–200, 208
John of Grimestone, 2–3
John of Reading, 165–66
Johnson, Eleanor, 22, 24, 122, 216, 239n12, 248n32, 251n70
Judgment, Last, 97, 129, 163–64, 171–72, 197, 202, 210. *See also* Fifteen Signs of Doomsday (motif); portents, of apocalypse
Julian of Norwich, 59, 63, 89

Kempe, Margery, 241n19
Kimmerer, Robin Wall, 12, 27, 89
kin, 3–4, 10, 16, 34, 52, 63, 78, 124, 130, 134–38, 144, 212, 220, 232n83, 261n19. *See also* oddkin
King, Pamela, 39, 74
Kiser, Lisa, 133–34
Knighton, Henry, 165–66, 171–72
Kolve, V. A., 132–33, 244n76, 244n78
kynde (personification), 18, 168, 216–17, 252n91

Langland, William: exemplarism of, 170, 252n85; treatment of natural disasters, 156. *See also Piers Plowman*
Larkin, Phillip, 190
Laudato si', 12–13, 260n90
Leopold, Aldo, 14
Life of Adam and Eve (*Vita Adae et Euae*), 82, 237n58
Little Ice Age, 5, 20–22
Lochrie, Karma, 12, 168
Lot's Wife, 100, 130–31, 139–45, 244n74, 245n106
Lucretius, 106
Lydgate, John, "The Fifftene Toknys aforn the Doom," 203–7, 259n77

MacFarlane, Robert, 16
macrocosm, 7, 53–55, 100, 121, 133, 175, 225n23
Mandeville's Travels, 146, 148, 246n116
Masciandaro, Nicola, 68, 70, 234n12, 235n22, 236n42
Matthew Paris, 17, 156–60
McAvoy, Liz Herbert, 229n17
medieval climate anomaly, 20–21, 227n9
medieval warm period. *See* medieval climate anomaly
memento mori, 2, 43, 56, 58, 124. *See also ars moriendi*
Merchant, Carolyn, 64, 224n21, 226n46, 234n8, 234n11

microcosm, 7, 29, 32, 132–33, 175–76, 216, 220; human body as, 31, 34, 53–55, 100, 176, 225n23
Middle English Genesis and Exodus, 114, 244n68
Middle English Metrical Paraphrase of the Old Testament, 51, 99, 114–15, 140–41, 230n45, 244n68
Milton, John, *Paradise Lost*, 81, 112, 115
Minnis, Alastair, 32, 47, 66, 228n9, 229n19, 231n54, 231n60, 232n76, 232n82
Mirk, John, *Festial*, 199–201, 258n56
Mitchell, Allan, 24, 233n96, 240n19
Mitchell, Joni, 64
mortality. *See* death
Morton, Timothy, 6, 11–12, 14, 53, 59, 77, 90, 160, 234n118 (chap. 1), 234n1 (chap. 2), 254n12
Muir, John, 4
Mum and the Sothsegger, 25, 252n89

Nelson, Ingrid, 57
Nelson, Maggie, 16, 217
Nersessian, Anahid, 160, 226n48, 248n19, 249n41
Newhauser, Richard, 106
Nixon, Rob, 106, 108, 225n32, 260n90
Noah's Wife, 130–38, 244nn74–75, 244n79
Northern Homily Cycle, 59, 197–99
nostalgia, 32, 63–65, 69–74, 85, 233n112, 235n24; definition of, 236n36
Novacich, Sarah, 138, 229n17, 233n102

oddkin, 14, 133–34
Ordinalia, 79–81, 245n89
origin narratives. *See* Bible: Genesis; cosmology
ostentatio vulnerum, 190, 199, 208–9, 259n85. *See also* wounds
otium, 68, 74–75. *See also* pastoral (mode)
Ovid, *Metamorphoses*, 66–67

pastoral (mode), 40, 67–68, 90–91, 158, 161, 226n46, 235n26; elegies, 235n15; and technology, 67, 235n24
pastoral care, 217–18
Patience (poem), 109, 243n51, 243n57, 245n106
Pearl (poem), 109, 230n40
penance: of Adam and Eve, 82–88; aim of apocalyptic sermons, 154, 163, 196; for ecological exploitation, 239n90
performance: as creation, 35, 75; as process, 33–35, 39, 47; virtuality of, 229n22, 229n27
pestilence. *See* Black Death; plague
Piers Plowman, 160–71, 216–19; apocalypse in, 216, 218–19, 248n23, 249n50; climatological interpretation in, 19, 169–71; ecological crisis in, 24–25, 151, 156, 160–62, 249n45; on learning to love, 216–17; preaching in, 98, 163, 166–68, 196, 251n69; wonders in, 46, 160–61, 168–69

plague, 5, 24, 97–102, 109, 163, 176, 216; in the Bible, 98–99; definition of, 98–99; Justinian, 21, 100; as punishment, 98–101. *See also* Black Death
plant blindness, 38
plants, 29, 33, 37–43, 55, 157–58. *See also* trees
Play of Adam (*Ordo representacionis Ade*), 72–73, 193–94
pollution, 64, 226n1
Polychronicon, 73–74, 171, 243n47
Popa, Maya C., 130
portents, of apocalypse, 6, 10, 97, 152, 154, 167, 173, 187–201, 210–11, 251n68; temporality of, 166–67, 253n5. *See also* Fifteen Signs of Doomsday (motif)
predation. *See under* animals
Pricke of Conscience, 201–3, 206; window in York, 184–85, 253n1
primitivism, 66–69, 234n12, 235n22, 235n25
punishment: catastrophes as, 97–102, 104–5, 110, 154, 160–63, 167, 173; as result of the Fall, 44, 47, 232n82
punishment paradigm, 100–102, 104, 163, 240n22, 251nn68–69, 254n6. *See also* Rigby, Kate

quarries, 15, 21, 91, 103
"Quindecim signa" (lyric), 202, 258n69

repentance, 65, 83–84, 163, 196, 239n90
resilience, 2, 65, 81–82, 89
responsibility, 9, 12–13, 24, 52, 59, 63, 69–70, 74, 90, 101–2, 132–35, 145, 149–50, 178, 210, 214–15, 217–18
Reynolds, Evelyn, 224n12, 241n24, 252n92
Rich, Adrienne, 109
Rigby, Kate, 100–101, 104, 159, 255n17
Ritchey, Sara, 228n11, 234n7
rivers, 23, 84–88, 97
Robertson, Kellie, 54, 56, 223n4, 225n23, 226n46, 233n95
Romance of the Rose, 40, 67
romances, 40, 82, 109, 161, 224n14
Rudd, Gillian, 40, 225n44, 228n16, 233n100, 251n79

Saint Maurus's Day windstorm, 164–67, 196
salt, 141; cost of, 23; pillar of, 100, 130, 141–43, 146; produced from Dead Sea, 148
Samalas volcano eruption, 21, 157
Sanders, Scott Russell, 103
Scranton, Roy, 7, 211–12, 225n24, 225n26
sermons, 55, 59; about catastrophes, 98–99, 154, 163, 167–68, 239n7, 257n41, 257nn43–45; including the Fifteen Signs, 191, 196–201. *See also Cleanness* (poem)
Simonie, The, 23
Sir Gawain and the Green Knight, 109–10
Smith, D. Vance, 56, 167, 249n42

INDEX

Smith, Zadie, 151
Sodom and Gomorrah, 100, 108–10, 126–30, 139–46, 241nn22–23
soil. *See* earth
South English Legendary, 201
Spahr, Juliana, 61, 71
Spearing, A. C., 112, 122, 147, 216, 242n27
Stafford, William, 13
Staley, Lynn, 229n17
Stanbury, Sarah, 67, 105, 109, 141, 144, 243n58, 244n64
Steel, Karl, 69, 203, 231n60, 235n22, 235n31
Stevens, Wallace, 30, 34, 47
Stewart, Susan, 33
stones: as apocalyptic sign, 188, 200, 205; relation to human body, 54–55
storms, 19, 98, 102, 163–68; associated with Great Flood, 115–20; fall of angels compared to, 112; of fire, 128. *See also* Saint Maurus's Day windstorm

technology (*techne*), 11, 22, 65–70, 234n11
tokens. *See* portents, of apocalypse
Towneley plays: "The Creation," 50–51, 230n38; "Noah," 131–35; "Second Shepherds' Play," 25
trees: destroyed by storms, 2, 21; in Eden, 30, 38–41
Trevisa, John, 55, 73–74
Trokelowe, Johannes de, 23
Tsing, Anna, 147, 226n58, 238n82, 242n35

vulnerability, 3, 32, 69, 91, 129, 179, 243n56. *See also* wounds

wastelands, 80–81, 109, 127, 141, 146–48, 216
Watson, Nicholas, 224n15
weather, 19–25, 46, 104, 113, 127–28, 151–79, 181, 211
Weil, Simone, 214
White, Lynn, Jr., 10–12, 32, 64, 225n38, 236n33
wilderness, 88, 101
wildfires. *See* fires
Wilner, Eleanor, 30
Wimbledon, Thomas, 196
wind, 25, 38, 127–28, 146, 157–60, 164–67, 197. *See also* Saint Maurus's Day windstorm
witness, 105–10, 122–24, 130–31, 139–46, 151, 187–90, 196–98, 202–7, 220
wonders, 10, 22, 107, 110, 119, 129, 143, 153–54, 160–61, 167–69, 173, 189, 197, 200–201, 247n10, 249n40
Woolf, Rosemary, 57, 223n6, 236n41
wounds, vii, 6, 9–10, 27, 64, 69, 85, 95, 98–99, 148, 153, 184, 190–91, 196–201, 207–10. *See also ostentatio vulnerum*
Wycliffe, John, 172, 253n100; on Creation and Fall, 229n19, 232n82, 236n45

York, England, 34–35, 58, 184–85
York plays, 34–57, 71–79: "Creation," 35–47, 215; "Creation of Adam and Eve," 48–52, 57, 75; "Adam and Eve in Eden," 52; "Fall of Man," 75; "The Expulsion," 71, 74–79; "The Flood," 131, 136–38; "Last Judgment," 209–10

Zagajewski, Adam, 201
Zeeman, Nicolette, 162, 168, 261n13